Evaluating
RESEARCH

Evaluating RESEARCH

Methodology for People Who Need to Read Research

Francis C. Dane
Saginaw Valley State University

Los Angeles | London | New Delhi
Singapore | Washington DC

For information:

SAGE Publications, Inc.
2455 Teller Road
Thousand Oaks, California 91320
E-mail: order@sagepub.com

SAGE Publications Ltd.
1 Oliver's Yard
55 City Road
London EC1Y 1SP
United Kingdom

SAGE Publications India Pvt. Ltd.
B 1/I 1 Mohan Cooperative Industrial Area
Mathura Road, New Delhi 110 044
India

SAGE Publications Asia-Pacific Pte. Ltd.
33 Pekin Street #02-01
Far East Square
Singapore 048763

Printed in the United States of America

Library of Congress Cataloging-in-Publication Data

Dane, Francis C., 1952-
Evaluating research : methodology for people who need to read research
Francis C. Dane.
    p. cm.
Includes bibliographical references and index.
ISBN 978-1-4129-7853-8 (pbk.)
  1. Research—Evaluation. 2. Research—Methodology. I. Title.

Q180.55.E9D355 2011
001.4—dc22   2009029109

This book is printed on acid-free paper.

13 14 15 16 17 9 8 7 6 5 4 3

Acquisitions Editor:	Vicki Knight
Associate Editor:	Lauren Habib
Editorial Assistant:	Ashley Dodd
Production Editor:	Catherine M. Chilton
Copy Editor:	Kim Husband
Typesetter:	C&M Digitals (P) Ltd.
Proofreader:	Sally M. Scott
Indexer:	J. Naomi Linzer Indexing Services
Cover Designer:	Arup Giri
Marketing Manager:	Stephanie Adams

Contents

Preface

Welcome to the world of research. Having taught research methods in one form or another many times over many years, I know that you probably are taking this course because it is required and not because you have an intrinsic interest in understanding and using research. Whether you do or do not have an intrinsic interest in research, I have written this text with you, the student, foremost in mind. My goal is to enable you to have the knowledge required to evaluate research and critically use empirical results as you attempt to analyze and implement policy in your role as administrator, educator, or policy analyst.

I have tried to present the material with a style designed to pique your interest. I thoroughly enjoy research, the methods employed to produce it, and the application of research results to policy analysis and implementation, and I have tried to convey that enjoyment throughout this manuscript. I admit to a straightforward attempt to help you achieve that same level of enjoyment. For those who are thrilled about this course, welcome to the family; for those not so thrilled, I hope to welcome you to the family by the time you finish reading this book. All of you will, I hope, develop a greater appreciation for the ways in which consuming research can add to our understanding of the way the world works and how we can enhance our efforts to improve the world.

Trying to convey my enjoyment of research is not the only aspect designed to make your mastery of the material more efficient. The running glossary is one example. The first time a new term is introduced, it appears in **boldface** type. Definitions appear in the text in *italics*, so you don't have to interrupt reading to find the term in the back of the book. Just in case you can't remember a definition and can't remember where in the text the definition is, there is also an end glossary.

Throughout the text, statistical concepts and procedures are paired with the research methods for which they are appropriate. Those of you who have had a statistics course will find this provides a convenient review. Those of you who have not had a course in statistics will find this to be a helpful introduction. You won't become proficient at statistics from the material in this text, but you will learn how statistics and methodology are part of the same process.

Finally, I encourage you to contact me with your reactions to the book. I would appreciate any comments, good or bad, you have about this book. Send an e-mail to me; my address is fdane@svsu.edu. If you prefer to send anonymous comments, my postal address is SE 161, Saginaw Valley State University, University Center, MI, 48710, USA. Compliments are always delightful, but complaints are the source of improvement. If you don't like something, let me know. I'll try to change it in the next edition. In the meantime, I hope you enjoy your sojourn into research. It really is exciting.

Frank Dane
Midland, MI

Acknowledgments

Although the "author line" contains only my name, this book was not written without considerable input from many different people. There are too many to list everyone, but some deserve specific mention. I am grateful to Vicki Knight, SAGE Acquisitions Editor, for seeing the promise in the prospectus and for the many suggestions for improving the draft. Everyone else at SAGE who was involved in the project also deserves a great deal of gratitude. They made the process of transforming a prospectus into a book the smoothest, least trying, and most efficient in my experience with publishing; pay attention to the names listed on the copyright page and thank them if you ever run into them, for they, too, made this book possible.

The reviewers who provided careful, informed commentary on the prospectus, outline, and draft also deserve thanks, for they improved the content more than I could have done on my own. They include John Bartowski (University of Texas at San Antonio), Juliana Fuqua (California State Polytechnic University, Pomona), Yoonsook Ha (University of South Carolina), Charles S. Reichardt (University of Denver), Linda Renzulli (University of Georgia), and Wendy Weller (State University of New York, Albany). Ann Garcia (Saginaw Valley State University) provided extensive technical assistance in the preparation of the submission draft during many enjoyable exchanges.

Although there is not room to name them individually, the students who endured multiple pre-publication drafts of the book while enrolled in MAS 625 at Saginaw Valley State University also are deserving of acknowledgement. I am also grateful to Joni Boye-Beaman and Mark Nicol, sequential MAS Program Directors, and Don Bachand, then Dean of Arts and Behavioral Sciences, for their tolerance and encouragement as I reconfigured the 625 course from research production to research consumption.

I have lost count of the number of people who piqued my interest in, provided information about, and generally enhanced my knowledge about, skills in, and experience with conducting research as well as my passion for communicating about research. As with the students in MAS 625, there are too many to list, but I do have to mention Jackie Dane Fussell, partly because it was she who first taught me the value and thrill of satisfying curiosity, and partly because I can imagine her saying, "What, you wrote a book and didn't mention your mother?"

Finally, the greatest acknowledgement, gratitude, and thanks are reserved for Linda Dane. Her companionship, love, trust, encouragement, confidence, and all things valuable are without limit.

CHAPTER 1

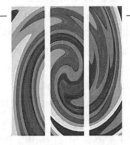

Introduction

How can our intellectual life and institutions be arranged so as to expose our beliefs, conjectures, policies, positions, sources of ideas, traditions, and the like—whether or not they are justifiable—to maximum criticism, in order to counteract and eliminate as much intellectual error as possible?

—W. W. Bartley III (1962, pp. 139–140)

Overview

This chapter is an introduction to research. Like most introductions, it is a broad overview of what is to come. Admittedly, it is also an attempt to pique your interest. You will learn what research is and what the goals of research are. You will also learn about a number of different research projects, projects that illustrate that no single research method is necessarily better than any other. Part of this process is learning about a general framework for understanding and evaluating research conducted by others so that you may inform your own plans and decisions about policy, programs, traditions, and the other aspects of life to which Bartley referred in the opening quote. You will learn how the remainder of this book fits into the overall approach toward learning about research and becoming an informed, critical consumer of research. Finally, you will learn how to begin searching for research articles.

INTRODUCTION

You may have a song (or two) to which you have attached so much meaning that you want to stop everything when you hear it and concentrate on listening and conjuring memories associated with the song. For me, that song is "Who'll Stop the Rain?" (Fogerty, 1970) performed by Credence Clearwater Revival. For those of you who have not heard the tune, the rain is a metaphor for the confusions and mysteries of life. Somewhere behind all those rain clouds is the sun, answers to the mysteries of life. Although everyone has been looking for the sun, the singer continues to wonder who'll stop the rain. As you read this, you may be wondering the same about research, the course you are taking, and this book. What you need now is some sun, but all you see is rain. I'll try to provide some sun, although I don't promise to clarify the mysteries of life.

Because you have been involved in public policy, either implementing or developing it, I need not point out how important public policy has been, is, and will be in our lives. I also need not point out that public policies and programs don't always work out the way they should; they often involve unintended consequences, are sometimes more costly than necessary, and occasionally don't do much of anything. In Fogerty's words, public programs can become "five year plans and new deals, wrapped in golden chains." Like noted methodologist Donald Campbell (1969, 1971), I believe understanding research methods will help you to learn more about public policies, programs, and related topics sufficiently to remove some of those golden chains. In our complex and rapidly changing world, we can no longer afford the luxury of being armchair theorists—of making up explanations as we go—as we search for understanding and try to make the world a better place. We need to use research to sort out various explanations and programs we already have, as well as to point the way to more useful explanations and programs. But incorporating research into policy analysis and implementation must involve more than accepting on faith what "the experts" write. The plethora of dissemination outlets for research reports enables just about anyone to claim to have published a scientific report, often without any review, so we can no longer count on the experts to be, well, experts. We need to become experts ourselves, not in conducting research, but in critically evaluating research done by others so that we can determine whether or not the latest research is any good and is applicable to the public interest problem to which we are devoting our administrative attention.

Therefore, this book is about research: what it is, how to evaluate it, how to tell people about it, and how to use it. It is about trying to find an answer to the question posed by Bartley, and it is about stopping the rain. As you read further, you will come to realize that research is one of the means by which people avoid making intellectual errors. That is, research is a part of life, a particularly exciting part of life that involves trying to discover the whys and wherefores of the world in which we live. As you read further, you will learn about research. I hope you will also have some fun and maybe, just maybe, you might even find the sun.

Definitions

It is always best to start at the beginning when attempting to learn a new topic, and for research that beginning is a definition of research. Unfortunately, it is not easy to arrive at a single definition of research. Just about everyone who has written about research has offered one or another definition. For example, Nachmias and Nachmias (1981) defined it as "the overall scheme of scientific activities in which scientists engage in order to produce new knowledge" (p. 22). Although research is conducted by scientists, it is also conducted by nonscientists. Of course, scientists and nonscientists tend to do research differently, a difference you will be learning about throughout this book, but that doesn't mean nonscientists necessarily do research poorly. Kerlinger (1973) doesn't restrict research to scientists in his definition, "systematic, controlled, empirical, and critical investigation of hypothetical propositions about the presumed relationships among natural phenomena" (p. 11), but he added other restrictions. Research is not always systematic, and it is not always controlled. The more systematic and controlled research is, the better it is, but even poor research is still research.

I could go on citing other definitions, but that would only end up boring you to tears. When it comes down to what is important, the definition of research is rather simple. **Research** is *a critical process for asking and attempting to answer questions about the world*. Sometimes asking and attempting to answer questions involves a questionnaire, sometimes an interview, sometimes an experiment, and sometimes an entirely different method. Simple definitions, however, can be misleading. There is more to research than its definition, or this would be the last page of the book.

Research, as a critical process, is one of the tools we use to achieve Bartley's state of maximum criticism. We do so not by pointing out only negative qualities of a particular public interest program but by examining all of its qualities—good, bad, or indifferent. Whether the program involves drug rehabilitation, nutrition for children, educational efficiency, safety and security, or any of the other myriad issues to which public policies are directed, the ultimate subject of our criticism is human behavior, something about which all of us already know a great deal. That knowledge, however, can sometimes get in our way. If, for example, we fail to examine critically some aspect of human behavior because "everyone knows it is true," then we have fallen short of the goal of an empirical approach to policy analysis. Researchers, instead, should be like a little child who continually asks "why?" Of course, we are more sophisticated than little children, but we need to return to research to evaluate the answers we obtain to our questions. As critical questioners, we need not believe every answer we obtain. For that matter, research enables us to ascertain whether or not we have even asked the appropriate question.

One of the appropriate questions we must ask is, simply, "why pay any attention to research?" To answer this, we must make a brief foray into **epistemology,** *the study of the nature of knowledge, of how we know what we know.* In the late 19th century, Charles Peirce (1877) codified the four primary methods we use to decide how we know what we know: (1) a priori method, (2) authority, (3) tradition, and (4) science. As we consider each of the four methods, keep in mind that there are questions that are more amenable to one of these methods than another; no method of knowing is best for all questions.

Also known as logic, intuition, and sometimes faith, the **a priori method** defines knowledge as *anything that appears to make sense, to be reasonable.* There are some advantages to the a priori method, not the least of which is the ease with which we can develop certainty or relieve ourselves of doubt. Thus, Descartes (1637/1993) employed the a priori method to arrive at his famous decision about how he could be certain that he was real, that he (and the rest of us) existed: cogito ergo sum. As you might suspect, developing certainty is also the chief disadvantage of the a priori method; it is all too easy to close enquiry prematurely because we hit upon a reasonable answer. Thus, many people are certain that most medieval people believed the earth was flat (Russell, 1991), some are certain that aliens from outer space have abducted people (Carroll, 2005), and others are certain that the best way to prevent teen pregnancy is by teaching abstinence (O'Donnell et al., 2007). Of course, not all knowledge developed via the a priori method is wrong; the quality of knowledge derived in this way is a function of the quality of the reasoning employed by the individual producing the knowledge.

In the context of epistemology, **authority** involves *believing something because the source of the knowledge is accepted as inherently truthful.* As children, for example, we believed our parents because they said so. Sometimes the belief was correctly placed—stove burners can be hot—and sometimes not—tooth fairies do not exchange our baby teeth for money or prizes. As adults, we rely on authority as an epistemological method when we accept a physician's diagnosis, or any other expert's conclusion, on the basis of the individual's status as an expert. This can lead to positive outcomes, such as a much-needed prescription for hypertension medication, or it can lead to negative outcomes, such as sterilizing people because they are "mentally defective" (Gejman & Weilbaecher, 2002). When we rely on authority for knowledge, the quality of the knowledge rests upon the quality of the authority.

Tradition involves *believing something because of historical precedent, because it has always been believed*. For example, we tend to eat oysters only in months that include an "r" in the name. The reasoning is sound; warmer weather makes safe storage and transportation more difficult, and bacteria are more plentiful in warmer water (Miliotis & Watkins, 2005), but rapid refrigeration at harvest makes the tradition less important now than it was before such techniques were developed. A very different tradition, shaking hands when meeting someone, may have its roots in demonstrating that one is not capable of holding or reaching for a weapon (Morris, 1971). Such concerns are not as relevant as they once were, but the tradition continues with a very different rationale. We now believe we can determine someone's personality from his or her handshake, and we use that belief to project a desired impression of ourselves (Chaplin, Phillips, Brown, Cianton, & Stein, 2000). We continue to engage in the behavior because "we've always done it that way," and continue to believe knowledge is produced from the tradition, even when the original reasons no longer make sense. Thus, what we know from tradition may be useful but only as long as the original reasons for the tradition are valid.

Science, *the use of systematic, empirical observation to improve theories about phenomena,* enables us to develop knowledge by testing our explanations of the world against what we can observe in the world. For example, we know that training nurses in advanced cardiac life support techniques (ACLS) increases the success of in-hospital cardiopulmonary resuscitation about fourfold (Dane, Russell-Lindgren, Parish, Durham, & Brown, 2000). The researchers systematically compared the resuscitation outcomes of people who had an ACLS-trained nurse call the code with the outcomes of people who had a nurse not yet trained in ACLS discover the patient in distress. Prior to that study, many people believed ACLS training for nurses would benefit patients who required resuscitation, but that explanation was not tested. Unlike other ways of knowing, however, science includes continual testing of explanations. As you will learn in the next chapter, no theory is ever accepted as true, never again to be examined. Similarly, science continues to develop new questions based on obtained answers. For example, other researchers have demonstrated that nurses trained in ACLS are as capable of leading a resuscitation attempt as are physicians (Gilligan et al., 2005). Thus, while the knowledge we obtain from science is only as good as the data generated from research, the continual generation of data serves to produce an accumulation of knowledge in which misinterpretations of data are corrected instead of perpetuated.

In summary, the four different ways of knowing are equally useful, depending upon the questions being asked and the knowledge desired. Science cannot, for example, determine how we can know we are real, and a priori reasoning cannot determine whether ACLS training for nurses will increase the success rate of resuscitation attempts in hospitals. Science cannot explain why we began to shake hands, but tradition cannot determine whether ACLS-trained nurses can lead a resuscitation attempt as well as physicians. Science is best used to gain knowledge about empirically testable ideas or explanations. That covers an extremely large number of phenomena but does not cover all phenomena. I hope to convince you that science, through empirical research, is an effective way to make decisions about the utility of public service programs.

Table 1.1	A Summary of Epistemological Methods
Method	Process for Establishing Knowledge, Deciding What Is Truthful
A priori	Accepting information because it makes sense or is reasonable through the application either of intuition or deductive logic
Authority	Accepting information because the source is believed to be inherently truthful or knowledgeable
Tradition	Accepting information because it has always been accepted in one's family, government, society, culture, or other socialization unit
Science	Accepting information because it was obtained through systematic, empirical observation

GOALS OF RESEARCH

The ultimate goals of research are to formulate questions about testable phenomena and to find answers to those questions. Nestled within these are other goals toward which researchers strive. No one can ask all of the questions, and no one can find all of the answers to even a single question, so we need to find some way to limit what we attempt to do. The immediate goals of research—exploration, description, prediction, explanation, and action—provide us with a strategy for figuring out which questions to ask and which answers to attempt to find.

Exploration

Exploratory research involves *an attempt to determine whether or not a phenomenon exists.* It is used to answer questions of the general form, "does X happen?" Exploratory research may be very simple, such as noting whether or not men or women (boys or girls) are more likely to sit toward the front of a classroom. If one or the other gender does sit in front more often, then we may have discovered a social phenomenon that merits further investigation (Okpala, 1996).

Exploratory research may also be very complex, and sometimes the object of exploratory research is the research process itself. For example, Durkheim's (1951/1897) classic study of suicide statistics involved looking for patterns among a variety of different characteristics. Religious denomination was among them, and Durkheim found Protestants were more likely to commit suicide than Catholics. He also found city people, and people living alone, were more likely to commit suicide than were rural people or those living with a family. From such patterns, Durkheim concluded that anomie, a lack of integration into a social network, was one of the major factors leading to suicide. Many social scientists continued to use existing statistics to elaborate Durkheim's initial theory. Durkheim had explored suicide and noted anomie as a major influence, and other researchers attempted to elaborate on his notions.

Jacobs (1967), however, noted that researchers were generally failing to consider another important source of information about suicide, the notes left behind by those who committed the act. His analysis of the content of such notes revealed that many people valued some degree of uncertainty in their lives. Believing that they knew what the future was going to be like—depressing—was extremely uncomfortable for them, and presumably such people preferred the uncertainty of death to the certainty that life would continue to become worse.

Jacobs's research does not replace Durkheim's monumental work, but it does add much to our understanding of suicide. Both researchers explored the same topic, and each arrived at a different answer. Durkheim's answer was anomie; Jacobs's answer was too much certainty. Just as Durkheim's initial exploration opened many new avenues for research, so does Jacobs's exploration. Neither researcher was testing a particular theory, although both researchers eventually arrived at a theoretical framework for their explorations. Neither researcher discovered suicide, but their explorations did lead to discovering systematic aspects of suicide.

Description

Descriptive research involves *examining a phenomenon to characterize it more fully or to differentiate it from other phenomena.* For example, suppose that, based on Okpala (1996), I wanted to investigate the gender differences in seating preferences more fully by defining exactly what is meant by the "front" of the room. I could partition the class into halves, quarters, and so on in order to determine the proportion of each gender in the ever-smaller front sections. Or I might visit different classrooms to determine the extent to which such behavior is related to the type of subject matter, the size of the room, or some other characteristic.

The example above may appear to be a bit innocuous, but meaningful research programs have been initiated with even less impressive beginnings. Munsterberg (1913), for example, began his inquiries into the consistency and accuracy of eyewitness testimony after wondering about his own perceptions following a burglary at his home. He wondered why he thought, and testified, that the burglars had broken through a basement window when they had actually forced open a door. Since he first questioned his own perceptions and began conducting systematic research on the topic, a number of researchers have been investigating eyewitness accuracy and applying their results to courtrooms and other settings (Greenberg & Ruback, 1982; Parker, 1980; Toglia, Read, Ross, & Lindsay, 2007; Wrightsman, 1987). Empirical attempts to describe more comprehensively the limits of eyewitness accuracy have been conducted from the time of Munsterberg's first musings to the present, and they are likely to continue well into the future. Indeed, even the most recent studies on eyewitnesses have some basis in the research Munsterberg conducted at the beginning of the previous century.

Perhaps the most extensive descriptive research is that conducted by the U.S. Bureau of the Census. The goal is to count and describe the characteristics of the entire U.S. population, and the impact of this research is extensive. Billions of dollars in federal, state, and municipal aid shift with the changing population. Congressional districts appear and disappear, and hundreds of researchers rely on these data to assess the representativeness of their own research samples (e.g., Bowen et al., 2004).

Descriptive research captures the flavor of an object or event at the time the data are collected, but that flavor may change over time. The U.S. Census Bureau, for example, repeats its very costly research every 10 years and engages in interim data collection every year (see U.S. Bureau of the Census, 2008). Other research results may change even more rapidly. Research on unemployment is conducted monthly, and public opinion polls about certain issues may be conducted as often as every day. Research results are not timeless, simply because change is one of the complexities inherent in our world. Thus, descriptive research can be used to examine change by comparing old results with new.

Prediction

Sometimes the goal of research is prediction, *identifying relationships that enable us to speculate about one thing by knowing about some other thing.* While this may seem complicated, it really is not. We all conduct and use **predictive research** every day. We know, for example, about the relationship between hours on a clock and the probability of a certain business being open. Or we understand the relationship between a thermometer reading and the necessity of a coat when going outside. Those who create and use college entrance examinations use research to demonstrate the relationship between the scores on such tests and performance in the first year of college (Camara & Kimmel, 2005) or graduate school (Kuncel, Hezlett, & Ones, 2001). The importance of such predictive research can be inferred from the number of truth-in-testing laws passed by various states in the United States (Lennon, 1982).

Knowing someone's score on a college entrance examination enables us, as a result of predictive research, to speculate about the individual's ability to complete the first year of college. As some colleges and universities have more, or less, difficult curricula, admissions committees use the relationship between first-year performance and test scores to set lower limits for accepting entering students. Of course, there are those who obtain very high scores on such examinations and flunk out in their first year, and those who obtain low scores and do very well. Such exceptions point out that predictive research enables us to speculate, or make informed guesses, but does not lead to absolute certainties.

Explanation

Explanatory research involves *examining a cause-effect relationship between two or more phenomena.* It is used to determine whether or not an explanation (cause-effect relationship) is valid or to determine which of two or more competing explanations is more valid. For example, Sales (1972) used explanatory research to test an explanation derived from Marx's claim that religion is the opium of the people. If religion is a form of opium (figuratively, of course), then one might expect membership in religious organizations would increase during times of economic hardship. People need opium more when things are bad than when they are good. Previous research, however, evidenced no relationship at all between economic indicators and religious membership.

Sales, after reading that research, noted that the other researchers had not made distinctions among different kinds of religions. He attempted to make distinctions between religions by using the psychological concept of **authoritarianism**. Those high in authoritarianism *submit to authority figures, are ethnocentric, and are preoccupied with strength or power* (Adorno, Frenkel-Brunswick, Levinson, & Sanford, 1950). Even though the concept was originally developed to describe people—a personality construct—Sales applied it to religions and created categories of authoritarian and nonauthoritarian religions. Using various economic indicators and church membership records, Sales was able to demonstrate that membership increased in authoritarian religions but decreased in nonauthoritarian religions during times of economic hardship. Thus, the overall effect was no change in religious membership, just what previous researchers had found, but the overall lack of relationship masked an important difference among religions. Authoritarian religions are more likely to provide definite prescriptions for living, and such prescriptions are consistent with the "opium" notion to which Marx was referring in his theory.

Sales's results do not prove that Marxist theory is correct, but the theory can be offered as a possible explanation of his results. As you will discover time and time again, it is not possible to prove that a theory is correct. However, Sales's use of psychological, sociological, and economic concepts was fruitful, and his research provides us with a better understanding of, and an interesting way to study, phenomena such as the increased popularity of fundamentalist religions and similar organizations during difficult times (Hilton, 1981; Willey, 2002).

Action

Research can also be used to attempt to do something about a particular phenomenon. **Action research** refers to *research conducted to solve a social problem* (Lewin, 1946). Action research can involve any of the previously mentioned goals but adds to such goals the requirement of finding a solution, doing something to improve conditions. For example, Becker and Seligman (1978) noted that many people continue to run their air conditioners even though the outside temperature is lower than the temperature inside their house. To address this problem, Becker and Seligman conducted an experiment to test potential solutions to this instance of wasted energy. They created four different groups by providing some people with a chart showing them how much energy they were using, other people with a light that flashed whenever the outside temperature was lower than the inside temperature, still other people with both chart and light, and still others with neither chart nor light. They measured the amount of electricity used by each of the four groups and discovered that the charts did not alter people's energy efficiency. The signaling device, however, decreased electricity consumptions by about 16%. Through their action research, they provided a solution to the problem of wasted electricity: a simple signaling device.

There are, of course, a variety of different theories that could be used to explain why the signaling device worked and the charts did not, but testing those theories was not of interest to Becker and Seligman. They did, however, rely on such theories to implement their study. They inferred from other research, for example, that feedback can be used to alter people's behavior, and so they selected two different forms of feedback, charts and flashing lights, as possible solutions to the problem. Action research, in general, is an extremely important aspect of science, for it is through action research that we are able to test applications of other research results. We might all want to make the world a better place, but the complexity of the world requires that we test proposed solutions to problems before applying them on a large scale.

Table 1.2	The Five Goals of Research Expressed as Abstract and as Concrete Questions	
Abstract Questions	**Concrete Questions**
Exploration: Does it exist?	Do suicide notes contain any information about people's motivations concerning suicide?
Description: What are its characteristics?	How accurate are eyewitnesses?
Prediction: To what is it related?	Are SAT scores related to first-year GPA in college?
Explanation: What causes it?	Do economic changes cause changes in membership in religious organizations?
Action: Can this be used to solve a problem?	Can feedback about outside temperature be used to help people to conserve energy?

Research goals affect the methods used to complete a research project, and they affect the ways in which we attempt to evaluate, and eventually apply, research. It would not be appropriate to reject research because it did not meet goals it was not designed to meet. We should not, for example, devalue Becker and Seligman's research because they did not explain why flashing lights created more efficient use of energy. Explaining why was not part of their project. We also cannot, in general, apply research results to goals different from the original goals of the research. Sales's research, for example, explored the utility of suicide notes. He discovered suicide notes provide useful information about suicide. However, we would be reaching well beyond the initial goals of the research if we used Sales's results to claim that people commit suicide only because they prefer the uncertainty of death to the certainty of depression. Thus, we need to understand the initial goals of every research project, but understanding the goals is only the beginning of evaluating research.

EVALUATION OF RESEARCH

Before we apply research results, before we accept them as reasonable, we need to be able to know whether or not they are worthwhile. We need to evaluate research results and the methods used to produce them, and we do so critically. Critical evaluation involves noting both positive and negative aspects, the good and the bad. Critical evaluation also involves noting the indifferent and irrelevant, the things to which research is not related.

For those of us who conduct formal research, the need for evaluation is obvious. We have to be able to determine whether or not our research is worthwhile, if for no other reason than to prevent wasting our time. But even if we never conducted any of our own research, we would still need to know how to evaluate research. Whether or not we conduct research, we all use research to help us understand the world around us and to make decisions about how to improve the world while we develop, change, or implement policy. As consumers of research, we need to be able to determine which research project is relevant and which is not. To construct a systematic framework for evaluating research, I have borrowed some familiar questions from journalism: who, what, where, when, how, and why. These questions will be used throughout the remainder of the text, which also allows me to provide a preview of what is to come in subsequent chapters.

Who

The "who" of a research project involves three different questions. These include asking who are the researchers, the participants, and the consumers. The answers, of course, vary from project to project, and all have something to do with how one evaluates the project.

Asking about the researchers involves more than simply discovering their names. What we really want to know is something about the characteristics of the researchers, their competence and their biases. We presume researchers are competent until we learn otherwise, but once we learn otherwise, we tend to be unwilling to consider their research seriously. For example, I know of no one willing to place a great deal of faith in research conducted by Sir Cyril Burt in light of his fraudulent research on intelligence (Hearnshaw, 1979). Few things arouse the ire of researchers more than fraudulent research reports. Because research reports are the major source of information about research, and because they serve as the basis for evaluating research, they must be as accurate as possible. Outright fraud is extremely rare, but even the most competent researchers are susceptible to biases.

Researchers' biases affect the direction of their research, just as our own biases affect the manner in which we evaluate our own and others' research. We would not be too surprised to learn, for example, that a longtime believer in extrasensory perception conducted a study that supported its existence. We might, however, be more likely to accept the same results if the study was conducted by a known critic of extrasensory perception. There is no reason to believe that one or the other researcher is any better, but we tend to believe people more when they are presenting a position counter to their known beliefs (Dane, 1988a). Whether or not we agree with the biases of other researchers, we must be aware of them and of our own biases and be sensitive to their influence in the evaluation process.

Participants in a research project are also an important consideration in the evaluation of research. Suppose we were interested in studying how jurors arrived at their verdicts in a criminal trial. It might not be particularly useful to ask college students to decide on a verdict, simply because college students are not similar to the majority of people who serve on juries (Ellison & Buckhout, 1981; Kerr & Bray, 1982; Simon, 1975). On the other hand, if we happen to be using a trial setting to investigate how people make decisions, then it would be reasonable to ask students to decide about a portion of trial evidence. There is no reason to suspect that students make decisions differently than anyone else makes decisions. Simply determining who the participants are is not sufficient. Critical evaluation involves assessing the fit between the purpose of the research and the participants involved in it.

Sometimes, records about people, organizations, programs, or other objects are the participants in research. The data source in Jacobs's (1967) study was suicide notes, not the people who wrote them. We would not expect those writing such notes to have had an interest in the outcome of the research, but self-presentation, concern for the impression one makes upon others, may be an important aspect of any research project. Participants, or those creating records that may be used for research, have a tendency to want to make themselves look good. Even people who write suicide notes expect someone to read them, and the extent to which self-presentation plays a role in the research project should always be assessed.

The intended consumers of research also play a role in one's ability to evaluate a project. Researchers tend to write their reports for other researchers as opposed to the general public. They often use jargon that they expect readers to understand. At this point, the phrase "a 2 × 2 factorial design" probably doesn't mean much to you, but it denotes a specific research design. The design carries with it a variety of assumptions, implications, and techniques, all of which would be very time-consuming, not to mention boring, to describe every time someone wrote about it. Inability to understand jargon makes it difficult to evaluate research, which is one of the reasons for the glossary in this text.

On the other hand, too much jargon makes it difficult for anyone except another expert to understand the report. Although publicity and political differences were probably the primary motives, misinterpretation of procedures and conclusions contributed to Wisconsin Senator Proxmire's creation of the Golden Fleece Awards in the 1970s (Baron, 1980). Sometimes, consumers may want to limit research. Shaver (1981, 1982), for example, noted the Reagan administration's budget restrictions on social science research were politically motivated. Many of the budget cuts directly affected research designed to assess the impact of the administration's economic programs. Similarly, a nonscientist member of George W. Bush's administration altered scientific reports on global warming and greenhouse gases (Revkin, 2005). Sensitivity to the consumers of research is a necessary part of the evaluation process, including noting the absence of research.

What

The "what" of research concerns the topic as well as the theory on which the research is based. Theory includes the overall **worldview**, *the basic set of* *untestable assumptions underlying all theory and research.* It should be obvious that different research topics require different methods. Attempting to interview people who have committed suicide is ridiculous, not to mention macabre. On the other hand, an interview or survey is entirely appropriate for a project dealing with energy use. What may not be so obvious is that different questions about the same research topic may require different methods. If researchers are interested in perceptions about electricity use, interviews may be just what they need to use. But if they are interested in actual electricity use, then they might do as Becker and Seligman (1978) did and read meters instead of asking people how much electricity they used.

Through the theory they use as they derive their research questions, researchers also affect the manner in which they conduct the research. Sales (1972), for example, specifically tested Marxist theory, so he included economic conditions, one of the major components of Marxist theory, as one of his research measures. If he instead was interested in theories about psychological depression, he probably would have used some sort of depression scale and ignored economic indicators. Both economics and depression may be related to membership in a religious organization (Jenkins, 2003), but which gets included in a single research project is determined by the theory from which the research question is derived. The evaluation of research involves assessing whether or not what is included in research is appropriate to the theory on which it is based.

Beyond the level of theory, worldview also plays an important role in research. Kamin (1974) pointed out that researchers were willing to accept the notion that men and women did not differ in intelligence, and so those developing intelligence tests generally excluded from intelligence tests items that produced gender differences. They were not, however, so willing to accept the notion that racial and ethnic minorities were as intelligent as themselves. Thus, early measures of intelligence did not exhibit a gender bias but did exhibit a number of racial and ethnic biases. Political beliefs may also affect the topic one selects for research (Frank, 1981).

Worldviews also affect the way in which research results are interpreted. A current example is the debate between those favoring the creationist (including intelligent design) and evolutionist explanations of the origin of our planet and the humans who inhabit it (Durant, 1985; Poling & Evans, 2004). I am simplifying the issues considerably, but it is fair to note that the followers of each worldview base their conclusions (more or less) on the same data, the physical world. The creationists conclude that the world is about 10,000 years old, and that it and humans result from divine intervention. They reject the scientific methods used to obtain data that are not consistent with their beliefs. Evolutionists conclude the earth is billions of years old, that humans evolved from other species, and they reject untestable, theistic events as valid sources of data. Evolutionists do not accept what is written in religious documents as scientific evidence, and creationists do not accept the scientific data produced by evolutionists. Clearly, worldviews affect the conclusions as well as evaluations of research in this debate, just as worldviews affect evaluations of all research.

Where

The "where" of research includes the physical and social environment in which the research was conducted. Certain conditions are possible in one setting but not in another, and some settings do not allow certain types of research to be conducted at all. We cannot, for example, legally study jury deliberations in any systematic fashion by recording what occurs in the deliberation room, although some researchers have been able to do so under extraordinary circumstances (Devine, Clayton, Dunford, Seying, & Pryce, 2001; Ellison & Buckhout, 1981; Simon, 1975). Similarly, we cannot ethically examine reactions to an emergency by shouting "fire" in a theater. On the other hand, we can study simulations of juries, as well as simulations of emergencies. Bringing trials or emergencies into a research laboratory may introduce an element of artificiality, but artificiality alone is not grounds for devaluing a research project. Just as it is with other evaluation questions, it is necessary to engage in critical assessment of the relationship between the physical setting and the research goals.

The influence of the social environment may include very general aspects of the society as well as cultural biases. Someone doing research in a country without a jury system, Japan for example, might never decide to use a jury simulation to study group decision making. Similarly, the belief in the United States and Canada that beauty was in the eye of the beholder kept social scientists from systematically studying the effects of physical attractiveness until the 1960s. The first few studies about physical attractiveness, however, blew that belief right out of the water. After decades of research and its attendant publicity, few of us have any trouble responding to a question that begins with "On a scale from 1 to 10, how attractive is . . . ?" and even fewer of us doubt our rating will agree with those of many others (Adams, 1977; Rhodes, Halberstadt, Jeffery, & Palermo, 2005).

When

The time frame of a particular study may, of course, alter its utility, but it can also be the major purpose of the study. Science operates on the basis of cumulative knowledge most of the time (see, e.g., Fleck, 1979). Each bit of information is supposed to add to what is already available. The results of a particular study may be extremely valuable at one point in time but may only bring a yawn after years of research on the topic. Demonstrating, for example, that social class exists in the United States might well bring a yawn, and perhaps questions about why one is wasting time on such trivial research. On the other hand, a demonstration that social class no longer exists in the United States would arouse considerable excitement and disagreement. Research should not occur in a vacuum but should be placed in a context of the existing information about the research topic.

Changes in conditions over time may themselves be the focus of research, particularly with respect to whether or not a particular social program is still needed. Similarly, the passage of time may have an impact on research. For example, in a study involving **deception**, *providing false information about the research project*, the longer the study lasts the more likely it is that the deception is no longer feasible. If a study involves an interview, an extremely long interview may lead to fatigue or boredom, affecting the responses of the participants or the interviewer's ability to record responses accurately. Of course, the explanation is not time, per se, but changes in other conditions that occur with the passage of time. Nevertheless, the context of a research project and its length must be considered a part of a critical evaluation of the project.

Why

We have already dealt with many of the reasons why research is done. To the goals already mentioned—exploration, description, prediction, explanation, and action—we can add contracts and curiosity to the list of whys that affect research.

Contract research is conducted because someone hires a researcher specifically for the purpose of conducting the research. The Pepsi Taste Challenge is an example, although not necessarily a representative one. Research firms were hired to conduct the taste tests, but the results belonged to Pepsi. (I've often wondered whether or not the results would have been released had they not favored Pepsi, but I think I know the answer.) The primary consumers of contract research are those who pay the bills, and they have considerably greater impact than most researcher consumers. In contract research, the consumer, rather than the contracted researcher, typically has control over the research process and almost always has control over the release of the results. In some cases, the exact methodology of the study may be kept secret, in which case it is impossible to evaluate the research critically. Nevertheless, the fact that research was contracted by a specific organization does not, per se, mean that the research is inherently faulty.

When research is conducted only to satisfy someone's curiosity, critical evaluation is also rather difficult. On the other hand, only the researcher needs to evaluate curiosity-motivated research that is not made public. Sometimes, however, such research is also of interest to others, and the researcher ends up publishing the research in one form or another. In such cases, the research should be evaluated as critically as any other research.

How

The goals of research affect its methods, and so we turn to some of those methods as a way to preview the remainder of this text. The design and procedures are likely to be the most critically evaluated aspects of research and so deserve the greatest amount of attention.

The "hows" of research range from the manner in which one obtains an idea to the ways in which one writes about the research results, and understanding each of these is useful in our attempts to consume research conducted by others. Nestled between these two activities are issues concerning ethics, design, data analyses, and interpretations. In addition, there are many aspects of research that may or may not be relevant to a particular research project. Scale construction and obtaining large, representative samples are just two examples of such aspects.

Like most of life, research can be extremely boring if you only read about it with no particular purpose in mind. Although you may not be able to apply everything discussed in this text, you can think about the relevancy of various topics to your public policy interests throughout the text. As you continue to read, think about how you might use the information you are reading in your current position or your intended profession. Imagination cannot replace activity, but imagination is better than nothing. At some point, and I hope it is soon, you may be in a position to prepare a research-based policy paper. If you have thought about it ahead of time, you'll be able to take advantage of the opportunity.

CONDUCTING A RESEARCH REVIEW

The relationship between research and theory is an extremely strong one. Research results are always placed in the context of existing theory, and existing theory provides a framework for new ideas about what to research. There is no official starting point in this relationship, but I have chosen to begin the discussion of how to review research with choosing a topic.

Choosing a Topic

The first step in conducting a research review is to choose a topic. There are no rules for this step, but there are some general guidelines. Sources for research topics are infinite, for anything may stimulate a research question. Indeed, anyone can come up with any number of research questions, but the trick to conducting a research review is to develop a good question, one that is likely to have been addressed by researchers. Recognizing and formulating a researchable, empirical question takes a little practice and requires some understanding of research methods, but one does not have to be an expert in research methodology to begin the process. Perhaps the most important suggestion that can be made about deciding upon a question upon which to base your review is to limit your questions to topics that are particularly interesting to you. I can think of no more boring task than reviewing research on a topic in which I have no interest.

You may be assigned a topic for review by a supervisor who wants empirical information on a specific policy or program. Barring such an assignment, however, you need to consider various sources for information about potential review topics. One excellent source is the policy manual for your place of employment. Page through the manual until you find a section on an interesting topic. Read the section and think about questions you would like to ask the author of the policy manual or think about reasons why the policy might have been developed; either will provide you with a starting point for a research review. If there are references in the manual, use them to gather more information about the topic and the research related to it. Another good source for research topics is a research journal. Choose a journal relevant to your discipline or scope of activities and scan the table of contents until you find a topic of particular interest. Read the article to find out what issues and questions are being addressed. Again, think about questions you would like to ask the author if you had the opportunity.

In addition to policy manuals and journals, take the time to ask coworkers or supervisors about their own questions about policy or administrative issues. If one or more of their interests coincide with yours, you have yet another source of information, but do not ask him or her to do your work for you. Discovering the policy interests of colleagues is always a good idea, but discovering interests and asking for major input into your own work are two very different things.

Once you have developed a question, regardless of its source, you have begun the research review process. The next step is to become familiar with your topic. This point may seem too obvious to bother making, but more than a few reviewers have begun amassing sources only to discover that they were woefully unprepared to interpret those sources. If your review involves a formal theory, read about the theory and its related research. If your interests are not tied directly to a formal theory, reading about issues related to your interests is likely to result in some familiarity with the applicable formal theory. Remember that, explicitly or implicitly, all research is based on one or more theories.

Operationalization

Once you have chosen a topic and become familiar with a theory related to it, the next step is to consider the range of **operational definitions**—*concrete representations of abstract theoretical concepts*—that could be related to your interests. Heat is a theoretical concept, for example, and the number of units on a thermometer is one operational definition of it. Sales (1972) operationalized one component of Marxist theory, "opium" or the reduction of stress, in terms of membership in a religious denomination. The operational definition of a concept is not the same as the concept itself, but it does represent the concept. A score on an intelligence test, for example, is not the same thing as intelligence. Campbell (1969) coined the term **definitional operationism** to refer to *the failure to recognize the difference between a theoretical concept and its operational definition.* Leahey (1980) used the phrase "myth of operationism" to label the same problem. Theoretical concepts must have operational definitions before we can do any research related to the theory, and we need to maintain the distinction between a concept and its operationalization. You will need to consider the variety of different ways in which the policy concepts of interest to you can be operationalized, or made concrete, through research. You do not have to know all of the possible operational definitions of concepts in which you are interested, but it helps to consider some of them before beginning your research review. Operational definitions can be extremely useful as key words in a search.

When you have an operational definition of a concept, it is called a **variable**—*a measurable entity that exhibits more than one level or value.* A thermometer reading is a variable, for it is measurable and it exhibits more than one level. Similarly, Sales's use of religious denomination is a variable; it is measurable and could be either authoritarian or nonauthoritarian. Other examples of variables include a score on an intelligence test, a rating of 1 to 10 on a scale of physical attractiveness, words related to depression in suicide notes, and the presence or absence of a gun in an eyewitness situation. Variables need not be numeric, but they must vary; there must be more than one level, at least the presence or absence of some quality.

Once you have some operational definitions for the theoretical concepts of interest, you will soon understand how those variables are used to form **hypotheses**—*statements that are used to describe a relationship between variables*. An hypothesis is a concrete statement analogous to an abstract relationship described in a theory. Sales tested the hypothesis that economic hardship and religious membership are related; worsening economic conditions should be accompanied by increased membership in authoritarian, but not in nonauthoritarian, religious denominations.

You may recognize the phrase "reverse psychology," the name used to describe the attempt to induce someone to behave in a manner that is contrary to suggestion. Brehm (1966) proposed reactance theory to explain this phenomenon. Briefly, **reactance** refers to *the proposition that whenever someone's perceived freedom is threatened, the person is motivated to reassert that freedom*. The salesperson who tells you that several other people are interested in the last remaining item, for example, may be trying to threaten your freedom to purchase the item in hopes of motivating you to reassert that freedom by purchasing it immediately. When a freedom is completely eliminated, reasserting that freedom involves increasing the attractiveness of something that represents the freedom. If you need a particular journal article for a paper and cannot find it, the importance of the article increases as you search for it. If you discover that it is permanently lost, you may even decide that it is no longer possible to complete the paper.

Mazis (1975) conducted a test of reactance theory by capitalizing on a serendipitous opportunity. The Dade County (Florida) authorities outlawed the sale, possession, or use of cleaning products containing phosphates in the early 1970s. When the law was passed, some manufacturers were prepared and were immediately able to sell their brand-name products without phosphates. Other manufacturers were less well prepared, and it was several months before their brand names reappeared on the shelves without phosphates. Mazis compared people who were able to continue using their favorite brand of laundry detergent to those whose favorite brand was temporarily unavailable. According to his research hypothesis, people who could no longer use their favorite brand should exhibit an increase in its perceived value, whereas those who could continue to use their favorite brand should exhibit no change in its perceived value. The results were consistent with the hypothesis; the temporary elimination of certain brand names was accompanied by an increase in their perceived value, and manufacturers unprepared for the new law actually benefited from it by an increase in customer loyalty to their products. You may not be interested in reactance theory as a psychological theory, but you may be interested in reactance theory if a policy change under consideration involves reducing perceived freedoms.

For any particular theory, the number of ways in which a concept may be operationalized is limited only by the imagination of the researcher. We cannot, however, evaluate variables solely on the basis of creativity. You probably would not want your instructor to be creative when operationalizing your knowledge of research methods in terms of your body temperature and award the highest grades to the most feverish students. This may be a creative approach, but it is not valid. **Validity**, in general, refers to *the extent to which a claim or conclusion is based on sound logic.* There are many specific kinds of validity in research, and we will eventually discuss all of them, but the relevant validity here is **construct validity,** *the accuracy with which a variable represents a theoretical concept.* Validity, including construct validity, is assessed through consensus.

If you agree with Sales's use of authoritarian versus nonauthoritarian religious denominations as a variable representing Marx's concept of "opium," then you consider it to be a valid variable. If you agree with the logic Mazis used to represent a threatened freedom with a banned laundry detergent, then Mazis's variable is valid. The consensus of science is not merely popularity—it is based on logic derived from the theory—but it is agreement. Sometimes, however, the popularity of a particular variable leads to its misuse as an operational definition. Deutsch (1980), for example, commented that extensive use of games, particularly the Prisoner's Dilemma, as an operationalization of conflict was "mindless—being done because a convenient experimental format was readily available" (p. 63). The mere existence of a valid operational definition is not sufficient reason to use it in research or to use it in a review of research; whatever research variables you include in your review should be based on a logical analysis of the theory, policy, or issue to be addressed in your research question.

By the time you have an interesting research question, have found an applicable theory, policy, or program for your question, and have (at least temporarily) decided upon some operational definitions, you have become intimately involved in the cyclical practice of science (see Figure 1.1).

Figure 1.1	The Cyclical Nature of the Practice of Science

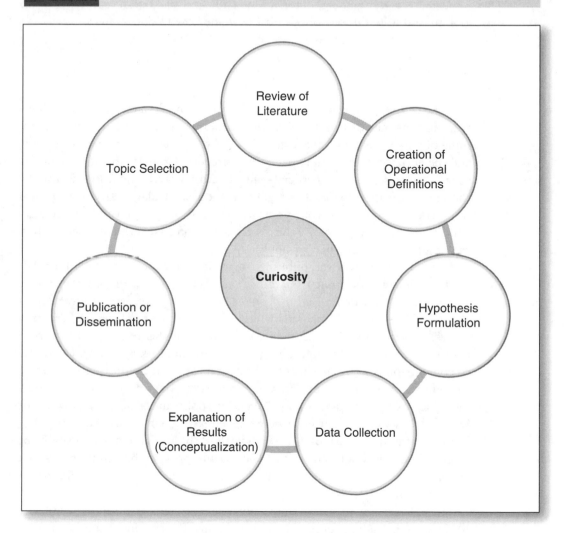

FINDING RESEARCH

Before one can use research to inform public policy decisions, one has to be able to find research reports, what researchers refer to as "the literature." Despite use of the definite article, there is no one, single literature; instead **literature** is *the generic term used to refer to any collection of articles, chapters, and books* *that are relevant to a particular topic.* Knowing that "the literature" is out there, somewhere, is a beginning, but is not much help if one doesn't know where to look to find it. In this section, we will examine how to find sources.

Published Sources

Some of the best, as well as some of the most overlooked, sources for literature are introductory textbooks. They contain a great deal of information, some of which you may have forgotten since you took an introductory course, and the good ones have many pages of references. Granted, the information is usually discussed at a superficial—introductory—level, but there is usually enough information to decide whether or not a particular theory or empirical study could be related to your policy interests. Once you have identified relevant information, you can use the reference section to determine where to find the original article, chapter, or book.

Other good sources for published material are general content journals, such as *Journal of Policy Analysis and Management, Education Policy Analysis Archives,* or *Journal of Comparative Policy Analysis: Research and Practice.* These journals include material on a variety of policies and research topics, and they usually include a combination of theoretical and empirical articles. If you page through these journals, or more likely, scan their tables of contents online, you are likely to find a fair amount of information related to your policy interests. You can also peruse somewhat more specialized journals, such as those in psychology, education, political science, social work, or whatever discipline might be closely aligned with your policy interests. Your library maintains a list of the periodicals it holds, and it can usually be searched online by subject or title. The list will provide the call numbers that enable you to locate current and back issues of the journal in the library or URLs for online access.

Journals are not the only sources for relevant literature, although they are likely to be the major sources. Every year, Annual Review, Inc. publishes a series of volumes, titled *Annual Review of . . . ,* for most of the major disciplines dealing with human behavior. Other review series, often titled *Advances in . . .* can be found by perusing the library's electronic card catalog by title.

Electronic card catalogs are also useful for locating professional and trade books on specific topics. Some of these books present new theories, and others may be edited volumes that review a variety of different but related research programs. You might also want to locate and peruse the American Library Association's *Guide to Reference Books* (Balay, 1996), which contains a list of reference volumes on almost any subject you can imagine. Don't let the 1996 copyright date deter you from using it; annual supplements keep it current.

Finally, the bookshelves of willing faculty may be one of the best starting points for your search. When you ask them for potential sources on a topic, be as specific as you can. For example, I would not know what to suggest to someone who wanted information about the general topic of jury decisions; there are too many places to begin. You need to have given your policy issue some thought and narrowed the topic before someone else can provide useful suggestions about specific books.

Skimming through new issues of journals or annual series is one way to develop your research idea and to find information related to it. Indeed, you have probably taken enough courses to have a good idea about which journals or series are likely prospects for perusal. Let us move on, then, to some very specific tactics for tracking down information you have decided you need.

Key Topics

One of the best tactics for locating relevant literature is searching for specific topics. Once again, textbooks are a great starting point. A glance at the table of contents and the index will let you know whether or not there is anything in the book that is relevant to your policy issue.

When you know some of the key topics relevant to your research idea, there are even faster methods for locating related literature. You are probably familiar with a few indexing or abstracting services available through your library's search databases, such as ProQuest, a compilation of empirical journals, newspapers, general magazines, and other publications, all of which can be searched via one or more keywords. ProQuest covers a wide range of topics, and the articles contained in it reflect such general coverage. You will need to pay close attention to the types of articles that are generated from any search you conduct.

In 1964, the U.S. Office of Education established the Educational Resource Information Center (ERIC), which is currently maintained by the National Institute of Education. ERIC is an indexing and abstracting service, available electronically through most libraries, that deals specifically with research on educational topics. Although originally established to reference only educational topics, ERIC now indexes an increasingly wider range of topics related to human behavior. With a little creative use of synonyms for topics of interest, you should have little difficulty using it.

Another, somewhat specialized indexing and abstracting service is PsycINFO, which is searchable via preselected keywords as well as everyday words that might appear in abstracts, titles, and the like. Like psychology, just about every discipline has a searchable database of articles. Which databases are available through your library will depend upon the extent of the subscription services. It is not possible for me to describe, or even list, all of the available indexes, nor would it do much good for me to try to guess which, in print or on computer, your library might have. The easiest way to find out what is available to you is to talk to one of the reference librarians.

I have not provided very many details about how to use any of the indexes or abstracts because it is much better to find out from a person rather than a textbook. Local options vary so much on most computerized indexes, even if it is officially the same index, that my telling you about how my library's index works could be a waste of time. It is worth your effort to get the information from your local reference librarian. I have been assured that most reference librarians really do enjoy showing people how to use the services they offer. One reference librarian likened it to showing off one's favorite toys. Another said that reference librarians enjoy talking about their reference services almost as much as professors enjoy talking about their research—now that's enjoyment.

Key Authors

In almost all but the newest areas of research, there are likely to be key researchers—people whose names are known and who do a great deal of writing in the field. Milgram is a key researcher in obedience, Baron in aggression, and so on. If you have exhausted your key topics or cannot think of any key topics, one way to continue your literature search is by examining the work of key authors. You may discover key authors from perusing textbooks or general journals or by reading whatever material you were able to discover through a key topic search.

Chances are, however, that the research of key authors will be dated, just as the research by Milgram and Baron is relatively old by research standards. You may have to go back several years in a journal before noticing the regular appearance of any individual. After you have a key author's name, however, you can use the index issue of more recent journals to determine whether or not the author has published in that journal for the volume(s) included in the index issue. The index issue is usually the last issue in a given volume or the last issue of the calendar year. Alternately, you can use the search databases available through your library to search for articles by a particular author. Don't be surprised to find that most authors publish in a variety of areas—Milgram did not limit his research only to obedience—so expect to find unrelated articles as well as related articles.

Of course, the farther back in time you have to go to find a key author, the more likely it is that the author is no longer researching in the topic in which you are interested. Milgram, for example, is no longer alive and so is obviously not currently publishing on the topic of obedience. But, as you pay attention to the authors of studies, you will begin to see a pattern of coauthors, which, over time, may help you track down the most recent articles. Even if one or more of your key authors is no longer publishing on your topic, pursuing a particular author may lead you to a key study.

Key Studies

Sooner or later in your search you will find an article that seems perfectly related to your policy issue—a key article. Once you have found them, key articles are one of the most effective bases for a comprehensive literature search. The reference section of the key study will list relevant research reports that were published before the key study was published. Consulting those references provides the means for discovering related research in the relative past.

Key articles are a great find, but I can imagine you asking "What if my key article is ten years old?" If you have found the key article through an electronic database, you can use the key terms listed for that article to discover additional articles related to the same key terms. This helps you to overcome the problem associated with any differences between the specific key terms used by the database organizers and the key terms you think they should have used when organizing the database. If it is available through your library, you also can use the *Social Science Citation Index* (SSCI). The Citation Index portion of this reference tool enables you to find related articles published after your key article.

The Citation Index consists of a list of key articles arranged alphabetically by the first author's last name. Under each key article entry is a list of additional articles, each of which included the key article in the reference section or in a footnote. Because the author(s) of the listed article included the key article in its references, you are almost guaranteed that the listed article is in some way related to your key article. By locating and reading the articles listed under one or more of your key articles, and by systematically tracking down those articles in the Citation Index, you can very quickly bring yourself up to date on research related to your key article, even if the initial key article you used was 20 years old.

Unpublished Studies

Not all of the empirical and theoretical work related to your policy issue idea can be found in published sources. One reason is that books and journals are subject to a publication lag. The author obviously wrote the material before it was published and collected the data before the article was written. Even after an article or book is accepted for publication, it will not appear in print for at least four months, and sometimes it may take as long as two years to appear in print. Thus, there will always be research more recent than that contained in any given published article. Unfortunately, as a beginner in research you will have to accept this limitation; checking the most recent issues of appropriate journals is about as current as you can get. After you have been consuming research for a while, you will become acquainted with others who do research in the same field. Talking to your professional colleagues is about the only way to find out how to access prepublication copies of the very latest research.

Some of the references you obtain in your search will be found in either *Dissertation Abstracts International* or *Masters Abstracts International*. These publications contain abstracts of doctoral dissertations and master's theses, respectively, and have indexes through which you can find dissertations and theses related to various topics. In both publications, however, the abstracts are very short, about 300 words, and you will have to write to University Microfilms to get a copy of the entire research report. Before writing, however, check with faculty members; they may already have a copy and may be willing to lend it to you.

Finally, a caution about using the World Wide Web general search engines (e.g., Google, Yahoo, AOL). Using these will certainly produce many hits for almost all key words, and some of these may actually be research articles, but the majority of the material is likely to be more opinion than research. You might be able to find good background information, but you are likely to find more information than you are able to peruse efficiently. For example, a search via Google for the terms "abstinence," "sex," and "education" turned up nearly 700,000 hits, clearly too many to wade through in order to find research on the effectiveness of abstinence-only sex education. Adding "effectiveness" to the list of terms in hopes of reducing the number of hits backfired; the number increased to 2.9 million. In contrast, a search using the same three terms via ProQuest, after checking the "scholarly article" option, produced only 199 hits, which was reduced to 16 documents by adding "effectiveness" to the search terms. Sixteen documents, one of which turned out to be a key article, were much easier to peruse than 2.9 million documents.

Enough reading for now; go develop a topic of interest and search for some research articles.

SUMMARY

- Research can be defined in many ways, the most general of which is a process through which questions are asked and answered systematically. As a form of criticism, research can include the question of whether or not we are asking the right question.
- The ultimate goal of research is to be able to answer the questions asked. However, exploration, description, prediction, explanation, and action are different ways to ask the same question.
- Exploration involves attempting to determine whether or not a particular phenomenon exists.
- Description involves attempting to define a phenomenon more carefully, including distinguishing between it and other phenomena.
- Prediction involves examining the relationship between two things so as to be able to make educated guesses about one by knowing something about the other.
- Explanation also involves examining the relationship between two things but specifically involves trying to determine whether or not one causes the other.
- Action involves using research to attempt to solve a social problem. Action research may involve any of the other goals of research, but it includes a specific application.
- Evaluating research involves the questions who, what, where, when, how, and why. Researchers, participants, and consumers of research may all affect the outcome of the research, as well as the manner in which the outcome is interpreted.
- The topic, theory, and worldview on which research is based are also involved in evaluating research critically, as are the physical location of the research and the social climate in which it is conducted.
- Research results are not timeless, mainly because the world itself is dynamic. Changes in research results, however, can themselves become the focus of research.

- Contract research often requires special consideration of the potential impact of those contracting the research. Similarly, research conducted for the sake of personal curiosity is rarely evaluated as critically as scientific research. However, all research that becomes public should be subjected to equally stringent evaluation and criticism.
- Searching for research reports is best done through search engines designed for scholarly publications. Using key terms, key authors, and key articles, as well as textbooks, should provide you with a comprehensive set of reports, the literature related to the policy or program in which you are interested.

EXERCISES

1. Obtain a popular-press report (newspaper, magazine, blog, etc.) about a public policy and determine whether the information in the report is based on a priori reasoning, appeal to authority, tradition, or scientific content. (Note: there may be a mixture of types of epistemological methods represented in any given report.)

2. Obtain a popular-press report containing reference to scientific research. Decide what kind of purpose is attributed to the research. (Ideally, choose a report that contains enough information about the research so that you can later track down the article[s] on which the report is based.)

3. Using a new popular-press report or one you used in the other exercises, answer as many of the who-what-where-when-how-why questions as possible.

4. Identify a public policy in which you are interested and use the resources in your library to track down at least two empirical (research) articles that are relevant to that policy.

CHAPTER 2

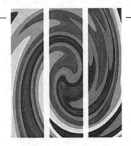

The Scientific Approach

It [science] is not perfect. It is only a tool. But it is by far the best tool we have, self-correcting, ongoing, [and] applicable to everything. It has two rules. First: there are no sacred truths; all assumptions must be critically examined; arguments from authority are worthless. Second: whatever is inconsistent with the facts must be discarded or revised.

—Carl Sagan (1980, p. 333)

Overview

This chapter contains a description of the scientific approach as it applies to the theory and practice of research. You will learn why science, despite being the best approach to research, is not subject to proof from outside its own logical system. Scientific knowledge and its growth are a function of agreement, and you will learn how agreement is facilitated by the use of inductive reasoning. You will also learn about distinctions between scientific and nonscientific research, various misconceptions about science, and the importance of theory in the research process. You will learn how to use theory and other resources to facilitate your understanding, critical evaluation, and application of research. Finally, you will learn about the ethics of consuming research.

INTRODUCTION

Many people think of scientific research as something done by intelligent-but-absent minded people wearing white coats while surrounded by strange-looking equipment with blinking lights. Some may think of scientists as despoilers of a simple, nontechnical lifestyle. Others may think of scientists as the harbingers of an idyllic age. None of these views is correct; one of the goals of this chapter is to dispel these and other myths about science. Science is not something one does; rather, it is an approach toward doing things, and one of the most important things scientists do is research. Scientists certainly do not all wear white laboratory coats, nor do we all use strange equipment, with or without blinking lights. Some scientists may be extremely intelligent or absent minded, but these qualities do not make a person a scientist; neither does adopting a scientific approach necessarily make someone intelligent or absent minded.

I noted in Chapter 1 that everyone, not just scientists, does research. What distinguishes scientific from other kinds of research is not the activity itself but the approach to the activity. Scientific research is, among other things, systematic. There are other guidelines about what is and what is not scientific research, as well as guidelines about what to do with scientific research once we have it, including ethical guidelines. Scientists know what these guidelines are, agree about them, and attempt to adhere to them. Nonscientists either do not know them or do not consistently use them. It is not research that distinguishes scientists from nonscientists; it is the approach one takes toward research. As we learned in Chapter 1, science is a systematic approach to the discovery of knowledge based on a set of rules that defines what is acceptable knowledge. Just as there are rules for such things as tennis or international diplomacy, there are rules for science. And just like tennis or international diplomacy, not everyone necessarily operates according to the same set of rules.

A PHILOSOPHY OF SCIENCE

Years ago I was discussing religion with a friend. We disagreed about a lot of things, but we were calmly discussing the relative merits of our personal beliefs. At one point I asked my friend to explain why she believes what she does. She replied very simply, "I believe it because I know it's true." Then I asked how she knew it was true, and she said, "I know in my heart it's true." She could not explain why she believes what she believes, any more than I could explain why I believe what I do about religion. We both thought we were correct, but neither of us could logically prove we were correct in any absolute sense. At best, we could point out we were not alone in our beliefs. Of course, most people accept the notion that there is no absolute proof when the topic is religious beliefs. What many people do not understand is that the same is true about science.

Any set of rules that defines what is acceptable, empirical knowledge may be called a **philosophy of science**. Among philosophers of science and among scientists, however, there is more than one accepted philosophy. This is partly because philosophers, like members of any other discipline, are developing, changing, and assessing new ideas and formulations in an attempt to improve upon what we know. Whatever their differences, however, all philosophers of science need to address the same four basic questions: (1) When is something true? (2) If we have more than one explanation, how can we tell which one is better? (3) How can we put what we know into practice? and (4) Why do we do it the way we do it?

In this chapter we will concentrate on a particular philosophy of science called nonjustificationism (Weimer, 1979). The name of this viewpoint is derived from the position that a scientific approach cannot be justified—proven valid—except through unproven assumptions; **nonjustificationism** is a *philosophy of science for which the major premise is that we cannot logically prove that the way we go about doing research is correct in any absolute sense.* While this conclusion may seem outlandish right now, the remaining discussion should help you understand why this outlandish conclusion is quite logical and not at all inconsistent with a scientific approach to understanding the world.

When Is Something True?

This first question to be answered through any philosophy of science is usually called the question of **rational inference**—*the difficulty inherent in supporting any claim about the existence of a universal truth.* Just as when my friend and I were discussing religious beliefs there was more than one truth, there is more than one solution to the problem of rational inference. In order to be scientific, whatever we accept as our answer to the question of when something is true, i.e., our interim solution to the rational inference problem, must be based on **facts**—*phenomena or characteristics available to anyone who knows how to observe them.* Recall Sagan's (1980) second rule of science: whatever does not agree with the facts is wrong and must be changed or rejected completely. Although the statement is simple, deciding how to go about the process is a little more complex.

Behavioral scientists, for example, are interested in understanding how people interact with each other at a variety of different levels. We want to understand as much about people and human phenomena as possible. No matter how many facts we have, however, we cannot understand them until we have a way to summarize those facts. Summarizing facts—making them comprehensible—is what theories are all about.

But anyone can make up a theory about human behavior. Given enough time, just about everyone in the world could articulate some sort of theory for any given phenomenon. Thus, we have the equivalent of a very large warehouse that is full of theories. This imaginary warehouse contains as many different theories about people as there are people in the world, multiplied by the number of different theories each of those individuals has for each of the various phenomena that make up human behavior. Clearly, we need to imagine a very large (and probably quite disorganized) warehouse. Of course, each discipline has its own warehouse of theories, so deciding what to do with all of the theories in all of the sciences can be somewhat daunting, but it is not impossible.

At a very simple level, all we have to do is compare each theory in the warehouse to the facts: if the theory does not fit the facts, we change it or throw it out of the warehouse. This process may sound good, but it just does not work that way. Theories are made up of **concepts**—*abstract words that are used to represent concrete phenomena.* We can point to concrete examples of concepts, but the concepts themselves are abstract. For example, conflict, as a theoretical concept, is not the same thing as a family argument or a revolution. Family argument and revolution are, of course, concrete examples of conflict, but they are only examples and not complete definitions. No matter how compellingly practical a concept may be, it is only an approximation of reality, and any given concrete phenomenon is only an approximation of a concept (Wartofsky, 1968). Theories symbolize or represent the real world in which we live and behave, but the concepts within the theories are not the same thing as the real world. Because concepts are abstract and the facts we rely on to test them are concrete, deciding whether or not a theory fits the facts is rather difficult.

This difficulty arises because we must rely on inductive reasoning when fitting facts to a theory. **Inductive reasoning** is *a process of generalization; it involves applying specific information to a general situation or future events.* Let me illustrate with a story about a college instructor of mine who consistently arrived 10 minutes late for class. About three weeks into the semester, I came to the conclusion that he would continue to do so, which meant I could sleep an extra 10 minutes on those days and still arrive "on time" for class. This conclusion was a generalization, an inductive inference. Based on the instructor's specific behavior—arriving late during the first three weeks—I attributed to him a general or abstract quality—tardiness—and used that abstract concept to predict his behavior in the future. Unfortunately, it never occurred to me he would show up on time for the midterm exam, and I developed cramps in my hand trying to write fast enough to make up for the time I lost by arriving late. It was a rather painful way to learn that inductive reasoning does not necessarily lead to absolute truth.

Despite the inability of inductive reasoning to lead us to absolute truth, we must rely on it in any scientific approach to research. We simply cannot let all those theories pile up in the warehouse until we have all of the facts; nor can we wait for all the facts before we begin to construct theories to put in the warehouse. Instead, we simply accept the notion that inductive reasoning is the best process of generalization we have until something better comes along.

Had I waited until after the midterm exam before attributing tardiness to my instructor, I could have saved myself some writing cramps (and perhaps gotten a better grade on the exam). But even then I could not have been sure that he would be on time for the final exam, nor could I be certain that he would not begin arriving on time after the midterm. Of course, I could have just arrived on time myself every day, but that would have meant missing out on hours of extra sleep accumulated across the entire semester. I weighed the alternatives and constructed my theory about his behavior. After he showed up late the first day after the midterm, I reverted to sleeping an extra 10 minutes, but I showed up on time for the final exam. I adjusted my initial theory to fit the new facts, but I did not wait until I had all of the facts before constructing my new theory.

I have simplified the arguments involved in this issue, but the basic point of the rational inference problem is rather simple: inductive inferences cannot be proved true, but we need to use them to construct theories until we have evidence to the contrary. If we have enough contrary evidence, we can throw a theory out of our warehouse, but that does not mean that any of the theories remaining in the warehouse is true. We are left with no choice but to provide support for a theory by trying to show that alternative, competing theories are not true. If we make a prediction from a theory and test the prediction, and if the prediction fits the facts, then we have *not* proved the theory to be true; instead, we have failed to prove that the theory is false. It is difficult to think in terms of double negatives—Theory X is not not-true—but that is the logic forced on us by the rational inference problem. Thus, research in which we test between two competing theories is better than research in which we test only one theory, because comparing theories is one way to deal with the rational inference problem.

How Can We Tell Which Theory Is Better?

The absence of absolute truth does not limit what we can learn in a scientific approach, but we are faced with a particular path in our quest to learn about behavior and other real-world phenomena. We can, as I mentioned above, test between two different theories and decide which one is better. Testing between theories is like a grand tournament in which every theory is pitted against every other theory; the theory with the best win-loss record at the end of the tournament is the winner. Of course, that does not mean that the winning theory is true—only that it is the best theory we have until another, better theory is entered in the tournament. Like all tournaments, the tournament of scientific theories has some rules about which theories are entered and how many times a theory has to lose in order to be eliminated.

The rules of the grand tournament of science bring us to the problem called **criteria for growth**—*finding standards that can be used to decide that one explanation is better than another*. We all know, for example, that as an explanation of the apparent movement of the sun across the sky, current theories of astronomy are more accurate (but less poetic) than the myth of Helios, the sun god, waking every morning and driving his fiery chariot across the sky. We would scoff at anyone who seriously believed the Helios explanation, just as any ancient Greek would have scoffed at our current theories. How we came to decide that astronomy is better than mythology involves our criteria for growth: paradigms and facts.

Theories, whether in or out of our imaginary warehouse, do not exist in a vacuum. Every theory is related to at least one other theory through shared concepts or propositions. Kuhn (1962) was the first to use the term paradigm (pronounced "pair-a-dime") to describe such groups of related theories. A **paradigm** is *a logical system that encompasses theories, concepts, models, procedures, and techniques*. The earth-centered solar system, for example, was once a paradigm in physics, just as instinct was once a paradigm in psychology (McDougall, 1908). At the time McDougall was theorizing about human behavior, the predominant explanations included some notion about instinctual processes; there was an instinct for survival, one for aggression, and so on. New observations about behavior were interpreted in terms of existing instincts, and if new observations did not fit, then new instincts were invented to account for the observations.

During a period of time in which a particular paradigm is accepted, which Kuhn referred to as a period of normal science, research is directed toward solving problems related to matching current theories with observations. At such times research tends to be directed toward refining theories, toward trying to make them better, such as inventing new instincts to fit research observations. New research and the refinements of theories add to the strength of the paradigm, which in turn leads to the perception that the paradigm, including its associated theories and procedures, is the best way to explain what goes on in the world.

Eventually, however, problems with the paradigm emerge as more and more information cannot be fit into the existing theories. I note "eventually" because no matter how reasonable or useful a paradigm may be, it, too, is based on inductive reasoning and thus cannot be considered to be universal truth. When enough problems emerge and an alternative paradigm, complete with its own theories and procedures, arises that fits the observations better, then the old paradigm gives way to a new one during what Kuhn calls a scientific revolution. Thus Galileo started a scientific revolution with his notion of a sun-centered solar system, although it took years before the followers of the earth-centered paradigm accepted the new paradigm. Then the new paradigm becomes *the* paradigm and the field returns again to normal science, until the next paradigm shift occurs.

Underlying all of normal and revolutionary science is reliance on facts. Observations are considered to be facts when people can point to concrete examples of the observation. Although it may seem **tautological** to require facts to be observable, that very requirement is one of the reasons McDougall's instinct theories eventually gave way to modern explanations of behavior; there was no way to observe—to be able to point to concrete examples of—the processes by which instincts influence behavior. Today, of course, we have some evidence for instinctual processes as one of several possible explanations for some behaviors (see, for example, Lea & Webley, 2006; Snyder, 1987), but we do not use instinct as the primary explanatory concept for all behavior.

In addition to being observable, facts must also be **objective**. Within a scientific approach, **objectivity** means *that an observation can be replicated, observed by more than one person under a variety of different conditions.* If I am the only researcher who can demonstrate a particular effect, it is not objective. If, however, several others note the same effect under different conditions, then we have a fact, an objective observation that needs to be incorporated into existing theories.

Thus, during normal science, theories are compared on the basis of their fit into the existing paradigm as well as our ability to use them to account for the existing facts. During revolutionary science, comparisons occur between old and new paradigms, but the basis for such comparisons remains the existing facts. Then, upon return to normal science, theories within the current paradigm are again evaluated in terms of their fit with the facts. It is important to note, however, that because a new paradigm may redefine what is an acceptable fact, the facts may change from time to time (Fleck, 1979).

How Can We Put What We Know Into Practice?

By now you may be having some serious doubts about how a scientific approach can be a path to anything except confusion. There are no absolute truths, and sometimes what were once considered to be facts are no longer considered to be so. We have arrived at the problem of **pragmatic action**—*determining how we should go about putting a scientific approach into practice*. Essentially, those who adopt a scientific approach must get together and decide how they are going to use that approach. The solution to the problem of pragmatic action, the answer to the question of how we put what we know into practice, lies in agreement.

Just as legal theorists assume that a decision made by 12 jurors is better than a decision made by one juror, scientists agree that evidence obtained by a number of different researchers is better than evidence obtained by one researcher; that is, objective data—repeatable observations—are agreed to be better than subjective data. The greater the number of researchers who produce the same research results, the more we consider those results to be facts to which we must fit our theories; notice that the theories must fit the facts, not the other way around. A variety of reasonable arguments support this agreement about objectivity, but no one can prove, in any absolute sense, that the consensus is correct. As Sagan suggested, it is not perfect, but it is the best we have.

One of the problems inherent in the use of objectivity is the variety of different research methods available to study any particular phenomenon (see, e.g., Watson, 1967). When researchers use different methods to study the same phenomena, they often come up with different observations. Consensus, then, must extend into agreement about which research methods are appropriate for which research questions, as well as agreement about whether or not a particular method was used properly. Essentially, that is what this book and the course you are taking are all about. You cannot rely solely on the assumption that the experts have used the correct research method to answer their question; you must be able to determine yourself whether the methods used by the researchers fit the way in which you want to use the research results.

For example, in the early years of research about differences between men and women, one of the more common methods was to select a group of men and a group of women, have both groups do something such as solve math problems, and then compare the performances of the two groups. If the performances of the groups were different, then the researchers concluded that the results reflected basic differences between the two sexes. Deaux and Major (1987), however, presented convincing, empirical arguments that such things as the context of the situation, self-presentation strategies, researchers' and participants' beliefs about whether or not the sexes ought to be different, and a variety of other factors can change the results obtained from such methods. Therefore, the potential influence of such factors must be considered before we conclude that gender differences reflect basic differences between men and women.

We now know that simply comparing a group of men to a group of women is not an effective way to examine gender differences. Then again, everyone "knew" back in the old days that such simple comparisons were the best way to study gender differences. Even though we rely on consensus for such purposes as fitting theories to facts and even for deciding what is a fact, we must keep in mind that a new consensus might emerge after we have obtained more information. Still, there can be no scientific approach without consensus.

Why Do We Do It the Way We Do?

Every time I discuss consensus as the basis for a scientific approach, I can hear my mother saying, "Would you jump off a cliff just because everyone else is doing it?" That was her response, for example, to my wanting to stay out late because my friends' parents allowed them to stay out late; I am sure you have heard the same response when you have tried to use similar reasoning, or you have provided the same response when your children used that reasoning. What we have come to, then, is the problem of **intellectual honesty**—*the individual scientist's ability to justify the use of science itself*. If we can never prove that theories are true, if paradigms are only temporary, and if facts and methods for gathering them may change, then why would we ever accept a scientific approach as a valid way to learn anything?

Consider a simple survey of students' attitudes about current grading practices. In order to understand and apply that study, we must rely on a great deal of background information. We must accept research about students' reading levels when examining the questionnaire, accept research that suggests that a survey is a reasonable way to measure attitudes, accept research concerning the best way to format the questions on the survey, accept research about which statistics are appropriate to analyze the data, and so on. All of that research comes from within a scientific approach, and we are using that information to add more facts to the same scientific approach. Where does it all end?

The solution to the intellectual honesty problem—the answer to why we do it the way we do—can again be found in Sagan's quote at the beginning of this chapter: it is "by far the best tool we have." We do it the way we do it because we have not found a better way. Very simply, we adopt a scientific approach because we have a certain amount of faith in it because it works; or as my grandfather used to say, "If it ain't broke, don't fix it." Note, however, that the faith is placed in the approach itself, not in any particular theory that comes from the approach.

Recall the debate between evolutionists and creationists mentioned in Chapter 1. Theistic intervention (active causation by a god, not necessarily the existence of a god) serves as an explanation for creationists because they have faith in their approach. Similarly, evolution serves as an explanation for evolutionists because scientists have faith in their approach. Neither side will be able to convince the other because they do not have any common ground of agreement; they place their intellectual honesty on two entirely different points of view (Bobkowski, 2007). If you refuse to place your faith in a scientific approach, no amount of argument on my part will convince you to do so. On the other hand, if you can accept the limitations of a scientific approach and still remain convinced it is the best tool we have for extending our knowledge about the world, then we can go on to discuss some of the differences between scientific and nonscientific approaches and we can begin to deal with the rules and guidelines of scientific research. But before moving on, see Table 2.1 for a summary of our discussion of the philosophy of science.

Table 2.1	Justificationist and Nonjustificationist Approaches to the Four Basic Questions Inherent in Any Philosophy of Science	
The Questions	**Justificationist Approach to Science**	**Nonjustificationist Approach to Science**
The rational inference problem: When is something true?	Facts → One correct theory	Facts → Many incorrect theories
Criteria for growth: How can we tell which theory is better?	Better fit with paradigm and facts	Better fit with paradigm and facts
Pragmatic action: How can we put what we know into practice?	Consensus → Correct paradigm	Consensus → Better, but not correct paradigm
Intellectual honesty: Why do we do science the way we do?	Science → Absolute truth	Believe science is the best way to obtain knowledge

SCIENCE AND NONSCIENCE COMPARED

I keep bringing up the notion that we all conduct research all of the time. We are all, in one way or another, gathering new information to increase our knowledge about our world. Such everyday research is not necessarily scientific, but it does provide us with a way to satisfy our curiosity. In addition to the points noted above, the differences between scientific and nonscientific research generally revolve around avoiding mistakes. Mistakes can occur when we make observations, when we interpret observations, or when we accept various misconceptions about what is included in a scientific approach toward research.

Observation

Whenever we observe something, we make errors; period, no exceptions, ever. The errors, which researchers generally call bias, come from selecting what to observe and interpreting what we observe, as well as from the act of observation itself. We cannot avoid bias entirely, but we can attempt to reduce error to a minimum and be aware of error that we have not been able to eliminate.

For example, what we decide to observe creates a form of bias because it prevents us from making other observations at the same time. This is an error of omission that results simply because we cannot be in two places at the same time. That does not mean that what we do observe is wrong or incorrect, but rather that it is incomplete. Essentially, we need to keep in mind that what we have been observing is not all that could be observed. For example, researchers before Jacobs's (1967) study on suicide notes had concentrated mainly on suicide statistics. Durkheim's (1951/1897) original work had led them in that direction, and that approach was certainly adding to our understanding of suicide. But suicide statistics would never have given us the kind of information that Jacobs was able to obtain from his analysis of the contents of suicide notes. The bias in this example involved looking in only one place, a bias that Jacobs corrected with his study. This is one of the ways in which science is self-correcting; new observations correct the errors of previous observations.

Of course, objectivity is another way to reduce, but not eliminate, the bias inherent in observation. When more people observe the same thing, under the same or different conditions, then the collection of observations becomes more accurate (less biased, more complete). Different observers, different situations, different locations, and different definitions of what to observe all contribute to the objectivity of data, and all reduce observation error. Realizing that all observation contains some amount of error or bias is an important part of a scientific approach to research, for it prevents anyone from saying, "Your results are wrong and mine are correct." If we accept the notion that everyone's data are a little bit wrong (contain some error, some bias), then we can concentrate on trying to figure out why our observations do not agree; that is, we can begin to refine our theories so that they more closely fit the existing facts.

Logical Analysis

The quality of observations is one distinction between scientific and nonscientific research, but it is far from being the only one. Once observations are made, we must interpret them and draw conclusions about them. We have already discussed the scientific reliance on inductive reasoning, so it should come as little surprise that induction plays an important role in data interpretation.

Suppose I look out my window and observe 90° displayed on the scale of a thermometer. I could, of course, reasonably conclude that the temperature outside my office is 90°, assuming I had reason to believe that my thermometer was accurate. Anyone else could also look out the same window and note the same reading, and they would probably come to the same conclusion. Inductive reasoning enters the interpretation process when we attempt to move our conclusions beyond the immediate area outside my window, beyond the immediate confines of the data collection environment. Beyond my window is the remainder of the campus, the town, the county, the state, the country, and so on. How far beyond our immediate observations we can reasonably interpret those observations is both a matter of inductive reasoning and yet another distinction between scientific and nonscientific research.

Given our general knowledge about meteorology, we could reasonably conclude that the temperature around campus and town is about 90°. I would be reluctant to speculate about temperature across the state, as would most people. The same reluctance applies to interpreting data collected in a research project: how far we **generalize**, *relate findings gathered from the research situation to other situations*, is limited by common sense and background information about the research topic. If college students participated in a study about jury decision-making processes, I would feel comfortable generalizing the results to actual jurors by claiming actual jurors may use the same decision-making *processes* that the students used. However, I would not feel comfortable claiming that actual jurors would make the same *decisions* that the students did. The way in which students and actual jurors go about making decisions may be the same, but the decisions produced by that same process may be quite different because they may pay attention to different information (have different biases) and may have different life experiences with which to interpret the information they receive. **Overgeneralization**—*drawing conclusions too far beyond the scope of immediate observations*—brings scientific research into the realm of nonscientific research.

Research Reports

From time to time you may find yourself reading a research article in which it appears as though the researchers designed their study to test a theory, collected data, and supported the theory discussed in the introduction of the article. You should know, and the researchers should know, that logic does not enable us to support a theory. Yet they write such phrases as "research supports the theory of. . . ." or "the theory of X has received a great deal of empirical support." In such cases the language of scientific research appears to conflict with scientific philosophy.

Keep in mind that the reason that research cannot support a theory is that "support" for a theory comes not from finding results consistent with a theory but from failing to find results that do not fit the theory. Remember the double negative logic of science: Failing to disconfirm a theory is the only empirical way to provide support for a theory. But support for a theory does not mean the same thing as proof that a theory is correct. It is a little too verbose to write "a number of researchers have attempted to disconfirm theory X and have failed to do so" continually, and so we sometimes write "theory X has received empirical support."

Most authors of research articles create the impression that the researchers knew, from the start, exactly how the major results of the study would come out. Instead, research is often conducted with extremely little certainty about how the results will turn out. The researchers are not trying to hide their inability to predict the results accurately; rather, they are succinctly providing a theoretical context for their results. No matter how unexpected the results of research may be, they cannot contribute to what we already know unless they can be placed into a theoretical context.

For example, when I was asked by a defense attorney to consult on the voir dire (often called "jury selection") process in a criminal trial, I took advantage of an opportunity to interview the jurors after the trial. What I noticed from these interviews was that jurors who seemed very different on the basis of such characteristics as age and socioeconomic status also ended up on opposite sides of the hung jury resulting from the trial (Whitman & Dane, 1980). If you read the publication that resulted from those interviews, it appears as though I had a very logical theoretical framework before I conducted the interviews and that I found support for the theory in the results of my study. Not so.

I did have an initial theoretical framework before conducting the research, but it was nowhere near as logically organized as it was presented in the article. It was more like a hunch based on what I knew about jury behavior and social psychology. However, a scientific approach to research does not involve telling everyone about hunches; it involves presenting research results that help evaluate theories. So after interpreting the results, I wrote a very logical, organized, theoretical introduction to the article so that my presentation of the research results made sense in the context of the introduction. Kerr (1998) refers to such writing as HARKing (Hypothesizing After the Results are Known) and notes that there are costs associated with such writing. As a general rule, HARKing ought not to be done without an explicit statement that one has done so. As a consumer of research, however, you will find it difficult to determine whether or not an author has engaged in HARKing.

Definitive Studies

Although any study may satisfy someone's curiosity about a particular issue, no study ever satisfies scientific interest in an issue. That is, despite the fact that one often hears the phrase used in one or another context, there is no such thing as a **definitive study**—*a research project that completely answers a question*. Because any particular phenomenon is extremely complex, someone will always ask, "But what if. . . ?" Such questions point out the need for additional research. Proposing that a definitive study can exist produces premature closure of activity; as Yogi Berra is supposed to have said about a baseball game, "It ain't over 'til it's over." It is, of course, difficult to argue with such logic. Within a scientific approach to research, it is not over until it is no longer possible to ask "What if?"

Although definitive studies may not exist, there are highly influential studies that set an entire research program, or series of programs, in motion. These studies have a great deal of **heuristic value**—*they stimulate additional research activity*. Milgram's (1963) research on obedience is one example of a study with high heuristic value. It not only generated a great deal of controversy concerning research ethics; it also stimulated extensive research on compliance of individuals and groups. Munsterberg's (1913) studies of the accuracy of eyewitnesses' recollections, many of which were demonstrations conducted in the classroom, were also highly heuristic. Many examples of current research on eyewitnesses can be traced to one or another of his demonstrations.

As an administrator, you should neither look for nor believe you have found a study that conclusively proves whether or not a program is effective; you won't find such a study because they simply don't exist. You will, however, find many claims that others have found such a study. I recently searched for the phrase "science proves" on Google and turned up about 93,700 Web sites, not all of which were quack sites, which merely demonstrates that there are many individuals who don't understand the limitations of science. In case you are interested, another search for the phrase "research proves" resulted in about 158,000 Web sites; a quick scan of some of those sites convinced me that many writers confuse *prove* with *demonstrate*, a confusion that could lead to erroneous conclusions about the value of a program or policy.

Determinism

Perhaps the most misunderstood concept in a scientific approach to research is **determinism,** the *assumption that every event has at least one discoverable cause.* As defined here, determinism means nothing more than "events do not happen by themselves." We assume that there is always a causal agent and that the agent can be discovered through a scientific approach to research. If you think about it at all, you will realize that there could not be science without determinism. The purpose of psychology, for example, is to understand the causes of human behavior; if we did not assume that every human behavior had at least one cause, then there would be no point to trying to understand the causes of human behavior.

Many people, however, incorrectly mistake determinism for **predestination,** the *assumption that events are unalterable.* The two assumptions clearly are not at all similar. Indeed, there is some notion in determinism that once we are able to discover the cause of an event, we can alter the cause and thereby alter the event. There may, of course, be theories that include the assumption of predestination, and some of those theories may be tested through scientific research, but predestination is an aspect of a specific theory and not an assumption inherent in science.

Table 2.2 contains a summary of the differences between what is and what is not included in a scientific approach to research. Although there may be many other comparisons that could be drawn, you should have enough background in philosophy of science to begin putting it into practice.

Table 2.2	Comparisons Between Science and Nonscience	
Science Is	**Science Is Not**
A way to obtain new information	An activity per se
Described by a philosophy	Defined by only one philosophy
Generalizing from facts	A way to prove theories true
Grounded in paradigms	Blind acceptance of tradition
Based on consensus	Relying on personal authority
A matter of faith	Uncritical faith
Deterministic	Predestination
The best approach we have	Refusing to search for a better approach

ETHICS OF CONSUMING RESEARCH

I continue to be amazed that codes of ethics for researchers, particularly those who do research on human beings, did not emerge until the middle of the 20th century. To that point, the public, including researchers, assumed that scientists had sufficient integrity so as to make formal guidelines and regulations unnecessary, but the torture and other inhumane treatment of concentration camp inmates by the Nazis during World War II convinced the world community that guidelines were necessary, and The Nuremberg Code was enacted (Nuremberg Military Tribunal, 1949). The code emphasized the importance of **informed consent**, *the process of ensuring prospective participants have all the knowledge they need to make a reasonable decision concerning their participation*, and a balance of risks and benefits such that the latter outweighed the former (Gorman & Dane, 1994). Expansion of the code for physicians and other medical researchers resulted in the Declaration of Helsinki (World Medical Association, 1964), which further clarified the relationship between research and treatment.

In the United States, breaches of research ethics, again primarily in biomedical research (see, e.g., Jones, 1993), led to the passage of the 1974 National Research Act. The act included creation of the National Commission for the Protection of Human Subjects of Biomedical and Behavioral Research (National Commission for the Protection of Human Subjects of Biomedical and Behavioral Research, 1979; Seiler & Murtha, 1981), the purpose of which was to recommend an overall policy for research with human participants. The commission provided a report that led to a number of changes in the ways in which biomedical and behavioral research is conducted. Eventually, a formal set of regulations was adopted in the United States ("Final regulations amending basic HHS policy for the protection of human research subjects," 1981; "Protection of Human Subjects," 2001) that included establishment of institutional review boards (IRB) to conduct prior review and continuing oversight of all human subjects research conducted within the purview of any institution or organization that received federal funds. Similar developments in other countries have led to nearly global adoption of some form of guidelines or regulations concerning the conduct of human subjects research (Office for Human Research Protections, 2007).

The existing regulations and guidelines provide considerable direction as researchers attempt to balance the mutual obligations of developing new knowledge (Cook, 1981; Mindick, 1982) and treating individuals involved in our research with proper consideration (Dane, 1990). If you find yourself in a position to conduct research, or direct others to conduct research, you should become familiar with these guidelines and regulations. For the purpose of consuming research, however, it is more important to understand the principles that are used to guide the development of such regulations and to recognize the ways in which these principles apply to research consumption.

Ethical Principles of Research

In the Belmont Report, the National Commission for the Protection of Human Subjects of Biomedical and Behavioral Research (1979) established three principles by which all research should be guided—respect for persons, beneficence, and justice—and to these have been added trust and scientific integrity (Dane, 2006, 2007b; Dane & Parish, 2006). These five principles will form the basis of our discussion of the ethics of research consumption.

Respect for Persons

Respect for persons is a principle derived from the ethical theory proposed by Immanuel Kant (1788/1997), from which we obtain the admonition never to use another human being merely as a means to an end; that is, this principle involves maintaining others' **autonomy,** *the ability to direct oneself, particularly through the exercise of independent processing of information.* We see this implemented, among other ways, in the presumption of informed consent for research participants. In the context of research consumption, respect for persons involves giving researchers proper credit, representing others' work accurately, and providing comprehensive information to those who will benefit from our consumption of research.

At this point in your academic experience you are well familiar with the requirement to use quotation marks or other, similar conventions whenever you use someone else's words; to do otherwise is plagiarism. The purpose of this convention is to ensure that the individual who wrote the words receives credit for having done so and to prevent readers from thinking that the words are ours instead of the original author's. Similarly, whenever we obtain information from another source or use an idea obtained from someone else's work, we give credit by citing the source from which we obtained the information or idea; again, this prevents readers from thinking that the information or idea is original to us. Giving researchers proper credit, however, involves going beyond the usual conventions to avoid plagiarism; we also do so through the manner in which we write about the research. Thus, we should refer to the authors, not to unnamed "researchers" or "research" (see, e.g., American Psychological Association, 2001). For example, when describing the research mentioned in Chapter 1, we should write "Sales (1972) demonstrated an increase in membership in authoritarian religions during difficult economic times" instead of writing "Research has shown an increase in membership in authoritarian religions during difficult economic times (Sales, 1972)." While both sentences provide credit to Sales for the information, the former makes it clear that Sales conducted the research; the latter refers only to Sales as the source of the information and could mean that anyone conducted the research about which we learned from reading Sales.

Just as we respect others by giving them proper credit as the sources of the information we use, we also respect others by representing their work accurately. Obviously, we want to convey correctly information we obtain from others, but accuracy goes beyond "getting it right" in the sense that we must avoid oversimplifying research results. Rector (2002), for example, reported that an evaluation of the Not Me, Not Now abstinence-only advertising campaign (Doniger, Riley, Utter, & Adams, 2001) included a reduction in pregnancy rates among 15-year-old teens but did not report that Doniger et al. also found no change in pregnancy rates among women aged 17. The failure to report the additional results oversimplifies the results, and could mislead those reading the report, leaving them to think that the change in pregnancy rates was longer lasting than it actually was. Conveying the complications sometimes demonstrated in research can be difficult, but our ethical obligation to respect individuals, those who reported the research and those who will read our review of that research, requires that we overcome such difficulty. Accurately reporting results also involves making sure that our readers understand what was measured in the research we review. The Union of Concerned Scientists (2006), for example, reported numerous examples in which government reports concerning abstinence-only sex-education programs labeled various programs as effective without noting that *effective* was defined in terms of attendance or changes in attitudes about sexual behavior; actual sexual behavior was not measured in the research included in these reports. There is, of course, nothing wrong with considering attitude change to be a desired outcome, but it is inaccurate, and therefore undermines autonomy, when one implies that changes in attitudes toward sexual activity are synonymous with changes in sexual behavior, per se.

Finally, we demonstrate respect for persons when our reports about research are comprehensive, when they include all relevant research and not just those studies that conform to our preferences or those of our intended audience. Imagine your reaction upon reading about a researcher who reported only part of the data, only those data that were consistent with a conclusion drawn by the researcher even before data were collected. I hope your reaction would include outrage and a general conclusion akin to "that's not right" or "that's dishonest." Indeed, such behavior would be evidence of a lack of respect for one's audience through undermining autonomy by misleading the readers; it would be dishonest. A failure to present all relevant studies in a review of research, too, would be similarly dishonest. The key word in the previous sentence is "relevant." As of this writing, a quick search of the ProQuest database of publications yields 157 articles in scholarly journals on abstinence-only sexual education, 21 of which also include the key term *evaluation*. Thus, a review of the effectiveness of such programs would not necessarily need to include all 157 articles but most probably should include the 21 articles involving evaluations. Similarly, the same search conducted through Google yielded about 99,900 sites for "abstinence-only sex education," which would be impractical to review, but only 55 sites when the phrase "evaluation report" was added to the search box, a much more manageable number of sites to examine. Between the 21 ProQuest articles and the 55 sites identified through Google, one would have a very good start to meeting this ethical obligation to include relevant material.

In summary, respect for persons, in the context of consuming research, involves giving credit where it is due, accurately reporting research procedures and results, and comprehensively reporting the available, relevant research. To do anything less undermines the autonomy of our audience; it reduces the accuracy or amount of information for decision making available to our audience members.

Beneficence

While researchers have an ethical obligation to generate new knowledge (Cook, 1981; Mindick, 1982), they also have an ethical obligation to do so in a manner that promotes the public good (National Commission for the Protection of Human Subjects of Biomedical and Behavioral Research, 1979). The notion that knowledge is beneficial in and of itself has a long tradition in Western thought (see, e.g., Plato, 2005), and so, to some extent, researchers satisfy both ethical obligations simply by producing new knowledge. As research consumers in the role of administrator, policy analyst, or policy implementer, we also have an ethical obligation to promote the public good, to engage in beneficence (Cooper, 1998; Svara, 2007). We, too, partially fulfill that obligation simply by producing new knowledge.

It may seem strange to think that a reviewer of others' work produces new knowledge—after all, the information already exists in the original research reports we review—but a good review goes beyond simply noting what others have found in their research. Yet even simply noting what others have done can be beneficent in the sense that a list and description of sources in a single document makes information available in a more convenient format. Nevertheless, a good review involves using the information in existing sources to make a particular point, to draw a conclusion that would not have been obvious from reading only one or two of the original sources.

Of course, one can argue that adopting an empirical approach to policy analysis is itself another way in which to promote beneficence. As noted by Mead (1969), increases in knowledge often precipitate fear about how that knowledge will be used. In the context of policy implementation and analysis, a careful review of research knowledge about the effects of the program can be used to reduce such fear. Reviews can be used to identify ways to improve programs, as opposed to recommend only "yes" or "no," in much the same way that research is used to improve scientific theories. The absence (or insufficiency) of empirical research can be used to promote additional research on a specific program or a social problem in general. Many people also tend to be afraid of empirical program or policy evaluation as a result of experience or hearsay regarding misuse of such efforts (see, e.g., Posavac, 1994), but a careful, comprehensive review of research can be used to allay such fears. Thus, the ethical obligation of beneficence, promoting the public good, is relevant to reviewing research for program or policy analysis; indeed, the obligation can be met by ensuring widespread dissemination of research reviews.

Justice

In the context of conducting research, the ethical obligation for justice refers generally to ensuring that risks and benefits associated with research are distributed equally throughout the population (National Commission for the Protection of Human Subjects of Biomedical and Behavioral Research, 1979). For example, toward the end of the 20th century a great deal of attention was focused on the underrepresentation of women included as subjects in biomedical research (Mastroianni, Faden, & Federman, 1999). This meant that men were much more likely to benefit from the results of such research and that too little attention was paid to women's health issues, which eventually came to be perceived as patently unfair or unjust. More recently, we see that the risks associated with stem cell research are being inequitably borne by those governmental regions that allow such research (Dane, 2007a).

It may seem puzzling to think in terms of risks associated with reviewing existing research: After all, how likely is it that someone could be harmed by your writing about research that has already been done? But reviews can have considerable impact, particularly when they are used to evaluate social programs and policies. Jensen (1969a), for example, reviewed research on intelligence, particularly twin studies, to inform efforts related to **compensatory education**—*attempting to raise the educational level of individuals whose education has been disadvantaged for one reason or another.* Among other questionable aspects of his review was the combination of his noting that "all of the major heritability studies reported in the literature are based on samples of white European and North American populations, and our knowledge of the heritability of intelligence in different racial and cultural groups within these populations is nil" (1969a, p. 64) and, 20 pages later, using heritability data to support the claim that genetic factors were the primary explanation of the differences in intelligence-test scores between Whites and Blacks in the United States. The erroneous conclusion, however, was not merely an example of "could be better" writing; Brazzill (1969) noted that only five days after Jensen's research made headlines in Virginia newspapers, defense attorneys in a school integration suit were quoting from Jensen's article to support their claim that school systems should remain segregated. The defense attorneys and the newspaper article about Jensen's research appeared to have completely ignored the qualifications that Jensen included in his article and a subsequently published reply to critics (Jensen, 1969b). Jensen, fulfilling his ethical obligation, wrote a letter to the editor in response to the misapplication of his results, but by that point the damage was done.

Again, we return to the notion that careful writing is important, but meeting one's ethical obligation of justice involves going beyond careful writing. You have already read about the difficulties inherent in generalizing from research results, and this becomes particularly relevant when reviewing research for program evaluation or policy analysis. It becomes quite important to consider the range of research subjects included in the relevant research and compare that range to the diversity of individuals who are to benefit from a program or will be affected by a policy. If most evaluation research involved teenagers, for example, fulfilling the obligation of justice would include an explicit, comprehensively presented caution about applying the research to a program for younger children, as well as an explicit call for research that included younger children.

At the heart of the concept of justice with respect to empirical policy analysis is the notion that Campbell (1969, 1971) referred to as the experimenting society, which involves both a willingness to evaluate the outcomes of programs and policies and the willingness to try new programs without guaranteeing that the outcomes will be positive. If policy makers and others present a new program as some sort of guaranteed treatment or cure for a particular social problem, then they become committed to the program and very reluctant to reverse their positions and admit that the program was less effective than required or to alter the program substantially in light of empirical research. Once reputations are on the line, there is a strong tendency to find ways to describe the program as effective or valuable even in the face of empirical information to the contrary. Despite considerable research on the lack of effectiveness of Drug Abuse Resistance Education, also known as Project DARE (Lynam et al., 1999), the commitments, one could argue "guarantees," of those who initially and continue to tout the program (see, e.g., Dillon, 2006) have created considerable pressure to maintain the program. It is, of course, not possible to calculate how much time and money could have been saved if, instead, those involved in the program had adopted an "experimenting" approach and incorporated all relevant empirical research into subsequent planning and implementation. Few would argue with the notion that societal resources should be allocated equitably, fairly, or otherwise justly, and this ethical obligation applies equally to an equitable allocation of resources to programs proportionally to their effectiveness. Reviewing research and applying the results of that research is one way to fulfill this obligation.

Trust

As we learned earlier, the enterprise of science relies heavily on trust. Although a scientific approach is self-correcting, scientists have to rely on each other, trust each other, because it is logistically impossible to double-check everything, to look over each scientist's shoulders to ensure that he or she is doing exactly what was presented in a research report. Thus, those reading about our research on the effects of training nurses in advanced cardiac life support (ACLS) (Dane et al., 2000) have to trust that we correctly identified which nurses were trained and which were not, that we correctly identified which patients survived a resuscitation attempt and which did not, that we actually conducted the statistical analyses that we wrote about, and so on. The self-correcting nature of science will determine whether or not the sample we used was unique—if no one else can replicate the results we obtained, then our sample was unique—but ultimately, the entire scientific community must trust that we did the research the way we described doing the research.

So, too, those reading our reviews of research must trust that we actually read and understand the research reports we include in our reviews; they must trust that we made a good-faith effort to identify all relevant research reports, and so on. Our willingness to enter the scientific community as consumers of research thusly engenders an ethical obligation to be as trustworthy as those who produced the research being consumed. Beyond simple honesty, those who will read our reports and those who will be otherwise affected by the content of our reports are owed a high degree of competency in the construction of those reports.

Particularly in the areas of public policy, all those who are affected by such policy must place a considerable amount of trust in those who develop, analyze, and implement such policy. Indeed, some authors (e.g., Cooper, 1998; Svara, 2007) argue that maintaining public trust may be the most important ethical obligation of program administrators and others who work in areas affected by public policy. As with other ethical obligations, honest, comprehensive, careful, and expert review and application of research brings us quite far along the path of fulfilling the obligation of trust. Independently evaluating the quality of the research, for example, meets this obligation much better than merely accepting researchers' conclusions because they're the experts. We know that the self-correcting nature of research means that, indeed, errors are made; thus, we become part of the self-correcting process by critically examining research we review. Even though we may have biases about what conclusions we would like to include in our review, either for or against a particular program or policy, we have an obligation to set aside those biases and ensure that our conclusions are based on sound, methodological principles rather than on personal preferences.

Scientific Integrity

The ethical obligation for scientific integrity involves having respect for the scientific process itself and acting accordingly. For researchers, this involves, quite simply, "doing good research" in all that the phrase entails (Committee on Assessing Integrity in Research Environments, 2002). For consumers of research, this involves adopting a scientific approach to reading, understanding, and reporting on others' research, even if one is not actually a scientist. Thus, it involves behaving like a scientist when using science as the basis for commenting on programs or policies.

In addition to intellectual honesty, accuracy, fairness, and respect for those involved directly and indirectly, scientific integrity involves giving careful consideration to actual and potential conflicts and, if relevant, explicitly declaring those conflicts and comprehensively trying to overcome such conflicts. Just as in Chapter 1 we learned that one important part of critically reviewing research involves assessing the "who" of research, an important part of reviewing research ethically involves making potential readers aware of who we, the reviewers, are and what biases might have influenced our review. Although it is best to avoid conflicts of interest, it is probably not possible to do so entirely (Adams, 2007; Kimmelman, 2007; Pachter, Fox, Zimbardo, & Antonuccio, 2007). A program or policy you are reviewing may be the *raison d'être* for your department and an unfavorable review may put your position in jeopardy, or the program or policy may be a favorite of influential policy makers. In such circumstances, even the best attempt to be objective may not be fully successful. In a very well known study, for example, Rosenthal and Fode (1963) demonstrated that telling undergraduate researchers that rats were "bright" as opposed to "dull" resulted in "bright" rats performing better in a discrimination task. Similarly, Rosenthal and Jacobson (1966) demonstrated that, compared to a **control group** (*participants who receive no treatment or any set of participants to which the treatment group is being compared*), randomly assigned first- and second-grade students gained 10 to 15 IQ points after their teachers were falsely informed that the students had scored highly on a "test for intellectual blooming" (p. 115). (The effect was not obtained among students in Grades 3–8.) In neither study was there any evidence of cheating, such as falsely reported scores, among the researchers or teachers; Rosenthal et al. believed the effect was much more subtly produced, probably without the researchers' or teachers' intentional efforts or awareness.

Given that we cannot avoid conflicts of interest entirely and that we cannot avoid bias entirely when we have a conflict of interest, you may be tempted to think that there is nothing to be done, that we simply cannot meet the ethical obligation for scientific integrity, but you would be mistaken in that conclusion. There are tactics we can employ to overcome bias in a conflicted-interest situation. Perhaps the most important of these is becoming aware of the conflict (Cain, Loewenstein, & Moore, 2005). In the Rosenthal et al. studies (Rosenthal & Fode,

1963; Rosenthal & Jacobson, 1966), for example, neither the student researchers nor the teachers were aware that the information presented by the experimenters could bias them; you are in a much better position because you are now aware that even seemingly innocuous information can produce bias. Knowledge of potential bias is necessary but not sufficient; we also need to consider carefully and objectively how the bias could affect our decisions about the research we are reviewing. In other words, we need to think critically about our own thought processes and make our reasoning explicit (Moore & Loewenstein, 2004). Cooper (1998) refers to this as the "*60 Minutes* Test," as in thinking about how we would explain our decision if we were facing one of the interviewers on the CBS television show. Thus, while we make notes about one or another research project, we should keep asking ourselves questions such as these: Is this note correct? Would the project researchers agree with my characterization of their research? or Could someone else argue with my notation? As well, the text in our review must also match the notes we have taken.

In general, then, the ethical obligations with respect to consuming research are somewhat different than those for conducting research, despite the obligations having been based on the same five principles: respect for persons, beneficence, justice, trust, and scientific integrity. With the exception of scientific integrity, as opposed to integrity in general, you probably noticed that the obligations are very much the same as those included in the code of ethics, guidelines for responsible conduct, or other requirements established by the professional organizations of which you are a member. When we are functioning as experts, we must pay considerable attention to the actual and potential impacts we have on nonexperts. Similarly, when we function as research experts, we must pay attention to the actual and potential effects of our actions.

SUMMARY

- Science is not an activity but rather an approach to activities that share the goal of discovering knowledge. One of these activities is research.
- Like any approach, a scientific approach has limitations. These limitations include rational inference, criteria for growth, pragmatic action, and intellectual honesty.
- Rational inference is a limitation on the extent to which we can propose universal truths. Because we must rely on inductive reasoning for such proposals, we cannot prove their accuracy. Thus, we accept theories as temporarily correct, while always assuming that another, better theory is likely to come along.

- Criteria for growth is a limitation on the standards by which to judge the relative merits of explanations. Although such judgments are based on objective observations, we must be aware that the objectivity and relevance of observations are limited to the paradigm on which their relevance and objectivity are based.

- Pragmatic action is a limitation on the practice of research concerning methodological issues. Consensus, based on sound reasoning, is the way we decide how best to practice research.

- Intellectual honesty is a limitation on our willingness to accept a scientific approach. Placing one's faith in the scientific approach, however, does not involve believing in one or another particular theory.

- It is axiomatic that all observations contain some degree of error. Objectivity—the extent to which more than one observer can make the same measurement—decreases measurement error but does not eliminate it.

- Although research reports are written so as to place research results in a theoretical context, it is often the case that the theoretical context was logically derived after the research was conducted. This is a shortcoming when the author suggests that the hypothesis was derived prior to data collection.

- Despite the fact that a scientific approach includes the goal of comprehensively testing theories, there is no such thing as a definitive study. No study produces the final answer to a research question, in part because there is always the possibility that another theoretical context raises additional questions.

- One of the basic assumptions of a scientific approach to research is determinism—every phenomenon has at least one discoverable cause. Although people often confuse determinism with predestination, the two concepts are entirely different. Predestination refers to the belief that events cannot be altered.

- Regardless of the point at which one begins a research project, the project is always related to one or another theory. Variables—logically derived, concrete representations of theoretical concepts—are used to form hypotheses; it is hypotheses that are directly tested in a research project.

- Construct validity refers to the extent to which a variable represents a theoretical concept. Consensus is necessary for validity, but it is possible to misuse a variable on which consensus has been achieved. Avoiding the belief that a variable is the same as the concept it represents prevents such misuse.

- Ethics for scientific research were not formally codified until the second half of the 20th century. The first of these, The Nuremberg Code, was in response to the Nazi atrocities.

- There are five primary principles that guide ethical research: respect for persons, beneficence, justice, trust, and scientific integrity. These same principles can be used to guide ethical consumption of research.
- Respect for persons involves giving researchers proper credit, representing others' work accurately, and providing comprehensive information to those who will benefit from our consumption of research.
- Beneficence involves promoting the public good.
- Justice refers generally to ensuring that risks and benefits associated with research, including the consumption of research, are distributed equally throughout the population.
- Trust involves much more than honesty; those who will read our reports and those who will be otherwise affected by the content of our reports are owed a high degree of competency in the construction of those reports.
- Scientific integrity involves intellectual honesty, accuracy, fairness, and giving careful consideration to and, if relevant, explicit declaration of conflicts of interest and a comprehensive effort to overcome such conflicts.

EXERCISES

1. Find examples in which people have written or said things that indicate they do or do not understand the rational inference problem in science.

2. Find examples in which people have written or said things consistent with the notion of comparing one theory against another. (Note: This may be somewhat difficult because most popular-press reports usually mention only one theory, if any.)

3. Find examples of reports in which the author(s) claim(s) to be reporting a consensus about scientific conclusions. Can you determine the source of the reported consensus?

4. Find an example of what you think is biased reporting of research. Explain why you think it is biased. Can you think of any conflicts of interest you might have with the report?

CHAPTER 3

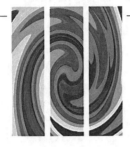

Reading a Research Report

People don't usually do research the way people who write books about research say that people do research.

—A. J. Bachrach (1981)

Overview

The purpose of this chapter is to provide you with an overview of how to read a research report. You will learn about a technique to enhance your critical-reading skills. You may not have enough knowledge about methodology and statistics to understand everything in a research report, but you will learn about general style, as well as the difference between what is typically included, what is sometimes included, and what is generally not included in a research report. You will also learn about the traditional organization of a research report.

INTRODUCTION

Good critical reading requires practice, thought, and awareness. The more critical reading you do, the more your reading will improve. The more you think about what you are reading, and the more you pay attention to what others have written about what they read—good or bad—the more your reading will improve. To become a better reader, read more and write about what you read. Beyond reading more, however, there are specific techniques that can be used to improve your critical-reading skills. One of these is the SQ3R method—Survey, Query, Read, Recite, and Review—a technique designed to enhance understanding while reading.

The SQ3R method of reading (Robinson, 1970; Vacca & Vacca, 1999), slightly adapted for higher-level materials (and readers), will help you to organize what you are reading. It takes a little practice and seems somewhat awkward at first, but it is well worth the effort. It is a very effective method for ensuring that one understands technical material.

The "survey" part of the technique represents obtaining an overview of the material to be read. For research articles, this can be accomplished by reading the title and abstract; you also should examine any tables and figures contained in the article. As you survey, you should "question," which involves asking as many questions as possible about the title, abstract, tables, figures, section headings, et cetera. Think about what each part of the report might mean, wonder how it fits with the rest of the material, wonder about how the graph or table was constructed, think about alternative words that could be used. The more questions you ask, the more focused your reading will be.

The first of the three *R*s stands for "read," which is an obvious component of reading a research report, but in this case the reading should be done actively. Don't just allow the words to pass in front of your eyes; try to answer the questions you asked during the survey phase of the process. As you encounter something you do not understand, stop to figure it out, look it up in a textbook or search online for information, and use other techniques to ensure you understand what you are reading before continuing. I find that "read" works best when I do it one paragraph at a time; I make sure that I understand each paragraph before attempting to read the next paragraph.

The second *R* represents "recite," which stands for articulating in your own words what you just read in the paragraph. I prefer to "recite" using my pen; I try to write, in my own words, the point that was made in the paragraph I read. Whether you actually recite or write, the purpose of this *R* is to test your knowledge of what you have read. Note that using a highlighter to mark passages you think are important is not sufficient; highlighting only marks the author's words. Instead, you should express the author's idea in your own words; either say or write what you think the passage means. If you can express the point in your own words, then you are more likely to understand the material. I used to write in the margin of whatever I was reading, but now I "recite" while taking notes in a document on my computer. My "reciting" forms an outline of what I've read, and the notes are very convenient for the final *R*, "review." Before you decide that you have read and understood a research article, review the notes you have made to make sure that those notes still make sense in the context of the entire article. You may discover, for example, that some of your earlier notes can be improved as a result of your more comprehensive understanding of the entire article.

That is about all I can include in this chapter about how to improve your reading, for to comment any more would require a one-on-one, in-person session. Instead, the remainder of this chapter deals with why and how to read a research report. There are some general (and a few specific) conventions adopted by those who write reports about research, and we will examine these conventions in this chapter. Obviously, I cannot provide comments about specific reports you may read, nor does it make much sense to predict the kinds of reports you will read. Therefore, the examples from reports that are included herein are from my own writing, which also enables me to provide some indication of the underlying purpose and intent concerning specific passages.

RESEARCH REPORT ORGANIZATION

The purpose of writing a research report is simple: to inform others about the research the investigators conducted. This simple purpose involves the assumption that others want to be informed about the research. Part of what writing a research report is all about is writing the report so that others will want to read it, but the audience for which most researchers write is other researchers. This means that authors of research articles focus on the things that they believe other researchers want to know—the theoretical and empirical background of the research, the procedures used to collect the data, the results of the data analyses and how they were obtained, and the conclusions drawn from the results—and they create that focus using a particular style. You will probably encounter a fair amount of jargon, such as the statement "The interaction effect was reliable," as you read reports. You need to be familiar with such jargon in order to understand the article. In addition to jargon, you also will encounter passive-voice writing, such as "the subjects were assigned randomly," which is more difficult to follow than material written in active voice, and most of what you read will be in the third person because researchers consider the primary focus to be the data, not who collected the data. Finally, you will encounter very succinct writing, which is much denser than, say, a novel or even an advanced textbook. In short, you should be prepared for reading much more slowly and much more carefully than you have previously done.

The organization of a report of empirical research is fairly standard among behavioral and social sciences—indeed, most sciences. In psychology, the standard is comprehensively described in the *Publication Manual of the American Psychological Association* (American Psychological Association, 2010). Slightly different formats may be used to present the organized material, but every research report is likely to contain an introduction, sections for method and/or procedures, results, discussion, and references, and a summary or abstract of the report.

The major sections—introduction, method, results, and discussion—are often described as analogous to an hourglass of information through which the author guides the reader. As depicted in Figure 3.1, the report begins with one

Figure 3.1 The Hourglass Analogy of the Research Report. The introduction begins leading the reader from very general issues to successively more specific issues until the results, the center point of the article, are presented. Then, the reader is led back from the very specific results to the most general implications of the results.

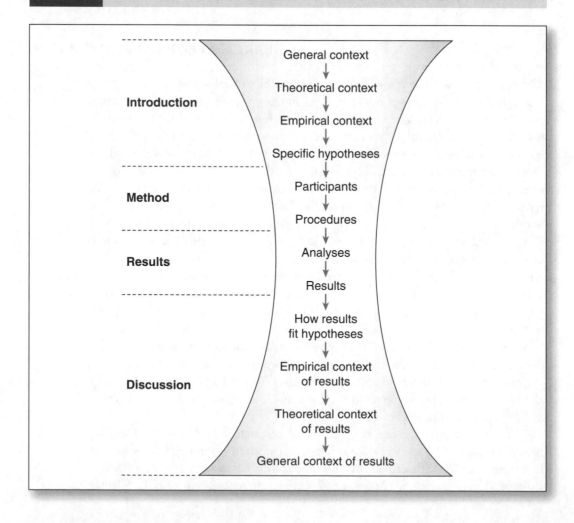

or more general statements that place the research in context, followed by increasingly more specific statements until the reader is informed of the intentions and hypotheses of the research. The method section includes information about how the data were collected, the results section contains what was found, and the discussion is used to bring the reader back to the general context. As the center of the hourglass, the results are the focus of the research report. For this reason, you cannot consider your understanding of the research to be more than a tentative idea until you understand the results.

Introduction

To explain the purpose of the research, most researchers include an introduction, which enables them to explain, and you to learn, how the particular project described in the report fits into the general scheme of inquiry.

General Context

Below is a portion of the first part of the introduction from the report Dane and McPartland (1983) wrote about research on judgments of the propriety of various public displays of affection:

Intimacy between two people is often inferred from the manner in which they relate to each other at a nonverbal level. Since the publication of Hall's (1959) *The Silent Language*, research on nonverbal indicators of intimacy has grown at a geometric rate, and touch occupies a primary position within the literature. Coverage ranges from rigorous reviews and theoretical proposals (Patterson, 1976, 1982) through textbook summaries (Kleinke, 1975; Malandro & Barker, 1983). Throughout this literature, however, authors have focused on people directly involved in interpersonal exchanges. Observers' reactions have been neglected.

Hall's volume, for example, is devoted almost entirely to interpreting nonverbal behaviors from the actors' viewpoints. He offers only a few examples in which the reader is asked to imagine amazement upon observing peculiar behaviors. Kleinke (1975) similarly devotes several pages to touching, but only from the perspective of involvement. Malandro and Barker (1983, p. 270) concluded "the sender and receiver recognize that touch carries messages that are often more dominant than the words we speak," but failed to mention inferences drawn by observers. A thorough review of the literature yields many more analyses of touch from participants' viewpoints, but no analysis of observers' viewpoints. (Dane & McPartland, 1983)

In two paragraphs, we presented the general area into which our research fit (nonverbal behavior), introduced the specific aspect on which we would concentrate (observer's reactions to touch), and provided several examples to buttress our argument that research is needed in this area. We established the beginning of the hourglass pathway through which we would lead the reader.

As a reader, you now know where to go for more general information about the topic because we provided references. You also know specifically what the research report is about—observers' reactions to interpersonal touch. Such context is important to understand if you are to understand the remainder of the report.

Literature Review

After presenting the general context of the research, authors next provide information about other research that is relevant to the specific project described in the report. Just as understanding the literature is an important part of designing a research project, understanding the empirical and theoretical context is important to understanding and interpreting the results of a project someone else conducted. Without knowing how this particular project fits into the grand scheme of knowledge, you are not likely to be able to make a judgment about the relative importance of the results for your purposes.

The literature review does not contain everything the authors ever read on a given topic; it is tailored specifically to place the individual project in context. Consider the following portion of a literature review:

A decade ago, Hunt (1974, p. 1) dramatized the frequency with which observers were exposed to public displays of intimacy by noting "the unprecedented spectacle of sexually normal young people stripping off their clothes and having intercourse out in the open." Indeed, about 70,000 people in the U.S. were arrested for "sexual misconduct" in 1980 (Flanagan & McLeod, 1983). Somewhere along the continuum from holding hands to sexual intercourse, observers' primary reactions to public touching change from a simple inference about intimacy to marked disapproval. At what point that change takes place is not known. For that matter, we can only assume the existence of general cognitive structures about reactions to interpersonal intimacy.

The paucity of research on observers' reactions to public touching involves only general attitudes. Excluding research on erotica presented through mass media, we found only one study on the topic. Crawford and Crawford (1978, p. 396) reported individuals' reactions to the statement "Public displays of affection are in poor taste" were highly correlated with items concerning public nudity, sexually explicit reading material, and so on. They concluded reactions to public intimacy are a subset of general attitudes toward sexuality. Conceptual leaps aside, it seems overly simplistic to assume reactions to observing public touching will mirror, in substance and form, reactions to engaging in the same behavior. (Dane & McPartland, 1983)

These two paragraphs from the center of our introduction (Dane & McPartland, 1983) accomplish three purposes. First, they provide the reader with information about existing research. Second, they provide some indication of the reasons that existing research is not sufficient. Finally, they lead the reader further into the hourglass to the point at which we presented specific information about our study:

The purpose of the present study is to assess individual attitudes toward the propriety of specific displays of intimacy in public. Relationships among different displays were explored to determine the extent to which attitudes reflect categorical reactions. Reactions to kissing and hugging, for example, may be considered similarly appropriate but distinct from reactions to mutual fondling or body contact *sans* clothing. In light of the issues addressed by Paul, Weinrich, Gonsoriek, and Hotvedt (1982), attitudinal differences concerning heterosexual and homosexual couples were considered likely. It would seem straightforward to predict that a male kissing another male in public would be judged less appropriate than a male kissing a female. It may also be the case that categorical reactions differ for heterosexual and homosexual couples. (Dane & McPartland, 1983)

Little by little, we led the reader from a very general statement about human behavior to a specific statement about our research, but we did it in relatively few words. Notice also that the above paragraph—the last paragraph of the introduction—included some predictions about what we expected to find in the research. Of course, those predictions were not really predictions; we had already analyzed the data and knew the outcome. The last paragraph of the introduction serves as a transition to the specific details of the research, just as this sentence serves as a transition to the next section about methods.

The Method Section

The method section of the report is the section wherein the researcher attempts to accomplish two things. First, the researcher provides enough information for you to understand how he or she collected the data and to decide whether or not the data collection is appropriate for your purposes. In one sense, the method section is a secondary introduction, for it serves to guide you to the results. The second purpose involves providing enough information to enable someone to replicate the research. Thus, the method section is also an archive.

Participants

The first subsection of the method section is usually a description of the participants. It contains information about who they were, how they were selected, and any other pertinent information. From Dane and McPartland (1983):

> The participants were 73 male and 113 female undergraduate volunteers attending a small state college in upstate New York. The median age was 19, and each received partial course credit for participating.

Brief though it may be, there is much to learn from these two sentences. We included information about how many, gender, regional location, and age. Other than the label "volunteers," there is no specific information about sampling procedures, but the label says it all. By calling them volunteers and not providing additional information about sampling, you can infer that the sample was an **accidental sample**; *the participants were included in the study because they were conveniently available.* Although information by omission may not be the best way to describe our sampling procedures, such is the convention in research reports. Thus, every word, even words not included, may be important to your understanding of the project.

Sampling

When researchers use a procedure other than accidental sampling, they will explain the procedure they used. You might, for example, read "Random digit dialing was used to obtain a random sample of residents in South Carolina. Business and other nonresidential phone numbers were eliminated, which produced the final sample of 600 residents." There is not a lot of detail, such as describing the computer program that generated the random phone numbers, unless the procedure is so unusual as to require such explanation. Thus, authors rely a great deal on the knowledge of their readers. You are expected to know enough about research methods and procedures to be able to interpret the two sentences about random digit dialing, so you need to be a very active reader when reading research reports.

Apparatus or Materials

The apparatus or materials subsection is included if the researcher used any special equipment or materials in the study. These descriptions are included so that others may duplicate the research procedures as well as to enable readers to understand the procedures. Of course, common equipment is usually not described; no one really cares what brand of pencil was used to record observations. We wrote:

> The face sheet of the questionnaire contained instructions for completing the instrument, and items concerning age, gender, and religious preference. The second and third page contained a list of 26 behaviors, ranging from holding hands to sexual intercourse, with instructions that each behavior was to be rated as to its propriety as a public display of affection. The seven-point rating scale ranged from a -3 (strongly inappropriate) to a $+3$ (strongly appropriate), including a labeled neutral point. Separate ratings were made for a male-female, male-male, and female-female couple, and the items were listed on the page in a randomly determined order. (Dane & McPartland, 1983)

Included in the above paragraph are examples of the types of items and a very explicit description of the response scale. Rarely is a copy of the actual instrument included. Only those readers interested in replicating the research exactly would need to see the entire questionnaire, so there's no need to add such lengthy material to the body of the report. If you need to see the exact instrument used in the study, you can always write to the researcher(s) and ask for a copy. Almost all researchers are happy to comply with such requests.

If the questionnaire had been described in a previous report, whether ours or someone else's, we would have provided a more general description of the instrument and referred the reader to the more detailed published description. Someone else might write, for example, "The questionnaire used by Dane and McPartland (1983) was used to obtain attitudinal information about a variety of public displays of affection." Such a statement would then be followed by a general description of the questionnaire, a description that would enable the reader to understand what was done without having to look up the Dane and McPartland reference. Until you become familiar with the measurement techniques used in your area of interest, however, I strongly recommend that you look up the original reference so you can be sure you understand the full scope of what was measured in the research.

Procedure

The procedure subsection contains details about the specific manner in which the data were collected. Enough detail is usually included to accomplish the archival purpose of this section, as well as to enable you to empathize with the participants. That is, the procedure is usually written from the participants' point of view, which is necessary to understand the participants' reactions (the results). In our report, we wrote:

> To ensure anonymity, participants completed the questionnaire in groups of 10 to 20. For each session, a male researcher described the study as an investigation of reactions to public displays of affection. Participants were asked to rate the propriety of specific displays of public affection, for which *public* was defined as any location where one could reasonably expect to be observed by others. It was explicitly noted that those who believed they would be offended by the task should complete only the face sheet of the questionnaire, but no one exercised this option. (Dane & McPartland, 1983)

Notice how much information we packed into the above paragraph. If you were reading actively, you now know that the questionnaire was administered anonymously and in small groups. You know what instructions were provided and how informed consent was attained. You don't know the exact wording of the instructions, but if that wording had been important to the data collection process, we would have provided a direct quote. Because the procedure involved completing a questionnaire, there was no need to describe manipulations of an independent variable or to describe graphically the physical environment.

Manipulations

When research involves experimental manipulations, they are described in sufficient detail for the reader to understand them and again from the participant's viewpoint. For example, you might read something like this:

Three different feedback groups were created. In the Positive Feedback group, we told participants they correctly answered 45 of the 50 test questions. In the Negative Feedback condition, we said they correctly answered only 5 of 50 questions. Participants in the No Feedback group did not learn about their performance.

Notice that the labels given to the various groups are informative labels. Notice also that, as an active reader, you will be expected to remember what those labels mean throughout the remainder of the article. When the procedure in the study is very complicated, researchers will sometimes provide a brief summary of the method and design before moving on to the results section.

The Results Section

As is implied by the name, the results section is where researchers report the results of the data analyses. It is the section around which the entire report is centered. Researchers want to be sure readers understand the results, and so they generally follow the rule of thumb used in oral presentations: Tell them what you are going to tell them, tell them, and tell them what you told them. Following this rule, however, does not mean the researcher will be redundant; instead, it means the information is often presented at three different levels. I'll provide examples as we move on to the preliminary and main subsections of the results section.

Preliminary Results

Just as the overall research report requires an introduction to prepare the reader for what is to come, the results section may include an introduction to prepare the reader for the main results. Depending on the procedures, there may be any number of things accomplished at the beginning of the results section.

If the researcher used a manipulation or selected participants on the basis of some pretest measure, the researcher will usually present information about the success of the manipulation or selection process. Thus, the first part of the results may include the results of analyses that are used to describe the impact of the manipulation or selection procedure. For example:

Participants rated their level of performance on a ten-point scale ranging from poor (1) to excellent (10). These ratings were used to determine whether the feedback manipulation was effective, and produced a main effect for Feedback when subjected to Analysis of Variance, $F(2, 59) = 10.25$, $p < .05$;

the manipulation was successful. Participants in the Positive Feedback group rated their performance ($\mu = 8$) better than those in the No Feedback group ($\mu = 5$).

Included is information about the manipulation, the result of the analysis, an interpretation of the result, and a clarification. The quote follows the rule—tell them three times—without writing the same thing three times. An active reader will learn new information from each repetition.

Other material in the preliminary results might include analyses of interrater reliability, descriptive statistics about the participants, information about data eliminated from the analyses, and any other results that move the reader toward the main results. How much information is included in a preliminary results subsection depends on the specific nature of the study. In the public displays of affection report, for example, we used the beginning of the results section to convince the reader that the participants' ratings were sensible:

Table 1 contains the overall mean propriety rating for each of the 26 behaviors, according to type of couple. The participants clearly discriminated among the items, which are ordered from most to least appropriate within ratings for the male-female couple. Of particular interest is the trend for female couples' behaviors to be rated consistently less appropriate than the male-female couples and, without exception, the trend for male couples' behaviors to be least appropriate. These trends are not overly surprising in light of Gross, Green, Storck, and Vanyur's (1980) findings concerning prevalent negative reactions to overt homosexuality. (Dane & McPartland, 1983)

I have not included the table from the article; it is too long to merit the space as an example here. The table in the report exhibited the properties described in the text. It is evident from the table that the participants rated holding hands, for example, as more appropriate than kissing, and so forth. The results are not surprising, but surprise was not the point. Rather, the purpose was to convince the reader that the data make sense, that the participants did what they were expected to do. In this case, active reading would enable you to make decisions about the extent to which we measured reactions in an appropriate way, that our participants were not atypical, and that the results we obtained are relatively consistent with related results reported by other researchers.

Another part of the preliminary results subsection may contain an overview of the statistical procedures used to analyze the bulk of the data. This part of the results section is usually included because it serves to orient the reader—to enable the reader to develop expectations about the kinds of information to come—but is sometimes neglected. Any transformations performed on the data will be included at this point in the results section. We wrote:

> To explore the potential structure underlying the ratings, separate factor analyses were conducted for each type of couple. Because the analysis was exploratory, all factors yielding eigenvalues greater than one were retained prior to orthogonal rotation. For all three couple types, four factors emerged, accounting for 64%, 72%, and 67% of the variance for male-female, female-female, and male-male couples, respectively. The order of emergence was identical across couple type, although specific item loadings differed among couple types for the fourth factor. (Dane & McPartland, 1983)

Active reading enables you to decide whether or not factor analysis is appropriate to the purpose. **Factor analysis** is *a statistical technique for investigating structure among a number of variables* (see Chapter 4). Essentially, it can be used to group variables together based on their correlations in much the same way that those who write college admissions tests group items into separate subject categories. Even though this paragraph dealt with preliminary results, we began to discuss some of the main results of the study. We pointed out, for example, that each of the three sets of ratings produced four factors. Beginning to present main findings in the last paragraph of the preliminary results is one way to provide a transition from one subsection to the next. As an active reader, you need to be attuned to such transitions so that you don't miss some main results that are presented in what appears to be a preliminary results section.

Main Results

When researchers report the main results of the study, they usually present the most central or most important results first, then present decreasingly important results. The same format is typically used for each result: a general description, more specific information, and finally relevant qualifications.

For each set of results, what question the result is supposed to answer is presented. In the above paragraph from our report, for example, we reminded the reader that we wanted to explore the structure of the propriety ratings. Then we restated the result in terms of the specific operational definition used to measure the variable. This is typically followed by a prose statement of the result, such as "The ratings produced four factors for each type of couple." Results are often interpreted as they are presented, but some researchers will present all of the results before engaging in interpretation. As an active reader, you want to think about the interpretation that is presented and make sure that you understand the interpretation and agree with it. If you are reading for a specific purpose, such as the preparation of a review of research for policy analysis purposes, you may also want to interpret the results in terms of the policy you are analyzing. The researcher's interpretation is not the only interpretation that is allowed. The statistical results are presented to support the conclusion, but you can draw a different conclusion if that conclusion makes sense with respect to the methods employed by the researcher.

Qualifications or elaborations of the results are presented using the same format: prose, numbers, and prose. For example, the excerpt below, which did not follow the above paragraph in the results section, concerns analyses conducted on the scores produced by the factor analyses mentioned above:

> Additional exploration of the reactions involved determining whether the participants' characteristics were related to their reactions. Item loadings were used to create weighted factor scores ranging from negative one (inappropriate) to positive one (appropriate). These were then subjected to a 2 (Gender) × (Religion: Catholic, Jewish, Other, None) × 4 (Factor Label) × 3 (Couple Type) Analysis of Variance.
>
> The analysis yielded a reliable main effect for Gender, $F(1, 172) = 4.10$, $p < .05$. Males ($\mu = 0.07$) considered the behaviors to be generally more appropriate than did females ($\mu = -0.05$). The only other reliable effect was a Factor Label × Gender interaction, $F(3,516) = 8.27$, $p < .0001$, for which the means are presented in Table 6. As is evident from the table, women rated all but the asexual behaviors as less appropriate than did men. (Dane & McPartland, 1983)

Each finding is first presented in prose, then in numbers, and then again in prose. Each statistical analysis is clearly identified, and each effect is accompanied by its level of statistical significance. For the simpler main effect, however, the means were included in the text. The table (labeled Table 6 because it was the sixth one we included in the report) was used to clarify the interaction effect because it was more efficient to present the eight means in tabular form than in prose. Notice, however, that a prose clarification of the interaction was included in the text. The active reader is therefore able to compare the prose to the table and consider what other descriptions (more relevant to the reader's purpose) might also fit the table. The same point may be made about figures—graphs, pictures, and drawings—that are used to convey information more efficiently than it could be conveyed in prose or a table.

Notice also that each effect was accompanied by a small amount of interpretation, such as "males considered the behaviors to be generally more appropriate than did females." The active reader should think about such interpretation to make sure it is consistent with the numbers presented. The small amount of interpretation in the results section should not be accepted at face value; read actively and decide for yourself whether the interpretation is consistent with the numerical results.

Conclusions

The conclusions drawn from the results are placed in the discussion section of the report. This is where the researcher begins to expand the hourglass, beginning with a restatement of the main results. In some respects, the discussion section is the reverse of the introduction: Instead of leading the reader to the results (as was the case in the introduction), the researcher is leading you away from the results toward the general points he or she wants to make. The conclusions should logically follow from the results, but some researchers take the reader further from the results than others. It is unlikely that a published article will contain just any old thing in the discussion section, but it's certainly possible that a research report could contain conclusions that are less than apparent from the results.

Typically, the discussion is begun with a restatement of the main research question and a summary of the relevant results. For example:

In general, the data demonstrate that observers do make attributions about public displays of affection. Specifically, judgments about the propriety of the behaviors conform to expectations based on the level of sexual intimacy for the behavior. More important, the data show that propriety may be judged on the basis of categorical information about groups of behaviors. (Dane & McPartland, 1983)

This is a very full first paragraph for a discussion section. It includes a restatement of the research question: Do people react to intimate touching other than registering it as an intimate act? It also includes the point that observers' reactions may be categorical, and the conclusions are limited to the data collected. All this is done, however, without merely restating what has already appeared in earlier sections of the report. Even though the researcher is continuing along the path defined by previous sections of the report, the discussion section will not include a mere rehash of what has already been written; active reading continues to be a necessary skill. The discussion section will contain information not previously presented in the report, and you need to be prepared to consider critically the new knowledge and understanding of the study it contains.

Although we could not do it in the public displays of affection report, the discussion typically will also include efforts to relate the results to previous research on the topic. (We could not do it because there was no previous research.) The researcher will not mention every study ever done on the same topic but will provide enough information to place the results in a theoretical context. Differences between the researcher's results and those of previous researchers will usually be noted, but researchers are not likely to dwell on every detailed difference between their results and others' results. If the result is related to the policy you want to analyze, pay particular attention to noted differences and follow up with the cited article so that you understand those differences and how they may relate to the policy you are analyzing.

Toward the end of the discussion section, the researcher may present what he or she considers questions that remain unanswered despite the results or questions that are raised because of the results:

> Furthermore, research and theory that may be stimulated by the current exploration should include consideration of the discrepancies between heterosexual and homosexual behavior. For example, there is a considerably wider range of behavior that our participants considered sexual for homosexuals than for heterosexuals, even though the same behavior was rated for both couple types. It is clearly the case that observers process and react to the public behaviors of others, and it is time we began to include observers' inferences in our theories about the meaning of touch as a means of nonverbal communication. (Dane & McPartland, 1983)

Because the study was exploratory and the results may be limited to the sample we used, the suggestions about future research are rather general. The more specific the hypotheses with which the researcher has dealt, the more specific will be the recommendations that the researcher will include. The fact that there remain unanswered questions, however, should not be taken as an indication that the research was somehow insufficient, incompetent, or incomplete. A single research study almost always is about a single, very finite issue or question. You, as the active reader and eventual review writer, will be able to put all those little answers together to form a more general answer about the policy you are analyzing.

One last note about the discussion section needs to be made: The discussion section will probably not contain any surprises. Therefore, don't be lulled into thinking that the researcher has nothing new to present in the discussion section. Active reading is required to catch and process the sometimes subtle additions to what you already know about the project. There may not be any surprises, but if you think there is nothing at all new in the discussion, then you are probably not reading actively.

Other Sections

The introduction, method, results, and discussion sections constitute the bulk of the research report. There are, however, a few other sections that may appear in a research report. Even though they may not be included in the limelight, they are equally important in terms of the information an active the reader can glean from them. They include the abstract and the references. Again, the American Psychological Association's (2010) publication manual is an excellent source for additional information.

Abstract

Regardless of the length of the report, most reports will contain a summary, usually called an abstract and printed at the beginning. An abstract includes about 100 to 150 words, which is not many words in which to summarize a research report that may be as long as 25 pages. More than any other section of a research report, then, an abstract is incredibly succinct and requires active reading to decode. It also requires patience; you may have to reread an abstract several times before you understand all that it has to offer. Consider the abstract from the public displays report:

The purpose of this study was to explore observers' reactions to public, intimate behaviors. College students rated the propriety of imagined behaviors ranging from holding hands to sexual intercourse for opposite- and same-sex couples. Behaviors for the heterosexual couples were consistently rated as most appropriate. Factor analysis of the ratings yielded four categories: genital contact, other erotic contact, asexual contact, and an inconsistent factor that varied with type of couple. Suggestions for future research included potential underlying cognitive processes of observers and the need to incorporate such processes into current theories about nonverbal behavior. (Dane & McPartland, 1983)

Some people are tempted to read only the abstract of a research report. It does, of course, contain the main points of the complete report, but an abstract does not contain any of the qualifications and elaborations necessary to understand those main points. The abstract is essentially a teaser, but if you stop reading at the abstract, you will miss out on a great deal of information that may be helpful in your policy analysis. You have already read enough of the public displays report to know just how little of our results are contained in the abstract.

On the other hand, you may use the abstract to decide whether or not to read the full report. This is a perfectly legitimate use of the abstract; indeed, it is the purpose for which the abstract was written. If the abstract contains nothing that is relevant to your interests, then the full article probably will not contain relevant material, either. However, if there is one shred of relevance apparent in the abstract, you would do very well to read the entire article.

References

Any published material to which the researcher refers in the report will be referenced in what is called, straightforwardly enough, the references section. Styles for references vary from journal to journal, but the predominant style in the behavioral and social sciences is that recommended by the American Psychological Association (2010) in its publication manual. The references are an excellent source of additional material to read as you prepare your research review.

Enough. The only way to improve your reading skills is to read some research articles. So go and read a research report (but first read the summary).

SUMMARY

- Good reading requires practice, thought, and critical thinking. The more you do of any of these things, the more your reading skills will improve and the more efficiently you will be able to read research reports.
- The purpose of reading a research report is to find out about the results the researcher obtained. The results are the focal point of any research report.
- Research reports are organized in an hourglass fashion. First is presented information about the general phenomenon, then more specific issues related to the phenomenon, next the details about the research procedures, then the results, and finally interpretations that typically end as generally as the introduction began.
- Because scientific writing is succinct, active reading is required to obtain as much information from the article as the researcher put into it. Passive voice, third person writing, and past tense make it difficult to read a research report quickly. The SQ3R method of reading will help you read more efficiently.

- The introduction typically begins with a statement about the behavior of interest; then it should lead you logically and straightforwardly to the specific hypotheses of the study.
- The method section should describe the way in which the data were collected. It should contain enough detail to enable you to empathize with the participants and to replicate the study.
- The results section will sometimes include a preliminary exposition of the major types of analyses used. It will include all results obtained from the data, ordered so that the most important results are presented first.
- The discussion section usually opens with a brief summary of the major hypotheses and the results relevant to those hypotheses. Further generalization from the results proceeds in the same logical and straightforward organization used in the introduction.
- The abstract will include the main points of the complete report but will be extremely brief. You should not count on the abstract containing all that you need to know about the research.
- References may be useful in identifying and obtaining additional material relevant to the policy you are analyzing or background information that will be useful in understanding the specific information contained in the research report.
- Stop reading this book now, and go read a research report.

EXERCISES

1. If you have not already done so, practice the SQ3R method while reading this chapter.

2. Find a research article relevant to your interests (or use one you already have) and identify the paragraph(s) corresponding to Figure 3.1.

3. Using an interesting research article, identify parts that you do not understand. Make a list of the things you need to know in order to understand this article. Do the authors provide references that you can read for additional clarification?

4. Find a popular-press report of one of the articles you have found and compare the popular-press version to the research article.

CHAPTER 4

Conceptual Overview of Statistical Analyses

Aristotle could have avoided the mistake of thinking that women have fewer teeth than men by the simple device of asking Mrs. Aristotle to open her mouth.

—Bertrand Russell (Peter, 1980, p. 457)

Overview

The material presented in this chapter is a follow-up to the research strategies presented in Chapter 1. In addition to learning more about the strategies—exploration, description, prediction, explanation, and action—you will be given an overview of statistical analyses appropriate for each strategy. As I've written in previous chapters, research involves asking and attempting to answer questions. How the questions are asked determines the methods used to answer them, which in turn partly determine the answers. Another aspect of research that partly determines the answers is how statistical procedures are used to analyze the data. Therefore, research consumers need to understand the statistics used by the researchers whose

(Continued)

(Continued)

work they are consuming. Fortunately, at least for those who shy away from statistics and other mathematical topics, research consumers don't need to know how to *calculate* statistics. Instead, consumers only need to know enough about statistics to decide whether or not the researchers chose their statistics correctly and to critically assess the researchers' interpretations of their results. Thus, this chapter deals with what I refer to as conceptual statistics, which includes basic theory and principles; no calculations or formulas are included. For those of you who have yet to complete a course in statistics, the material will serve as an introduction to the concepts of statistical analyses.

INTRODUCTION

Research design and data analyses are interdependent; one makes little sense without the other. One situation researchers should always avoid is having data without a way to analyze them; researchers who don't avoid this situation engage in strange, sometimes inappropriate, ways to analyze their data in the hopes of salvaging something of their efforts. As a consumer of research, you need to know enough about statistics to determine that a researcher did not choose just any old analyses. As well, you need to know enough about statistics to interpret the results presented in empirical articles, even those written by researchers who knew exactly how to analyze their data. Thus, even though you don't have to worry about analyzing data, you do need to be able to figure out whether a researcher analyzed data properly and how the results of those analyses can be used to inform the program, policy, or issue you are addressing. The purpose of this chapter is to help you deal with others' analyses and results by providing an overview of current research strategies and the analyses most appropriate to them. The chapter is organized around the major research strategies: exploration, description, prediction, and explanation. (Action is not included as a separate research strategy because it almost always incorporates one of the other strategies.)

EXPLORATORY RESEARCH

As defined in Chapter 1, exploratory research is an attempt to determine whether or not a phenomenon exists. That is exactly what Bertrand Russell had in mind when he suggested that Aristotle ought to have looked in Mrs. Aristotle's mouth instead of writing a philosophical discourse on gender differences.

Appropriate Questions for Exploratory Research

Exploratory research is similar to the insistent question asked by columnist and *60 Minutes* commentator Andy Rooney: "Did you ever wonder about. . . ?" (see, e.g., Rooney, 2003). Anything is fair game when one tries to discover what is out there, wherever "there" may be. Some examples of exploratory research questions include these: Do people think differently about themselves than about others? What do jury members talk about during deliberations? Has anyone ever done research on this topic before? The last question is one of the questions we ask when conducting a literature review.

Exploratory questions tend to be rather general, but that does not mean they are necessarily frivolous or uninformative. At the very least, exploratory research satisfies personal curiosity, but good exploratory research also has **heuristic value** in that it *stimulates the researcher and others to conduct even more research.* For example, the attempt by members of the Chicago Jury Project to answer the question about what jurors discuss during deliberations has been the basis for hundreds, perhaps thousands, of other research projects about the behavior of jurors (Ellison & Buckhout, 1981). Nearly any question about the existence or nature of human behavior, or the lack thereof, is an appropriate question for exploratory research.

Appropriate Statistics for Exploratory Research

Just as the questions addressed through exploratory research are usually general, the data analyses used for exploratory research also tend to be general. Often, analyses for exploratory research are **qualitative analyses—** *nonnumerical analyses concerning quality rather than quantity.* For example, early research on conformity as a group process dealt with determining whether or not members of a group who initially disagreed with the majority changed their opinions during group discussions (Levine & Russo, 1987). The quality of the behavior—opinion change—was the focus of analysis; change was either there or it was not. Early researchers on this topic were not particularly interested in how much people's opinions changed, just whether there was a change.

Even when analyses are not qualitative, they usually include calculating descriptive statistics concerning central tendencies or averages—mean, median, and mode—or concerning dispersion of scores, such as range, interquartile range, and standard deviation. Sometimes, histograms or frequency polygons are used to graphically examine data in more detail or to more clearly present data. Travis (1985), for example, used charts of surgery rates in different areas of the United States to illustrate more clearly the discovery that elective hysterectomies were considerably more prevalent than either elective appendectomies or elective prostate surgery.

Other useful exploratory analyses include stem-and-leaf displays and scattergrams. Stem-and-leaf displays (Tukey, 1977) are an alternative to more traditional histograms or frequency polygons. A **stem-and-leaf** *allows one to visualize the entire data set as a distribution of scores, without having to lose information about what the specific scores are. They also enable one to informally to examine differences among groups.* Figure 4.1 contains a stem-and-leaf display for the publication dates of the references cited in a social psychology textbook (Dane, 1988a). The stem—the left side of the display—contains the root of the date, such as 187 for the 1870s or 196 for the 1960s. The leaf, the right side of the display, contains the remainder of the number, such as 1 in 1871. By examining the stem and the leaf, one can reconstruct the original score: 187 on the stem together with 1 in the leaf indicates the year 1871.

Traditionally, the digits in the leaf are ordered, increasing from left to right, as in the figure. Although not shown in this figure, one may use the same stem more than once if that makes the display easier to read. However, when doing so, researchers will usually use every stem the same number of times. Longer leaves indicate more data points, so researchers use the same spacing for all of the leaves. That way, the leaves represent the distribution of scores much as a histogram does but without masking the actual numeric values of the data.

Scattergrams, on the other hand, allow one to examine relationships between variables or between two different groups measured on the same variable. However, they are more likely to be used for descriptive and predictive research purposes, so we'll postpone discussing them until those sections.

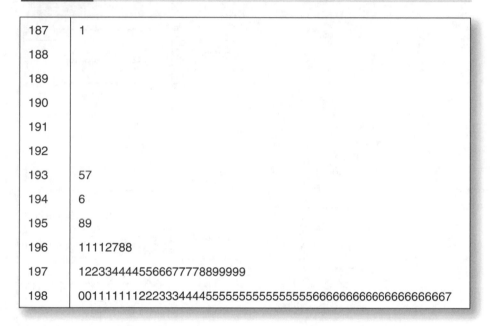

| Figure 4.1 | A Stem-and-Leaf Display of the Publication Years for the Citations Included in Dane (1988a). The stem, three-digit numbers along the left side, is the century and decade of the publication year. The leaf, the single-digit number extending to the right from the stem, is used to complete the year. Note how easy it is to recognize the relative abundance of later references compared to the relatively few citations from earlier years. Stem-and-leaf displays enable one to understand the frequencies included in an entire data set and understand the specific scores that comprise the data set. |

187	1
188	
189	
190	
191	
192	
193	57
194	6
195	89
196	11112788
197	12233444455666777788899999
198	001111111222333444455555555555555555566666666666666666667

In general, data analyses for exploratory research fall under the category of "interocular trauma" analyses: The effects are so apparent that they hit you right between the eyes, or they are not apparent at all. It is clear from Figure 4.1, for example, that there are more references from the 1980s than from any other decade; the length of the 198 leaves hits you between the eyes. Even if the effect in which you are interested is subtle, it becomes apparent because you are looking for it; it is either there or it is not.

The kinds of analyses appropriate for exploratory research are displayed in Figure 4.2. Now we're ready to turn our attention to descriptive research.

Figure 4.2

Both qualitative and quantitative analyses can be used to examine the data from exploratory research. Which quantitative statistics you will see in articles depends upon the nature of the research question; either central tendency, variability, or both may be included in an article. A variety of graphic presentations are also used to display information about the entire data set.

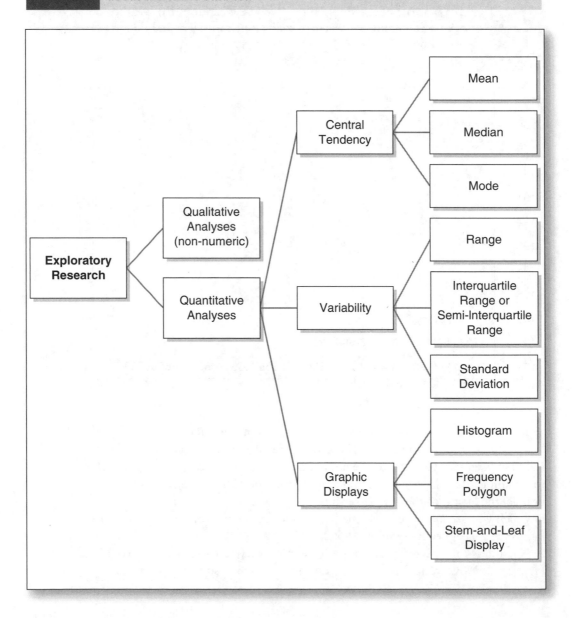

Descriptive research involves attempting to define or measure a particular phenomenon, usually by attempting to estimate the strength or intensity of a behavior or the relationship between two. Rather than assessing whether or not something is going on, descriptive strategies involve assessing exactly (more or less) what is going on.

Appropriate Questions for Descriptive Research

Questions for which a descriptive strategy would be appropriate are those in which the researcher explores the limitations of a phenomenon. These might include its distinctiveness from other phenomena, the extent to which it occurs in various situations, or its strength or quantity. Examples include such questions as these: Under what circumstances do people think differently about themselves than about others? How much time do jurors spend talking about evidence during deliberations? How many different operational definitions of this phenomenon have been used in previous research? These are, of course, descriptive versions of the exploratory questions presented in the previous section. Descriptive research does not necessarily involve different research topics, but it does involve different questions about those topics.

Usually, one of the purposes of descriptive research is to generalize—to relate the findings gathered from the research situation to other situations. Typically we want to generalize from the research participants to another group of people or to people in general. Obtaining an answer to the question about how much time the jurors in our study spend discussing evidence is considerably more useful if that answer can be extended to other jurors as well. Generalization requires **external validity**—*similarity between the physical and social aspects of the research environment and the target environment* (Shadish, Cook, & Campbell, 2002). Generalization also requires the use of inferential statistics.

Appropriate Statistics for Descriptive Research

When we attempt to generalize results, we make an inference about the relationship between the research participants and the target of our generalization. Imagine, for example, that we discovered that a particular sample of jurors spent an average of 50% of their deliberation time discussing evidence. If that research sample represents the entire population of jurors, then we might conclude that all jurors spend about 50% of their time in deliberations discussing evidence. That generalization requires the use of inferential statistics.

Inferential statistics are *values calculated from a sample and used to estimate the same value for a population.* That is, inferential statistics are estimates, based on a given sample, of qualities or quantities existing in a larger group of individuals. The basis for all inferential statistics is a mathematical principle known as the *central limit theorem.* Fully explaining the central limit theorem is beyond the scope of this book and is not really necessary for our purposes. However, most statistics textbooks include an explanation of it if you are interested (Nowaczyk, 1988; Wike, 1985; Winer, 1971; Witte & Witte, 2006).

One important aspect of the central limit theorem is that it enables us to use a sample to estimate a population if the sample has been obtained by **random sampling**—*a process by which every member of the population had an equal opportunity to be included in the sample.* Random sampling, then, does not mean just any old sampling procedure but one with a system that ensures that each person, place, or thing in the population has an equal chance of being included in the sample. Selection of a lottery winner, for example, is a random sampling procedure. The population includes every entry entered into the lottery, and each entry has an equal chance of being selected. If all entries are placed in the equivalent of a large box, mixed, and then chosen one at a time, then every entry in the lottery had an equal chance of being selected. (The fact that some people may purchase more than one entry doesn't change the fact that each *entry* has an equal chance of being selected.)

Another important aspect of the central limit theorem is that we can use it, if we have a random sample, to estimate the amount of measurement error associated with any values obtained from the sample. Once we have determined that a sample of jurors spends 50% of their deliberations discussing evidence, we can also determine the accuracy range of that estimate. When reporters announce that Candidate X has obtained 40% of the popular vote in an election, plus or minus 2%, they are reporting an accuracy range (± 2%) for the estimate obtained from their sample.

The types of inferential statistics used to analyze descriptive research data include some of the same calculations used for exploratory research, such as mean, median, mode, standard deviation, and so on. The difference is that these calculations are then used to make inferences, rather than simply describing the data collected from the sample. Other analyses include *chi-square* (also known as *crossbreak analyses*), correlation, factor analysis, *t* test, *analysis of variance* (also known as *ANOVA*), and meta-analysis. Although a detailed explanation of each of these procedures is not within the scope of this text, I will provide a brief overview of their use in descriptive research.

Chi-square analyses are *statistical techniques used to determine whether the frequencies of scores in the categories defined by the variable match the frequencies one would expect on the basis of chance or on the basis of predictions from a theory.* Chi-square analyses are used to make inferences when the data are categorical or nominal—involve measuring participants in terms of categories such as male-female, voter-nonvoter, and so forth. Chi-square procedures can be used to determine whether a relationship exists between two or more categorical variables or whether the categories obtained from one sample of individuals are similar to the categories obtained from another sample. Parish et al. (2000) for example, reported a relationship between type of arrhythmia and survival in their examination of in-hospital resuscitations. Not surprisingly, less severe arrhythmias were more likely to be associated with a successful resuscitation attempt. When the results of chi-square analyses are reported, you are likely to see text that looks something like $X^2 (2) = 5.7$, $p < .05$, where X^2 is the symbol for chi-square, the number in parentheses—in this case 2—reflects the degrees of freedom for the analysis, and the number after the equal sign reflects the actual value for the statistic. This value is then compared against values that should be obtained if the null hypothesis is correct, and this comparison is then used to determine the probability that the data represent the null hypothesis. The *p*, of course, is the symbol used to indicate the probability that the obtained result is due to chance or random error, which is then followed by the value for that probability.

Similarly, chi-square may be used to determine whether there is a relationship between gender and voting behavior, or it may be used to determine whether psychology majors are composed of a different ratio of men to women than are chemistry majors. Chi-square analyses are frequency analyses; they involve comparing the frequencies of various categories. Haberman's two volumes (1978, 1979) are excellent sources for more information about chi-square and other categorical analyses.

When research measures involve continuous variables, such as income, grade point average, age, intensity of emotion, and so on, correlational procedures are used to make inferences about relationships between variables. For example, the relationship between the size of a city and its crime rate can be described with correlational analyses. **Correlations** are *statistical procedures used to estimate the extent to which the changes in one variable are associated with changes in the other variable.* Essentially, a correlation coefficient is a number summarizing what may be observed from a **scatterplot**, *a graph in which corresponding codes from two variables are displayed on two axes.* When data analyses involve correlations, you are likely to see something like this: $r (42) = .37$, $p < .05$. The *r* is the symbol used for the correlation coefficient, the number in parentheses represents the degrees of freedom for the statistic—usually the number of pairs of scores minus one—and the number after the equal sign is the actual value of the correlation coefficient.

Figure 4.3 is a scatterplot representing a positive correlation using data from a study of medical students' scores on a measure of cynicism at the beginning of their first and second years of medical school (Roche, Scheetz, Dane, Parish, & O'Shea, 2003). Positive correlations reflect a direct relationship—one in which increases in one variable correspond to increases in the other variable. In Figure 4.3, it is clear that students who were more cynical than their peers during their first year of

Figure 4.3	A Scatterplot of the Relationship Between Scores on a Measure of Cynicism in the First and Second Years of Medical School. Students who scored high in the first year tended to score high in the second year and vice versa. The darker, denser areas of the plot indicate a greater number of overlapping points or higher frequency in the data set.

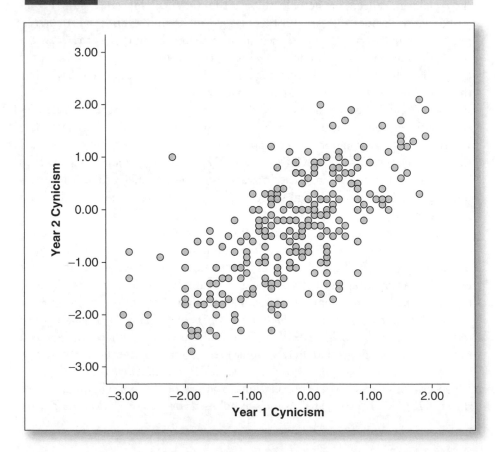

medical school were also more cynical than their peers in their second year of medical school. Notice that there are more overlapping data points in the center of the graph than at the edges of the graph, which also illustrates the general tendency for most of the students to score "average" on the measure of cynicism. If I could make Figure 4.3 a three-dimensional figure, you would see the higher frequency data points appear to come out from the page toward you.

Of course, not all variables that are related exhibit a direct relationship. Figure 4.4 contains the scatterplot of two variables one might expect to be

Figure 4.4

A Scatterplot of the Relationship Between Beliefs About Cynicism and Beliefs About Altruism. As the strength of the belief about cynicism increases, belief in altruism decreases. The darker, denser areas in the plot indicate a greater number of overlapping points or higher frequency in the data set.

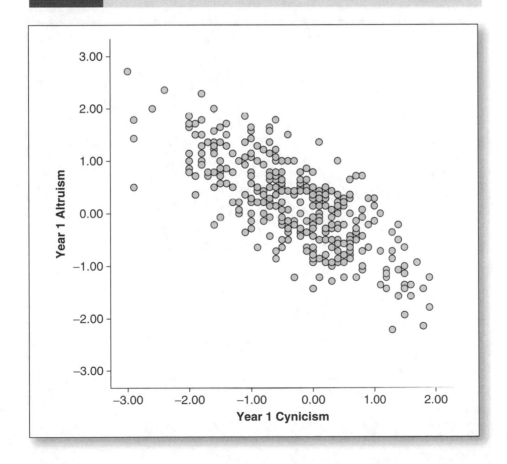

indirectly or inversely related, cynicism and altruism. Such a relationship would produce a negative correlation, indicating that increases in one variable are associated with decreases in the other. In Figure 4.4, it is apparent that medical students who are more cynical tend to be less altruistic than their peers (Roche et al., 2003).

And finally, Figure 4.5 contains the scatterplot of two variables that exhibit no relationship: a random number and first-year cynicism. Again, if I could produce the figure in three dimensions, the scatterplot in Figure 4.5 would

Figure 4.5   A Scatterplot of the (Lack of) Relationship Between Medical Students' Cynicism and Scores From a Random Number Generator. The circular pattern of the plot indicates that there is no relationship between the two variables. The denser pattern of dots in the center of the plot indicates that more people have average scores.

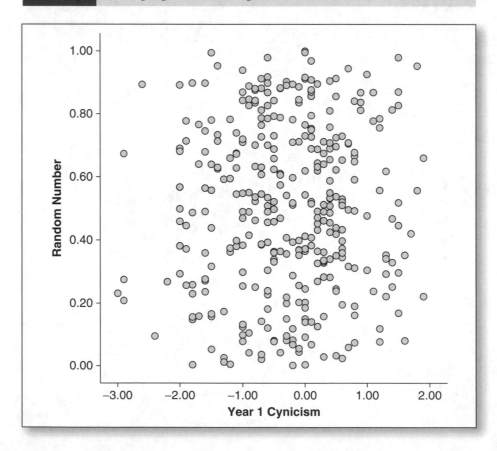

appear to be a bell with its base on the page and its top coming out toward you. Notice that both variables, cynicism and the random number, tend to exhibit more data points toward the center of their respective scales, again merely indicating that more people tend to have average cynicism scores and that the random number generator I used has an average of about 0.50. However, for any given random number, there is no particular cynicism score that is more prevalent, except the average score.

A very specialized type of correlational analysis is called **factor analysis,** *a statistical technique used to identify groups of variables that share variance in common or measure the same concept.* Another statistical procedure, known as *principle components analysis,* is conceptually similar to factor analysis; the math is somewhat different (Lindeman, Merenda, & Gold, 1980), but interpretation is essentially the same for our purposes. The principle underlying factor analysis is that any given variable probably measures more than one theoretical concept, and that the variance produced by employing more than one such variable can be rearranged so that all of the "pieces" of variance can be rearranged to reflect the different concepts measured by the collection of variables. Typical reports of results from factor analysis include a table in which factor loadings are used to show how strongly each variable is associated with the various dimensions (concepts) represented by the collective responses to the variables. An example of a factor analysis, including results, may help to make this descriptive procedure more understandable.

You are probably familiar with course evaluation forms, sometimes called student opinion forms, through which students have an opportunity to provide evaluative ratings about the course and instructor at the end of the semester. At my university, there are 21 primary feedback items (variables) included on the form, and these items are organized into sections about (1) instructor involvement, (2) student interest, (3) student-instructor interaction, (4) course demands, and (5) course organization. One question that can be asked about student responses to these variables is whether the students in my classes consider the separate sections of the instrument to be, indeed, separate. That is, we can ask whether the five separate sections measure five different aspects of the course experience or whether there is some smaller number of dimensions that can be used to describe students' reactions to my courses. The results of the factor analysis are displayed in Table 4.1, in which the section numbers and items are listed in the left column and the "rearranged pieces" of the items—the factors—are displayed in the five right columns. Each of the factors represents a concept measured by the pieces of the items. The numbers in those

Table 4.1	Factor Loadings Derived From Students' Responses to a Course Evaluation Form in Which the Items Were Arranged Into Five Separate Sections. Loadings in bold type indicate a sizable contribution of the item to that factor.

Section Number. Course Evaluation Item	Factor Loadings				
1. Instructor was enthusiastic	**.874**	.194	−.128	.270	.171
1. Instructor interested in teaching	**.831**	.317	−.097	.162	.052
1. Instructor's examples were helpful	**.887**	.196	−.114	.106	.129
1. Instructor concerned with students' learning	**.687**	.370	−.106	.239	.096
2. Student interested in learning	.143	.151	−.108	.133	**.889**
2. Student attentive in class	.218	.268	−.057	.240	**.832**
2. Student felt challenged intellectually	.383	**.489**	−.129	.263	.346
2. Student has become more competent	**.421**	.298	−.143	.226	.225
3. Instructor encouraged idea expression	.287	.336	−.011	**.621**	.207
3. Instructor explained conflicting viewpoints	.176	.030	−.116	**.644**	.183
3. Student has opportunities to ask questions	.174	.191	−.004	**.963**	.075
3. Instructor stimulated class discussion	.362	.185	.034	.046	.098
4. Instructor covered too much material	−.139	−.080	**.938**	.000	−.121
4. Instructor presented material too rapidly	−.102	−.024	**.926**	−.078	−.039

Section Number. Course Evaluation Item	Factor Loadings				
4. Out-of-class assignments too time consuming	−.053	−.029	.971	−.035	−.038
4. Assigned readings too difficult	−.027	−.226	.716	−.064	−.021
5. Instructor covered concepts systematically	.198	.618	−.124	.033	.069
5. Course was well organized	.350	.712	−.156	.142	.164
5. Instructor's presentations were clear	.444	.665	−.161	.287	.198
5. Direction of course was adequately outlined	.314	.923	−.023	.142	.168
5. Student enjoyed going to class	.326	.544	−.019	.351	.462

columns—the factor loadings—represent the extent to which the item contributes to the concept measured by the factor. Loadings can range from −1.00 to +1.00; generally, a loading of .4 or higher indicates a sizable contribution to that factor.

Although the results of the factor analysis contain five different factors, the items are not grouped statistically exactly the same way they were grouped on the course evaluation form. The four instructor items (Section 1) are grouped together in Table 4.1 on Factor 1, but part of the "student has become more competent" item loads on the same factor. Thus, we can conclude that a student's belief in his or her increase in competence is tied to his or her reaction to the qualities of the instructor. Similarly, from the loadings on Factor 2 we can conclude that students' opinions about how intellectually challenged they felt are related to the organization of the course. Factor 3 clearly involves the difficulty of the course and is the only factor that corresponds entirely to the section on the questionnaire.

Factor 4 represents the opportunities for participation provided to the students, but interestingly, the instructor's stimulation of class discussion is not a part of this concept. Factor 5 represents the students' interest and attentiveness, which is partly related to how much the students enjoyed the course. Interestingly, the student's overall enjoyment of the course is "pieced" into the student's interest and the organization of the material, but this is independent of course difficulty, the instructor's enthusiasm and interest in teaching, and the opportunities for participation. We could, of course, continue discussing these results for a long time, but you should have enough knowledge about factor analysis to understand how it can be used for descriptive research purposes.

More often than not, descriptive research involves trying to determine whether two groups differ according to some quality, such as whether women or men tend to commit more crimes or whether psychology majors or chemistry majors perform better on the Graduate Record Exam. Essentially, such research involves comparing the central tendency of one group with the central tendency of another, and the t test (for two groups) or ANOVA (for more than two groups) are the appropriate statistics. Both statistics enable one to determine whether groups have equivalent or different mean scores.

The principle underlying t tests and ANOVA is the assumption that both (or all) groups, whatever they may be, represent samples from the same population. Men and women, for example, represent two different samples from the same population (humans). If that assumption is correct—that is, if there are no fundamental differences between men and women; they are just humans—then the two samples should have the same central tendency, the same mean. To the extent that the two groups are different, one can conclude that the assumption about them being from the same population is wrong. Of course, that doesn't mean, in the case of men and women, that one group is not human. Instead, it means that, on whatever variable is being measured, the two groups represent very different populations of humans; they are not the same on whatever the measurement dimension may be. Most any statistical text will include descriptions of t tests and ANOVA. Nowaczyk (1988) and Wike (1985) are among the more readable; Winer (1971) is more advanced and technical.

When researchers report the results of a t test, you will see something like this: $t(45) = 3.67$, $p < .05$; "t" is, of course, the symbol for the t test, and the number in parentheses represents the degrees of freedom for the statistic. The number after the equal sign is the calculated value of the statistic. For ANOVA, you will see something like: $F(2, 27) = 3.50$, $p < .05$. "F" is the symbol for ANOVA and the number after the equal sign is the actual value of the statistical test. ANOVA has two indicators for degrees of freedom within the parentheses. The first of these represents (but is not equal to) the number of groups compared, while the second indicates the degrees of freedom for the error term.

One of the more complicated forms of ANOVA is *multivariate analysis of variance* (**MANOVA**), which is *employed whenever two or more dependent variables are analyzed simultaneously, usually because there is reason to believe that the multiple dependent variables are related in some way* (Lindeman et al., 1980). Essentially, MANOVA is analogous to employing regular ANOVA except that the "variable" analyzed is the factor, or common variance, of the several dependent variables that actually were measured. Imagine, for example, comparing the course evaluations of several members of a single department. In such a study, MANOVA would be used on each of the factors identified in Table 4.1 above.

In some cases, the data collected in a descriptive research project are the results of other researchers' studies, in which cases researchers often use meta-analysis to detect trends in published reports. **Meta-analysis** is the *collective name for the various quantitative techniques used to combine the results of empirical studies.* The term was coined by Glass (1976) and, since its initial development, has come to include a variety of different statistical techniques. What all of these techniques have in common, however, is that the unit of analysis is the statistical result of data analyses instead of the raw data collected by a researcher (Wachter & Straf, 1990). When reporting the results of a meta-analysis, researchers use **effect size**, which is *a statistical term for the estimate of the magnitude of the difference between groups or the relationship between variables.* The effect size from each study is combined with effect sizes from all of the other studies on the same phenomenon in order to determine, among other things, the average effect observed in the reviewed literature. For example, Kulik, Kulik, and Bangert (1984) used a meta-analysis of research published on the effects of practice tests upon scores on standardized tests such as the SAT. Based on their review of 40 studies, Kulik et al. were able to use effect size to estimate that the average increase in total score on an aptitude test, such as the SAT, was about 20 points for a student's completing a practice test.

Effect size can also be used in many other kinds of analyses, such as those used for predictive and explanatory research, a point to which we shall turn later in this chapter. The kinds of data and analyses for descriptive research are depicted in Figure 4.6. We next turn to a discussion of predictive research.

| Figure 4.6 | The kinds of quantitative statistics researchers typically use to analyze data from a descriptive study depends on the types of questions one is asking and the types of data one is using to attempt to answer them. |

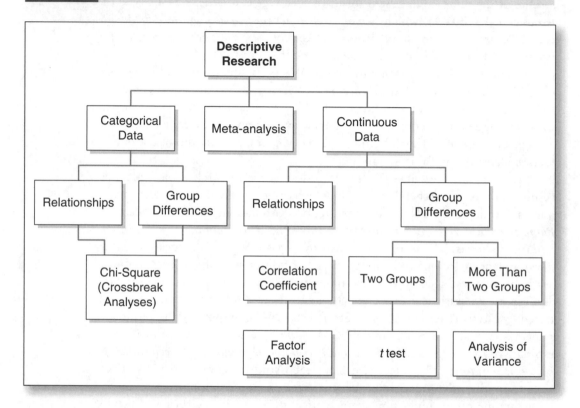

PREDICTIVE RESEARCH

Predictive research involves any study in which the purpose is to determine whether a relationship between variables exists such that one can use one of the variables in place of another. Such research may be done in order to avoid using one of the variables because it is too expensive or time-consuming or to avoid having to wait for an appropriate situation in which to use one of the variables. College admissions committees use the results of predictive research for accepting new students; it's too costly to wait an entire year to find out whether or not a student will do well enough to remain in school. Or one might try to predict jurors' decisions from their attitudes toward the legal system or try to predict whether or not an attempt at cardiopulmonary resuscitation is likely to be successful for a particular type of patient.

In any predictive research, the **response variable** is *the measure one would like to predict*, and the **predictor variable** is *the measure one hopes will predict the response variable*. These are, respectively, analogous to dependent and independent variables in an experiment. SAT score, for example, would be the predictor variable and first-year grade point average would be the response variable in the research admissions committees use to select students. Graduate admissions committees also make use of the Graduate Record Exam for the same purposes (Educational Testing Service, 1981).

Appropriate Questions for Predictive Research

Predictive research involves measuring relationships between two or more variables, and appropriate questions include any question that fits the general form "Is *X* related to *Y*?" or "Can *X* be used to predict *Y*?" Predictive versions of the questions used to illustrate exploratory and descriptive strategies would include these: Does someone's self-esteem predict the impressions formed about others? Is the amount of time jurors spend talking about evidence related to their verdict? Can I predict the outcome of my research from the research of others? Table 4.2 contains a summary of the ways in which these questions have changed as a function of the research strategy. Notice

Table 4.2	Exploratory, Descriptive, and Predictive Research Questions
Exploratory	Do people think differently about themselves than about others?
Descriptive	Under what conditions do people think differently about themselves than about others?
Predictive	Does someone's self-esteem predict the impressions formed about others?
Exploratory	What do jury members talk about during deliberations?
Descriptive	How much time do jurors spend talking about evidence during deliberations?
Predictive	Is the amount of time jurors spend talking about evidence related to their verdict?
Exploratory	Has anyone ever done research on this topic before?
Descriptive	How many different operational definitions of this phenomenon have been used in previous research?
Predictive	Can I predict the outcome of my research from the research of others?

that changes in the questions posed within any given topic are related to the answers one can expect to obtain.

Prerequisites for Predictive Research

Because predictive research involves assessing whether or not one variable can be used to predict another, researchers need to be able to determine the extent to which the separate variables actually measure what they are supposed to measure; that is, both variables must be valid. Equally important, however, is that both variables must be as reliable as possible. The requirement for very high reliability results from the fact that the predictive power of the predictor variable is limited to its reliability. If SAT scores, for example, are 80% reliable, then the best they can do is predict about 80% of first-year college grades. Put another way, if the correlation between random halves of the SAT test is only 0.89, then 80% is also the highest amount of variance we can expect to account for when using SAT scores to predict grades.

Statistics for Predictive Research

The types of statistical analyses used for predictive research are all based on **correlation**—*a statistical measure of the degree to which two or more variables are related.* In addition to correlation coefficients themselves, the other predominant statistical procedure is regression analysis.

A correlation coefficient generally consists of both an algebraic sign and a number. The sign indicates the direction of the relationship: positive for direct, negative for inverse. In predictive research, the sign is generally not important, except perhaps as a check on calculation accuracy. When our purpose is to predict one variable from another, it makes no difference whether we predict from a direct or inverse relationship. If you look back at Figures 4.3 and 4.4, for example, you should be able to see that one can predict cynicism in the first year of medical school equally well from altruism in the first year or from cynicism in the second year. What matters is the strength of the relationship, not whether the relationship is direct or inverse.

What is important in predictive research is the numeric value of the correlation coefficient. Correlation coefficients can range from −1.00 to +1.00; any coefficient outside this range results from calculation error. A coefficient of −1.00 represents a perfect, inverse relationship and enables prediction with

100% accuracy. Similarly, a coefficient of +1.00 indicates a perfect, direct relationship and 100% predictive power. Such coefficients, however, are extremely rare. A coefficient close to zero indicates no relationship at all and therefore no predictive power. The scatterplots in Figures 4.3 and 4.4 reflect coefficients of about +.70 and −.76, respectively. The square of the correlation coefficient is a measure of the amount of variance the two measures have in common, a measure of the extent to which the two variables measure the same concept. Thus, cynicism in the first and second years of medical school (Figure 4.3) share about 49% of their variance; something happens during the first year to change the students' cynicism about people (Roche et al., 2003).

More often than not, however, predictive research involves trying to construct a prediction equation, not simply determining the extent to which two variables are related. We might, for example, want to construct an equation to predict the amount of time jurors spend deliberating from the length of the trial. If we could construct such an equation, judges and other court personnel could use the equation to schedule other hearings during the deliberation. If a judge knew the jury was going to deliberate for about two hours, for example, the judge could schedule several short hearings during that time and still be ready to hear the verdict when the jurors have finished deliberating.

Regression analyses are used to construct such prediction equations. A **regression equation** is *a formula for predicting a score on the response variable from the score on the predictor variable.* In general, regression equations take the form $Y' = bX + c$, where Y' is the predicted score, b is the regression coefficient, X is the score on the predictor variable, and c is a constant (the point at which the prediction line crosses the ordinate or Y axis on a graph). One example of a regression equation with which you are probably familiar is the expression used to convert Fahrenheit temperatures into Centigrade temperatures. For Centigrade to Fahrenheit conversions, the equation is $F = 1.8C + 32$. Predictions from a regression equation are approximate and depend on the strength of the relationship between the two variables: The stronger the relationship—the closer the correlation coefficient is to either −1.00 or +1.00—the more accurate the prediction. Fahrenheit and centigrade temperatures are highly correlated simply because they are both highly valid and highly reliable measures of the same thing (heat). The amount of prediction error is very small; however, it is not zero. There is always some error in any measurement, and therefore, there is always some error in any prediction made from a measurement. Estimating the margin of error associated with predictions also falls under the category of regression analysis. Although the mathematics involved are beyond the scope of this text, almost any basic statistics text contains the information you would need.

There are times when more than one predictor variable is used in research, such as when a college admissions board uses SAT scores, high school grades, and high school ranking to predict first-year college grades. In such instances, the analysis known as **multiple regression** (*a statistical technique for estimating simultaneous correlations among any number of predictor variables and a single, continuous response variable*) is used. Although considerably more complicated in terms of mathematics, multiple regression relies on the same basic principles as correlation and simple regression. Kerlinger (1979) contains a very readable introduction to multiple regression. When there is more than one predictor variable, the regression equation is expanded to reflect this, and a multiple regression equation might look something like $Y' = b_1X_1 + b_2X_2 + b_3X_3 + c$, where b_1 refers to the regression coefficient for the first predictor, X_1, and so on through c, the constant. Researchers are not likely to report a regression equation in this form, however; the results in Table 4.3 are a more customary presentation of the results from a multiple regression analysis.

The results in Table 4.3 come from a study of medical students' attitudes about people in general (Roche et al., 2003). The response variable in this analysis is cynicism in the first year of medical school, and the predictor variables include beliefs about people's trustworthiness, strength of will, and altruism (also measured in the first year of medical school). Notice that all three variables are significant predictors of first-year cynicism, but trustworthiness is the strongest predictor. The column labeled t reflects the fact that a type of the t test is used to determine whether or not the regression coefficient for each predictor is significantly different from zero.

Table 4.3	Results of a multiple regression analysis in which first-year cynicism among medical students is predicted from beliefs about (1) the trustworthiness of people, (2) the strength of will displayed by people, and (3) how altruistic people in general are.		
Variable	Coefficient	t	p
Constant	−.030	−0.646	.519
Altruism	−.346	−6.788	.001
Trustworthiness	−.680	−12.693	.001
Strength of will	−.107	−2.191	.029

Regression analyses, both simple and multiple regression, come in many different forms, but the essence of each form is that one or more predictor variables are tested for its (their) relationship to the response variable. In logistic regression, for example, the response variable is a nominal or **categorical measure** (*determining the presence or absence of a characteristic; naming a quality*), which requires different mathematics to calculate the results but produces the same kind of results (regression coefficients). In path analysis, one or more intermediate variables are included in the model such that predictors are used to predict the intermediate variables, which in turn are used to predict other response variables. This enables researchers to understand the sequencing of the predictors; for example, high school grades predict SAT scores, and SAT scores predict first-year college grades. This sequencing enables researchers to understand the process by which one variable influences another, but the results are interpreted the same way one would interpret a simple regression result. Similarly, structural equations analysis is used to examine the predictive power of factors derived from factor analysis, but the results are interpreted much the same way one interprets multiple regression results.

EXPLANATORY RESEARCH

The purpose of explanatory research is to test whether or not one or more independent variables can cause one or more dependent variables. A single explanatory research project, however, will not involve all the potential causes for a given effect, but instead will concentrate on a few. As you learned in Chapter 1, the purpose of explanatory research is to demonstrate that one variable can cause the other, not to demonstrate that the independent variable is necessarily the only cause.

Appropriate Questions for Explanatory Research

Questions for which explanatory strategies are appropriate are those in which a causal relationship is being considered. Using the same topics as in previous sections, these might include these: What causes people to think about the reasons for their behavior? Do different instructions about reasonable doubt affect the length of jury deliberations? Why are my results different from those obtained in previous research? You should also recall from Chapter 1 that explanatory research requires that the researcher be able to manipulate the independent variable and randomly assign participants to the different levels created through manipulation.

Appropriate Statistics for Explanatory Research

You have probably guessed by now that explanatory research involves the use of inferential statistics. If so, you are correct. Because experimental procedures involve creating different groups representing the different levels of the independent variable, inferential statistics are used to determine the extent to which the different groups actually perform differently on the dependent variable. If you can reject the assumption that the groups represent samples from the same population, then you can conclude that the independent variable had some effect.

Any statistical analyses designed to detect differences in central tendencies, such as *t* test and ANOVA, are appropriate for analyzing explanatory research data. If the dependent variable is a categorical variable, such as verdicts from a jury decision, then chi-square analysis can be used to detect differences between the groups. Contrary to what you might expect, the complicated part of explanatory research is ensuring the internal validity of the research design, not the statistical procedures used to analyze the data obtained from the design. Thus, there are no "special" statistics used for explanatory research. You are likely to encounter any and all of the previously described statistical analyses when reading explanatory research.

SUMMARY

- Research design and analyses are interdependent. How a project is designed partly determines the statistics the researcher uses to analyze the resulting data. However, lack of familiarity with statistical procedures may limit your ability to interpret a particular set of research results.
- Designs can be categorized in terms of their purposes: exploration, description, prediction, and explanation. Different purposes involve different designs and, therefore, different statistical analyses.
- Analyses for exploratory research tend to be qualitative rather than quantitative. They involve determining whether or not something has happened and are rarely complex.
- Analyses for descriptive research tend to be simple, inferential statistics that enable the researcher to summarize the data he or she has obtained, usually through measures of central tendency, as well as to estimate values for the population to which the researcher wishes to generalize. However, when questions about interrelatedness of variables are addressed, factor analysis may be used to describe those relationships. When describing or summarizing the results of existing research is the purpose of the study, meta-analysis is used.

- Predictive research analyses are all based on correlational techniques in which analyses are used to determine the extent to which one variable is related to another variable. When specific predictions are required, regression analyses can be used to construct prediction equations.
- Explanatory research generally involves comparing the various groups created through the manipulation of the independent variable, and appropriate analyses include any that can be used to determine whether or not the groups created can be assumed to belong to the same overall population.

EXERCISES

1. Using your library's databases, search for and read an article containing a stem-and-leaf display.

2. Using your library's databases, search for and read an article containing results from a multiple regression analysis.

3. Using your library's databases, search for and read an article containing results from an analysis of variance (ANOVA).

4. Go to the Web site of the American Statistical Association (www.amstat.org), the Statistical Society of Canada (www.ssc.ca), or the Royal Statistical Society (www.rss.org.uk) and explore the site to find ways to obtain additional information or contacts when you need statistical information in the future.

CHAPTER 5

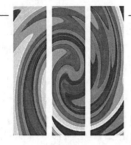

Sampling

I don't like turnips, and I don't like liver. Call it prejudice if you wish, but I have no intention of ever trying either again just to make sure I don't like them. I am sure.

—Andy Rooney (1982, p. ix)

Overview

In this chapter you will learn about the principles and procedures researchers use to select the people or things from which they obtained data. You will learn about terminology used to describe sampling, as well as the theory and importance of sampling distributions. You will also learn about the difference between the two major types of sampling procedures: probability and nonprobability sampling. In addition to learning about the various procedures, you will learn about the advantages and disadvantages of each. Finally, you will learn that understanding the limitations on applying results that stem from the sampling choices made by researchers is an important part of consuming research and applying it to policies and programs.

INTRODUCTION

Like columnist and *60 Minutes* commentator Andy Rooney, most people have an aversion to one or another type of food. They've tried it, didn't like it, and insist there is no need to try again. When I was in college, I hated coconut. I tried it several times and disliked it each time I tried it. You would have had to pay me a semester's worth of tuition to get me to eat anything with coconut in it. One night, eating at the home of a friend, I asked for a second piece of cake. My friend was very surprised. She knew I didn't like coconut, and she knew that her mother had included coconut in the cake. She thought I was eating the first piece just to be polite. When she told me, I was equally surprised, as well as curious. Had my tastes changed? What was going on?

No, my tastes had not changed. Instead, I had become a victim of sampling error. Until I ate that cake, all I had ever sampled was processed coconut, which I continue to dislike. Eventually I learned that fresh coconut had been used in the cake. I had generalized from my limited experience with processed coconut to all coconut; I had stereotyped all coconut on the basis of my experience with only processed coconut.

Generalizing from a sample is something that every one of us does every day. We may be attempting to answer a question about people without including all people in our sample. We may see one episode of a television program and decide never to watch the program again, watch one of a director's movies and decide to see more of them when we get the opportunity, and so on. Avoiding incorrect generalizations due to sampling error is what this chapter is all about. Before learning how to avoid sampling error, however, we have to learn a little of the jargon associated with sampling.

When discussing **sampling**—*the process of selecting participants for a research project*—scientists tend to use a great deal of jargon. One reason for all the jargon is that we need to be able to communicate very specific notions about sampling to those who will read our research reports, and very specific notions often require jargon. You need to understand the jargon to be able to read others' reports.

Sampling unit and **sampling element** are both used to *refer to a single "thing" selected for inclusion in a research project*. If the researcher samples people, then a person is the unit or element. If television shows are sampled, then a single program is the unit, and so on. *All possible units or elements that can be included* make up the **population**. A population is an abstract concept, something that cannot be seen or measured, even though it consists of concrete units. The population of the United States, for example, can be estimated but it cannot be accurately counted because one can never be sure one has counted everyone; someone could be hiding, for example, or a new person could be born after the researcher has already counted "everyone" in a particular location.

Instead, research is done on a **sample**—*a portion of the elements in a population*. Any part of a population is considered a sample, and any given sample can be a part of more than one population. You and two of your classmates, for example, are simultaneously a sample of your class, a sample of university students, a sample of students in general, a sample of the people living in whatever country in which you may reside, and so on. A sample, then, is a concrete portion of a population, probably of more than one population.

Although a sample is a portion of a population, technically the sample is not selected from the population. Instead, samples are selected from a **sampling frame**—*a concrete listing of the elements in a population*. Again using you and your classmates as examples, I could select you from the registrar's list of all students at your campus, which would then be the sampling frame, but I could never be sure that the registrar's list included the entire population. Some students may be left off the list, some may be included on the list even though they are no longer students, and so forth. Essentially, the sampling frame is the largest possible sample of a population; it is everything that can be selected.

A **parameter** is *a value associated with a population*. It is an abstract value simply because we cannot calculate, for example, the mean of a population if we don't know how many units are in the population and cannot measure the entire population. Instead of calculating parameters, we have to estimate them from **statistics**—*values associated with samples*. Most people think *statistic* refers to statistical analyses, such as correlations, but the term applies to any value calculated from a sample. Because a sample is always concrete, we can calculate statistics. When we use statistics to estimate parameters, the statistics are inferential statistics. However, because they are estimates, inferential statistics always contain some amount of error, usually error resulting from the sampling process.

Sampling error is the term applied to *the extent to which a sample statistic incorrectly estimates a population parameter*. Consider, for example, the taste I had associated with coconut. Because I had sampled only processed coconut, that test contained some sampling error. I used that taste, however, to make inferences about all coconut (the population of coconut), just as a sample statistic is used to make an inference about an entire population. The more error involved in the sampling process, such as my ignoring raw coconut, the greater the sampling error of an inferential statistic.

If you had asked me how confident I was about my reaction to coconut before I ate that piece of cake, I, like Andy Rooney, would have told you I was 100% certain. That would have been a statement about a **confidence level**—*the probability associated with the accuracy of an inferential statistic.* I might have said the probability of my disliking any coconut you gave me was 1.00, a probability we now know was an overestimate. Indeed, a confidence level of 1.00 is always an overestimate, for no statistic can be 100% accurate. There is always going to be some sampling error, a confidence level less than 1.00, simply because we can never be sure exactly what is and is not included in any given population.

Enough jargon. You now know that units and elements are things and that they make up populations and samples. Populations are abstract collections of everything, whereas samples are only a portion of things in the population. A sampling frame is the largest sample that can be obtained from a population; it is almost every thing in the population. Further, statistics are sample values, which are often used to estimate population parameters (values). Any statistic contains some amount of error, which can be determined by calculating the confidence level associated with the statistic. Whenever a sample is taken from a population, there is always some sampling error. Fortunately, under certain conditions we can estimate sampling error, which is what we turn our attention to next.

SAMPLING DISTRIBUTIONS

In this section we will deal with the basis for estimating sampling error and confidence limits. If you have had a course in statistics, you've probably seen this material before. But if you are like most of us, you can always use a review. If you have yet to complete a statistics course, this material is necessary to understand the reasons for most of the sampling procedures discussed later in the chapter.

The basis for all statistics dealing with sampling distributions is sampling theory. We will use a running example in which we are interested in discovering the mean grade point average (GPA) of the students in a fictitious methods class. We will have to assume that everyone in the methods class constitutes a population, which also means we will not be able to calculate the mean GPA of the entire class. We will use fictitious numbers, including the fiction that there are 35 students in the class; the data are reflected in Figure 5.1.

The simplest way to discover the mean GPA in the class is to ask everyone to report his or her GPA. But not everyone may be willing to report his or her

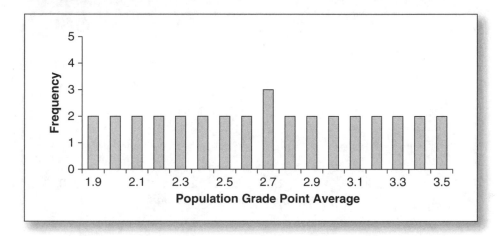

Figure 5.1 The Population of 35 Grade Point Averages Obtained From a Fictitious Class of Students

GPA, or some may be absent on the day the data are collected. Suppose a researcher, who is also a member of the class, asks four people in the class to report their GPAs: the people sitting in front, behind, to the left, and to the right of the researcher. They report GPAs of 3.5, 2.0, 2.2, and 1.9, and the researcher adds her own GPA of 3.2. We now have a sample of five students and can calculate the sample mean:

$$(3.5 + 2.0 + 2.2 + 1.9 + 3.2) / 5 = 2.56$$

The question is whether 2.56 is a reasonable estimate of the mean for the entire class. The answer is that we have no way of knowing: The researcher might have asked four other people and obtained a different sample mean.

The Population

Suppose that the distribution of grade point averages in the entire class is the distribution illustrated in Figure 5.1; the distribution of the sample is shown in Figure 5.2. The mean of the population is 2.70, which is not exactly the same as the sample mean of 2.56. Clearly, the sample statistic is not an accurate estimate of the population parameter, but you should already know that statistics are never perfectly accurate.

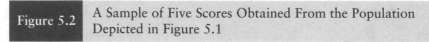

Figure 5.2   A Sample of Five Scores Obtained From the Population
Depicted in Figure 5.1

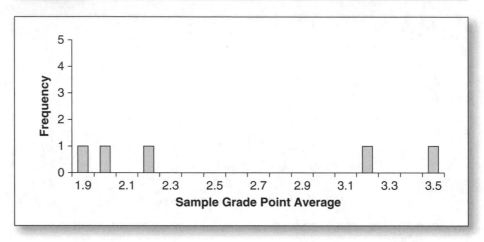

Notice how flat the population distribution is in Figure 5.1—2.70 is the only value for which there are three scores; all the rest have two scores. Of course, in a real research project, we would only be able to guess the shape of the population distribution, although we could make that guess on the basis of the shape of the sample distribution. The point is that the population of scores is not a normal, bell-shaped distribution; nor does it have to be for sampling theory to be applicable. What is required, however, is that the sample be selected randomly from the population.

Random Selection

The key to being able to use a sample statistic to estimate a population parameter is the manner in which the sample is selected. **Random selection** includes *any technique that provides each population element an equal probability of being included in the sample.* Choosing the four people sitting closest to the researcher in the classroom does not provide everyone in the class an equal chance of being included in the sample, and so the sample illustrated in Figure 5.2 is not a random sample. Therefore, we have no way of being able to estimate the amount of error included in that sample. If, however, the researcher put the names of everyone in class into a hat and drew out five names, she would have obtained a random sample. Later in the chapter you will learn about the variety of ways in which a random sample can be obtained, but they are all basically derivations of this "everyone's-name-in-a-hat" procedure.

Standard Error

If a sample has been randomly selected from the sampling frame, it is possible to estimate the amount of error in the sample by taking advantage of certain properties of sampling distributions. A **sampling distribution** is *a distribution of statistics created by repeatedly selecting random samples from a population*. Assume that instead of the four people around her, the researcher randomly selected five students from her class. If she calculated the mean GPA of that sample and then repeated the same procedure another 199 times, she might obtain the sampling distribution presented in Figure 5.3.

Compare Figures 5.3 and 5.1. Although the two distributions have almost identical means, their shapes are very different. The population distribution in Figure 5.1 is very flat, whereas the sampling distribution in Figure 5.3 is peaked and considerably less spread out. Even though there are more scores in the sampling distribution—200 compared to 35 in the population—the variability of the sampling distribution is smaller. The standard deviation of the population is 0.48, whereas that for the sampling distribution is 0.21, less than half than that of the population. This is always the case; sampling distributions exhibit less variability than does the population distribution.

Figure 5.3	The Sampling Distribution of Means Obtained From 200 Randomly Selected Samples of Five Grade Point Averages From the Population Depicted in Figure 5.1

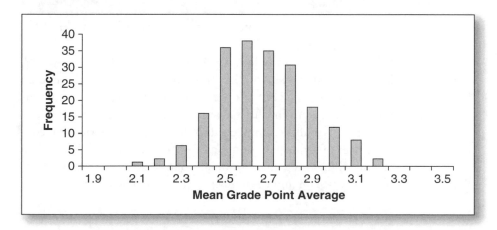

The **standard error** of a statistic is *the standard deviation of its sampling distribution*. Even though it is a standard deviation like any other standard deviation, it merits a special name because it comes from a sampling distribution. Thus, for our example, the standard error of the mean—the standard deviation of the sampling distribution illustrated in Figure 5.3—is 0.21. The standard error is what enables us to determine the amount of sampling error that exists in any random sample we select—but only when the sample is selected randomly.

Once again, however, we must come back to the real world of research. It is fine to run around generating sampling distributions, but that requires a great deal of time and effort, as well as more information about the population than is usually available. But if a single sample has been randomly selected, the researcher doesn't need to generate sampling distributions. Because the first sample selected was not a random sample, we won't use it; let me instead demonstrate with the first sample I selected in order to create the sampling distribution in Figure 5.3. That sample consisted of GPA values of 1.9, 3.3, 2.7, 2.6, and 3.4.

The mean of this random sample is 2.78, and its standard deviation is 0.61. As sample statistics, they are supposed to be estimates of the population parameters, and forgetting about the fact that we actually know what those parameters are, we can estimate the population mean and standard deviation to also be 2.78 and 0.61, respectively. In order to calculate the standard deviation of the sampling distribution of means—the standard error of the mean—all we have to do is apply the formula below:

$$S_{\bar{x}} = \frac{S}{\sqrt{n}},$$

where $S_{\bar{x}}$ is the standard error of the mean, S is the standard deviation of the sample, and n is the size of the sample.

Substituting the values of our sample yields $0.61/\sqrt{5} = 0.27$. Recall, however, that the actual standard deviation of the sampling distribution pictured in Figure 5.3 is 0.21, which is close but not the same as our calculated value for the standard error of the mean. The difference results from the fact that the calculation formula is based on the assumption that the sampling distribution contains an infinite number of samples. A sampling distribution, then, is actually an abstract notion, something we can approximate but cannot actually produce. Because we cannot generate an infinite number of samples, no concrete sampling distribution is ever going to have exactly the same standard deviation as the value calculated from the formula, except through coincidence.

Confidence Intervals

What remains to be done is to determine the amount of sampling error in our sample, which involves calculating a **confidence interval**—*the inclusive, probabilistic range of values around any calculated statistic*. Remember that at the beginning of this exercise we wanted to estimate the mean grade point average of everyone in the fictitious methods class; that is, the population mean. Our sample mean, 2.78, is an estimate of the population mean, but we also know that it is an imperfect estimate. The population mean may or may not be 2.78, but it certainly ought to be close to 2.78. The question, then, is how close? What is the range of values around the sample mean that could reasonably include the population mean; that is, what is the confidence interval of our statistic?

We could, of course, simply say the population mean is somewhere between 0.0 and 4.0, and we would be absolutely correct. But that would be uninformative; we knew that before we collected any data from the sample. But the more restricted we make the range of values, the less sure we can be about whether that range contains the population mean. What we must decide, then, is how sure we want to be. Or put another way, what are we willing to accept as the probability that the range we select is wrong? In most sciences, the rule of thumb for being wrong is a probability of .05—five chances in 100 of being wrong.

We can take advantage of the central limit theorem in order to create our confidence interval. We know from that theorem that about 95% of all scores in a normal distribution fall within about two standard deviations of the mean. Because a sampling distribution is composed of an infinite number of randomly selected samples, any sampling distribution is normally distributed. Therefore, we can infer that 95% of our sample means should fall within plus or minus two standard errors of the mean. Our estimate of the population mean is 2.78, and our estimate of the standard error is 0.27. Thus, we can be 95% certain that the true population mean is somewhere between $[2.78 - 2(0.27)]$ and $[2.78 + 2(0.27)]$ or somewhere between 2.24 and 3.32. The probability that we are wrong is .05. By starting with a sample of five students, we have estimated that the mean of the population is between 2.24 and 3.32. In doing so, we made use of sampling theory and the central limit theory, and we had to calculate a sample mean, a sample standard deviation, and the standard error of the sample mean.

Sample Size

If the confidence interval we estimated above is too wide for your liking, you can achieve a smaller interval by increasing the size of the sample. Look again at the formula used to calculate the standard error of the mean:

$$S_{\bar{x}} = \frac{S}{\sqrt{n}}.$$

Notice that the square root of the sample size is in the denominator of the formula. What this means is that the larger the sample size, the smaller the standard error of the mean. A smaller standard error of the mean results in a smaller confidence interval. To get a smaller confidence interval, select a larger sample.

Figure 5.4, for example, contains a sampling distribution of 200 samples, but the size of each of the samples is 10. This distribution was created from the

| Figure 5.4 | The Sampling Distribution of Means Obtained From 200 Randomly Selected Samples of 10 Grade Point Averages From the Population Depicted in Figure 5.1 |

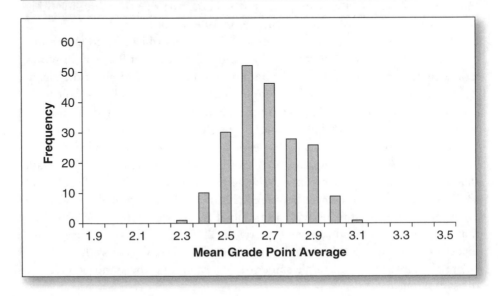

same population as that depicted in Figure 5.3, but this distribution is considerably narrower. The standard deviation of the sampling distribution for $n = 10$ is 0.16, whereas that for $n = 5$ is 0.21.

Although I could continue to illustrate sampling distributions with larger and larger sample sizes, you can see the relationship between sample size and standard error by examining Figure 5.5, which was created by assuming, for illustration purposes, that the standard deviation of the sample was 10. The size of the sample, indicated on the abscissa (X axis), varies from 10 to 1,000, but the standard deviation of the sample remains at 10. As the sample size increases, the size of the standard error decreases. The change, however, is not linear. When the sample size changes from 10 to 50, the change in the standard error is considerable. Beyond samples of 50, however, increasing the sample size does not dramatically affect the standard error. Thus, it is not always reasonable to attempt to obtain the largest possible sample.

| Figure 5.5 | The Relationship Between Standard Error of the Mean and Sample Size. All samples have a standard deviation of 10. |

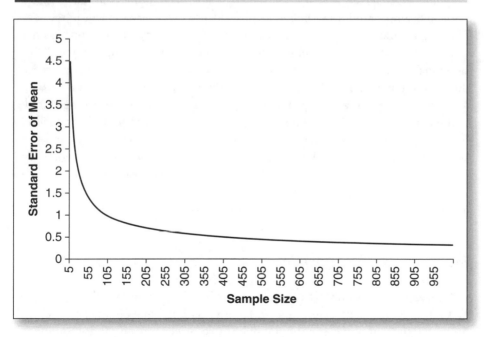

PROBABILITY SAMPLING

The foregoing discussion of sampling distributions relied entirely on samples resulting from a random sampling procedure. To create the distributions in the various figures, I used a computer to generate 200 random samples from a population that contained 35 grade point averages. As mentioned before, whenever one can obtain a random sample, one can rely on the central limit theorem and the properties of the normal distribution to determine the amount of sampling error in a sample. In general, **probability sampling** is *any technique that ensures a random sample*; that is, a technique that ensures that every element in the sampling frame has an equal chance of being included in the sample. There are a number of variations on the names-in-the-hat example discussed before, and we turn our attention now to describing those variations.

Simple Random Sampling

Names selected from a collection of name tags in a hat and a list of random numbers generated by a computer program are both examples of **simple random sampling**—*techniques that involve an unsystematic random selection process*. Basically, simple random sampling involves identifying every element in the sampling frame and choosing among them on the basis of any planned process that also ensures that every element has an equal opportunity of being selected. When sampling frames are too large for slips of paper in a hat or some similar procedure, a random number table can be used. A random number table is exactly what its name denotes: a table containing random numbers or numbers arranged in no particular order. Random number tables usually contain thousands of random numbers, but most researchers now use random number generators contained in software such as Microsoft Excel, SPSS, SAS, and so on. The importance of a random number table, or random number generator, is that each number is independent of every other number, which is exactly what is required to ensure that each entry has an equal probability of being selected for the sample.

Systematic Random Sampling

Simple random sampling can be a rather inefficient way to select a sample. With a very large sampling frame and a large sample, one could spend several hours paging through a random number table or generating random numbers with a computer. **Systematic random sampling** is accomplished by *choosing* *elements from a randomly arranged sampling frame according to ordered criteria.* Frequently, systematic random sampling is accomplished by choosing every 10th, 15th, or some other *n*th element in the sampling frame. Just as in simple random sampling, however, several decisions need to be made before a researcher can begin.

First, and most obvious, the researcher needs to decide the size of the sample. If, for example, one wanted a sample of 50 people from a sampling frame containing 900, then a proportion of 50/900 = 0.055 of the entire sampling frame. Inverting that proportion, 1/0.055 = 18, provides the *n*th or multiple to use in the procedure; that is, if a researcher wanted 50 people from a sampling frame of 900, he or she would choose every 18th person.

Second, one needs to decide on a starting point in the sampling frame list. Again, finger pointing or some other unsystematic means is recommended, which could include using a random number generator to decide which element is to be the first element selected. If, for example, a researcher randomly put her finger on Element 14, then the sample would include Numbers 14, 32, 50, 68, and so on until she had all 50 elements.

As described above, systematic random sampling produces the same result as simple random sampling: a random sample. Both procedures require a list of the sampling frame, but systematic random sampling requires that the list be in random order. If the elements in the sampling frame list are not randomized, problems will arise whenever there are simple or periodic trends in the sampling frame listing.

Simple trends are *systematic and consistent changes in some quality inherent in the sampling frame elements.* For example, a mailing list a researcher obtained from someone else may be ordered in terms of postal codes. Depending on the starting point the researcher chooses and the proportion sampled, a postal code order may result in some codes, such as those for underpopulated areas, being skipped in the sampling process; thus such codes would not have an equal chance of being included. If the researcher selected every 30th name, postal codes represented by fewer than 30 names may not be included at all.

Periodic trends are *cyclic changes that repeat throughout the sampling frame.* Babbie (1983), for example, mentioned a study in which the sampling frame consisted of soldiers arranged in squads. Each squad contained 10 soldiers, and the sergeant's name was always listed first in each squad. A researcher who systematically sampled every 10th soldier obtained a sample composed entirely of sergeants, simply because his starting point happened to be a sergeant's name. The other members of the squad never had a chance to be included in the sample, and it was not, therefore, really a random sample. Similarly, a list of students arranged according to year in school and grade point averages could result in sampling only seniors. Thus, before using any sampling frame list for systematic random sampling, a researcher must be sure the list is in random order. Without a randomly ordered listing, systematic random sampling is not truly random.

Stratified Random Sampling

Both simple and systematic random sampling procedures require a list of the sampling frame and that the elements in the sampling frame are relatively homogeneous. If a sampling frame is not homogeneous but instead contains subgroups, such as seniors, juniors, and so forth in a listing of university students, then the researcher may need to represent those subgroups in the sample. Whenever subgroups of a population are necessary for research purposes, stratified random sampling results in less sampling error than occurs in either simple or systematic random sampling.

Stratified random sampling is accomplished by *using random selection separately for each subgroup in the sampling frame*. Stratified random sampling for a sampling frame of university students would involve either simple or systematic sampling within the senior class, the same procedure within the junior class, and so on until all classes are represented in the sample. The subgroups within the sampling frame are treated as though they were separate sampling frames themselves.

By using stratified random sampling, one can be sure the sample will contain equal or some other proportionate numbers of males and females, people with ages above and below 30, or any other subgroups that are desirable. If a researcher wants to select a specific number of each subgroup's members, the technique is called **probability sampling with quotas**. In that case, one establishes a quota for each subgroup and then randomly samples members of that subgroup until the quota is met. The key, however, is using a random sampling procedure within each subgroup so the final sample is indeed a random sample.

Cluster Sampling

Simple, systematic, and stratified random sampling procedures are all variants of the basic name-in-a-hat process described earlier. Essentially, the entire sampling frame is listed and elements are randomly selected from it. Sometimes, however, researchers do not have a list of the sampling frame and cannot obtain one. One would not, for example, be likely to be able to find or generate a sampling frame list for all college students in the United States. When sampling frame lists are unavailable, researchers use **cluster sampling**—*randomly selecting hierarchical groups from the sampling frame*. The groups included in the sampling frame are called clusters, and one samples finer and finer gradations of clusters until one is at a level at which one can obtain a list of elements.

To select a random sample of 500 college students in the United States, for example, a researcher could first create a sampling frame consisting of a list of colleges and universities (my encyclopedia has one, and there are other sources for such a list). Using simple random sampling, one could randomly select, say, five colleges from this list. Then, from those clusters, one could randomly select 100 students from each college to obtain a random sample of 500 college students residing in the United States. Figure 5.6 illustrates this sampling procedure.

Usually, whenever the sampling frame is so large that one needs to use cluster sampling, one will very likely need to include some sort of stratification as well. To obtain a sample of U.S. college students, for example, one probably wants to be sure to include some students from small, medium, and large institutions or some from each of the four regions of the country. Once the strata are selected, the researcher might also want to select various levels of students—graduate students, seniors, and so on—within each college.

Figure 5.6   A Two-Stage Cluster Sampling Procedure for Obtaining a Random Sample of 500 College Students in the United States

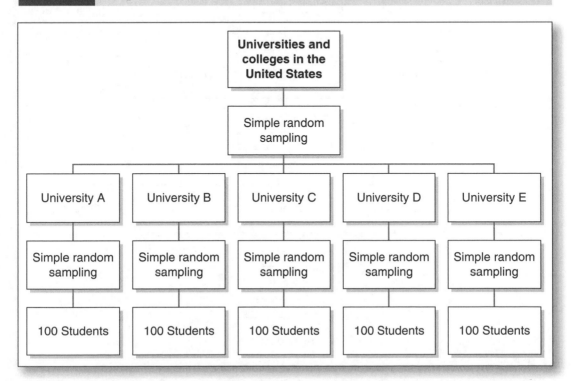

Such a multistage, stratified cluster sampling process is illustrated in Figure 5.7, wherein the figure is simplified by displaying only part of the process.

Figure 5.7   A Multistage Stratified Cluster Sampling Procedure

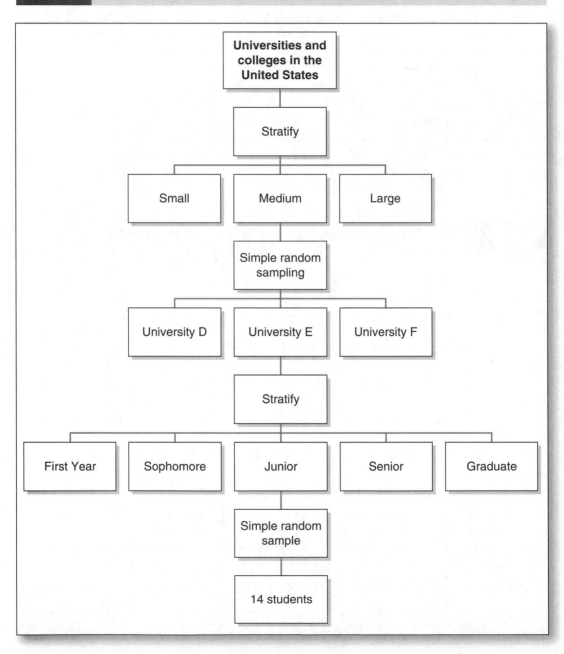

Combining different probability sampling procedures is not uncommon, and it is acceptable to combine any two or more probability sampling procedures. So long as one limits oneself to random selection procedures, one is free to be as creative as is necessary to obtain the desired sample. What is not acceptable, however, is combining probability with nonprobability sampling procedures.

NONPROBABILITY SAMPLING

Unlike probability sampling, **nonprobability sampling** refers to *any procedure in which elements have unequal chances for being included*. If one chooses elements on the basis of how they look, where they live, or some other criteria, the researcher limits the chances of those who do not meet the criteria. There are several different types of nonprobability sampling procedures, but they all have one thing in common: When a nonprobability sample is obtained, one cannot estimate sampling error. Because nonprobability samples are not random samples, it is usually impossible to determine the appropriate sampling distribution, which is required for estimating sampling error.

Accidental Sampling

The most common procedure for obtaining a nonprobability sample is **accidental sampling**—*selection based on availability or ease of inclusion*. As you might guess, the person-on-the-street interviews often shown during local newscasts are examples of accidental sampling. The interviewer selects whoever is willing to talk in front of the camera, and the sample is further made accidental by selecting the most intelligible respondents for broadcast on the air. Accidental sampling is also called availability sampling, but it is likely to be mislabeled as "random" by those who do not understand the nature of a truly random selection process.

Those who mistakenly refer to accidental sampling as random sampling tend to argue that they didn't use any selection criteria at all. Instead, they claim they interviewed the first 25 people to walk out of, say, a movie theater. But that does, in fact, involve selection criteria. Specifically, selecting the first 25 people out of the theater limits the chances of inclusion of those who sat near the front, those who stayed to watch the credits, those who were so moved by the movie they sat for a while to regain their composure, or those who for some other reason delayed their departure.

One of the best examples of the problems that may be encountered when attempting to generalize from an accidental sample is the embarrassment of the editors of *The Literary Digest* ("Landon, 1,293,669: Roosevelt, 972,897," 1936) when they used an accidental sample to predict the outcome of the 1936 U.S. presidential election. Their problem was, simply, that their prediction was incredibly wrong. They initially sent out 10 million ballots and obtained a sample of 2 million returns. Those returns indicated a 57% to 43% margin in favor of Alf Landon over Franklin Delano Roosevelt. Instead, Roosevelt obtained about 63% of the actual popular vote.

With such a large sample, even an accidental sample, someone unfamiliar with sampling theory might expect the sampling error to be very small. But that's exactly the point underlying our knowledge about sampling theory: No matter how large the sample, there is no way to estimate sampling error without a random sampling procedure. Unfortunately, the editors of *The Literary Digest* had used telephone books and automobile registration records in their sampling frame. In the mid-1930s, telephone and automobile owners tended to be among the wealthier members of the population, and wealthier voters, then as now, tended to vote Republican.

The editors' sample was composed primarily of Republicans, which explains why they predicted that the Republican candidate, Landon, would be the winner. The standard error of their sample would have been extremely small, but *only* if the editors had wanted to predict the voting patterns of Republicans. Of course, Republicans were not the only voters to vote in the 1936 election, and the editors ended up looking rather silly.

Purposive Sampling

For some research projects, particularly exploratory or pilot projects, researchers may want to obtain a sample of specific individuals. **Purposive sampling** refers to *procedures directed toward obtaining a certain type of element*. If one were developing a questionnaire designed to measure prejudice, for example, one might want to include in the sample both members of a known bigoted group, such as the Ku Klux Klan, and members of, say, the National Association for the Advancement of Colored People. If the questionnaire was valid, the former group ought to score considerably higher than the latter. Although the two samples would enable the researcher to assess validity, the researcher would still have no logical basis for attempting to generalize the results to any particular population.

Quota Sampling

One of the many ways in which those interested in such things attempt to predict the outcomes of elections is **quota sampling**—*selecting sampling elements on the basis of categories that are assumed to exist within the population.* At first glance, quota sampling appears to be the same as stratified random sampling, but there is an important difference. In stratified random sampling, elements are randomly selected within the stratified groups. Quota sampling, on the other hand, is more akin to stratified purposive or stratified accidental sampling. Presumed subdivisions of the population, not a concrete listing of the sampling frame, are the bases of the selection process.

For those interested in predicting the outcomes of elections, quota sampling usually involves selecting voters from what are called key precincts, those that exhibit a good track record of outcomes similar to the overall election results. There may be a historical reason to believe that the precinct results will match the overall results, but the continuation of that match cannot be guaranteed. If there has been a shift in the population in the precinct or a shift in the thoughts or activities of the voters in the precinct, then the precinct results will no longer match the overall election results. Indeed, political scientists use changes in the predictive ability of key precincts as a measure of political shifts, such as growing conservatism, for one example.

Although quota sampling may produce a sample that appears to be a miniature version of the population, the appearance is more illusory than real. It is possible to obtain certain percentages of males and females, Blacks and Whites, wealthy and poor, and so on, but failure to select randomly within those categories makes it impossible to determine the amount of sampling error. Despite its apparent attractions, research based on quota sampling should not be generalized without considerable thought given to the possibility of changes in the population.

Quota sampling led to the famous 1948 photograph of President-elect Harry Truman holding a newspaper with the infamous headline DEWEY DEFEATS TRUMAN. Based on the 1940 census, the correct percentages of various types of voters had been included in a quota sample, but the percentages had changed since the census. In the intervening eight years, the need to increase production to support U.S. efforts during World War II had led to a major shift in the population from rural to urban areas. The 1940 census figures did not reflect that shift, and the quota sample used by the newspaper had underestimated urban voters (who tended to vote Democrat). The early election returns from key precincts chosen on the basis of the outdated census information, coupled with the desire to be the first on the street with the election results, produced the incorrect headline.

REPRESENTATIVE SAMPLES

The primary goal of any sampling procedure is to obtain a **representative sample**—*a sample that resembles the population within an acceptable margin of error*. The phrase "within an acceptable margin of error" should immediately clue you in on the fact that probability sampling procedures are required for representative samples, simply because sampling error can be estimated only for randomly selected samples.

Of equal importance, however, is the phrase "resembles the population." Random selection, simply because it is random, may result in a sample that does not resemble the population. The odds are against such an occurrence, but some likelihood exists. In a predominantly male college such as the U.S. Air Force Academy, for example, a simple random sample might well not include any female students. If the population evidences distinct subgroups, some stratification will be required to obtain a representative sample.

Alternatively, some types of research projects do not require that much attention be paid to sampling procedures. We already noted that exploratory projects may not require a probability sample; an accidental or purposive sample may be all that is needed. One of the more difficult practices for many to understand is the use of volunteer participants in experimental research. When I conducted jury decision research, I was often asked, for example, "How can using college students tell you anything about what real jurors will do?" (see, e.g., Dane & Wrightsman, 1982). To understand why sampling may not be important in experimental research, it is necessary to recall the purpose of explanatory research.

The purpose of explanatory research is to demonstrate that one variable causes another (for more detail, see Chapter 7). By using an accidental sample, one can do exactly that. Whatever the undefined characteristics of the population from which the sample came, we know that the population includes the independent variable as a characteristic because it was manipulated in the sample. Even though we do not know anything else about the imaginary population from which the sample was selected, we do know that the sample represents a population that has experienced the different levels of the independent variable. Therefore, the inferential statistics used to examine group differences are based on a random sample—a random sample of individuals exposed to the manipulation—and sampling error can be estimated. Of course, one cannot generalize the experimental results to any particular population, but that is not the main purpose of experimental research.

SUMMARY

- A unit or element is any one thing selected for inclusion in a research project. Populations are abstract collections of elements that can be defined by a sampling frame. Samples are selected from the sampling frame—the concrete representation of the population.
- Parameters are values exhibited by a population and, like the population, are abstract. Statistics—values obtained from a sample—must be used to estimate parameters. All estimates, however, contain some amount of sampling error, which must also be estimated in order to determine the accuracy of the statistic.
- A sampling distribution is a distribution of statistics that could be obtained from repeated samples drawn from the same population. Confidence intervals can be calculated by taking advantage of the nature of sampling distributions, which is defined by the central limit theorem. The standard error of a statistic is the standard deviation of its sampling distribution, and it can be estimated if the sample was selected on the basis of some random sampling procedure.
- Simple random sampling involves identifying all elements in a sampling frame and using a procedure that provides every element an equal chance of being included in the sample. Systematic random sampling also involves a listing of the sampling frame, from which elements are selected by some systematic procedure. A stratified random sample includes dividing the sampling frame into subgroups—strata—from which random samples are separately selected.
- Cluster sampling can be used whenever a listing of the entire sampling frame does not exist. Increasingly more specific elements are randomly selected until one reaches the level at which one can randomly select the elements to be included in the research project.
- Nonprobability sampling includes any sampling procedure that does not result in a random selection process. Accidental sampling involves selecting whatever elements are convenient, whereas purposive sampling involves selecting specific units of interest. Quota sampling involves an accidental or purposive sample selected from presumed subgroups in the population. Regardless of which nonprobability sampling procedure is used, sampling error cannot be estimated.

- A representative sample is any randomly selected sample that resembles the population. Most, but not necessarily all, random samples are also representative. Whether or not a sample represents a population of interest can also depend on the purposes of the research project.

EXERCISES

1. Using your library's databases, find an article in which the authors tried to obtain a simple random sample and any of the other types of probability samples.

2. Using your library's databases, find an article in which the authors obtained an accidental sample.

3. Using your library's databases, find an article in which the authors tested the representativeness of their sample.

CHAPTER 6

Measurement

Whenever you can, count.

—Sir Francis Galton

Overview

The purpose of this chapter is to present an overview of measurement theory. You will learn more detail about operational definitions, reliability, validity, and techniques for determining how reliable and valid an operational definition may be. You will also learn about different levels or dimensions of measurement and the implications of these levels for statistical analyses, which will enable you to decide whether or not researchers used appropriate analyses. In addition, you will learn about the construction of measurement scales: how to decide the appropriate use of scale, how to evaluate the reliability and validity of scales, and information about various formats for scales. Finally, you will learn more about the relationship between variables and the concepts they are used to represent.

INTRODUCTION

Everybody thinks they know what measurement is. It is what you do, for example, when you use the bathroom scale to determine how much you weigh. You step onto the scale, read the number, and you have measured your weight—simple, straightforward, uncomplicated. But using that bathroom scale is only a small part of the overall measurement process, most of which occurs long before you step onto that scale. Somewhere along the line you learned about the relationship between those scale numbers and your weight; you may not think of "relationship" in those terms, but that, too, is part of the measurement process. Also, someone designed and built the scale; that's part of the process. Someone, perhaps the same person, tested the scale for accuracy and consistency; that's part of the process as well. You may have taken the measurement process to its completion when you used the scale, but you only did the easy part. For everyday purposes, being an uncritical end user of measurement may well be enough, but when trying to understand research well enough to apply results to policies or programs, we need to understand the measurement process well enough to make critical assessments of the research under consideration.

There are a variety of different definitions of measurement, but all of them include the notion that **measurement** is *a process through which the kind or intensity of something is determined* (Adams, 1964; Allen & Yen, 1979; Anastasi, 1982). What kind or what intensity doesn't much matter; the process of measurement is essentially the same whether one is measuring religious denomination (kind) or weight (intensity).

The entire measurement process is a series of procedures that moves us from a theoretical concept, such as weight, to a concrete representation of that concept, such as the numbers on a bathroom scale. We all think we know a great deal about measurement because we all do it every day. But we also make a great many errors in our everyday measurement. For example, I once owned a car with a defective speedometer; it read about 15 miles per hour faster than it should. I knew about it and compensated for it. I knew that a reading of 75 miles per hour was really only 60 miles per hour. Every once in a while, however, someone riding with me would look over at the speedometer and then would begin looking around for patrol cars or look at me as though I was crazy for driving so fast. When I noticed this, I tried to work the speedometer's inaccuracy into the conversation. I knew what the relationship between the concept of speed and the speedometer's representation of it was, but first-time passengers did not, and it sometimes caused them problems.

Dimensionality

Measurement is used to represent theoretical concepts and most concepts in the behavioral and social sciences have more than one dimension, more than one quality that defines them. **Dimensionality** refers to *the number of different qualities inherent in a theoretical concept*. Consider, for example, the concept of social status. Some of its dimensions include occupational prestige, ethnicity (unfortunately), popularity, educational prestige, financial resources, and so on. To attempt to represent all of these dimensions in a single measurement would be impossible. Instead, those who want to measure social status select one, or a few, of the dimensions.

Regardless of which dimensions are selected, however, the researcher is measuring only a part of the overall concept. For example, you might consider financial resources to be inadequate as a sole measure of social status and decide to combine financial resources and educational prestige. Someone else may add popularity, and so on, but no one would be able to include everything. For this reason, as well as others, measurement is always incomplete. Whatever is measured is only part of the actual theoretical concept. Measurement represents concepts, but no measure can be considered to be the same thing as the concept itself.

MEASUREMENT LEVELS

In addition to there being any number of dimensions inherent in any theoretical concept, any dimension may be measured at one of four different levels of measurement: nominal, ordinal, interval, and ratio. Each level involves making finer distinctions within levels of the concept being measured, and each level limits the types of statistical procedures that can be used to analyze the data. The simplest level, nominal, enables one to make distinctions among categories, such as using the school one attended to measure educational prestige. The other three levels—ordinal, interval, and ratio—involve finer and finer gradations among the levels of the concept being measured.

Nominal Measurement

As you might expect from the term, **nominal measurement** involves *determining the presence or absence of a characteristic; it is naming a quality.*

Because naming a quality usually involves creating categories, nominal measurement is also called categorical measurement. By naming or labeling things, we are able to distinguish among them just as your name distinguishes you from other people. Good nominal measurement, however, requires being able to categorize a person or object into mutually exclusive categories. Your name, therefore, is not a particularly good nominal measurement because other people may have the same name. Using your name does not allow one to distinguish between you and another person with the same name, although it does enable one to categorize you along with others who share your name. If we want to distinguish among individuals, a Social Security number (in the United States) is a good nominal measurement. Unless the Social Security Administration has made an error or someone has stolen your number, you are the only person with your number, and one could use the number to distinguish you from everyone else.

Sometimes the label used in nominal measurement is a number, as in the example of a Social Security number. It distinguishes you from other people, but the number itself has no meaning beyond its use as a label. When I did research on jury decisions (e.g., Dane, 1985), I usually used a "1" for a guilty verdict, a "2" for not guilty, and a "3" for not guilty by reason of insanity. The numbers represent only categories, not intensity. A verdict of "3" is no higher or lower, no more or less intense, than a verdict of "2." For this reason, nominal or categorical measurement imposes restrictions on data analyses and interpretations.

The major restriction on data analysis involves central tendency statistics or averages. The only appropriate central tendency statistic for nominal data is the **mode**, which is *the most frequent score in a set of scores*. Suppose, for example, that 20 people in a jury study voted guilty, 15 voted not guilty, and five voted for the insanity plea. Using the numerical assignments I described above, the modal response would be "1" (guilty).

Neither of the other two measures of central tendency, mean and median, is appropriate for nominal measures. The **mean**, which is *the arithmetical average of a set of scores*, is calculated by adding all the scores and dividing by the number of scores. The mean of the verdict scores described above would be $[(20 \times 1) + (15 \times 2) + (5 \times 3)] / 40 = 1.625$, a meaningless number because the values that went into the calculation had no mathematical meaning. Because the numbers assigned to the verdict preferences are only labels, computing the mean makes no sense. The same applies to the **median**, *the 50th percentile score, which separates the lower and upper halves of a distribution of scores*. There are 40 scores in the sample verdicts, so the median would be between the 20th and 21st score, halfway between "1" and "2," or "1.5." The median, too, is meaningless for nominal measurement scales.

The above limitations do not mean that researchers cannot use statistical analyses on nominal data, only that they cannot use analyses that involve adding, subtracting, multiplying, or dividing the scores. They can count the number of scores, just as I did to determine the mode of the distribution. Therefore, chi-square analyses are the most appropriate statistics for such data. Essentially, **chi-square analyses** are *statistical techniques used to determine whether the frequencies of scores in the categories defined by the variable match the frequencies one would expect on the basis of chance or on the basis of predictions from a theory*. Any introductory statistics textbook can be accessed to obtain a more detailed description of chi-square procedures.

Ordinal Measurement

There are a variety of situations in which researchers want to do more than determine the presence or absence of a characteristic. Some assessment of intensity or degree is required; perhaps some way to order responses on a continuum is desired. **Ordinal measurement** involves *ranking or otherwise determining an order of intensity for a quality*. Letting people know you are in the top 10% of your class, for example, is making use of an ordinal measurement scale; you are reporting your rank within your graduating class.

Ordinal measurement identifies the relative intensity of a characteristic, but it does not reflect any level of absolute intensity. If you are in the top 10% of your class, for example, I know you are doing better than most of the students in your class (congratulations, by the way). But your class ranking doesn't enable me to determine how well you would do at, say, Harvard, or at Basket-Weaving State College, unless you happen to be attending one of those institutions. I also cannot determine how much better you are than the bottom 90% of your class. Ordinal measurement is like the place finishes at a horse race: The winner might be barely a nose ahead of the second-place finisher or might have won by 10 lengths. For this reason, comparisons among ordinal values are somewhat limited, but not as limited as those among nominal values.

The limitations on ordinal data result from the fact that ordinal measurement involves ranking the scores. Calculating a mean for a set of ordinal scores is about as nonsensical as it is for nominal scores. The mean for ordinal scores is the center of the ordinal scale, which doesn't change. If there are 10 scores, for example, then the mean of those ranks is always going to be 5.5; if there are 20 scores, the mean is 10.5, and so on. In this case the mean is determined by the number of scores in the set, not the values of the scores that were ranked. Chi-square analyses can be applied to ordinal data, but that involves treating the ordinal ranks as though they were nominal categories. It can be done, and the results can make sense, but the researcher who does this loses the ordered nature of the ordinal measurement. More generally, any statistical technique that involves comparisons on the basis of the median is appropriate for ordinal data. If you need to learn more about median-based statistics, Witte and Witte (2006) is a good source for such analyses, as is Conover (1998). Conover's book is more comprehensive, but it is also more technical.

Interval Measurement

When more specificity is required, researchers attempt to attain an interval level of measurement. **Interval measurement** involves *a continuum composed of equally spaced intervals*. The Fahrenheit and centigrade temperature scales are good examples of interval measurements. A change of one degree anywhere along the continuum reflects an equal amount of change in heat; the interval "degree" is equal along the entire scale. With interval data, researchers can compare different scores more specifically than they can with either nominal or ordinal measures. Recall that with ordinal measurement you know that a value of 5 is different from a value of 10, but you don't know how much different. With interval measurement, you know that a value of 5 is exactly five units different from a value of 10, the same difference as that between 10 and 15.

What we do not know when we use interval measurement, however, is exactly what one interval represents in terms of the quality being measured. For example, the most well known use of interval measurement in the behavioral sciences is the IQ score or intelligence quotient, even though there is some disagreement about its status as an interval measure (Anastasi, 1982). Although it is not possible to determine exactly how much intelligence is represented by a single IQ point, it is possible to make comparisons between scores. The difference between the scores 100 and 110, for example, reflects the same amount of intelligence (whatever that is) as does the difference between 120 and 130. How much intelligence is represented by 10 points is unknown, but 10 points is 10 points anywhere along the scale.

This limitation of interpreting interval measures—not knowing the meaning of one unit—results from the fact that interval scales involve arbitrary numbers that represent anchor points on a continuum. For the centigrade and Fahrenheit scales, the arbitrary anchors are the temperatures at which water changes states (freezes and boils): 0 and 100 degrees centigrade and 32 and

212 degrees Fahrenheit, respectively. Similarly, on the IQ scale the arbitrary anchor point chosen was 100, a point that purportedly reflects an intellectual capacity consistent with one's physical age.

Despite the arbitrary anchor values used for interval measurements, there are few limitations on the types of analyses that can be applied to interval data, provided, of course, that the analyses are appropriate for the questions being asked. If researchers wish to determine relationships between variables, correlational analyses are appropriate; if they wish to examine differences among groups, any statistic that involves comparing means, such as analysis of variance, is appropriate.

Although the arbitrary values for interval data do not restrict the statistics that may be used to analyze the data, the arbitrariness of the anchors does limit the ways in which we may interpret statistical results. Suppose, for example, that you have one group with an average IQ of 150 and another with an average IQ of 75. Statistical analyses indicates that this difference was reliable, and you would like to interpret it. It is, of course, true that the mean IQ of one group is twice that of the other, but that does not mean you can claim that one group is twice as intelligent as the other. Because the numbers of an interval scale are arbitrary, it is never clear exactly how much intensity is reflected by any given number on the scale. Thus, the values produced from interval measurement cannot be interpreted the same as numbers used to count things. If you have 10 dollars and I have 5 dollars, then you have twice as many dollars. Counting numbers have an absolute zero, which brings us to ratio measurement.

Ratio Measurement

To interpret numbers used to measure a variable without restrictions, the researcher must have used a ratio level of measurement. **Ratio measurement** involves *a continuum that includes a value of zero representing the absence of a quality*. When physicists measure temperature, for example, they use the Kelvin scale, on which a value of zero represents the complete absence of heat. There are no negative values on the Kelvin scale because there cannot be less heat than no heat at all. Thus, 100 degrees on the Kelvin scale represents twice as much heat as 50 degrees. The same cannot be said for either the Fahrenheit or centigrade scales. That the latter two scales contain a zero point does not make them ratio scales because the zero points on those two scales do not represent the absence of heat.

In the behavioral and social sciences, very few measurements conform to the requirements for a ratio scale, and what few there are have been constructed for the purpose of providing examples of ratio scales. Income, for example, has a zero point that represents the absence of earnings. Therefore, someone who earns $20,000 has an income twice that of someone who earns $10,000. However, income is usually used to represent some aspect of socioeconomic status, and when it does, it no longer conforms to ratio-level requirements for measurement: Someone with zero income does not have zero socioeconomic status. If you believe you have encountered a ratio level of measurement while reviewing research, you should be very skeptical; be sure that zero means "nothing," the complete absence of the concept being measured.

Before you read on, see Table 6.1 for a summary of our discussion of measurement levels. It is important that you understand the different types of measurement levels that are used in research and the implications those levels have for interpreting research results. Most researchers get it right when they are interpreting their own results, but you are very likely to be in a position to reinterpret another researcher's results. If you do not get it right, then your review of a policy may mislead others into making a policy change that has an incorrect empirical basis.

Table 6.1	Summary of Measurement Levels		
Level	What's Measured	Example	Central Tendency
Nominal	Distinctions	Guilty/not guilty	Mode
Ordinal	Relative position	Socioeconomic status	Median
Interval	Arbitrary amounts	Intelligence quotient	Mean
Ratio	Actual amounts	Age	Mean

RELIABILITY

Knowing what level of measurement was used in research is only part of the measurement process. Another part involves understanding how reliable, or consistent, the measure is. A variety of different techniques are designed for such purposes, and all of them rely on the extent to which one version of the measure is related to another version of the measure.

The extent to which two things are related can be measured through **corre-lations,** *statistical procedures that estimate the extent to which changes in one* *variable are associated with changes in another*. A positive correlation coefficient means the two variables are directly related, a zero coefficient indicates no relationship, and a negative correlation indicates an inverse relationship. When assessing the reliability of a measure, correlations involve different versions of the measure instead of different variables. What follows is a brief description of the various ways in which such assessments are typically accomplished and reported in research articles.

Interrater Reliability

Whenever subjective judgments or ratings made by more than one person are part of the measurement process, the appropriate technique for determining reliability is interrater reliability. As implied in the name, **interrater reliability** is *the consistency with which raters or observers make judgments*. Using a very simple example, interrater reliability would involve the extent to which you and a friend agree about the temperature after reading the same thermometer. If you and your friend write down your daily temperature readings for a couple of weeks, the two sets of readings could be correlated. The higher the correlation coefficient (I'm assuming it would be positive), the greater the reliability of your measurements.

Another example can be drawn from studies in which physical attractiveness is measured. Such studies typically involve two or more raters making judgments about physical attractiveness on a scale from 1 to 10 (Adams, 1977). Each rater assigns a scale number to each person being rated, and interrater reliability is estimated by correlating the ratings from one judge with those from another. If the measurement process is reliable, there should be a high, positive correlation between any two judges.

Proper use of interrater reliability techniques requires observers or raters to make independent ratings. If one rater merely copies the ratings of another, for example, all that would be tested is the other rater's ability to copy correctly; that's not reliability. Collaboration among observers or judges is not allowed. Of course, collaboration does not have to be as obvious as copying one another's ratings; even minimal discussion will destroy the independence of the ratings. Raters should make their ratings as though they were taking a final exam: no copying, no idea sharing, no peeking. Collaborative ratings tend to appear to be more consistent, but the consistency is artificial. What you will often read in a research report, however, is that ratings were made independently and then disagreements were resolved through discussion. For example, Parish et al. (2000) tested interrater reliability for judgments about cardiac arrhythmias and then resolved the few discrepancies (the correlation was above 0.90) through discussion before including the rhythm categories in their analyses. Resolving discrepancies through discussion is perfectly acceptable, so long as interrater reliability was assessed before the discussions occurred.

Test-Retest Reliability

One of the most readily apparent ways to estimate reliability is **test-retest reliability**, *consistency estimated by comparing two or more repeated administrations of the measurement*. Despite its name, the test-retest technique does not require using a formal test as a measure; indeed, it is based on the same principle as that involved in interrater reliability. Instead of repeating measurements by using more than one rater, test-retest reliability involves repeating the measure simply by making the measurement again after some period of time has elapsed. One required assumption is that the characteristic being measured does not change over the time period; another assumption is that the time period is long enough so that one can rule out participants' memory as the basis for the second set of scores. Test-retest reliability, like interrater reliability, is estimated with correlations: The correlation between the two administrations of the measure is the estimate of reliability. For example, Roche, Scheetz, Dane, Parish, and O'Shea (2003) assessed the reliability of the attitude measures they employed by calculating correlations between scores obtained annually as students progressed through medical school.

When the measurement does involve a formal test, another prerequisite for using the test-retest technique is the absence of practice effects; that is, taking the first test should not make participants more knowledgeable or more aware of what's being measured. Because test-retest reliability involves assessing relative change between the two administrations, practice effects will undermine the basis of the reliability assessment.

Alternate-Forms Reliability

When test-retest reliability is not possible, either due to practice effects, rapid changes in the characteristic being measured, or extended memory for previous responses, the appropriate technique is alternate-forms reliability. **Alternate-forms reliability** involves *comparing two different but equivalent versions of the same measure*. The name of this procedure is doubly descriptive, for there are two different ways to implement it. One procedure involves giving the same group of people different versions of the measure at different times; this is analogous to the test-retest procedure. The other procedure involves giving the same measure to different groups of people.

When it is possible to use different forms of a measure for the same group of people, scores from one version of the measure are correlated with scores from the other. The procedure is exactly the same as that for test-retest reliability, except that different versions of the measure are repeated. The required assumption is that the two different forms are, in fact, different but also equivalent insofar as they both measure the same concept. Different-but-equivalent forms might involve merely changing the order of items in a multiple-item measure, or it may involve constructing entirely different items. Different addition items on a math test, for example, would be equivalent, but addition problems on one version and division problems on the other would not be equivalent. Similarly, differently phrased questions about attitudes toward a single topic would be equivalent, but questions about two different topics, such as sex education on one form and math education on the other, would not.

Sometimes, it is not possible to measure the same group of people more than once. In such situations, dividing a single group into two distinct subgroups may serve the same purpose. If, for example, a researcher gave the same test to everyone in the group and then randomly divided the group into two subgroups, he or she could compare scores between the groups to estimate reliability. Instead of correlational analyses, however, the researcher would use means, standard deviations, or some other distributional descriptors to determine the extent to which the two groups scored the same. One could, for example, use analysis of variance or chi-square for the comparison. If one divided the group randomly, there should be no difference between the two subgroups, and any difference that does emerge may reflect a lack of reliability.

Split-Half Reliability

There may be times when one cannot measure the same people more than once and cannot get enough participants to divide them into subgroups large enough to run the appropriate statistical analyses. If the measurement the researcher is using contains more than one item, such as some sort of questionnaire, then the split-half technique is used to assess reliability. **Split-half reliability** involves *creating two scores for each participant by dividing the measure into equivalent halves and correlating the halves*. Each half of the measure is then treated as though it were a complete version of the measure. Essentially, the split-half technique involves creating equivalent forms by dividing the measure, rather than the group of participants, in half. The scores on the two halves are then correlated, just as with the alternate forms procedure. Again, the stronger the correlation is, the greater the reliability.

The major prerequisite for the split-half procedure is the ability to create equivalent halves of the measure. One way to do this is to separate the odd- and even-numbered items. Note, however, that this is only one way to split the measure. Ideally one should create and correlate all possible halves of the measure and then use the average correlation coefficient as the measure of reliability. This process can be incredibly cumbersome and tedious. A 10-item measure, for example, can be split into halves 252 different ways. To create and correlate all those possible halves would take more time than it's worth. Even if one automated the procedure, one would still end up using a great deal of time and effort, not to mention paper for all the printouts.

Fortunately, Rulon (1932) developed a formula that enables researchers to split a measure only once and obtain an estimate of the average correlation that would result from the longer procedure of creating all possible halves. Rulon's formula is an inferential statistic. By calculating a correlation coefficient from a single split-half, it enables one to estimate the average correlation coefficient one would obtain from all split-halves. As with other statistical procedures, providing details or formulas for Rulon's procedure is beyond the scope of this book. The procedure is not all that complicated, however, and Rulon's article is not difficult to read and understand. So if you find yourself in need of Rulon's formula and cannot find a copy of the Rulon article, most measurement textbooks, such as Allen and Yen (1979), contain a description of the procedure.

Item-Total Reliability

When researchers use a measurement that includes more than one item, it is often necessary to determine the reliability of the individual items. If someone developed a questionnaire to measure attitudes toward insanity pleas, for example, he or she should determine the reliability of each item. Being confident about the reliability of each of the items enables one to be confident about the reliability of the entire measure.

Item-total reliability is *an estimate of the consistency of one item with respect to other items on a measure.* As you might expect, the procedure involves correlating the score on one item with the total score on the rest of the items. The total score represents everything else being measured, and the item-total correlation is therefore a measure of the relationship between the single item and everything else.

If a measure contains a large number of items, calculating all of the item-total correlations can be a very time-consuming and laborious process, even when one uses a computer for all of the calculations. Kuder and Richardson (1937) developed a shortcut formula that can be applied to the entire measurement, much like Rulon's (1932) shortcut for split-half reliability. It is known as the Kuder-Richardson 20 (K-R 20) formula and can be found in their original article and in most measurement textbooks. Anastasi (1982), for example, includes the Kuder-Richardson 20 formula as well as alternative formulae for various measurement levels. Also, most software packages, such as SAS and SPSS, include the procedure.

The result of the Kuder-Richardson 20 formula is a single correlation coefficient that is an estimate of the average of all of the coefficients that would be obtained from a true item-total procedure. It is an inferential statistic. If the correlation is high—0.80 or higher is usually sufficient—then all of the items are reliable and the entire instrument is reliable. If the coefficient obtained from the formula is low, then at least one of the items is unreliable, and one would have to examine each of them to discover the unreliable one(s). That examination would, of course, involve calculating separate item-total correlations for each item. As with most research procedures described in articles, however, you would be likely to read only the final result, the correlation coefficient, instead of the long, drawn-out process used to produce the reliable measurement.

Table 6.2	A Summary of Reliability Procedures	
Procedures	**Conditions**	**Analyses**
Interrater	Multiple judges	Correlation between raters
Test-retest	No practice effect	Correlation between scores
Alternate forms		
2 forms, 1 group	Equivalent forms	Correlation between scores
1 form, 2 groups	Random assignment	Between-group differences
Split-half	Equivalent items	Rulon's split-half
Item-total	Multiple items	Kuder-Richardson 20

As noted, you are likely to read only the "final number" for a reliability analysis, so we note that it is generally accepted that a correlation (or K-R 20 result) of 0.80 or higher represents good reliability. Some researchers are willing to accept a reliability value as low as 0.70 as evidence of adequate reliability. What amount of reliability you consider sufficient will depend upon the purposes you have for the research results you are interpreting. The more important the policy you are considering, the more reliability you should consider sufficient for your purposes.

VALIDITY

Reliability is a necessary condition for quality measurement, but it alone is not sufficient. Reliability is only the extent to which the measure is consistent. Before accepting any researcher's use of any measure, you must make sure it is valid. **Validity** refers to *the extent to which a measure actually measures what it is supposed to measure*; whether, for example, a questionnaire about the insanity plea really measures people's attitudes toward the insanity plea. Just as there are different ways to estimate reliability, there are different techniques for estimating validity. Which of the following techniques a researcher reports using depends on both the specific requirements of the study and the facilities available.

Face Validity

Suppose your instructor gave you a test in your research methods class, but the test contained only differential calculus problems. You would probably complain, claiming the test was not fair, and you might even contend that the test was invalid. You would be using face validity as the basis of your complaint. **Face validity** is *consensus that a measure represents a particular concept*. It is sometimes called **expert validity** or **validation by consensus**. When face validity involves assessing whether a measure deals with a representative sample of the various aspects of the concept, it is also called content validity. Whatever it is called, it is based on the notion that a good measure should look like a good measure to those who are in a position to know; those whose opinions matter should agree that a measure is measuring what it's supposed to measure.

Face validity is a rather limited test of validity. It is, after all, not much different from claiming "my mother said so," except that "an expert" replaces "my mother" in the claim. Although appeals to personal authority are not sufficient grounds for argument in a scientific approach, an appeal to expert authority can be used as a starting point in the process of evaluating a measure's validity. If a researcher cannot demonstrate face validity, the researcher is likely to have a difficult time convincing others that a measure is valid. Sometimes, however, face validity is the only type of validity assessed for a particular measure; it then falls to you to determine whether or not the validity of the measure is sufficient for your purposes.

Concurrent Validity

Just as face validity relies on authoritative experts, concurrent validity relies on authoritative measurements to establish validity. **Concurrent validity** involves *comparing a new measure to an existing, valid measure*. The difference between concurrent and face validity is that one relies on an existing, valid measure instead of the consensus of experts; one relies on data instead of opinion. Concurrent validity is a specific form of criterion validity; the existing measure is the criterion against which the new measure is validated. The comparison is usually accomplished by correlating the old and new measures in much the same way that alternate form reliability is determined, but sometimes you'll read that the researchers used regression analyses or a Bland-Altman analysis (Bland & Altman, 1986). Assessing concurrent validity is one of the major starting points for most predictive research projects. When a researcher develops a new measure of intelligence, for example, concurrent validity would be assessed by correlating the new measure with either the Stanford-Binet (Laurent, Swerdlik, & Ryburn, 1992) or Wechsler Adult Intelligence Scale (Ryan & Ward, 1999). The higher the correlation coefficient, the more valid is the new measure.

It is not too difficult to understand the major limitation of concurrent validity: The new measure cannot be any more valid than the old measure to which it is compared. If the validity of the existing measure was established through face validity, for example, then the use of concurrent validity is actually an approximation of face validity. It is always important, therefore, to determine how the validity of an existing measure was established before using it as a comparison in concurrent validation. For those of us who consume research, this may involve tracking a particular measure through the literature to discover the original basis for its validity. It can sometimes be a tedious process, but it is worth the tedium to avoid basing a policy or program recommendation on results obtained from a measure that does not have demonstrable validity.

Predictive Validity

Predictive validity is another specific form of criterion validity, except that **predictive validity** is *established by comparing a measure with the future* *occurrence of another, highly valid measure.* The most well-known example of predictive validity is college entrance examinations and their ability to predict first-year performance in terms of college grades. For predictive validity, one simply administers the new measure, waits for an opportunity to use the comparison measure, and then compares the two. The comparison measure is usually a very different form of measurement, such as grades versus a multiple-choice test, or it is an unquestionable standard to which all other, similar measures are compared (such as grades for college performance).

The same limitations for concurrent validity apply to predictive validity procedures: How the validity of the comparison measure was established limits the validity of the new measure. Usually, however, the limitation is not as important because the new measure is being developed specifically to predict the existing measure; that is, the existing measure is considered valid by definition. With college entrance examinations, for example, grades are by definition valid measures of college success. Whether or not that should be the case is an entirely different question, one we cannot address here. If another standard is chosen, then the new measure is compared to that.

Construct Validity

Construct validity involves determining *the extent to which a measure represents concepts it should represent and does not represent concepts it should not represent.* It is similar to an essay question in which you are asked to compare and contrast two different but possibly related concepts. Construct validity involves both making comparisons between a new measure and existing, valid measures of the same concept and contrasting the new measure with existing, valid measures of a different concept. It also involves testing the extent to which comparisons and contrasts are affected by the method used for the measure (Campbell & Fiske, 1959).

The first part of construct validity is called **convergent validity**—*the extent to which a measure correlates with existing measures of the same concept.* It is similar to concurrent validity but involves one important difference: Convergent validity includes comparisons with more than one existing measure. A new measure of college success, for example, would be compared not only to grades but to employment after graduation, perceived success, and so on. Ideally, the existing measures should involve at least two different measurement methods, one of which is the same method as the new measure. For example, a new questionnaire on attitudes toward insanity pleas should correlate highly with both an existing, valid questionnaire about insanity pleas and participants' verdicts for a simulated trial in which insanity was a plea.

Using different measurement methods for the existing standards enables the researcher to test the extent to which the correlations between the new and existing measures are related to the type of measurement method used. Two questionnaires about the insanity plea, for example, would be somewhat correlated by virtue of the fact that they are both questionnaires. If the new measure correlates both with another questionnaire and with some different method, such as simulated verdicts, then the researcher can be more comfortable with the new measure's validity. It is the same principle behind using multiple-choice and essay questions on the same examination: Some people might do well with one or the other simply because they are familiar with that particular answer format, but a student who does well on both formats is more likely to know the subject matter.

The second part of construct validity is called **divergent validity**—*the extent to which a measure does not correlate with measures of a different concept.* Again using a questionnaire about the insanity plea as an example, testing divergent validity might involve contrasting the new measure with a valid questionnaire about the effectiveness of parole procedures. As a measure of attitudes toward the insanity plea, the new measure should not correlate highly with a measure of attitudes toward parole; they are two different concepts. Using different measurement methods for the contrasting measures again ensures that any lack of correlation does not result from different methods per se. If someone were to include all of the above measures in the same study and were to calculate all of the correlations, the researcher might obtain the correlation matrix presented in Table 6.3, which illustrates results indicating that the new measure is a valid measure of attitudes toward the insanity plea.

Table 6.3	Correlation Coefficients for High Construct Validity				
	New NGI[a]	Old NGI	Verdict	Parole Q	Parole D
New NGI[a]	1.000	.950	.890	.216	.220
Old NGI	.950	1.000	.900	.116	.198
Verdict	.890	.900	1.000	.105	.026
Parole questionnaire	.216	.116	.105	1.000	.960
Parole decision	.220	.198	.026	.960	1.000

a. NGI = Not guilty by reason of insanity.

EPISTEMIC CORRELATION

At the beginning of this chapter (and in Chapter 2 as well) we learned that a measure represents, but is not the same thing as, a theoretical concept. There may be several different dimensions of a concept, of which the measure taps only some. There are also many different operational definitions for any theoretical concept, and no measure can tap all of them. Therefore, any measure, no matter how valid and reliable, represents only a portion of the total theoretical concept.

Any score obtained from a measure contains two components: a "true" score component and an "error" score component. The true component refers to the validity of the measure; it is the part of the measure that is doing what it is supposed to do. The error component reflects all of the things that can go wrong in the measurement process. The fewer things that go wrong, the smaller the error component. It is an accepted axiom of measurement theory, however, that the error component is never equal to zero; there is always, without exception, some error involved in any measure.

The theoretical relationship between the true component of a measure and the concept it represents is called an **epistemic correlation**. Despite its name, an epistemic correlation cannot be calculated; it can only be logically determined. Consider, for example, annual income as a measure of social status: Even though we all know that a higher income indicates a higher social status, it includes only one dimension of the concept. Thus, within certain limitations, we know that there is a positive epistemic correlation between income and social status. We cannot calculate that coefficient, but we can be reasonably certain that it is positive.

Before researchers can interpret data, and certainly before we could reinterpret results obtained in a study using income as a measure of social status, however, we would also need to know what level of measurement—nominal, ordinal, interval, or ratio—annual income represents. Annual income obviously cannot represent a ratio level because zero income does not reflect zero social status. Once you have given the matter some thought, you will realize that income probably does not represent an interval level of measurement, either. To merit interval level status, an income change of, say, $10,000 would have to represent the same amount of change in social status at any amount of income; clearly, this is not so. A change from zero income to $10,000 represents a considerably larger increase in social status than does a change from $1,000,000 to $1,010,000. The best we can do with income as a measure of social status is declare it an ordinal scale.

On the other hand, the very same measure—income—could be an interval or perhaps a ratio scale if used to represent a different theoretical concept. If, for example, someone used income to represent contribution to the tax base, it may be an interval level of measurement. Although an economist might disagree about its being at the interval level of measurement, the point is that the epistemic correlation must be evaluated before we can interpret results. Even though we cannot calculate it, we must make a logical decision, based on the concept itself, about the correlation between the concept and its measure. Understanding theoretical concepts and the measures used to represent them are equally important parts of good research consumption. We now turn our attention to more complicated forms of measurement, those involving multiple items used to measure a concept collectively.

SCALING

Because no measure is perfectly reliable or perfectly valid, researchers often use some sort of triangulation process to zero in on the concept they are trying to measure. In my high school physics class, for example, we always made three measurements and used the average of those three measurements as the recorded data value. The reason for using three measures was not apparent then, but it is now: Using the same measure three times and recording the average increases the overall reliability of measurement; an average reduces random error.

In the behavioral and social sciences, however, researchers rarely have the luxury of making the same measurement more than once. Putting a ball bearing on a balance three times is very different from asking a person to answer the same question three times; the latter usually involves little more than testing someone's memory of his or her first answer. Similarly, measuring the crime rate in a city three times requires the assumption that the rate does not change over time, which is not a safe assumption.

Instead of making the measurement three times, we usually measure the same concept in several different ways. One way to accomplish this is to use a **scale**—*a measurement instrument that contains a number of slightly different operational definitions of the same concept*. If you have ever completed a questionnaire that seemed to contain many similar questions, you have first-hand experience with a scale. Simply generating a number of seemingly redundant questions, however, does not a scale make.

The key to the notion of a scale is the phrase "slightly different operational definitions." Each item on a scale is a different operational definition of the same concept, and combining the items into a scale allows the researcher to zero in on the concept from a variety of different directions. All of the general measurement principles outlined above apply to scales. For example, scales can operate at any of the four different levels of measurement—nominal, ordinal, interval, or ratio—and all must be tested for reliability and validity. Scales, however, usually provide several advantages over single-item measures; one such advantage is a higher level of measurement than any of the individual items that together constitute the scale itself.

Common Aspects of Scales

Perhaps the best way to learn how to evaluate scales is to learn how they are developed. For that reason, we begin with ways in which researchers generate scale items. Then, after you understand how a scale is constructed, you will find it considerably easier to learn about how to evaluate and interpret results obtained from someone else's scale. There are a number of different ways to generate scale items, and they differ as a function of the type of scale being constructed. Details about item generation will be covered shortly, but first we need to consider some common aspects of all forms of scales.

Face Validity of Scale Items

First among the general issues surrounding scale item generation or evaluation is the face validity of items. Although face validity is not a necessary characteristic of every item on a scale, at least some of the items must demonstrate face validity. On the other hand, there is no reason to include items that are clearly not face valid, no matter how interesting they may seem to be. The general (if ungrammatical) rule of thumb for generating scale items is the same as that for generating invitations to a family reunion: "If it ain't related, it ain't included." If you cannot understand the relevance of items included in a scale, then you should have some doubts about the validity of the scale, doubts that should be overcome by the researcher's report of reliability and validity analyses. You may have to backtrack a few research articles to find the results of such analyses, but as I noted earlier, backtracking is well worth the trouble if you plan to use the results of a scale to make recommendations concerning an important policy.

Instructions for Completing Scales

Face validity ensures that you and other researchers will understand the items included on a scale, but that doesn't mean respondents will know what they are being asked to do. The most elegant or the most face-valid scale will be useless if the people who are to complete it cannot understand the instructions or don't know what's being asked of them.

Any instruction about how to complete the scale should be worded clearly and simply. If at all possible, examples of anything respondents are to do should be included. Similarly, items that make up the scale must be clear and understandable. Questions that require information unavailable to respondents, for example, cannot be either reliable or valid because the respondent would only be guessing. If the people who complete a scale are not likely to know the size of the federal deficit, for example, it makes little sense to ask them whether they think it is too large. Similarly, asking for information respondents may consider to be none of the researcher's business is likely to lead to a number of missing, or intentionally inaccurate, responses. If the researcher is trying to measure honesty, for example, it probably is not a good idea to ask people how often they cheat on their income tax returns unless the researcher can ensure that they will provide an honest response. Thus, be sure you understand the instructions given to participants before you interpret the results someone obtained using a scale.

Item Bias

Perhaps the most important consideration common to all scale items is **item bias**—*the extent to which the wording or placement of an item affects someone's response*. An item may be biased for a variety of reasons; some are more subtle than others. Perhaps the best (worst?) example of a biased item comes from a survey sent to me by my former congressional representative in the days when the Strategic Defense Initiative (SDI; also known as Star Wars technology) was a hotly contended issue. The survey was devoted to defense spending, and the first item was "Do you favor increasing defense spending to prevent Communist aggression?" This item has just about everything wrong with it that could possibly be wrong.

First, the item is a **double-barreled item**—*a single item that contains two or more questions or statements*. The item raises two issues, one concerning increases in defense spending and another about Communist aggression. Some respondents are likely to have opposing views on the two topics and would find it difficult to respond. They might, for example, oppose Communist aggression but not wish to increase defense spending. You might also have noticed the item was emotionally worded. Communist aggression was an emotional flag—something few American citizens would advocate, regardless of their political views or opinions about defense spending. The item is also ambiguous; there is no indication of how much of an increase the respondent is being asked to advocate or reject. Similarly, there is no indication of the type of Communist aggression to be prevented. All of these forms of bias make it extremely difficult for someone to respond to the item in any manner other than without thinking about it.

Perhaps the most important among the item's shortcomings is the fact that few, if any, respondents would have access to the kind of information required to make a rational decision. For example, not many people had an idea about how much money was currently being expended for defense, let alone that amount of defense spending set aside specifically for preventing Communist aggression. Nor did many people have any idea how much more money might be needed to prevent Communist aggression.

Finally, the placement of the item as the first in a series about defense spending introduced bias throughout the series. The implicit link between increases in defense spending and Communist aggression made it difficult for respondents to say no to other items about increasing defense spending. Once someone has agreed with the notion that increasing defense spending is a good idea for preventing Communist aggression, for example, that person will find it difficult to disagree with other items about increasing defense spending. I was not at all surprised when the representative voted in favor of all increases in defense spending, including SDI, claiming he was simply doing what his constituents had requested. Heavily biased scale items may be politically useful, but they have no place in good research.

Formats for Scale Items

Just as there are a number of different types of item bias, there are a number of different formats through which to present an item. The simplest of these is the **forced-choice format**—*a response format in which respondents must choose between discrete and mutually exclusive options*. The following item is an example:

	Yes	No
Should defense spending be increased?		

The respondent is forced to choose between increasing spending or not, hence the name "forced choice." The forced-choice format is most appropriate when responses can be easily categorized.

More often than not, however, responses are not so easily categorized. One's response to changing defense spending, for example, may be more a matter of how much to change, rather than simply to change or not to change. In such cases, the graphic format is the most widely used response format. The **graphic format** involves *presenting a continuum on which respondents make a choice.* Illustrated below are a number of different ways to use a graphic format:

What is your opinion on changing the level of defense spending?

1	2	3	4	5
It should definitely be decreased		It should remain the same		It should definitely be increased

The respondent is still required to make a choice, but the choices reflect positions on a continuum. It is even possible for someone to choose a position between 3 and 4, and in such cases a graphic format can include "markers" between the points, as shown here:

What is your opinion on changing the level of defense spending?

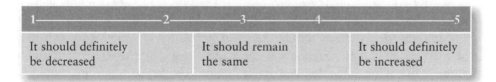

1	2	3	4	5
It should definitely be decreased		It should remain the same		It should definitely be increased

Other versions of the graphic format include presenting only the labels for the endpoints of the continuum, presenting additional labels along the continuum, including more numbers along the continuum, and so forth. Regardless of the variations in its appearance, the graphic format reflects a continuum of responses. The respondent is presented with a graded choice rather than a forced choice. Whatever version of the graphic format researchers may use, however, you should be sure that the endpoints reflect legitimate responses. The extreme endpoints should not be so extreme that no one would consider them to be potential responses. Researchers will typically report the endpoint labels for items in their research reports.

Providing response alternatives in a graphic format is not the only way to present a continuum of responses. The itemized format can be used to accomplish the same purpose. Instead of presenting a continuum of responses, the **itemized format** involves *presenting a continuum of statements representing various choice options*. Each statement is a response, and together the statements reflect a continuum of potential responses. The graphic item illustrated above could be presented through the itemized format as follows:

☐ Decreasing the level of defense spending is absolutely essential to the well-being of our country.

☐ Keeping defense spending at its current level is the best thing to do right now.

☐ Increasing the level of defense spending is absolutely essential to the well-being of our country.

Note that the first item represents one extreme, the second item represents a neutral point, and the third item represents an extreme that is the opposite of the first. Of course, more than three items would normally be included in an itemized format, but three are enough for illustration purposes. Instructions for the illustrated items would include asking respondents to place a mark in the box corresponding to the item that best represents their opinions. The essence of a graphic format, a continuum of responses, is presented with a series of statements. Respondents must choose one of the statements (they cannot choose between two represented positions), so the items must be very carefully chosen to represent an adequate gradation of responses.

Although the itemized format seems to be relatively straightforward, it is often very difficult to generate a series of statements that reflect a continuum without including some double-barreled items. The key is to ensure that only one aspect of the issue varies from statement to statement. It would be biased, for example, to include the notion of protecting the country under the "pro-increase" items and include the notion of social welfare under the "anti-increase" items. When interpreting research in which the itemized format was used, you need to be sure that neither the opening statement nor the response items are double-barreled.

Sometimes it makes sense to ask respondents to weigh the relative importance of specific issues. The **comparative format** involves *making direct comparisons among various positions*. One example of the comparative format, again using defense spending, appears here:

Which of the following ways to increase the defense budget is most preferable?

    a. increase the size of the national debt

    b. increase income taxes

    c. increase other types of taxes

    d. decrease money spent on social welfare programs

    e. I prefer not to increase the defense budget.

In another version of this format, respondents could be asked to rank the presented alternatives from most to least preferable. Regardless of which version is used, however, the comparisons must be distinct and legitimate.

We've only briefly touched on a few of the many different types of item formats used in research. The formats you encounter depend on the respondents to whom the researcher administered the scale and the concept measured with the scale.

Types of Scales

Just as items should be examined critically when interpreting research, the manner in which researchers combine those items should match their research purposes and match your interpretation of their research results. For this reason, some of the major types of scales currently used are presented below.

Thurstone Scales

One of the levels of measurement described previously, interval measurement, is extremely difficult to attain with a single item; equal spacing of alternatives in a graphic format is not the same as equal intervals. Interval measurement, however, can be approximated with a scale constructed using the Thurstone technique. Invented by Thurstone and his colleagues (1929, 1931; Thurstone & Chave, 1929), its formal name is the **equal-appearing interval technique**; it *contains a series of items, each of which represents a particular point value on the continuum being measured*. It is an itemized format scale designed so that the items reflect specific points on the response continuum.

In the construction of a Thurstone scale, many items are generated such that each item represents a particular point of view about the concept to be measured. This initial pool often contains as many as 200 items, which are then rated by at least 20 judges on an 11-point scale representing the full range of positions concerning the concept. After all of the items have been generated and judged, the scale values assigned by the judges for each item are tabulated and the median value used as the actual scale value of the item. The selection criteria for the final list of items are those with scale values closest to whole numbers with the smallest semi-interquartile ranges. The **semi-interquartile range** is a *measure of variability or degree of dispersion calculated by halving difference between values representing the 75th and 25th percentiles in a distribution of scores*. This procedure results in an approximation of an equal-interval measure. The respondent is asked to check any of the items that reflect his or her opinion. Ideally, respondents should check only one item, partly because using the equal-appearing interval scale involves assuming that respondents' opinions are sufficiently defined to make it difficult for them to agree with more than one item. A respondent's score is the scale value of the item selected. Sometimes, however, respondents will choose more than one item, in which case the respondent's score is the median of the scale values for all items selected.

Likert Scales

One alternative to the time- and labor-intensive effort required to construct a Thurstone scale is the technique developed by Likert (1932). Known as a Likert (pronounced lick-ert) scale, this technique also begins with generating a pool of initial items. The **Likert scale** *consists of items reflecting extreme positions on a continuum, items with which people are likely either to agree or disagree*. The items are typically presented in a graphic format that includes endpoints labeled with some version of "agree" and "disagree." After a pool of face-valid items has been generated, the entire pool of items is administered and an item analysis is completed, usually employing the item-total correlation. Items with the most extreme (positive and negative) item-total correlations are selected for the final version of the scale, which produces a unidimensional, interval-level measure of the concept about which the items were written. Once the final list of items is selected (usually about 20 items), scores for the measure are determined simply by adding the values of the responses, which is why the Likert scale is also called a **summative scale**, a label applied to any *scale for which scores are calculated by summing responses to individual items*.

Guttman Scales

The Thurstone and Likert techniques were designed to use more than one item to measure the same concept. Thurstone's technique should produce items ordered along a unidimensional continuum. Even though Likert's technique does not produce ordered items, it too should produce a unidimensional scale. Guttman (1944), however, criticized both techniques, claiming that neither resulted in a truly unidimensional scale.

The problem, according to Guttman, is that one respondent could obtain the same score as another respondent, even though the two respondents had agreed with or checked completely different items. To Guttman, this prevented the Thurstone and the Likert scale from being truly unidimensional. On a **Guttman scale**, it is possible to *order both the items and the respondents on a single, identifiable continuum*. The Guttman scale is also called either a scalogram scale or a **cumulative scale**.

Perhaps the best way to describe a Guttman scale is to illustrate the response pattern of an ideal or perfect scale, presented in Table 6.4. If the items are ordered on a continuum from easiest to most difficult to endorse, the pattern of responses forms two triangles. The upper right triangle consists only of zeroes, whereas the lower left consists of ones. From this pattern, it is possible to deduce exactly which items were chosen by any respondent simply by knowing the respondent's score.

Table 6.4	Proportion of Respondents Agreeing With Each Item on a Perfect Guttman Scale									
Scale	Item Number									
Score	1	2	3	4	5	6	7	8	9	10
0	0	0	0	0	0	0	0	0	0	0
1	1	0	0	0	0	0	0	0	0	0
2	1	1	0	0	0	0	0	0	0	0
3	1	1	1	0	0	0	0	0	0	0
4	1	1	1	1	0	0	0	0	0	0
5	1	1	1	1	1	0	0	0	0	0
6	1	1	1	1	1	1	0	0	0	0
7	1	1	1	1	1	1	1	0	0	0
8	1	1	1	1	1	1	1	1	0	0
9	1	1	1	1	1	1	1	1	1	0
10	1	1	1	1	1	1	1	1	1	1

Everyone who agreed with Item 10, for example, also agreed with Items 1 through 9. If a Guttman scale is perfect, only those who agreed with Items 1 through 9 would also agree with Item 10, only those who agreed with Item 1 would also agree with Item 2, and so on. To some extent, this is also what should occur with a Thurstone scale, but the results of a Thurstone scale rarely turn out that way. The advantage of the Guttman technique is that the item analysis is designed to ensure that a nearly perfect pattern of responses will occur.

Items are generated for a Guttman scale in much the same way as for the other scales; one writes an initial pool of items that exhibits face validity and covers the range of possible opinions. For a Guttman scale, however, the items will eventually be ordered on the conceptual dimension. Once written, items are administered to a sample of respondents, who are asked to check every item with which they agree. The scores from the initial group of respondents are then subjected to a very different item analysis called a scalogram. A **scalogram analysis** basically is *a determination of the extent to which the pattern of actual responses fits the ideal pattern of a Guttman scale*. The pattern displayed in Table 6.4 is an ideal pattern against which a set of 10 items would be compared. Items are removed from the initial pool of items if they don't fit the ideal pattern using a statistic called the **coefficient of reproducibility** (CR), *the proportion of fit between a perfect Guttman scale and one's data* (Anastasi, 1982). A CR greater than .90 is sufficiently high to conclude that the scale items form a reliably unidimensional scale (Edwards, 1957).

Semantic Differential Scales

The Thurstone, Likert, and Guttman scaling techniques have three things in common: They involve the preparation of a pool of items that exhibit face validity, they require some sort of analysis in order to select a final set of items, and they are designed specifically to measure unidimensional concepts or a single dimension of multidimensional concepts. In this section, we turn to a rather different measurement scale, one that does not share any of the above commonalities. The **semantic differential scale** is *designed to measure the psychological meaning of concepts along three different dimensions: evaluation, potency, and activity*.

Developed by Osgood, Suci, and Tannenbaum (1957), the semantic differential scale is not used to measure how much of a particular quality (such as social status) someone has or how much someone believes in a particular concept (such as human trustworthiness) but rather what someone understands a particular concept to be—that is, the subjective meaning of a concept. Instead of measuring respondents' attitudes toward research methods, for example, one might use a semantic differential scale to measure what people think research methods are. The meaning of the concept being measured is defined by the general dimensions of evaluation, potency, and activity.

Evaluation refers to *the overall positive or negative meaning attached to the concept*. Such labels as good, bad, attractive, and dirty may be part of the evaluation dimension. **Potency** refers to *the overall strength or importance of the concept*. Potency includes such labels as strong, weak, superior, and useful. **Activity** refers to *the extent to which the concept is associated with action or motion*. Such labels as fast, slow, active, passive, and deliberate qualify for the activity dimension. Thus, an individual's subjective perception of research methods might be good (evaluation), important (potency), and exciting (activity). One of the main advantages of the semantic differential scale is that the same list of adjective pairs can be used to measure the meaning of a variety of different concepts: research methods, education, social welfare, prisons, and many other concepts. An additional advantage is the existence of a variety of sources for more complete lists of adjective pairs. Osgood et al.'s (1957) book contains such lists, as does Snider and Osgood (1969), Jenkins and Russell (1958), and Kerlinger (1972). Equally important, however, is the fact that researchers have the ability to add or delete as many adjective pairs as may be appropriate for the concept they want to measure.

Q-Sort Scales

Just as the semantic differential scale is typically used to measure the meaning of concepts, a **Q-sort** is a *scale used to measure an individual's relative positioning or ranking on a variety of different concepts*. The Q-sort technique was adapted by Stephenson (1953) and has remained popular among researchers interested in measuring characteristics of individuals. One way to further describe the Q-sort technique is to consider it to be a combination of Thurstone and semantic differential scaling, for aspects of both techniques are involved. Various items representing different concepts are generated. The respondent then sorts these items into ranked positions on the dimensions of the concepts. The items used in Q-sort scales should be face valid, and double-barreled items should be particularly avoided because of the multidimensional nature of the technique.

Administration of a Q-sort is almost identical to the item analysis phase of Thurstone scaling, with one very important difference: With the Q-sort technique, it is the sorters who are being measured, not the items. Sorters (participants) are asked to categorize the items on the basis of some dimensional criterion. Unlike the Thurstone procedure, however, the sorter is also asked to make the number of items in the categories conform to a normal distribution. For example, if 100 items were to be sorted into 11 categories, the sorter would be instructed to distribute the items such that the number of items in each category would approximate the distribution below:

Number of items:	3	4	7	11	15	20	15	11	7	4	3
Category number:	1	2	3	4	5	6	7	8	9	10	11

Of course, the number of items to be placed in each category will depend both on the number of items in the initial pool and the number of categories. After the initial pool of items (between 60 and 90 is the recommended number) has been sorted, the category number assigned to each item is used to calculate correlations between the various individuals who did the sorting. That is, sorters become the variables in the calculation of correlation coefficients, and the category numbers assigned to the different concepts become the scores for the variable. The results of these analyses are usually displayed in a matrix labeled by the sorter's name or other identification along the top and side and containing correlation coefficients as matrix entries. From this matrix it is possible to identify sorters who are similar to each other. Again, despite its similarity to the Thurstone technique, the emphasis of the Q-sort is on the sorters themselves, not on the items they are sorting.

Sociometric Scales

The Q-sort technique is most useful for measuring various aspects of an individual or a few individuals. The scaling technique we next consider is most prevalently used for descriptive research among groups. A **sociometric scale** is a scale *designed specifically for measuring relationships among individuals within a group* (Proctor & Loomis, 1951). Sociometric scales—sometimes called sociometry—have also been used to measure social choice (Kerlinger, 1973). Very simply, the technique involves asking members of a group to make choices among other members of the group.

Consider, by way of example, the other members of your research methods class. Which three people do you most like? Which three do you like the least? Such questions are the basis of a sociometric scale. If every person in your class answered these two questions, there would be enough information to be able to construct a profile of your classmates—a "who's who" in terms of popularity.

Of course, the questions might just as easily be worded in terms of working with, eating with, or doing anything else with others in your class. Similarly, one could inquire about the people with the most and least financial status, intelligence, or any other concept of interest; the questions depend entirely on the researcher's purposes. The question(s) may be asked by way of a questionnaire, an interview, or observations of behavior. For example, without asking anyone anything, a researcher could observe the pattern of conversation within a group. Scores could be assigned on the basis of how many times each person talks to every other person, thereby measuring popularity, perceived expertise, friendliness, or any of the myriad of reasons why people talk to each other. If written or verbal questions are posed, the response format could be forced-choice, graphic, or any other suitable format.

Reliability and validity of the items used on a sociometric scale depend, primarily, on simplicity and face validity; that is, the simpler and more specific the question(s) used, the more reliable the measure. Similarly, the more directly the questions pertain to the theoretical concept under consideration, the more valid the measure.

SUMMARY

- Measurement is the process through which we translate the kind or intensity of a theoretical concept into a concrete variable. Most concepts include more than one dimension, not all of which can be easily included in a single variable.
- There are four different levels of measurement, all but one of which involve limitations on data analyses, interpretations, or both.
- The nominal level of measurement is the simplest and involves categorical distinctions of kind. Statistical analyses involving frequencies or the mode as the central tendency are the only appropriate analyses.
- The ordinal level of measurement involves degrees of intensity and reflects only relative amounts. Frequency analyses may be appropriate, but central tendency analyses based on the median are more likely to be the best analyses for such measures.
- The interval level of measurement represents intensity on an equal-interval continuum. The continuum, however, is composed of arbitrarily assigned values and does not contain an anchor for the absence of the quality being measured. Although there are no limitations on appropriate analyses, interpretations should not include multiplicative comparisons such as "twice as much."

- Ratio levels of measurement are extremely rare, perhaps nonexistent, in behavioral and social sciences mainly because the zero point of the measure must represent the absence of the quality being measured. If achieved, however, there are no restrictions on analyses or interpretations.
- Reliability involves the extent to which a measure is consistent, and it can be estimated through a variety of different techniques. All of these techniques, however, generally involve comparisons between different versions of the measure.
- Interrater reliability can be assessed when there is more than one person making ratings or judgments. It is accomplished by correlating one rater's scores with another rater's scores.
- Test-retest reliability involves presenting the same measure to the same people at two different times and then correlating the scores. Alternate forms reliability involves presenting the same people with two different versions of the same test and again correlating the scores. Alternatively, the same test can be given to two randomly divided subgroups and then compared with appropriate central tendency analyses.
- Split-half reliability involves comparing random halves of a multiple-item measure using a formula invented by Rulon. An alternative for multiple-item measures is item-total reliability, which involves comparing each item score with the total score using the formula invented by Kuder and Richardson.
- Validity refers to the extent to which a measure is related to its theoretical concept. Face validity refers to consensus about the relationship, whereas concurrent validity refers to the correlation between a new measure and one that has otherwise been demonstrated to be valid. Concurrent validity is one form of criterion validity. Another form of criterion validity, predictive validity, refers to the correlation between a new measure and a standard that is, by definition, valid.
- Construct validity refers to multiple comparisons with existing, valid measures of the same concept and multiple contrasts with valid measures of a different concept. The new measure should correlate highly with the former measure and not at all with the latter measure.
- An epistemic correlation is the derived relationship between a measure and its theoretical concept. It cannot be calculated but must be used to determine the level of the new measure.
- Measurement scales are used whenever one item is not sufficient to represent the complexity of a concept or when it is not feasible to repeatedly use the same operational definition.

- Every item on a scale has the potential to produce a biased response. Thus, every item should be examined for bias. The format for presenting a scale should be chosen to maximize respondents' understanding of the scale.
- The Thurstone technique is used to create a scale that represents the full range of positions toward the concept being measured. It, like the Likert technique, approximates an interval level of measurement. The Likert scale involves creating a series of extreme position statements to which respondents are asked to react through a graphic format. The Guttman scalogram technique ensures a true interval level of measurement, but it is more difficult to use than either the Thurstone or Likert techniques.
- The semantic differential scale is used to measure the psychological meaning of a concept; it consists of a series of adjective pairs that can be categorized in terms of evaluation, potency, and activity. Unless a set of adjective pairs has already been demonstrated to be reliable and valid, factor analysis is required to demonstrate these qualities.
- The Q-sort technique is typically used to assess the reactions of a small group of respondents. The emphasis of measurement is on the relative meaning of items included on the scale.
- The sociometric technique is most often used to assess relationships within a defined group, including a general measure of cohesiveness. Although essentially a technique that measures choices among the group members, the wording of the criteria for the choices can include nearly any concept in the behavioral sciences.

EXERCISES

1. Using any of the articles you have found so far, or after finding a new article, identify the types of measurement levels reflected by the variables included in the article.

2. Find an article in which the authors report on the reliability and/or validity of at least one of the measures used in the research. Determine the type of reliability and/or validity assessment employed by the researchers.

3. Find an example of each of the different types of measurement scales.

CHAPTER 7

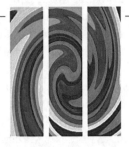

Experimental Research

That [continuity and progress] have been tied to careful experimental and theoretical work indicates that there is validity in a method which at times feels unproductive or disorganized.

—Aronson (1980, p. 21)

Overview

The purpose of this chapter is to provide you with the information you need to evaluate experimental research, specifically, research designed to test cause-effect hypotheses. You will learn about a variety of problems that must be considered when consuming the results of an experiment. For each of the major designs discussed, appropriate data analyses are suggested so that you can critically evaluate results, and general considerations about reading reports are addressed. Specific criticisms of each design will also be examined.

INTRODUCTION

To some people, experimental research is the highest peak of scientific research. To others it is the valley of darkness through which promising scientists must walk before they can do "meaningful" research. To most people,

experimental research is *the general label applied to methods developed for the specific purpose of testing causal relationships.* Like Aronson, I sometimes feel that experimental research can be unproductive and disorganized, and at other times I feel that experimental research is the best possible design for almost anything. I never feel as though it is the valley of darkness, but whatever negative feelings I may sometimes have are more than offset by the thrill of demonstrating that a cause-effect relationship exists where I predicted one would be. Experimental research may involve the most complicated research designs—that is, until one gets the hang of it—but it is the only way to obtain a definite answer to the question of *why* something happens. That is because experimental research is the only way to test causal hypotheses directly. Although the word *experiment* is used in a variety of ways in everyday language, an experiment has some very specific characteristics and has a narrower meaning when used by researchers than when used in everyday language. The specific meaning when used in the context of research has to do with a process called causal analysis.

CAUSAL ANALYSIS IN EXPERIMENTAL RESEARCH

Causal analysis—*the logical process through which we attempt to explain why an event occurred*—should not be new to you. It is, for example, the basis for explanatory research (see Chapter 1). Within the framework of experimental research, causal analysis includes a combination of three elements—temporal priority, control over variables, and random assignment—the presence of which enables us to test cause-effect hypotheses and interpret the results in terms of why something has occurred.

Temporal Priority

One of the requirements of causal analysis is knowledge that the suspected cause precedes the effect. Even though the simplicity of this requirement is readily apparent—something that will happen tomorrow cannot cause something that happens today—the concept can sometimes get a little confusing. For example, the unemployment figures that will be released tomorrow cannot affect today's decision to invest in the stock market; on the other hand, *speculation* about what tomorrow's unemployment figures might be *can* affect that decision. It is not tomorrow's event that affects today's behavior but today's speculation about tomorrow that affects today's behavior. **Temporal priority,** *the requirement that causes precede their effects*, is a stringent requirement, and we must be careful to understand exactly what is being considered a cause. Figure 7.1 illustrates temporal priority.

Figure 7.1	Sensible and Nonsensible Temporal Priority				
Sense			Nonsense		
Before	→	After	Before	←	After
Cause	→	Effect	Effect	←	Cause

Because the requirement of temporal priority is obvious, it is often assumed that temporal priority exists when in fact it may not. Consider, for example, the temporal priority involved in Jacobs's (1967) research on suicide notes discussed in Chapter 1. Jacobs's content analysis of suicide notes led him to conclude that people committed suicide because they believed the uncertainty of what might happen after death was preferable to the perception of certain, continued depression in their lives. One question Jacobs was not able to address directly was, "Which came first?" Did people decide to commit suicide because they preferred the uncertainty of death, or did they decide to commit suicide and then justify that decision by writing notes about the uncertainty of death? There is, of course, no way to answer this question using Jacobs's data; and there may be no ethical way to answer this question with any data, for in order to do so we would have to conduct a study in which we exerted control over someone's level of depression. Thus, to justify the label *experiment*, a study must *demonstrate* temporal priority; researchers are not allowed merely to assume that temporal priority was established.

Control Over Variables

Because temporal priority is often difficult to establish through logic alone, experimental research invariably involves exerting some control over the research environment. Some of that control involves keeping certain things constant, such as the form used to collect the data or the setting (whether in or out of a laboratory). Some things cannot be held constant, and they are called, sensibly, variables. One way to establish temporal priority is to manipulate the **independent variable**—*the suspected cause under consideration*. In order to test Jacobs's hypothesis experimentally, then, we would have to be able to depress a group of people to the point at which they were suicidal and then compare them to a group of people who were not depressed. Obviously, such research would violate just about every principle of ethics discussed in Chapter 2. Let's continue this discussion with a more feasible experiment.

In a study investigating the effects of the judge's instructions concerning reasonable doubt on jurors' verdicts, different types of instructions were presented to different groups of students role-playing jurors (Copenhaver & Dane, 1987). All of the students watched a videotape of a trial, which included instructions from the judge. Different groups of students saw a different version of the videotape. Some students received the standard instructions concerning reasonable doubt, whereas others received instructions that included a percentage, something like, "Reasonable doubt means you must be at least 90% sure the defendant committed the crime." Each of the students was then asked to vote either guilty or not guilty and to answer a few other questions. The independent variable was instructions concerning reasonable doubt, and it was controlled by manipulating the videotape presentation.

We were primarily interested in whether or not subjects given the percentage instructions would return verdicts different from those returned by subjects given the standard instructions concerning reasonable doubt. *The effect under investigation* is the **dependent variable**, which in this example is the verdict. The dependent variable (verdict) is dependent on the suspected cause (instructions concerning reasonable doubt). Because we used videotape to present the trial, we were also able to control all of the other aspects of a trial—the attorneys' opening statements, witnesses' testimony, and so on—by keeping them constant. The only aspect of the trial that differed from one group to the next was the instruction concerning reasonable doubt, the independent variable. The research hypothesis is illustrated in Figure 7.2.

Figure 7.2	An Example of an Experimental Research Hypothesis	
Judge's instruction	**→**	**Juror's verdict**
Independent variable		Dependent variable
Suspected cause		Effect under investigation

Random Assignment

Despite the use of videotape to control all aspects of the trial in the previous example, there remain other, equally plausible explanations for the different verdicts that the mock jurors produced. For example, perhaps one group of jurors just happened to be more lenient, or perhaps another group was composed mainly of people who believed that defendants are always guilty. To attempt to control all of these other possible causes by manipulating them and including them as additional independent variables would soon require more groups of people than would be possible. Instead of attempting to manipulate all other possible explanations, we relied on **random assignment,** which includes *any procedure that provides all participants an equal opportunity to experience any given level of the independent variable.* Thus, every subject had an equal chance of being assigned to the group receiving the standard instructions or to one of the groups receiving percentage instructions.

Because random assignment ensured that each participant was equally likely to experience any given level of the independent variable, there should be just as many lenient jurors in one group as in any other group, just as many hanging jurors in each group, and so on for any other variable we might be able to imagine but cannot control by making it constant and thus no longer a variable. Random assignment does not involve actually controlling extraneous variables; instead, it enables us to equalize their effects across all levels of the independent variable. The lenient jurors were, for example, still lenient, but the potential effect of lenient jurors was spread equally across all groups. Thus, the only thing that systematically differed among the groups was the independent variable, instructions about reasonable doubt.

DEMONSTRATION VERSUS DEMOGRAPHY

The combination of temporal priority, control of variables through manipulation, and random assignment is what makes a research study an experiment, what makes it possible to test cause-effect hypotheses. That same combination, however, tends to produce a somewhat artificial environment. In real trials, jurors rarely see a videotape of a trial, as did the students in Copenhaver and Dane's experiment, and although jurors are randomly selected to sit in the jury box, attorneys are able to challenge any juror and have that juror removed if it is apparent that the juror is strongly biased about the case. Copenhaver and Dane allowed any biased students to remain as jurors, although they equalized such effects through random assignment. Does the fact that the experimental jury is not exactly like an actual jury mean that the experiment has nothing to do with jury behavior? The answer is a resounding *no*.

Experimental research is not supposed to produce an exact replica of natural phenomena. That's not heresy but rather a recognition that experimental research has a very specific purpose—to test cause-effect hypotheses— and conclusions drawn from experimental research are drawn about the cause-effect relationship. In Copenhaver and Dane (1987), the conclusions we drew concerned how the different instructions produced different verdicts. We were not attempting to draw conclusions about whether or not our students would arrive at the same verdicts as actual jurors. On the other hand, we did expect that the differences apparent in our experiment—the effects of the instructions—would also be apparent with a sample of actual jurors.

The issue here is the difference between *demonstration* and *demography*. In our experiment, we demonstrated that percentage instructions concerning reasonable doubt produced different verdicts than did the standard instructions. Demography involves the question of how often we can expect those same differences to occur in courtrooms. Demonstration relies on the extent to which the independent variable is the only systematic difference among the groups. If the verdicts are different and the instructions are the only variable that could have caused those differences, then we have demonstrated a cause-effect relationship.

Demography, on the other hand, relies on **mundane realism**, which refers to *the extent to which the experience of the participants is similar to the experiences of everyday life*. If actual jurors were highly similar to the students who participated in the research, heard and saw the same evidence we presented in the videotape, and received the same instructions from the judge, then we would expect those jurors to behave much as our students behaved. But different trial evidence, different attitudes among the jurors, different instructions from the judge, and other variables would detract from the mundane realism of our experiment. We can claim that percentage instructions *can* cause different verdicts, but we cannot claim that they *always will*. Of course, replicating the experiment—for example, with a different set of evidence or with a different group of people role-playing jurors—and obtaining the same set of results would add to the generalizability of the cause-effect relationship we demonstrated in the first experiment. Eventually, enough replications with the same results would lead to the conclusion that different instructions usually produce different verdicts. Because there are no absolute truths in a scientific approach, however, we could not change "usually" to "always," no matter how many replications we completed.

ALTERNATIVE EXPLANATIONS FOR RESEARCH RESULTS

When the purpose of research is explanation—testing cause-effect hypotheses— every effort must be made to ensure that the independent variable is the only systematic influence on the dependent variable. The results of experimental research typically involve detecting differences among groups as measured by the dependent variable. Therefore, we need to be sure that the independent variable is the only preexisting difference among those groups. Temporal priority, manipulation of variables, and random assignment are the general requirements of an experimental design, but there are specific preexisting differences, called alternative explanations, that must be eliminated in order to make valid inferences from experimental research. As a critical consumer of research, you need to understand alternative explanations before you can determine whether or not a causal conclusion expressed in a research report is warranted. Campbell and Stanley (1963) literally wrote the book on alternative explanations, and much of the following discussion relies heavily on their classic volume.

History Effects

A **history effect** is *produced whenever some uncontrolled event alters participants' responses*. Usually the event occurs between the time the researcher manipulates the independent variable and the time the researcher measures the dependent variable. Sometimes a history effect is caused by a truly historical event, but more often than not it is produced by more commonplace events.

Generally, random assignment enables one to eliminate the likelihood of a history effect. If, for example, there had been a great deal of publicity about crime during the time we were conducting our experiment on judge's instructions, random assignment would ensure that, whatever the effects of that publicity might be, the effects would be equalized across the different levels of the independent variable. Figure 7.3 depicts an experimental design that can be used to eliminate history effects in that experiment.

Figure 7.3	Controlling History Effects Through Random Assignment

Maturation Effects

In some sense, maturation is a catchall alternative explanation. **Maturation** refers to *any process that involves systematic change over time, regardless of specific events*. From a causal point of view, the passage of time is not the cause of the process but is merely the most convenient indicator of whatever process may be affecting participants. Most experiments do not last long enough for maturation to occur in the everyday sense of the word—people growing older—but maturation also includes such things as fatigue, boredom, thirst, hunger, and frustration. If, for example, the percentage instructions were considerably longer than the standard instructions, then the participants hearing that particular instruction may have become bored or tired, and a systematic difference between groups other than that produced by the independent variable would have been introduced into the experiment.

The design involving random assignment illustrated in Figure 7.3 would provide some protection against maturation but not necessarily enough protection. Maturation effects could remain an alternative explanation of results if we did not ensure that the videotapes representing the different experimental conditions were the same length.

At this point, you should realize that control over much more than the independent variable is necessary for good experimental research. Not only did Copenhaver and Dane need to control the independent variable, they needed to control the type of trial presentation and the length of the trial as well. The need to control so many factors made it impossible to conduct our experiment in a real courtroom, for the legal system just does not allow people to play around with trials that way. The need for even more control will become apparent as we continue to consider additional alternative explanations of research results.

Testing Effects

Recall from Chapters 2 and 6 that measurement always involves some sort of error. How one phrases questions, for example, can affect the responses one receives. In experimental research, **testing effects** are *changes in responses caused by measuring the dependent variable*. Testing effects can occur in a variety of ways. One might, for example, measure the dependent variable more than once, thereby creating the possibility that responses on the second measurement reflect memory of the first responses. Similarly, testing effects can occur when there is more than one dependent variable: One cannot measure all of the dependent variables simultaneously—one of them has to be measured first—and participants' responses to the first dependent variable might alter their responses to subsequent measures of that variable.

As the study concerning judges' instructions about reasonable doubt was described earlier, testing effects should not have presented a problem. The dependent variable—verdict—is measured only once. Although there were other dependent variables, the primary one was verdict, and it was measured first. Of course, the participants' choice of verdict probably did affect their responses to other, secondary measures, but those secondary measures were not critically important to the research hypothesis. For example, participants who decided the defendant was guilty suggested considerably harsher punishments than did those who indicated the defendant was not guilty. Such testing effects make the dependent variable "punishment" suspect, simply because the participants may have suggested punishments merely to be consistent with their verdicts instead of on the basis of some other reasoning process.

The most obvious means for eliminating testing effects are to measure dependent variables only once and to measure the primary dependent variable before any other measures. Testing effects may also be avoided through random assignment if one cannot avoid multiple measurements of the dependent variable. Suppose, for example, that we measured each juror's verdict separately, then had them deliberate as a group, and then measured each juror's verdict after deliberation. Comparing the postdeliberation verdicts to the predeliberation verdicts would enable us to assess the extent to which verdict preferences changed during deliberation. However, that assessment of change is subject to testing effects. Jurors could have, in fact, changed their preferences during deliberation but then reported no change in order to appear consistent or nonconformist. (There may also be some other aspect of self-presentation operating.) But if participants are randomly assigned to the different groups, then such self-presentation effects, or any other effects for that matter, are likely to be equalized across the groups.

Instrumentation Effects

Beginning researchers, and even some experienced ones, can become confused about the difference between testing effects and instrumentation effects. Such confusion likely occurs because the two terms seem to refer to the same problem. They are not the same, however, and should be considered separately. **Instrumentation effects** are *changes in the manner in which the dependent variable is measured*; they are problems caused by inconsistent operationalization of the dependent variable or by inconsistently measuring participants' responses. Testing effects, on the other hand, are produced by the act of measuring something, even if the measurement itself is consistent.

In the context of the current example, instrumentation effects would be a viable alternative explanation if we had used different forms to record verdicts for the different groups of participants. Similarly, offering some, but not all, of the participants an alternative decision, such as "guilty but insane," would have introduced instrumentation effects.

To avoid instrumentation effects, control over operationalization of the dependent variable is critical. The logic of experiments may fall apart completely if those who experience different levels of the independent variable also experience different dependent variables. It may seem obviously foolish to use different versions of the dependent variable for different groups, but there are circumstances that might make such foolishness relatively easy to overlook. Even something as apparently innocuous as differences in the quality of copies of the form used to record the dependent variable can cause instrumentation problems. If one group has copies that are more difficult to read than the other group's copies, that discrepancy violates the logic involved in having the independent variable as the only systematic difference between the groups. Of course, as a consumer of research, you probably are not going to have access to the kind of detailed information that enables you to determine whether or not instrumentation effects have occurred in any particular study. Nevertheless, you should be attuned to potential clues of instrumentation effects when reading the method section of an article.

More often than not, instrumentation effects become a problem when the operational definition of the dependent variable depends on someone's judgment. Subjective measures, such as someone's rating of the quality of an essay, are subject to various problems. For example, the person making the judgments may grow tired, bored, or careless, and such changes are, in fact, changes in the dependent measure. In this case, because the instrument is the person making the rating, changes in the rater become instrumentation effects. Randomizing the order in which the ratings are made, perhaps by mixing the essays such that they are not grouped according to levels of the independent variable, is usually sufficient to equalize the likelihood of such maturation effects as fatigue.

Similarly, not allowing raters or judges to be aware of the level of the independent variable experienced by the participant reduces the likelihood of instrumentation effects. A **blind rater** is *someone who is unaware of either the research hypothesis or the experimental group from which the responses came.* When you read research reports containing such phrases as "the observers were blind to conditions" or "blind raters were used," it doesn't mean the observers had a vision deficit. Rather, it means the observers or raters did not know to which experimental group those being observed belonged.

Statistical Regression Effects

In the context of alternative explanations of research results, statistical regression effect does not refer to a particular type of data analysis. Rather, **statistical regression effect** is *an artifact of measurement that occurs when extreme scores are obtained and the person is tested again at a later time.* Someone who scores extremely high or extremely low on a measure is likely, if tested again, to obtain a second score that is closer to the average than was the first score. The person's score is said to regress toward the mean because the score moves back to the average score, either from an extreme high or an extreme low. Because Copenhaver and Dane used a dichotomous measure of verdict—guilty versus not guilty—their study is not subject to statistical regression effects.

On the other hand, most continuous variables, such as a rating from 1 to 10, an IQ score, and crime rates, include the assumption that the overall distribution of responses should conform to the normal distribution, the bell-shaped curve. Most scores bunch together near the mean of the distribution, and the frequency of scores decreases as the scores become more distant from the mean. Therefore, the probability of obtaining extreme scores is lower than the probability of obtaining scores closer to the mean. Think of the distribution of grade point averages of undergraduates at your school. Most undergraduate students have a grade point average somewhere between a 2.0 and a 3.0; the number of students with a 4.0 or a 0.5 is relatively low. Thus the probability of your running into someone with a 4.0 GPA is considerably lower than the probability of your encountering someone with a 2.5 GPA.

The statistical theory gets a little complicated, but the essential point is that extreme scores, whether extremely high or low, probably result from random measurement error—are an artifact or a fluke—rather than from a truly extreme level of whatever is being measured. Because extreme scores in a normal distribution are, by definition, unlikely to occur, the more reasonable explanation for an extreme score is that it was produced through measurement error. Thus, when someone with an extreme score is tested again, chances are good that the random measurement error will not recur and that the person's second score will not be as extreme as the first score. If I took an intelligence test and scored an IQ of 160, most people (including me) would declare that score to be an artifact, a fluke, and would demand a retest. The retest would likely produce a lower score, one that is closer to, but not necessarily identical to, the average IQ of 100.

Statistical regression effects, like testing effects, are a problem only when the dependent variable is measured more than once. Only random assignment can be used to avoid them. However, statistical regression effects can become a problem even when an implicit measure of the dependent variable is used. For example, a teacher might select students he or she believes to be the brightest students and give them special assignments designed to further improve their abilities. If subsequently the students exhibit no change in their abilities, perhaps as measured by an alternate-form examination, then the lack of difference could be due to the fact that the assignments were ineffective or due to statistical regression. That is, some of the "brightest," as measured by the teacher's perceptions, are probably not as bright as the teacher perceived them to be. Subsequent measurement would produce a score closer to average. But if the special assignments are actually making such students brighter, then the net result would be no change. Statistical regression brought the scores down, and the assignments brought them back up again, leaving the scores right where they started. Of course, the students did receive some benefit—improved abilities—from the assignments, but statistical regression prevented that benefit from being reflected in their scores. Note that such an experiment would also be subject to instrumentation effects; a teacher's perception and a written examination are not the same operational definition of the dependent variable.

Selection Effects

The last example of a statistical regression effect also involves a specific example of alternative explanations known as selection effects. A **selection effect** is *produced by the manner in which the participants were recruited or recruited themselves*. That is, selection effects occur because some characteristic of the participants differs systematically across the experimental groups. Once again, random assignment eliminates selection effects because the characteristic is equally distributed across the randomly assigned groups. In Copenhaver and Dane's experiment, some of the students may have believed that, in general, defendants are guilty and may therefore have decided before the videotape was shown that the defendant in the specific trial was guilty. If more of such students ended up in one group or the other, their verdicts would produce a difference that was not related to the independent variable: instructions concerning reasonable doubt. By now you should be getting the idea that random assignment is an integral part of any experiment.

Sometimes, however, random assignment is practically or ethically impossible. In such cases, a technique called matching provides a second-best alternative. **Matching** is *assigning participants to groups in order to equalize, across groups, scores on any relevant variable*. If, for example, we were conducting a study in an actual courtroom with real jurors, we would not be able to assign jurors randomly to conditions—whatever they happen to be—because doing so would mean we would undermine the defendant's right to due process. We might, instead, try to measure their beliefs about defendants and consider those beliefs as part of the research design. We could then compare those who were biased against defendants with those who were not and assess the extent to which biases affected their verdicts.

The problem with using matching to overcome selection effects is, very simply, that one can never be sure one has included all of the relevant variables in the matching process. We might, for example, have to match jurors on bias against defendants, on experience with crime, on the number of crime shows they watch on television, on their level of intelligence, and so on. There is no limit to the number of different things that might affect their verdicts, and so there is no limit to the number of different variables on which the participants would have to be matched. Even though matching does provide an alternative when random assignment is not possible, it is not as effective as random assignment. Thus, consumers should be much more critical, and skeptical, about tests of cause-effect explanations that include matching instead of random assignment. Sometimes, matching is the only available technique to a researcher, but that doesn't mean that it is as good as random assignment in controlling selection (or other) effects.

Mortality Effects

Borrowed from animal research terminology, **mortality effects** are *caused by the loss of participants during a project*. Those of us who use human participants prefer the term **attrition**, but mortality remains the official term. Mortality is a specific type of selection effect, one due to participants' choosing to leave, rather than join, the research project. In Copenhaver and Dane's study, mortality effects were not an operant consideration, although they could have been if any students had opted to retract their consent to participate in the study.

Random assignment is considered a safeguard against mortality effects because the number of participants likely to retract their consent is considered to be roughly equal across different groups. Random assignment, however, cannot be considered a *cure* for mortality effects, for one experimental group could in fact contain a disproportionate number of dropouts. Suppose, for purposes of illustration, that 10 students in the percentage instruction condition dropped out but only two students in the standard instruction condition did so. It would be difficult to interpret any differences between the two conditions because we would have no idea which verdict the students who dropped out would have returned. Any interpretation could be qualified by the phrase "for those who remained in the study," but it would be appropriate to wonder about the reason for the differential dropout rate. The reason could be, for example, that people are not willing to decide on verdicts when given a percentage instruction concerning reasonable doubt, or it could be something else related to the research hypothesis.

When you read a study in which mortality effects are likely to be of concern, either because the procedure was long or there are multiple sessions, read carefully to determine whether the researchers used a combination of random assignment and some preliminary measure of the dependent variable. Such a design is illustrated in Figure 7.4. The design will not prevent participants from retracting their consent, but it will enable the researchers to determine the extent to which those who dropped out differed from those who stayed.

Figure 7.4   Assessing Mortality Effects Through Experimental Design

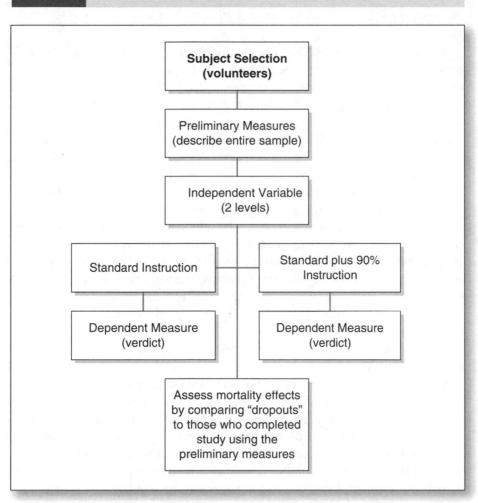

Comparing scores on the preliminary measure will provide some indication—but not conclusive proof—about any differences that may exist. If the dropouts were different from those who stayed, then the researcher has a potential problem with mortality effects and you need to add that to the mix of issues you include in your critical analysis of the study. If the two groups score the same on the pretest measures, then there probably are no problems. Furthermore, the researcher can use change scores—the difference between the preliminary measure and the dependent variable—to assess effects due to the independent variable.

Participant Bias

We have already noted that research participants can be affected by **self-presentation,** their *concern about the perceptions the experimenter and others may form* about them as a result of their responses in the project. This is one example of **participant bias**—*any intentional effort on the part of participants to alter their responses.* Another example may involve participants' concerns about revealing sensitive information simply because they believe it is none of the researcher's business what they think. Generally, any **evaluation apprehension—***concern about being observed*—can produce participant bias.

Random assignment helps to reduce such types of participant bias because, as usual, random assignment equalizes the distribution of apprehensive participants across experimental groups. The only way to avoid participant bias completely is to prevent the participants from being aware that they are being observed, but such a practice brings in the ethical problem of justifying disregard of informed consent. Participants sometimes are unaware that they are in a research project, but this occurs very infrequently and the amount of control exerted in an experiment makes such lack of awareness even more unlikely.

In addition to evaluation apprehension and related forms of participant bias, participants may intentionally attempt to help or hinder the research efforts. The **beneficent subject effect** occurs *when participants are aware of the research hypothesis and attempt to respond so as to support it.* Suppose, for example, that students role-playing jurors became aware of the purpose of Copenhaver and Dane's study. Some of them may have believed that we preferred the percentage instructions and may have provided verdicts they thought would help support that idea. Perhaps some of them attempted to predict what actual jurors would decide in the case, instead of making their own decisions about the verdict. Although such an effect might be interesting in its own right—why would these jurors care what we preferred?—it would certainly have made our study worthless for its original purpose.

The opposite, the **maleficent subject effect,** occurs *when participants are aware of the research hypothesis and attempt to respond so as to undermine it.* In this case, jurors might alter their verdicts to make it seem as though the percentage instructions are less effective than the standard instructions, or they might attempt to predict what actual jurors would decide and then return the opposite verdict. Again, participants' interest in the project might be an interesting topic of study, but interest so expressed is not conducive to the purposes of the research. The only way to prevent either effect is to prevent participants from becoming aware of the research hypothesis. This is known as keeping the participants blind and is analogous to keeping raters of subjective dependent measures in the dark about the hypothesis. In some projects, a **double-blind procedure** is used; that is, *the raters (or investigators) and participants are unaware of the research hypothesis or of group memberships related to that hypothesis.*

Blind and double-blind studies may involve concealment of the research hypothesis by preventing awareness of participation itself or they may involve some sort of deception. Both procedures—preventing awareness and deception—pose ethical problems and are considered only after it has been determined that simply withholding information about the specific research hypothesis will not prevent participant bias; efforts to attain methodological rigor must be balanced with consideration of the ethical treatment of participants (Gorman & Dane, 1994).

Experimenter Bias

Participants are not the only people who may alter their behavior during an experiment. **Experimenter bias** refers to *the experimenter's differential treatment of experimental groups.* In the jury experiment, there was considerable potential for experimenter bias. As much as we wanted to remain objective scientists, we had some definite ideas about what differences might result in response to the standard instructions and the percentage instructions, and it would have been extremely difficult to keep those ideas from having some sort of subtle influence on our behavior during the project.

The logic of the experiment required us to treat all groups exactly the same; the only systematic difference between the groups was supposed to be the manipulated independent variable, the instructions concerning reasonable doubt. About the only way for us to be sure we would not exhibit experimental bias would be to remain blind to experimental conditions. Thus, in order to control the length and quality of the trial across conditions and our awareness of the independent variable condition for any given group, we decided to present the trial via videotape. By having one person choose which videotape would be shown and the other person serve as the experimenter, the experimenter could remain blind to experimental conditions when showing the tape. Eventually, of course, the experimenter would hear which instruction was on the tape, but, by then, all he had to do was pick up the data collection forms as the participants walked out the door.

As you read other researchers' method sections, therefore, pay particular attention to their efforts to avoid experimenter bias and all of the previously discussed alternative explanations. Just because experimenters are not blind to conditions, for example, does not mean that there was no experimenter bias exerting effects upon the results. Experimenters who are not blind, subjects who are not randomly assigned, or any of the other aspects of the research that might alert you to potential alternative explanations, however, should be considered very carefully so that you, as the consumer of the research, can decide whether or not any of these alternative explanations pose a problem for interpreting the results. You should not assume there is experimenter bias simply because the results section did not contain the phrase "the experimenter was blind to conditions," but you also should not assume that there are no alternative explanations just because the study was published.

EXPERIMENTAL DESIGN

Fortunately, not every experiment is subject to every alternative explanation described above. On the other hand, every alternative explanation must be considered a potential problem until logic, control, or experimental design enables you to rule it out. In this section we'll consider the various experimental designs that can be used to rule out alternative explanations. **Design** refers to *the number and arrangement of independent variable levels in a research project*. Although all experimental designs involve manipulated independent variables and random assignment, different designs are more or less efficient for dealing with specific alternative explanations.

The design a researcher uses depends upon the research hypothesis the researcher has tried to test. Therefore, being familiar with a variety of different designs enables you to consume critically a variety of research projects as you attempt to inform policy empirically. The major factor in examining a design critically is not its complexity but the extent to which it provides internal validity. **Internal validity** refers to *the extent to which the independent variable is the only systematic difference among experimental groups* (Shadish, Cook, & Campbell, 2002). That is, the internal validity of an experiment allows you, as the research consumer, to conclude that the independent variable is the cause of the effects measured with the dependent variable. Just as every poker hand either wins or loses the pot, every design is either a winner or loser at internal validity, depending on the specific research hypothesis being tested.

In an effort to keep diagrams simple and easy to read, an *I* and subscripts will be used to denote levels of a single independent variable, and an *O* with subscripts will denote the dependent variable measured in the groups formed with the independent variable. Thus, the design of Copenhaver and Dane (1987) would be diagrammed as in Figure 7.5.

| Figure 7.5 | The Design of Copenhaver and Dane (1987) in Design Notation. This design is also known as the basic design. |

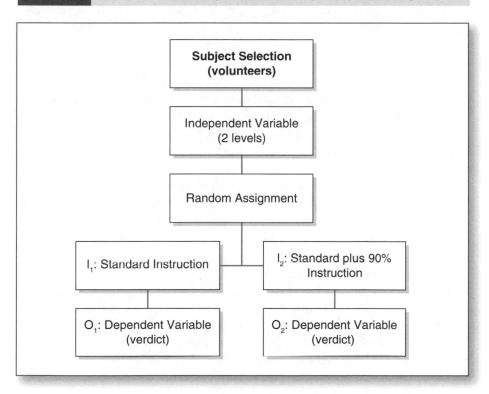

The Basic Design

The basic design is the simplest design that still qualifies as a true experimental design. Campbell and Stanley (1963) refer to it as the Posttest-Only Control Group Design, and it is essentially the design used by Copenhaver and Dane (1987). In the basic design (Figure 7.5), participants are randomly assigned to one of two different levels of the independent variable, and the dependent variable is measured only once. Coupled with careful control over procedures, this design effectively avoids most alternative explanations and provides a comparison between control (I_1) and treatment (I_2) conditions by comparing the dependent variable responses of the two groups, O_1 and O_2.

Data analyses for the basic design include any analyses in which central tendencies for two groups (O_1 and O_2) can be compared. These include a simple chi-square for categorical dependent measures such as verdicts, the Mann-Whitney U test for dependent measures composed of ranks such as best to worst drawings in an art contest or a t test or analysis of variance for continuous variables that do not involve ranks.

When this design is described in a research report, the author(s) will simply point out that participants were randomly assigned to different groups. You might read the following, for example:

> Participants were randomly assigned to receive one of two instructions defining reasonable doubt. In the standard condition, participants received instructions currently used in most jurisdictions. In the "percentage condition," the phrase "beyond reasonable doubt means you must be at least 90% certain the defendant committed the crime" was appended to the standard instruction.

The basic design is not necessarily limited to two groups, as can be seen in Figure 7.6. Different levels of the same independent variable, such as percentage instructions using the words "50% certain," "60% certain," and so on would also qualify for the basic design. In fact, Copenhaver and Dane included eight different levels of their independent variable: standard instructions plus percentage instructions ranging from 50% to 99%.

The basic design is most efficient for research in which the premanipulation state of participants—what they are like before they experience a single independent variable—is either not of interest or can be assumed to be unrelated to the independent variable. Neither change over time nor differential reactions to the independent variable as a function of some preexisting

| Figure 7.6 | The Basic Experimental Design With Three Levels of One Independent Variable |

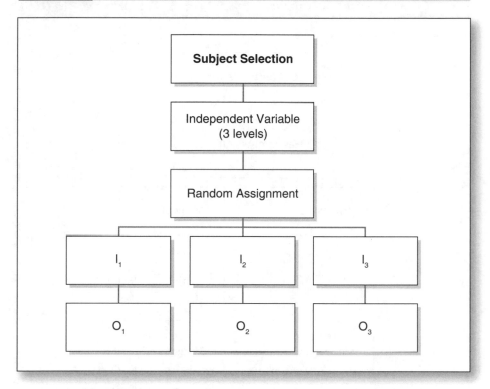

characteristic can be studied with the basic design, simply because there is no way to know anything about the participants before they experience the independent variable.

The Basic Pretest Design

The basic pretest design, as the name implies, involves adding a pretest measure to the basic design. The obvious reason for adding a pretest measure is to examine how much the independent variable causes participants to change. The basic pretest design, illustrated in Figure 7.7, is the design Campbell and Stanley (1963) call the Pretest-Posttest Control Group Design. In Figure 7.7, O_1 and O_3 refer to the pretest measure, the dependent variable measured

Figure 7.7	The Basic Pretest Design, in Which the Dependent Variable Is Measured Both Before and After Manipulation of the Independent Variable

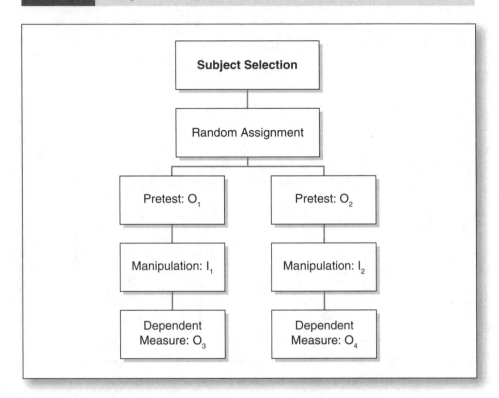

before the manipulation of the independent variable, and O_2 and O_4 refer to the dependent variable measured after the manipulation. Although not depicted in the figure, the basic pretest design can include more than two levels of the same independent variable.

Suppose, for example, that researchers were interested only in knowing what jurors thought the phrase "beyond a reasonable doubt" meant. They might first ask them to indicate, say on a scale from 0% to 100% certainty, where reasonable doubt lies. Then they could ask participants to view one of the videotapes used by Copenhaver and Dane and have the participants again indicate where reasonable doubt lies on the same percentage scale. Because the only differences among the videotapes were the instructions concerning reasonable doubt, they could use the data to determine the extent to which such instructions change individuals' perceptions about reasonable doubt. They would analyze the data by subtracting each participant's pretest response from his or her posttest response ($O_2 - O_1$ and $O_4 - O_3$) and treating the difference as though it were the only dependent variable. They could use a t test to compare the difference between the two groups.

The obvious advantage of the basic pretest design over the basic design is the ability to obtain information about the premanipulation state of the participants, to examine the change in scores. The disadvantage is that the pretest measure may affect participants' reactions to the independent variable; that is, asking participants first to provide their impressions about reasonable doubt could sensitize them to the instructions they will later see in the videotape (a testing effect).

Random assignment enables us to overcome the possibility of general testing effects, but the combination of pretest measures and manipulation of the independent variable may create another alternative explanation for the results. Campbell and Stanley (1963) call this alternative explanation a **testing-treatment interaction,** in which *participants experiencing one level of the independent variable may be more sensitive to testing effects than participants experiencing a different level of the independent variable.* Essentially, the pretest measure may make one of the levels of the independent variable, such as the percentage instructions concerning reasonable doubt, more forceful than it would have been without the pretest. This increased forcefulness of that particular level of the independent variable, then, is an artifact rather than a valid test of the variable's impact. The dependent variable in such cases measures both the effect of the independent variable and its combination with the pretest, instead of measuring the effect of the independent variable only. It is also possible that the pretest measure may make participants wonder about the purpose of the study and increase participant bias.

The Solomon Four-Group Design

The most effective design for dealing with the problem of testing-treatment interaction is the Solomon (1949) four-group design, illustrated in Figure 7.8. Although there are only two levels of the independent variable, four groups are required to assess the extent to which testing effects have occurred. It is important to realize, however, that this design does not eliminate the testing-treatment interaction but rather enables the researcher to determine whether or not it has occurred and, if it has, assess its impact. This design also enables

Figure 7.8   The Solomon Four-Group Design

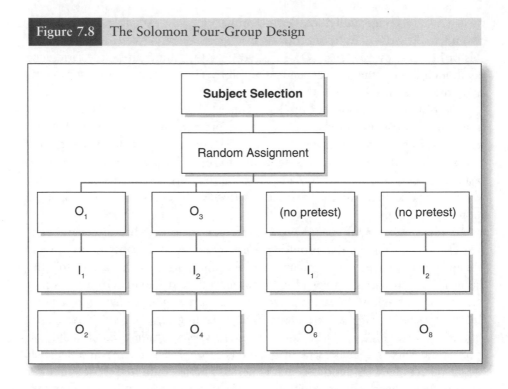

one to determine whether or not overall testing effects have occurred; that is, it enables the researcher to assess the effectiveness of the random assignment procedure.

If the I_1 level of the independent variable represents a **control condition—** *the absence of the manipulation*—then comparing O_2 with O_6 provides a test of the overall testing effect. The only difference between these two groups is the existence of a pretest measure, and any difference between these two groups would be due to the pretest. Comparing the difference between O_4 and O_8 with the difference between O_2 and O_6 provides an estimate of the testing-treatment interaction effect. If there is no interaction between testing and treatment, then the upper half of the design can be analyzed in the same way as the basic pretest design. If, however, there is a testing-treatment inter-action, the researcher can use the interaction to adjust statistically the size of the effect of the independent variable. As a research consumer, however, you will typically read only that the Solomon four-group design was used and that the researchers either found no testing-treatment interaction effect or found one and adjusted the results accordingly. However, your knowledge of this design will enable you to assess critically the results of studies in which researchers employed a pretest measure and did not assess testing-treatment interaction effects.

Unfortunately, the Solomon four-group design is not, in general, a very efficient design. It requires twice as many groups as the basic pretest design to examine essentially the same cause-effect hypothesis. The four groups depicted in Figure 7.8, for example, include only two levels of a single independent variable. The loss of efficiency is related to the need to test for the testing-treatment interaction. In general, the more the researcher needs to know, the more groups or participants will be required.

Factorial Design

Many research questions require inclusion of more than one independent variable in the design. For example, suppose I plan a study in which I want to assess the extent to which jurors rely on witnesses' nonverbal behavior (apparent nervousness and so on) in deciding on a verdict. At the same time, I also want to know whether it makes any difference if the witness is undergoing direct examination (questioning by the attorney on their side) or cross examination (questioning by the other side's attorney). This situation requires two independent variables: one for nonverbal behavior and one for type of examination.

Designs that include more than one independent variable are called **factorial designs**. In terms of our diagram scheme, a simple factorial design is illustrated in Figure 7.9, in which *A* refers to one independent variable and *B* refers to a second independent variable. Within the design, participants collectively experience all possible combinations of the two independent variables, but each participant experiences only one of these combinations. As with other designs, each of the independent variables can have two or more levels.

More often than not, the notation used in Figure 7.9 is not applied to factorial designs. As you probably discovered while attempting to decipher Figure 7.9, the notation is a little cumbersome. Instead, the notation used in Figure 7.10 is more acceptable for factorial designs. Figure 7.10 illustrates the two-variable jury study I just described. I've added identification numbers to the groups, called *cells* in the design, to make it easier to refer to them in further discussion. Usually, means, standard deviations, or some other summary statistics are presented in the cells when reporting research results.

| Figure 7.9 | The Factorial Design for Two Independent Variables, Each With Two Levels |

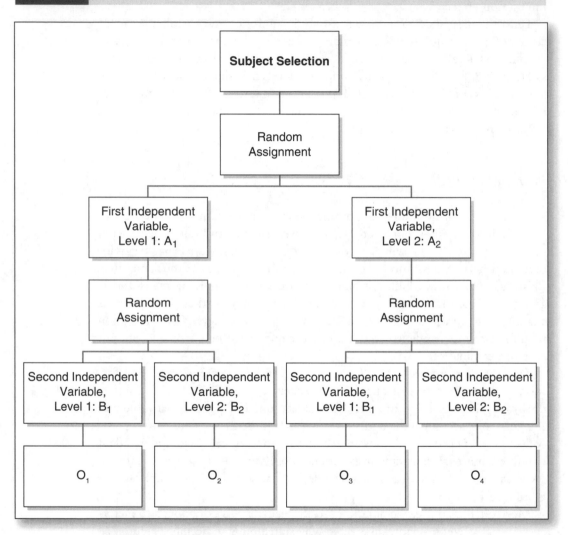

| Figure 7.10 | Typical Representation of a Factorial Design |

Direct (A_1)	Cross (A_2)
Cell #1: A_1B_1	Cell #2: A_2B_1
Cell #3: A_1B_2	Cell #4: A_2B_2

Note: A = type of examination; B = nonverbal behavior: nervous = B_1, calm = B_2.

In cell #1, participants will see a videotape of an obviously nervous defendant undergoing questioning from the defense attorney. In cell #2, different participants will watch the same videotape, but they will be led to believe that the attorney is the prosecutor. In cell #3, a calm-looking defendant will be questioned by his attorney, whereas in cell #4 the calm defendant will be questioned by the prosecutor. In order to control for such things as other physical characteristics of the witness and attorney, all participants will see the same attorney and the same defendant, but they will be told that the attorney is either the defense attorney or the prosecuting attorney. In order to control for what is being said—I'm only interested in nonverbal behavior—the sound will be turned off while the participants view the tape. The design depicted in Figure 7.10 is called a 2 × 2 factorial design—two levels of one independent variable combined with two levels of another independent variable.

The advantage of a factorial design is that interactions between independent variables can be tested. An **interaction** *occurs when the effect of one variable depends on which level of another variable is present*. In the study just described, perhaps a nervous defendant will be evaluated as more believable when undergoing cross examination than when undergoing direct examination. Because most people expect someone to be nervous when they are being challenged, it would be reasonable to expect someone to be nervous under cross examination, but it would not be reasonable to expect a defendant to be nervous when being questioned by the defense attorney. On the other hand, a calm defendant would be more believable when undergoing direct examination than when undergoing cross examination; someone being challenged and appearing calm might seem too rehearsed and so might be perceived as less believable. Thus, we expect an interaction between type of examination and nonverbal behavior; the effect of being nervous will depend upon whether it occurs under cross examination or direct examination.

The easiest way to illustrate an interaction effect is with a graph such as that depicted in Figure 7.11. The dependent variable, credibility, is represented on the ordinal or vertical axis of the graph, whereas one of the independent variables, nonverbal behavior, is represented on the abscissa or horizontal axis. Two different lines representing two levels of the other independent variable, examination type, complete the graph. Notice that the lines representing type of examination cross or intersect; this is the *sine qua non* (the essential characteristic) of an interaction effect.

It is not always the case, however, that including two independent variables in a research design will produce an interaction effect. It could be, for example, that a nervous defendant will always be less credible than a calm defendant, regardless of who is doing the questioning. If so, we would observe a

| Figure 7.11 | Illustration of an Interaction Between Examination Type and Nonverbal Behavior |

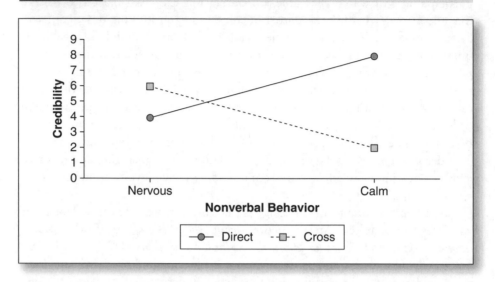

main effect—*an effect produced by a single independent variable*. Figure 7.12 illustrates a main effect for type of examination; nervous defendants are always less credible than calm defendants. Notice that the lines in Figure 7.12 do not

| Figure 7.12 | Illustration of a Main Effect for Nonverbal Behavior |

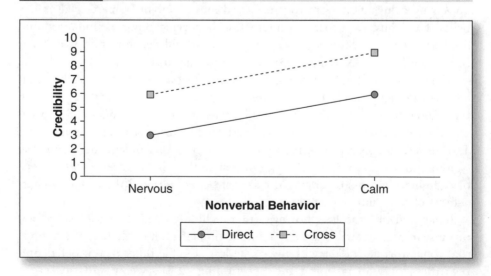

cross; they remain parallel. Parallel (or nearly parallel) lines on a graph such as those in Figure 7.12 are the hallmark of a main effect.

When data analyses indicate that the interaction is significant or reliable, it may not be important to interpret main effects that are part of the interaction. The interaction invariably makes the conclusion one would draw from the main effect wrong at least part of the time. For example, the data illustrated in Figure 7.11 reflect both a main effect for examination type and an interaction effect. The main effect is that, combined or averaged over nervous and calm defendants, the overall rating for cross examination (4) is lower than the overall rating for direct examination (6). However, it is clear from the figure that claiming the defendant is perceived as more credible under direct examination would be wrong when the defendant is nervous.

Instead of trying to interpret the main effect, most researchers will simply acknowledge its existence and then describe the interaction effect. I might write, for example, "an analysis of variance produced a reliable main effect for examination type, but it was superseded by the interaction between examination type and nonverbal behavior" and then proceed to describe the interaction or refer the reader to a graph that is similar to Figure 7.11. Of course, the quote is fictional—I haven't actually collected any data—but it does give you some idea about how researchers report interaction and main effect results. The temptation to interpret main effects that are superseded by an interaction is a rather strong one to which even seasoned researchers fall prey (see, for example, Dane & Thompson, 1985). Like so many other temptations, including oversimplification of results in general, it is best to avoid it.

The ability to detect and interpret interactions is the primary advantage of factorial designs. However, they can become methodological and interpretational nightmares when researchers try to accomplish too much with any one design. There is not much you, as a consumer, can do about an overly ambitious researcher, but keep in mind that, no matter how complicated a design may appear to be, factorial designs include only two types of effects, main effects and interaction effects. Don't allow yourself to be overly confused when trying to understand complicated factorial designs; interpret the results one main effect at a time and one interaction at a time.

Repeated Measures Design

Sometimes it is necessary either to expose participants to more than one level of an independent variable or to measure the dependent variable more than once for each participant. The basic pretest design, for example, is the simplest form of repeated measurement design, but that design does not involve exposing any participant to more than one level of an independent variable. A **repeated measures design** is *a specific factorial design in which the same participants are exposed to more than one level of an independent variable.* Repeated measures designs are also called "within subject" designs because the independent variable is manipulated within the same subject instead of between or across different subjects. Whether or not a repeated measures design is used by any researcher depends on the type of independent variables used and, of course, the hypothesis being tested. For some types of experiments, exposing participants to more than one level of an independent variable is illogical or impossible, and repeated measures designs also require some additional groups to test for order effects.

Suppose, for example, that I decide to use 10 participants in each of the four cells of the witness credibility study described earlier. Such a design is represented in Figure 7.13, in which participant identification numbers are entered in each cell; each participant experiences one and only one combination of the two independent variables. Such designs are also called **between-subject designs** because *the manipulations of the independent variables occur between participants.*

Figure 7.13	Subject Numbers for a 2 × 2 Between-Subjects Factorial Design	
Direct (A_1)	**Cross (A_2)**
A_1B_1: Subjects 1–10	A_2B_1: Subjects 11–20
A_1B_2: Subjects 21–30	A_2B_2: Subjects 31–40

Note: A = type of examination; B = nonverbal behavior: nervous = B_1, calm = B_2.

If I were to use a repeated measures design—expose any given participant to more than one level of an independent variable—the design of the resulting experiment would appear as in Figure 7.14. Each participant would see a nervous defendant undergoing direct examination and a different, calm defendant undergoing cross examination. I would be able to test more or less the same hypothesis with half as many participants. The "more or less" in the previous sentence refers to the different experiences in the two experiments: In the "between" design—illustrated in Figure 7.13—participants would see only one defendant; in the "within" design (Figure 7.14), participants would be exposed to two different defendants.

Figure 7.14	Subject Numbers for a 2 × 2 Repeated Measures Factorial Design
Direct (A$_1$)	**Cross (A$_2$)**
A$_1$B$_1$: Subjects 1–10	A$_2$B$_1$: Subjects 11–20
A$_1$B$_2$: Subjects 11–20	A$_2$B$_2$: Subjects 1–10

Note: A = type of examination; B = nonverbal behavior: nervous = B$_1$, calm = B$_2$.

More important, the repeated measures design depicted in Figure 7.14 would not be adequate for testing my original research hypothesis because the illustrated design would suffer from **order effects**—*changes in participant responses resulting from the sequence in which participants experience multiple levels of an independent variable.* The potential for order effects exists because participants would be exposed to the two defendants in different sequences: Participants 1–10 would first see a nervous defendant and then a calm defendant, whereas participants 11–20 would experience the opposite sequence. Whatever the sequence, part of their reaction to the second defendant could be due to their reaction to the first one. For participants 11–20, for example, the nervous demeanor of the second defendant might appear even more nervous coming after exposure to a calm defendant.

To correct for the alternative explanation of order effects, we would have to add additional participants and groups to the design. A corrected repeated measures design for the witness study might look like the design illustrated in Figure 7.15. Notice that all possible orders of nervous and calm defendants are covered in that design. Notice also that once again 40 participants are included

Figure 7.15	Design for a 2 (Nonverbal Behavior) × 2 (Examination Type) × 2 (Order) Repeated Measures Factorial Design	
Defendant (C)	**Direct (A$_1$)**	**Cross (A$_2$)**
First defendant (C$_1$)	A$_1$B$_1$: Subjects 1–10	A$_2$B$_1$: Subjects 11–20
	A$_1$B$_2$: Subjects 21–30	A$_2$B$_2$: Subjects 31–40
Second defendant (C$_2$)	A$_1$B$_1$: Subjects 21–30	A$_2$B$_1$: Subjects 31–40
	A$_1$B$_2$: Subjects 1–10	A$_2$B$_2$: Subjects 11–20

Note: A = type of examination; B = nonverbal behavior: nervous = B$_1$, calm = B$_2$; C = defendant.

in the design. The design in Figure 7.15 allows us to test the same research hypotheses tested in the design illustrated in Figure 7.13, as well as an additional hypothesis about the potential effects of viewing one defendant after viewing a second defendant.

For some variables, repeated measures designs are simply not possible. Some independent variable effects may last so long that they interfere with later, different levels of the same variable. Consider, for example, an experiment in which two different teaching techniques are being compared. A repeated measures design could not be used because students may learn so much material with whichever technique is used first that further learning under a second technique would be too slight to be measured. Whether or not you encounter such problems when reading about a repeated measures design depends on some researchers' selection of independent variables. Like any other design, repeated measures designs make sense for some research hypotheses but not for all research hypotheses.

Participant Characteristics

Before we leave design, let's consider the use of participant characteristics as independent variables. **Participant characteristics**, *sometimes called subject variables, are variables that differentiate participants but cannot be manipulated and are not subject to random assignment*. Participant characteristics include such variables as gender, age, ethnicity, amount of formal education, height, and so forth. They can be included in an experimental design, but because they are not subject to manipulation or random assignment, they cannot be considered true independent variables in an experimental design. When reading research reports, however, you will often find that they are described as independent variables or sometimes called **subject variables**.

In the witness study, for example, I could include participant gender as a variable in the overall design. This would involve treating men and women as though they represented two different levels of an independent variable, gender. If I were to analyze the data and observe a main effect for gender, however, it would be ludicrous to interpret such a finding to mean that being male (or female) caused people to view witnesses as less credible. Instead, it would be more reasonable to conclude that some other systematic difference between men and women caused the effect, but I would have no empirical basis for declaring what that systematic difference might be. It could be attitudinal, hormonal, perceptual, or any other potential difference (Deaux & Major, 1987).

When participant characteristics are included in an experimental design, conclusions about cause-effect relationships cannot be drawn from any effects associated with such variables. Despite this restriction, you would not have to look very long before finding a research article in which the author(s) did exactly that. Drawing cause-effect conclusions about participant characteristics seems to be an almost irresistible temptation to many researchers. When this happens, it usually results from a very logical consideration of the effect and the researcher's knowledge about related research. Suggesting potential explanations for a gender effect, for example, is certainly within the realm of scientific research. On the other hand, concluding that a gender effect results from differential attitudes when attitudes have not been manipulated in the design falls well outside the logic of experimental research.

DEMONSTRATION VERSUS DEMOGRAPHY AGAIN

Earlier in the chapter the primary purpose of experimental research was described as testing whether or not a cause-effect relationship can be demonstrated. This purpose does not automatically rule out generalizing the results of the experiment, but generalization (demography) is secondary to testing the relationship (demonstration). If generalizing well beyond the experimental environment is an important part of your intentions as a consumer, you need to ensure that your efforts in that direction are not affected by the internal validity of the experimental design. If random assignment is not consistent with generalization, you should not generalize as though random assignment didn't occur.

Overgeneralization is also something to avoid. Although overgeneralization is a potential problem in any research method, experimental research seems particularly prone to the phrase "research has proved." Random assignment is critical to experimental research, but experimental research is a process that also depends on replication for its effectiveness. Like any procedure based on probability theory, random assignment works in the long run but may not be effective on a one-time-only basis. Any research requires replication before we can rely heavily on the results.

You should realize that a single experiment does not *prove* that a cause-effect relationship exists; rather, it *demonstrates* the existence of the relationship under the conditions created by the experimental procedures. Those conditions include the specific experimenter, participants, operational definitions, and a host of other potential factors that differ from one experiment to another. A demonstration that something can happen does not mean it always will happen. The more carefully a researcher attempts to eliminate alternative explanations, the more likely the demonstration will be replicated by others. Conducting, and consuming, a valid experiment requires paying attention to all aspects of experimental research.

SUMMARY

- Experimental research methods are the only methods designed specifically to test cause-effect hypotheses. Experiments are accomplished by manipulating the independent variable, randomly assigning participants to the various levels of the independent variable, controlling or eliminating alternative explanations, and measuring responses via the dependent variable. The independent variable is the suspected cause; the dependent variable is the effect.

- Generalizing the results of an experiment well beyond the experimental situation is logically impossible, for the major purpose of most experiments is to demonstrate that the cause-effect relationship *can* occur, not that it always occurs.

- The logic of experimental research is that any difference between groups of participants as measured by the dependent variable is caused by their different experiences with the independent variable. Therefore, an experimenter must maintain internal validity—must rule out alternative explanations of any obtained differences.

- Alternative explanations are generally ruled out through the use of random assignment to conditions created by manipulating the independent variable. These alternative explanations include history effects, maturation effects, testing effects, statistical regression effects, selection effects, and mortality effects.

- Control over the experimental situation can be used to rule out instrumentation effects, participant bias, and experimenter bias.

- The basic design of an experiment includes different groups representing different levels of a manipulated independent variable to which participants are randomly assigned. Adding a pretest to this design enables us to measure change as a function of the independent variable. Care must be taken, however, to avoid an interaction between treatment and testing.

- The Solomon four-group design can be used to measure testing effects, including a testing-treatment interaction. This added ability to test effects decreases the efficiency of the design with respect to testing the research hypothesis.

- When more than one independent variable is necessary, factorial designs must be used to assess both main effects and interaction effects. Main effects are simple effects due to one variable, whereas interaction effects are those caused by a combination of two or more independent variables.
- Repeated measures may be used with any experimental design, but only if the effects of an independent variable are not so long lasting as to interfere with subsequent levels of the same or another independent variable. Designs with repeated measures must also take into account the possibility of order effects.
- Although often used in experimental research, participant characteristics cannot be considered valid independent variables. Also called subject variables, they may indicate the presence of a systematic difference, but they are not themselves considered to be causal agents.

EXERCISES

1. Find a research article in which the authors identify the research as an experiment. Determine whether the investigators established temporal priority and used random assignment.

2. Using the same or a different article, identify the design used in the research.

3. Using the same or a different article, examine the design and procedure carefully for each of the alternative explanations described in the chapter.

4. Find an article in which the authors describe an interaction effect. Identify the variables involved in the interaction and try to explain the interaction to someone who has not read the article.

CHAPTER 8

Quasi-Experimental Research

Participants were randomly assigned to the high and low IQ groups.

—Confused student's paper

Overview

Quasi-experimental research, as the name implies, includes research methods that approximate but are not truly experimental methods. In this chapter, you will learn about the major types of quasi-experimental designs and will also be exposed to the types of statistical analyses appropriate for these designs. The mathematics may be complex, but the principles are not. You will also learn about designs that involve only a single participant.

INTRODUCTION

For a variety of different reasons, some of which were not understood by the student quoted at the beginning of this chapter, it is simply not possible to assign participants randomly to the different levels of many independent variables. It is also not possible to manipulate many independent variables. One cannot, for example, manipulate participants' levels of intelligence; even if one found a way to make such a manipulation, doing so would be well beyond the boundaries of ethical research. On the other hand, one can manipulate participants' knowledge about specific topics—which is what the confused student did—but that's not the same as manipulating levels of intelligence. Similarly, a researcher cannot assign participants to different gender categories. For these and other variables that cannot be controlled, true experimental research is not possible. It is possible, however, to test research hypotheses with approximations of experimental research. But don't let such labels as "quasi" and "approximations" lead you to think that quasi-experimental designs are somehow not quite as good as "real" experiments for adding to our knowledge. Like all research designs, quasi-experiments are excellent for some, but not all, research questions. Understanding such designs, including their limitations, will enable you to expand greatly the amount of research you can apply to the policy issue or program under consideration.

In this chapter, we will concern ourselves with **quasi-experimental designs—** *research designs that approximate experimental designs but do not include random assignment to conditions* (Shadish, Cook, & Campbell, 2002). Although quasi-experimental designs do not involve so rigorous a test of cause-effect hypotheses as do experimental designs, they do provide worthy alternatives when experiments are impossible, impractical, or unethical. Many of the designs discussed below can be used to avoid a number of alternative explanations fully described in Chapter 9. Quasi-experimental designs cannot, per se, avoid all of the alternative explanations that threaten internal validity; instead, logical analysis replaces random assignment.

As alternatives to experimental designs, quasi-experimental designs can be used to ask nearly the same questions as those asked through true experimental designs. Testing cause-effect questions—explanation—is also the main purpose of quasi-experimentation. Although the questions are pretty much the same, the specificity of the questions differs greatly. Recall from Chapter 7 that experimental research involves asking whether the independent variable can be demonstrated to cause the dependent variable—whether, for example, judges' instructions concerning reasonable doubt can cause jurors to arrive at a particular verdict.

In quasi-experimental research, the cause-effect aspect of the question remains, but its emphasis changes. Instead of asking whether the independent variable *causes* the dependent variable, the question becomes whether an independent variable *is an indicator* of whatever the real cause may be. You cannot sensibly ask, for example, whether gender causes verdicts; gender per se is not a legitimate cause. Instead, you must ask whether verdicts differ as a function of gender, whether gender is an indicator of some unknown cause, whether whatever may be causing verdicts to change is strongly associated with gender. Observing that males and females systematically differ with respect to the unknown cause is not the same as claiming gender is the cause.

A more realistic example of quasi-experimental research is the study I designed a number of years ago to examine community reactions to field tests of genetically altered organisms (Dane, 1988b). Genetically altered organisms are bacteria created in a laboratory through gene splicing or through some other form of recombinant DNA technology (see, for example, Human Genome Project, 2007). Field tests of such organisms involve placing the organism in a natural environment outside the laboratory in which they were created. One manufacturer of such organisms was field testing an organism to determine how well it survives winter and multiple-crop planting. I was interested in the reactions of people living in and around the community where the field test was being conducted.

By measuring attitudes on a variety of issues before, during, and after the field test took place, I hoped to be able to draw some conclusions about attitudinal changes that coincided with the field test. Reactions to the field test were considered indicators of whatever changes may have taken place, but I could not conclude that the field test caused any of the changes that might have occurred. It would be reasonable to assume that the field test was causing some change, but observed changes may also have been due to coincidental changes in weather patterns, employment opportunities, or any number of other potential factors that happened to coincide with the field test (i.e., history effects). As you learn about the various designs available for quasi-experimental research, you will also learn about some strategies for limiting the number of possible alternative explanations.

TIME-SERIES DESIGNS

Time-series designs are *a type of extended repeated measures design in which the dependent variable is measured several times before and after the introduction of the independent variable*; that is, a series of measures is taken over a period of time. There are two types of time-series designs: interrupted time-series and multiple time-series.

Interrupted Time-Series Design

Interrupted time-series designs take their name from the notion that *the independent variable is an interruption of ongoing activities, a change in the normal stream of events*. For example, the field test mentioned earlier is a change in the ongoing experiences of the people living in the vicinity of the test. Figure 8.1 contains two examples of an interrupted time-series design.

In the research diagrammed in Figure 8.1a, each O represents a set of measurements of attitudes toward a variety of different issues. The field test was designed to continue for a period of time but would not have been permanent. However, because the effects of the field test may last considerably longer than the physical presence of the test, it may be more appropriate to consider the field test to be associated with a permanent change, as depicted in Figure 8.1b. Another relatively permanent change might be a change in the requirements for graduation at your college; the change, although not permanent in any absolute sense, would be permanent relative to your period of matriculation.

| Figure 8.1 | Time-Series Design for (A) a Temporary Independent Variable and (B) a Permanent Independent Variable |

O_1	O_2	O_3	O_4	O_5	O_6	O_7	O_8	O_9	O_{10}	O_{11}	O_{12}
				↑ Independent variable is implemented		↑ Independent variable is removed					

A. Interrupted time-series design for a temporary change. The independent variable is implemented and then removed.

O_1	O_2	O_3	O_4	O_5	O_6	O_7	O_8	O_9	O_{10}	O_{11}	O_{12}
				↑ Independent variable is implemented							

B. Interrupted time-series design for a permanent change. The independent variable is implemented and remains in effect for the duration of the study.

Whatever the research hypothesis under consideration, the measures obtained before the introduction of the independent variable (O_1 through O_5 in Figure 8.1) provide a way to determine the extent to which maturation and testing may be alternative explanations. If the results of those measures remain fairly stable, then testing and maturation are not likely alternative explanations. On the other hand, time-series designs are subject to history effects. If, for example, another chemical leakage incident such as that which occurred in Bhopal, India (Union Carbide Company, 2007) happened during the field test I was studying, I could not have determined whether any change in attitudes was associated with the field test or with the chemical leakage incident.

The analyses that are appropriate for time-series designs are forthrightly called time-series analyses. The mathematics of time-series analyses is beyond the scope of this book, but there are readable references you can consult on this topic (McDowall, McCleary, Meidinger, & Hay, 1980; Ostrom, 1978). Before doing so, however, you should have a solid background in multiple regression techniques. The essential basis of time-series analyses is a comparison between the preindependent-variable observations and postindependent-variable observations. For example, the preindependent- and postindependent-variable trends in Figure 8.2 are the same, indicating that the independent variable had no effect or that its effect was canceled out by some history effect.

Figure 8.2	Results for a Permanent Time-Series Design in Which the Independent Variable Appears to Have No Effect on the Dependent Variable

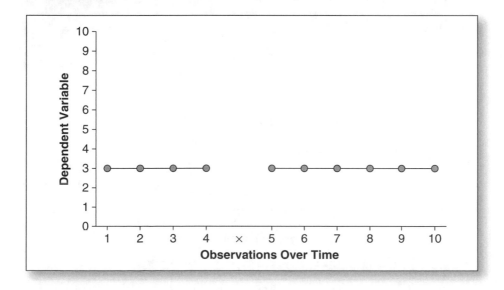

In Figure 8.2, whether or not the independent variable represents a permanent change does not alter the conclusion, although it does make a difference in the actual calculations of the time-series statistics. The results displayed indicate no effect at all for the independent variable. However, this interpretation must be qualified by the possibility that some history effect canceled what may have been a very effective independent variable. If the preindependent-variable trend is different from the postindependent-variable trend, then you may conclude there is an effect, which again must be qualified by the possibility that the effect is a history effect rather than a true effect of the independent variable. Figure 8.3 provides an example of a time-series study in which an effect was observed.

Drawing conclusions from a time-series design is not always as easy as is suggested in Figures 8.2 and 8.3, for quasi-experimental data are not always as straightforward as those presented here. More often than not, the trends observed before and after introduction of the independent variable cannot be described by a straight line. One reason for this difficulty is the lack of control one has in such research; because the researcher cannot manipulate the independent variable, he or she may not be able to control other variables that may

Figure 8.3	Results for a Permanent Time-Series Design in Which the Independent Variable Clearly Has a Dramatic Effect on the Dependent Variable

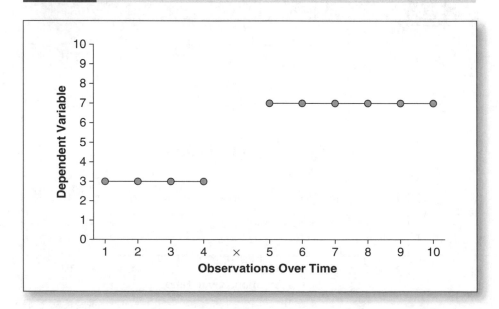

coincide with it. Consequently, the data become more difficult to interpret. The results illustrated in Figure 8.4 are far more representative of typical time-series data. Deciding whether the results shown in Figure 8.4 represent an effect for the independent variable or merely the continuation of an unstable trend requires a statistical decision, which is why we must rely on time-series analyses to interpret data from such designs.

Figure 8.4	Results for a Permanent Time-Series Design in Which the Independent Variable (X), Implemented Between Observations 4 and 5, May Have Had an Effect on the Dependent Variable

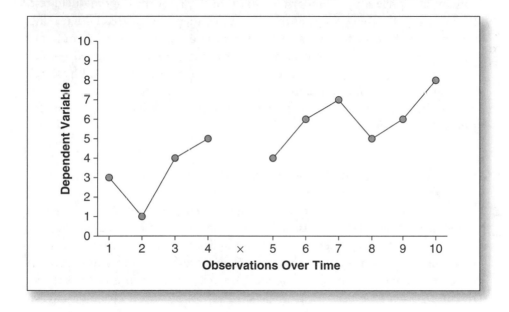

Multiple Time-Series Design

One variation of the interrupted time-series design is the multiple time-series design. In this design, two sets of observations are compared. As illustrated in Figure 8.5, one set of observations includes the manipulation, whereas the other set, which serves as a quasi-experimental control group, does not. The existence of the control group (Group 2 in Figure 8.5) guards against a history effect but only if the corresponding observations are obtained simultaneously. Analyzing multiple time-series data is considerably more complex in practice than is analyzing interrupted time-series data, but the theoretical basis for the analysis is the same.

Figure 8.5	Multiple Time-Series Design for a Permanent Change										
Group 1	O_1	O_2	O_3	O_4	$(IV)O_5$	O_6	O_7	O_8	O_9	O_{10}	O_{11}	O_{12}
Group 2 (control)	O_1	O_2	O_3	O_4	O_5	O_6	O_7	O_8	O_9	O_{10}	O_{11}	O_{12}

Returning to the community reaction to a field test as an example, Group 1 in Figure 8.5 would be composed of people living in the community where the field test is being conducted. Group 2 would include people in some other community, preferably a similar one that is unaware of the ongoing field test. If I measured the two groups at the same time, then it is less likely that a history effect will occur for one group but not the other. Of course, I could not be as sure about it as I could have been if I had randomly assigned participants to the two groups. However, with careful monitoring of the research environment and some common sense, one can all but eliminate history, maturation, instrumentation, and testing effects as alternative explanations for time-series designs.

REGRESSION-DISCONTINUITY DESIGNS

Time-series designs are **longitudinal designs**—*designs in which the same participants are repeatedly measured over time*. For some research projects, however, it is too expensive or otherwise undesirable to make repeated measurements. In such instances, cross-sectional designs are more appropriate. A **cross-sectional design** involves *one measurement of different groups that represent different time periods*. It might involve, for example, grouping participants according to the number of years they have lived in the community where the field test is occurring. Such a design, called a regression-discontinuity design, is illustrated in Figure 8.6.

The underlying logic of the regression-discontinuity design is the same as that for the time-series design. The different groups represent different amounts of experience with the independent variable. In Figure 8.6, for example, Group 8 could contain residents who have been living in the community for the longest period of time, and presumably the field test constitutes the greatest amount of change for them by virtue of the existence of more experience with the status quo. Group 5 would then contain residents who have lived in the community the least amount of time and therefore have not as much basis for comparison

Figure 8.6	A Regression-Discontinuity Design With Eight Groups	
Groups 1–4 do not experience the independent variable	Group 1	O_1
	Group 2	O_2
	Group 3	O_3
	Group 4	O_4
Groups 5–8 do experience the independent variable	Group 5	O_5
	Group 6	O_6
	Group 7	O_7
	Group 8	O_8

for the changes that may result from the field test. Group 4 in the control community would, in turn, have the longest period of residence in their community, and Group 1 would be the most recent residents in the control community.

The design is called a regression-discontinuity design because the groups that do not experience the manipulation (Groups 1 through 4 in Figure 8.6) are used to project expected values by way of multiple-regression analyses. These expected values are then compared to the actual values obtained from groups that experienced the independent variable (Groups 5 through 8 in Figure 8.6). The expected values are what would be expected if the independent variable had no effect.

Figure 8.7 illustrates the results from a regression-discontinuity design in which the independent variable apparently increased scores on the dependent variable. The line with squares represents actual scores, whereas the line with circles represents the scores that would be expected if the independent variable had no effect. The difference between the two lines represents the effect of the independent variable.

Although the regression-discontinuity design may seem to be more efficient than the time-series design, the relative efficiency of being able to obtain all measures at the same time is offset by the requirement of additional assumptions about the participants. Experience with the independent variable may be determined equivalently under both designs, but the regression-discontinuity design requires one to assume that the independent variable has not changed during the time period of interest. If, for example, a major incident occurred

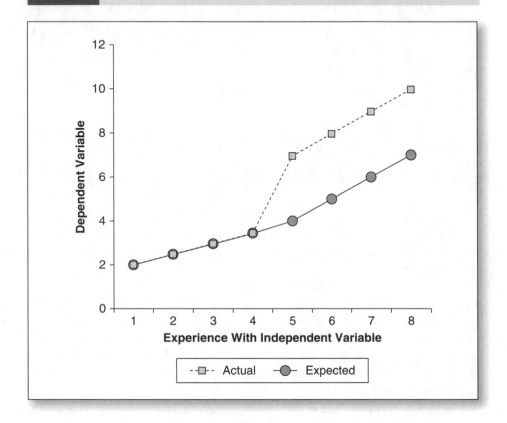

Figure 8.7 Ideal Results From a Regression-Discontinuity Design. "Expected" represents values expected if the independent variable had no effect.

during the field test, such as a demonstration by an environmental group, the independent variable would also change. It may also be that some of the more recent residents, who are assumed to experience less change in the community because they haven't lived there as long, moved to the community because they wanted to live someplace that was environmentally stable. Without careful monitoring of the ongoing activities and without attempting to measure the previous experiences of the participants, one cannot be sure the groups in a regression-discontinuity design differ only in amount and not in kind of the independent variable they have experienced.

Data analyses for regression-discontinuity designs, as you might expect from the name, involve regression analyses. Multiple regression analyses are used to determine whether the equations for the two lines in Figure 8.7 are the same. If the statistical analyses indicate that the two equations are not the same, then one can conclude that the independent variable had an effect, provided one can logically rule out alternative explanations. Like time-series analyses, the mathematics associated with multiple regression is beyond the scope of this book, but Kerlinger (1979) is an excellent source for this topic. For illustration purposes, however, you don't need to understand the math to understand the principle; either the two lines are the same or they're not.

NONEQUIVALENT GROUPS BASIC PRETEST DESIGNS

When it is not possible to make multiple measurements over time, to measure a relatively large number of different groups of participants, or to assign participants randomly to different levels of an independent variable, then an abbreviated combination of time-series and regression-discontinuity designs may be used. The design in Figure 8.8 should remind you of the basic pretest design described in Chapter 7. Except for the fact that participants are not randomly assigned to different conditions (a very important exception), the

Figure 8.8   The Nonequivalent Groups Basic Pretest Design

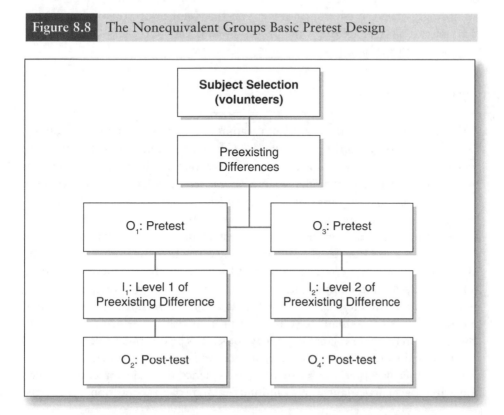

nonequivalent groups basic pretest design is identical to the basic pretest design. The use of pretesting (O_1 and O_3 in Figure 8.8) enables one to determine whether any change exhibited by those experiencing the independent variable also would have occurred in its absence.

Of course, the nonequivalent groups basic pretest design, like the time-series and regression-discontinuity designs, is subject to selection effects because it lacks random assignment to conditions. When it is necessary or otherwise desirable to use this design, alternative explanations must be ruled out through logical analysis rather than through random assignment and control over variables. Because it is highly similar to the basic pretest design discussed in Chapter 7, the statistical analyses used for the nonequivalent groups design are essentially the same: These include analysis of variance, the Mann-Whitney U test, and chi-square (Nowaczyk, 1988).

Matching, discussed in Chapter 7, provides an alternative to random assignment but is not as effective as random assignment for dealing with selection effects. Matching, you should recall, involves measuring the extent to which two or more groups differ on some preexisting characteristic, such as intelligence or experience, and adjusting the size of the independent variable effect accordingly. There is no end, however, to the number of potential variables that may require matching, and therefore one can never be sure one has matched participants on all relevant characteristics.

SELF-SELECTION

Although it may seem that random assignment is always preferable to quasi-experimental designs, such is not the case. There are a number of situations in which self-selection is the primary interest rather than an alternative explanation to be avoided. **Self-selection** refers to *any circumstances in which the participants are already at different levels of an independent variable*, usually because they have some desire to be at that level. Your own experience with class scheduling is an example. Unless you are very different from most students, you would rather be in a position to choose your courses than to have them randomly assigned to you by the registrar's office. When a research hypothesis involves a similar self-selection component, then a quasi-experimental design provides greater **external validity**—*the relationship between the research experience and everyday experience*—than does an experimental design. Self-selection is not always an alternative explanation; it may sometimes be the independent variable.

The key distinction between experimental and quasi-experimental research is the manner in which the participants experience the independent variable. Experimental participants are randomly assigned to conditions, whereas quasi-experimental research involves capitalizing on preexisting differences among participants. Whenever such preexisting differences are the focus of research, quasi-experimental designs may be more appropriate than their experimental counterparts. We next turn to considering designs in which there is only one participant.

SINGLE-PARTICIPANT DESIGNS

Known also as single-subject design, **single-participant design** is *a design specifically tailored to include only one participant in the study*. Whenever research interests center on a single person, perhaps a client experiencing therapy, single-participant designs are appropriate. They are also appropriate when the population of interest is so highly homogeneous that studying more than one member of the population is redundant. Learning studies involving experimental animals, for example, generally involve the assumption that one animal's reaction to the independent variable will be the same as any other animal's reaction. There are three types of single-participant designs: case study, baseline, and withdrawal.

Case Study Design

As the name implies, a **case study** involves *intensive study of a single participant over an extended period of time*. The most common example of such designs is a therapist monitoring a client's responses to therapy. By definition, therapy begins as soon as the therapist and client meet, so there is usually no opportunity to monitor the client before the independent variable—therapy—is experienced. Of course, self-reports from the client provide some information about pretherapy experiences, but that is not the same as directly measuring the dependent variable prior to the initiation of therapy. Using traditional design notation, a case study is illustrated in Figure 8.9. Of course, there is only a single participant and therefore no reason to include group numbers in the notation.

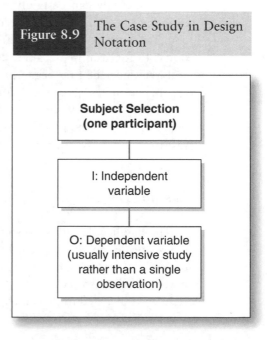

Figure 8.9 The Case Study in Design Notation

Subject Selection (one participant)

I: Independent variable

O: Dependent variable (usually intensive study rather than a single observation)

By now you should realize there are a host of alternative explanations to this design, which is essentially the basic design without random assignment. However, a series of logical assumptions may enable a researcher to rule out most of the alternative explanations (Dermer & Hoch, 1999). For example, in a therapy situation, it is reasonable to assume that a problem existed before the therapy began or the client would not have sought therapy. Thus, a measure of the dependent variable before initiation of the independent variable is not always necessary, although it can be used when appropriate and possible. More important, a case study involves a series of intensive, in-depth observations, and many of those observations may provide information that can be used to rule out additional alternative explanations.

For the most part, case study designs are utilized when the researcher is interested in what happens at the level of a specific individual, the specific conditions experienced by the participant. Similarly, as in all research, conclusions drawn from a case study should be limited to similar situations or participants. Although it is certainly possible to generalize from a case study, generalization comes from replication, repeating the study under different circumstances, in this case with a different participant. The major assumption underlying generalization is that the research participants represent the individuals to whom the generalization is applied, and a single research study rarely represents any larger group of people. Animals bred for research may be sufficiently homogeneous to allow generalizations, but people are rarely that homogeneous.

A case study can certainly be used to develop research hypotheses to be examined in later studies. Indeed, hypothesis generation is probably the most common purpose of case studies. Piaget's (1984) famous theory of child development, for example, came about through his case studies of individual children. Since he first began proposing hypotheses generated from case studies, many of his theoretical formulations have been supported empirically through a variety of different methods. There may be rare times, however, when one can reasonably generalize from a single participant, in which case researchers usually use a baseline design.

Baseline Design

The baseline design is, to some extent, an elaboration of the case study. In a **baseline design**, *preindependent variable measures are compared with postindependent measures for a single participant*. Illustrated in Figure 8.10, the baseline design is very similar to a time-series design, except that only one participant is included in the study. Multiple baseline measures may be taken, and one can use repeated measurements after a change in the independent variable regardless of whether or not the independent variable is manipulated. Indeed, the use of multiple measures as a baseline design is one of the ways in which researchers obtain sufficient data to rule out alternative explanations (Dermer & Hoch, 1999).

Just as with time-series designs, the measures in the baseline design are obtained before a change in the independent variable and are compared to those obtained after the change. If one can establish sufficient control over the research environment and can obtain sufficient measures to rule out alternative explanations, then the baseline design can be as powerful as any of the designs discussed in this or any other chapter. Laboratory rats raised in a controlled environment, for example, can generally be assumed to be so homogeneous as to make each rat representative of other laboratory rats. Testing the effect of an independent variable, such as the addition of sucrose to the animal's water, would enable one to demonstrate a

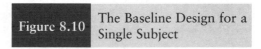

Figure 8.10   The Baseline Design for a Single Subject

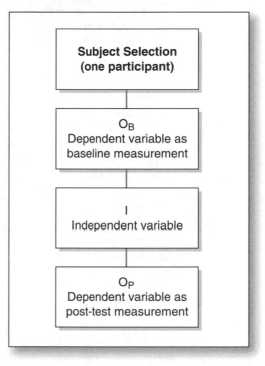

cause-effect relationship between the presence of sucrose and the animal's drinking behavior. If the researcher measured consumption of water prior to adding the sucrose and again after adding the sucrose, he or she would have a very powerful test of the effects of sucrose. Indeed, baseline designs using laboratory rats to test addiction to cocaine (Peele & DeGrandpre, 1998) are the basis for a number of antidrug television commercials that claim that rats prefer cocaine to food and will eventually starve to death before giving up cocaine in favor of food.

The strength of the baseline study is that the measure of the dependent variable before the change in the independent variable enables one to assess its effects. With the case study, for example, one can only guess about the preexisting state of the individual participant, even if that guess is based on self-reports from the participant. The baseline design allows one to measure premanipulation levels directly. Despite their strength, baseline studies should be replicated to assess actual generalizability of the results with greater confidence. Remember that if the researcher is interested only in that one, specific participant, there is no need for the researcher to generalize the results, but

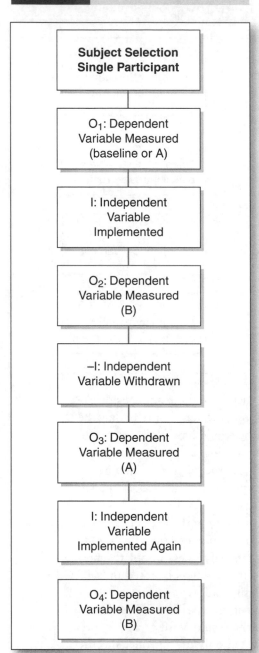

Figure 8.11   The Withdrawal Design

Subject Selection
Single Participant

O_1: Dependent
Variable Measured
(baseline or A)

I: Independent
Variable
Implemented

O_2: Dependent
Variable Measured
(B)

–I: Independent
Variable Withdrawn

O_3: Dependent
Variable Measured
(A)

I: Independent
Variable
Implemented Again

O_4: Dependent
Variable Measured
(B)

you need to generalize results in order to use them to inform a public policy (unless the policy applies only to that one research participant).

Withdrawal Design

Despite the strength of the baseline design, it is not the most powerful among the single-participant designs. That distinction belongs to the **withdrawal design,** in which *the treatment is presented and removed several times.* Known also as an A-B-A-B design, the withdrawal design involves measuring the dependent variable before the independent variable is manipulated, after it has been manipulated, again after the manipulation has been removed, and so on for as many repetitions as seems appropriate. The withdrawal design is illustrated in Figure 8.11, wherein it is easy to see why the design is also known as an A-B-A-B design.

Usually, the *A* condition or measurement refers to the baseline state of the participant—the state without the treatment or manipulation—and the *B* condition or measurement refers to the state of the participant while experiencing the treatment. At some point the treatment is withdrawn and the participant returns to baseline, after which the independent variable is manipulated again. Of course, this design may be used only if the independent variable can be manipulated. Even if the independent variable creates a permanent change in the participant, the withdrawal design enables one to measure its permanence, and additional measures can be used to assess how comprehensive the permanent effect may be.

Using the study of cocaine addiction in laboratory rats as example, one could measure food consumption, replace the food with cocaine, measure consumption, return the food, and so on so long as one thinks is necessary in order to demonstrate the effect. The same procedure could be used to measure reinforcement using something other than cocaine. On the other hand, one probably would not use a withdrawal design to study the effect of hypothalamic lesions, for once one induces lesions in an animal one cannot remove them, and thus the animal could never return to the baseline state. Permanence can be a difficult characteristic to ascertain. For example, in a therapy study with a human participant, the researcher may stop the therapy, but doing so does not necessarily negate all of the effects therapy has had thus far. Permanence involves more than removing the manipulation; the withdrawal design requires the removal of the *effects* of the manipulation, as well as its physical presence. The researcher must also be able to control alternative explanations, such as history, before drawing a cause-effect conclusion from a withdrawal study.

Data Analyses

Data analyses for single-participant designs tend to be extremely simple and straightforward. Because there is no variation among participants, there is no need for statistical procedures such as analysis of variance or regression. In general, single-participant data analyses tend to be "interocular trauma" tests; either the effect is so apparent it hits you between the eyes or it is not there. A researcher might, for example, graph the daily consumption of food in the rat study or graph a client's self-reported behavior problems. The graph should clearly demonstrate the effect, much as the graph of ideal time-series results in Figure 8.3 does. Because there is only one participant, there is little need for examining the margin of error associated with the conclusions; either the effect is there or it's not.

SUMMARY

- Although experimental designs provide the best way to test cause-effect relationships, there are times when experiments are not possible. At such times, quasi-experimental designs are preferred. Quasi-experimental designs lack random assignment.

- Time-series designs are longitudinal designs involving repeated measures of the dependent variable before and after implementation of the independent variable. The repeated measures can be used to assess maturation and testing effects.
- History effects can be assessed through multiple time-series designs, which involve simultaneously measuring more than one group of participants.
- Regression-discontinuity designs involve a single measure of the dependent variable across groups that differ along a dimension defined by the independent variable. They are cross-sectional designs that can be used when longitudinal designs are not feasible.
- When repeated measures or a large number of groups cannot be included in a research project, the nonequivalent groups basic design may be used to approximate an experimental design. In this design, two or more groups that have not been randomly assigned to conditions are measured before and after implementation of the independent variable.
- All quasi-experimental designs are subject to selection effects as an alternative explanation. Selection may, however, be considered a function of the independent variable if self-selection is part of the phenomenon being studied.
- There are also research hypotheses that can be tested with single-participant designs, but these are limited to hypotheses about the specific participant or involve the assumption that the participant represents a homogeneous group of others.
- In a case study, the participant is observed after the independent variable is introduced. A baseline design involves measuring the dependent variable before and after the independent variable is manipulated. In a withdrawal design, measures are taken sequentially with successive presentation and removal of the manipulation.
- If the independent variable can be manipulated and the research environment controlled, single-participant designs may be used to test cause-effect hypotheses but may lack the generality of more traditional experimental designs.
- Data analyses for single-participant designs typically involve graphic presentations instead of complicated statistical analyses. The effect of the independent variable is either apparent or not.

EXERCISES

1. Find an article in which the authors report on research based on a quasi-experimental design. Identify the variables that could not be manipulated.

2. Find an article in which the authors report on a study involving a time-series design. Determine which type of time-series design was used and identify the length of time the participants were observed.

3. Find an article in which the authors report on research involving a single-participant design. Consider each alternative explanation and decide whether any of them could have an effect on the conclusions drawn by the authors.

CHAPTER 9

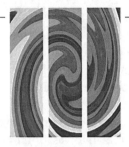

Survey Research

The latest research on polls has turned up some interesting variables. It turns out, for example, that people will tell you any old thing that pops into their heads.

—Caption from a cartoon by Charles David Saxon

Overview

The purpose of this chapter is to introduce the main issues and methods of survey research. Survey research includes methods in which participants are asked questions directly. The questions may be part of an interview schedule or a questionnaire and may be asked through one of several different procedures. It is extremely difficult to interpret the results of survey research if you know nothing about how those results are obtained, so you will learn about techniques for preparing survey instruments and which research purposes are most effectively accomplished via surveys. You will also learn how researchers administer a survey face to face or via the telephone (interviewing) and how they administer a survey through the mail (questionnaires). The relative merits of each technique will be discussed, and sampling issues specific to each technique will be examined. Finally, you will learn about general conventions for data analysis for survey research.

INTRODUCTION

Survey methods are probably the oldest methods in the researcher's repertoire, and they are the methods with which the general public is most familiar. All of us have asked people for information, and all of us have been asked by others to provide information. As humorously illustrated in the opening quote, however, there is more to survey research than simply asking other people to provide information. How researchers conduct scientific surveys and how to evaluate such research is what this chapter is all about.

Survey research is a general label applied to a variety of different research methods that share a common purpose. **Survey research** involves *obtaining information directly from a group of individuals*. More often than not, it includes interviews or questionnaires, but it is important to keep in mind that the use of an interview or a questionnaire does not, by itself, define survey research methods; the procedure is not what defines the method, but rather the method is defined by the manner in which the procedure is carried out.

Survey research methods involve obtaining information directly from the participants by posing questions. The questions may be presented orally, on paper, or in some combination, but the response comes from the person to whom the question is addressed at the time the question is asked; it is, so to speak, a live data collection technique. Thus, the researcher and the participant are working together to collect the data; the researcher asks and the participant answers. Even when questions are written on paper, you need to keep in mind the interactive aspect of survey research. Responses must be interpreted in terms of potential self-presentation effects and other effects related to recollection; thus, live does not refer to the researcher's being physically present while the questions are answered but instead refers to participants' awareness that someone (the researcher) is going to be learning about them through their responses.

Although interviewing and questionnaires may be part of any type of research project, the sample size helps to distinguish survey research from other methods. The sample size in survey research is generally large, although it is not possible to provide an exact range. A survey research project may include as few as 100 participants or as many as 300 million.

As you might expect, directly obtaining information from a group of participants is more efficient for some research purposes than others. Survey methods are most appropriate for description and prediction, although they may be used less efficiently for exploration and action. Even though surveys can sometimes be used for explanatory research, they typically are not used for explanatory research purposes because it is difficult to manipulate independent variables and assign participants randomly to conditions via survey techniques.

Description is perhaps the most frequent purpose for survey methods. The classic example is the U.S. Decennial Census, which includes a sample of hundreds of millions of participants. The relative frequency data obtained from the census are often used by other researchers as a basis for their sampling procedures, particularly those who want to obtain a sample representing a particular region of the country. On a smaller scale, the examinations you take in class can be considered a form of survey research. Your instructor, through a questionnaire called an exam, attempts to assess the relative amount of information you can correctly recall about the subject matter. Examinations, however, are missing at least one important ingredient of scientific research: The results are rarely reported to the scientific community.

The predictive survey research with which you may be most familiar is the use of college entrance examinations to predict first-year grades in college. The results of the research are reported, although their circulation is somewhat limited. A more traditional use of survey methods is the work of Hill, Rubin, and Peplau (1976), who attempted to determine the characteristics that predict the continuation or breakup of romantically involved couples. Although a number of variables were related to the status of the relationship, the predominant predictor was the general similarity of the two people. The more similar the two individuals in the relationship, the more likely they were to remain a couple during the two-year period of the study. We will come back to Hill et al.'s research, but first we'll briefly examine why survey research is inefficient for exploratory and action purposes.

Although survey research invariably involves either a questionnaire or an interview, you will soon learn that there is more to survey research than simply putting together a collection of questions. Surveys can be used for exploratory research, but not with any degree of efficiency. One of the first rules of survey research is to know what kind of information one wants to collect. The survey instrument should be designed on the basis of a research hypothesis, a condition antithetical to exploratory research. More often than not, designing a good survey study involves too much time and effort for exploratory research purposes.

If the intended effect of action research is to change the opinions of a large group of people, survey methods are an appropriate means by which to accomplish such research. Back (1980), for example, described the important role of surveys in an extensive program of research concerning population control. The surveys were used to assess the effectiveness of information campaigns designed to change attitudes about population control in general and birth control as a specific means. In the majority of action research, however, systematic observation or indirect measurement (see Chapter 10) is probably more appropriate. In the population control study, for example, the best measurement of the intended effect might be the birthrate in a selected target area. Survey methods may help to pinpoint reasons for a behavior change, but surveys may not be the most efficient way to measure the change itself.

In general, any question that can be expressed in terms of the relative frequency of information can be addressed through survey research. Put another way, whenever a researcher wants to know what a lot of people are thinking but doesn't necessarily need to know why they are thinking that way, survey methods can be used.

SURVEY CONTENT

There are three different types of information that may be obtained from survey respondents, the participants in a survey research project: facts, opinions, and behaviors. Although most surveys include all three types of information, we will examine them separately. The words used to label the different types of information may be familiar, but they have very specific meanings in the context of survey research.

A **fact** is *a phenomenon or characteristic available to anyone who knows how to observe it*. Often called sociological or demographic characteristics, facts include such variables as age, race, gender, income, and years of education. Facts are anything that can be verified independently. Hill et al. found that couples who were similar in age, education, and physical attractiveness were much more likely to remain in the relationship than were couples whose facts were not similar.

In most surveys, the word "fact" is somewhat misleading because respondents' self-reports are usually accepted without independent verification. That a survey fact can be verified doesn't necessarily mean that it will be verified, and respondents have been known to misrepresent themselves on a variety of different facts. Don't confuse the label as it is used in survey research with its use in everyday speech; just because someone says it's so doesn't make it so.

An **opinion** is *an expression of a respondent's preference, feeling, or behavioral intention*. Opinions can be objectively measured, but they cannot be verified independently. Suppose, for example, I declined a social invitation by telling my friends that I was going to stay home in order to finish writing this chapter. Thus, my stated intentions may have led my friends to believe that I intended to complete this chapter. But there is no way that those people could have verified that my intentions truly were to finish this chapter. I could have been going through the motions to make people think I worked hard, for example, while having no real intention of bringing the project to completion. As you read this now, however, you can verify the fact that I did complete this chapter, but at the time I wrote this no one could have verified my intentions. Indeed, even though you know that I finished writing the chapter, you don't know that I did that work the same evening I declined that social invitation.

Therefore, the major difference between facts and opinions concerns agreement about the ways in which the two can be operationally defined. A researcher can operationally define my age in terms of the date of birth on my birth certificate, for example, and encounter little or no disagreement about that operational definition; it has inherent face validity as well as inherent reliability (anyone who can read my birth certificate can calculate my age). However, there may be considerable disagreement about the face validity of defining my intention to complete this chapter in terms of my sitting in front of the computer; that I'm sitting here with the file open doesn't necessarily mean that I intend to finish the chapter. That differential consensus about operational definitions exists does not necessarily mean that facts are necessarily more valid than opinions. It does mean that the validity of facts is easier to establish than the validity of opinions.

Using agreed-upon operational definitions of opinions concerning closeness, love, traditional sex roles, and religiosity, Hill et al. (1976) found that all these variables were related to a successful relationship. In general, the more similar were the couple's opinions on these topics, the more likely the couple was to remain in their relationship.

The third type of survey content, **behavior,** *refers to an action completed by a respondent.* A typical behavior question may be worded something like, "How many times did you attend your research methods class this week?" Like facts, behaviors can be verified but only if a witness or indirect evidence can be obtained. Hill et al. (1976), for example, included questions about such behaviors as frequency of sexual intercourse and cohabitation. Clearly, the former is more difficult to verify than the latter. Interestingly, respondents' self-reports of these behaviors were not related to the success of their relationships.

Although opinions may contain a behavioral component, opinions involve intentions—How many times will you attend your class next week?—rather than actual completion of the behavior. Without verification, behaviors (and facts) can only be measured through self-reports. You must keep in mind that self-reports are not the same as verified, independent evidence; information from the two sources doesn't always agree.

Within any categorization system, there always seem to be things that do not fit cleanly. Knowledge is one of these things. Because most of their respondents were college students, Hill et al. attempted to assess knowledge through SAT math and verbal scores. Other researchers may measure knowledge in other subject areas, but the problem involves determining whether or not, for the purposes of analysis, knowledge should be considered a fact (an SAT score is verifiable) or a behavior (an attempt to remember information) or an opinion (a belief that the knowledge area is important). The resolution to the problem depends on the research purposes: If the researcher is using knowledge as an operational definition of a behavior, then treating the variable as a behavior measure is a solution.

Because most surveys include all three types of content, there is a tendency to disregard distinctions among them. Do not fall prey to this tendency. As you will learn later in this chapter, some types of content are best given precedence over other types of content. If you don't pay attention to the type of content in a survey, you may introduce considerable error into your interpretation of the results. The nature of self-report information already introduces some error into survey research (Phillips, 1971), and there is no point to adding more error through careless interpretation of survey results.

SURVEY INSTRUMENTS

Just as the dials, gauges, and lights on the instrument panel of an automobile provide the means by which a driver obtains information about the car, the items on a survey instrument provide the means by which a researcher obtains information about respondents. The item topics, instructions, item formats, and arrangement of the items can all have an effect on the information the researcher obtains. In this section, you will learn enough about these issues to evaluate the quality of survey research in order to interpret results more accurately. The discussion is equally appropriate for interviews and questionnaires, with the exceptions that interviewers can be trained to overcome some instrument shortcomings and questionnaires cannot be altered once given to respondents. The discussion is also relevant to any data collected through a questionnaire, even if the research is technically not survey research. Some of what you read below will not apply to your critical analysis if you are not able to see the actual instrument as it was presented to the respondents, but the general considerations can be used to evaluate instruments even when you are privy only to a summary of the instrument.

Survey Topics

Every survey instrument should have a topic—a central issue to which most of the items are related. Which topic is addressed, of course, depends on the researcher's interests and research hypotheses. The items included on a survey should be at least partially derived from theoretical interests. Although this may seem obvious and unnecessary, it is too often the case that researchers include items, sometimes create entire questionnaires, without giving enough thought to what questions are to be answered by the data. Such shotgun approaches to data collection rarely provide the wealth of informative data expected by those who use them, but that does not necessarily stop researchers from using a shotgun approach and, subsequently, reporting the results of the survey.

Some topics will be perceived as sensitive by the respondents, and questions dealing with these topics are likely candidates for responses based on self-presentation instead of accuracy. Data from such questions may be incomplete or reflect beliefs about what is appropriate. Respondents are generally unwilling to admit to illegal or socially deviant activities, for example, but they may also be unwilling to report even what seems to be innocuous information. In a one survey (Dane, 1988b), for instance, respondents were unwilling to identify their employer. They had no reservations about revealing what they did for a living, but did not want to tell us for whom they did it. Thus, survey results may often not contain information that you think should have been obvious for the researcher to include. The researcher may have included the questions, but may not have obtained enough responses to enable the data to be analyzed and reported.

That certain topics or items may be sensitive, however, does not automatically mean that a researcher will not be able to obtain information. **Anonymity**, which *exists when no one knows the identity of the person who provided the information*, or **confidentiality**, which applies when *there is a promise not to reveal the identity of the person who provided the information*, can facilitate respondents' willingness to reveal such information. Kinsey and his colleagues (Kinsey, Pomeroy, & Martin, 1948; Kinsey, Pomeroy, Martin, & Gebhard, 1953) were able to obtain interview responses on a topic as sensitive as sexual practices, and Hunt (1974) was able to obtain questionnaire responses on the same topic. When a researcher includes sensitive topics in a survey instrument, the researcher must be especially concerned about the validity of the data, but that does not mean that one cannot obtain valid data. Following ethical guidelines (Chapter 2) and treating respondents as one would want to be treated usually is sufficient to obtain cooperation.

Survey Instructions

The instructions for completing the survey instrument can be used to eliminate some of the response biases mentioned above through assurances of anonymity or confidentiality. Of course, one must be careful to be sure that one can guarantee anonymity or confidentiality if one promises to do so (Stone, 2002). False claims are unethical and usually cannot be justified simply in order to produce better response rates or more accurate responses. As a consumer of survey research, you may not have access to the specific instructions used by the researcher(s), but there is usually a summary of the instructions included in survey research articles. You need to consider those instructions as critically as you can in order to understand the way in which the instructions can affect the responses obtained in the survey.

The first part of any set of instructions should be a brief introduction to the study. When using a questionnaire, the instructions are usually placed on a cover sheet or in an accompanying cover letter. When conducting an interview, the introduction of the study is usually the first statement made to the respondents. The instructions should explain what the survey is about, how the results will be used, why the individual respondent's data are important to the study, and the level of anonymity or confidentiality with which the data will be treated. Ideally, the instructions will also include some mention of how respondents were selected to be included in the survey, such as random selection from the telephone book. The instructions don't need to contain great detail about the sampling procedures, but most respondents are interested in finding out how they came to be respondents and may become suspicious if they are not so informed.

More specific instructions about how to complete survey items are usually included throughout the instrument. Inclusion of sample items that illustrate the type of response or the length of responses for open-ended items tends to increase the amount of usable data (Dillman, 1978, 2007). If more than one topic is covered by the survey, the items for each topic are usually separated by brief explanations about the kind of information desired. Something as simple as "In this section, you are being asked to provide your opinion about several political issues" would be an adequate transitional explanation. In general, any point at which the topic or response format changes is a good point to include transitional instructions. Such instructions need not be extensive; they should provide a transition to avoid surprising respondents and inform them how to provide the information desired.

Survey Formats

The general layout of any survey instrument is not something to which you will be privy as a consumer, but understanding the variety of survey formats will enable you to evaluate survey results more critically because a great deal of information about the format can be gleaned from the more general description of the procedures that are included in comprehensive research reports. The format should, of course, be neat. One characteristic that contributes to neatness is space between items. Spacing prevents a cluttered appearance and makes it less likely that a respondent or interviewer will skip an item. Researchers who are tempted to make the instrument appear shorter than it is by crunching the items together generally have problems with inaccurate or missing responses. The respondent who begins to tire before turning the first page (or before noticing the interviewer turning the first page) is probably going to decide that the remainder of the instrument will require too much time and effort. Short is not necessarily better; what is better is anything that helps the respondent to understand.

Response formats for specific items were discussed in detail in Chapter 6, the chapter on measurement and scaling. However, some general considerations need to be addressed here. Regardless of the format selected, the researcher should be sure the respondents and interviewers understand how to use the format. If a researcher asks an open-ended question—the kind of question asked on essay exams—the researcher should be sure to allow sufficient space to write a response. If the respondent is to choose from among multiple choices, the choices should represent the range of possible responses and be mutually exclusive. If the response involves choosing a point on a continuum, then clear labels for the endpoints of the continuum should be included. Your ability to understand the labels used by the researcher is an indication of the likelihood that the respondents also understood the labels. For example, Crew (cited in Babbie, 1983) noted that the word *very* has different uses in different parts of the United States. In most parts of the country, *very* is an intensifier; it implies more of some quality. In some parts, however, *very* serves as a limiter; it implies less of some quality. As a consumer of research, you want to be sure that the researcher is aware of regional speech patterns and uses appropriate wording for items and response labels. The researcher can also communicate this to a reader who may have no knowledge of regionalisms.

Arrangement of Survey Items

The arrangement of items within the instrument is often to reduce response bias or other forms of unusable data. Within a section dealing with a particular topic, for example, the more sensitive items are generally placed toward the end of the section. Respondents should be gently led toward more sensitive items, not hit over the head with them.

For questionnaires, the first set of items should deal with the most interesting but least threatening topic and should be directly related to the overall purpose of the survey. At the beginning, the researcher is trying to get the respondent interested in completing the instrument, and one way to do this is to create the impression that the instrument actually does accomplish the purpose outlined in the cover letter. Dillman (1978) suggested creating one or two questions specifically for this purpose, if necessary. Such dummy questions would not be analyzed, but the impression they create may make analyses of other items more worthwhile. Factual items—age, race, and so forth—should be placed toward the end of the questionnaire.

For interviews, nonthreatening factual items—length of time at current address, age, and so on, but not income—are best placed first. They allow the interviewer to establish rapport without having to challenge the participant. Factual items help the interviewer to appear genuine and increase the likelihood that the respondent will indeed begin to respond; once begun, an interview is likely to be completed. As with a questionnaire, threatening items, even if they are factual, should be placed near the end of the interview. Thus, the same set of items would best be presented in somewhat different order for a questionnaire and for an interview.

In many survey instruments, some form of contingency item is necessary. A **contingency item** is *an item relevant only if a certain response was provided for a previous item*. A loan application, which is essentially a survey of your credit history, often requests a previous address if you have been at your current address for less than three years. Similarly, an item for which the respondent indicates that he or she is a registered voter might be followed by a contingency item such as "In what year, then, did you last vote in a national election?"

When only one or two contingency items follow a particular item, researchers usually offset them simply by using different margins. Different margins indicate that the item is special in some way, much the same way that different margins for extensive quotes in a manuscript indicate that the material is from a different author. If a series of contingency items is appropriate—say, 10 items for registered voters and 10 different ones for those not registered to vote—the researcher will usually instruct the respondent to skip to the appropriate section.

The order of items is important when leading respondents into sensitive topics and when dealing with contingency items. Order, however, can both create and eliminate response bias. People have a tendency to want to appear consistent (Judd & Park, 1993; Shepperd, 1997), and a series of items on the same topic may lead respondents to alter their responses to later items just to be consistent with their earlier responses. Not many people are willing to admit that they haven't voted in the last 10 years, for example, after they've indicated that voting is an important responsibility of every good citizen. Similarly, a series of items on one topic may influence responses to items on a different topic. Responding to 20 items dealing with the threat of terrorism, for example, is likely to alter responses to a subsequent series of items dealing with the defense budget. Response bias can occur as a result of the order of the items, even if the items themselves are not biased.

Unfortunately, there is little a researcher can do to prevent response bias due to the order of items. Randomizing the order of items may reduce the bias, but it is also likely to confuse respondents. Few people enjoy being questioned when the topic of inquiry is constantly changing. What can be done, however, is to estimate the extent to which order bias exists. If there is reason to suspect order bias, researchers might prepare different versions of the instrument and compare the responses, much the same way that researchers using a repeated-measures design in an experiment (Chapter 7) will test order effects. This procedure is best done when pretesting an instrument, but different versions of the final instrument may be required under some circumstances. If you don't read anything about dealing with response biases in an article, then you need to consider carefully the possibility that some of the survey results are, in fact, biased and adjust your interpretation accordingly. As with other threats to internal validity, it is not sufficient merely to suspect that bias might have occurred; a critical interpretation includes understanding explicitly how the bias may have occurred and how the bias may have affected the results of the research.

Pretesting Survey Instruments

I'll go out on the proverbial limb and state that pretesting is the most important phase of survey research. It's a sturdy limb; no survey data can be trusted fully unless the researcher can be sure the respondents understood the instrument and provided appropriate responses. In addition to editing the instrument to avoid various forms of bias, pretesting is required to ensure that assumptions made while editing were reasonable. If you read nothing about the researcher's having pretested a survey instrument, or there are no references to previous research in which the instrument was pretested, then you should become very suspicious indeed of the results.

Pretesting—*administering research measures under special conditions, usually before full-scale administration to participants*—involves giving a draft of the instrument to a relatively small group of people. Pretesting allows the researcher to fine-tune the instrument in much the same way that a bench check allows a technician to evaluate a part before installing it. Pretesting is not exactly the same as a pilot test, however, because the researcher is not trying to make a test run of the entire research procedure; only the measures are tested. When reading about survey research, check carefully to make sure that the researcher(s) used pretesting to check on the reliability and validity of the measures. It was during pretesting (fortunately) that I discovered that respondents were unwilling to identify their employers, even though they were willing to provide their job titles. I had to rewrite that part of the survey instrument, but rewriting was better than getting no data at all.

Some researchers also conduct a **pilot study**—*a small-scale administration of the survey using the exact procedures to be used for the full-scale project.* Normally, however, survey procedures are planned well enough to make a pilot study unnecessary. Unless the procedure involves some sort of manipulation to create different groups—an experiment using survey procedures to measure the dependent variables—there is usually no need to conduct a pilot study in addition to pretesting and you should not be concerned if the research article contains no mention of a pilot study.

ADMINISTERING SURVEYS

Every method for administering surveys has advantages and disadvantages, regardless of the amount of pretesting completed to facilitate proper administration. It is impossible to declare categorically that one method is better than any other. Research purposes, intended respondents, report audience, instrument length, and staff availability all enter into decisions about administrative procedures. Before interpreting any survey research results, carefully weigh the relevant aspects of the procedures used to collect the data.

Face-to-Face Interviews

In what was probably the first instructional volume on face-to-face interviews, Bingham and Moore (1924) described an interview as a conversation with a purpose. For our purposes, we can define an **interview** as *a structured conversation used to complete a survey*. The survey instrument provides the structure for the conversation, and collecting the data is the purpose.

The amount of structure in an interview depends on the amount of structure in the survey instrument. *Survey instruments that are essentially orally administered questionnaires* are called **schedules**, and they impose a high degree of structure on the interview. In some cases, schedules may consist of cards given to respondents; all the interviewer does is establish rapport, provide instructions, record responses, and answer the respondents' occasional questions (Gorden, 1969). Of course, establishing rapport, providing instructions, and answering questions are probably the most important things an interviewer does. Given the increased mistrust of strangers, however, a highly structured interview will probably produce a better response rate if administered through a mailed questionnaire or a telephone interview (Nederhof, 1981).

When items are likely to engender questions from respondents or the sequence of items is complicated, a structured interview is the most effective means for ensuring responses based on an accurate understanding of the questions. Structured interviews are also very effective when particular members of a household, such as the oldest person or employed individuals only, comprise the sample. In such cases, the interviewer will be able to ascertain the propriety of a potential respondent.

In a partially structured or **focused interview**, the *interviewer poses a few predetermined questions but has considerable flexibility concerning follow-up questions* (Merton, Fiske, & Kendall, 1956). Focused interviews are typically used when respondents consist of a specific group chosen for their familiarity with the research topic. A focused interview might be used to survey graduating seniors as part of an evaluation of the quality of a major program or for some other type of exit interview. As you might expect, it is also important that the interviewer be somewhat familiar with the topic; otherwise, the interviewer will be at a loss when the time comes to generate follow-up questions. The primary emphasis of a focused interview is gaining information about the subjective perceptions of respondents.

The major advantage of a focused interview is its flexibility, but that is also its major disadvantage. The flexibility enables the interviewer to explore more fully the opinions and behaviors of respondents; thus the total collection of responses should contain more and more varied detail than would the data from a structured interview. On the other hand, because not every respondent will be asked exactly the same questions, it is more difficult to interpret differences obtained when responses are compared. Thus, because some questions (and therefore some responses) will be unique to a given respondent, comparisons across respondents are best limited to the predetermined questions to which everyone responds unless the researchers have conducted a content analysis (see Chapter 11) of the responses.

Consider an exit interview, for example, in which everyone is asked why they are leaving their jobs. Some might say they were dissatisfied with their position, which would naturally lead to a follow-up question about specific aspects of the position. Others may say they are leaving to take advantage of a better offer, which would lead to questions comparing the new offer with the current position. Still others may be leaving to make a career change, which leads to entirely different follow-up questions. Although everyone has been asked why they are leaving, it would make no sense to compare the three groups' responses to follow-up questions. The entire set of responses from each participant, however, may be subjected to a content analysis in order to determine the main themes underlying the responses. Comparisons may then be made across respondents on the basis of the themes, rather than on the exact responses. When the *wording* of responses cannot be compared, the issues addressed by the responses may be comparable.

The least structured kind of interview is the unfocused or **nondirective interview**, in which *the interviewer encourages the respondent to discuss a topic but provides little or no guidance and very few direct questions*. I've included nondirective interviews here to provide the full range of structures available for interviews, but they are often not used to conduct a survey. With little or no guidance from the interviewer, responses from a nondirective interview are likely to be so idiosyncratic as to make analysis impossible. Nondirective interviews may be used to gather data in a single-participant design (see Chapter 8) or with a larger sample of extremely homogeneous respondents, but they are generally inappropriate for survey research.

Still, it is certainly reasonable to use a combination of interview structures within a single study. A combination of structures both ensures that at least a portion of the responses are based on the same questions and provides an opportunity to pursue a promising line of questioning with less structured probes. A **probe** is *a phrase or question used by the interviewer to prompt the respondent to elaborate on a particular response.*

If a researcher were conducting a survey of psychology majors, for example, about the relationship between satisfaction with research methods courses and intended career plans, one item on the schedule might involve having respondents rate, say on a 10-point scale, the overall utility of their most recently completed methods course. If a respondent rated the course toward the "useful" end of the continuum, the researcher might follow up with a focused question, such as "What about the course did you find useful?" Such nondirective probes as "What else?" or "Can you tell me more?" could be used to obtain more comprehensive information. Often, however, the most useful nondirective probe involves simply keeping the pen on the paper and waiting for the respondent to continue talking. Should a respondent begin to drift off the topic, a probe such as "That reminds me, I wanted to ask you about. . . ." will usually get the interview back on track.

Have you ever felt as though you were being interrogated by someone? Did you enjoy the experience? Unless you are remarkably fortunate, your answer to the first question is yes; unless you are remarkably weird, your answer to the second question is no. Most respondents would provide these same answers after being subjected to a poorly trained interviewer. An interview is a conversation with a purpose, but it is not an interrogation. First impressions are extremely important, and the impression one wants interviewers to create is that of a trustworthy, pleasant, and competent individual. Indeed, interviewers should, in fact, be trustworthy, pleasant, and competent. When reading about face-to-face interviews, then, it is important to consider how well trained the interviewers were.

Telephone Interviews

The telephone interview is an alternative to face-to-face interviews that has had a justifiably bad reputation for many years. At one time the primary problem with telephone interviews was, very simply, that not enough people had telephones. The size of the potential sample was relatively small, which introduced a fair amount of error into results obtained through telephone surveys. Today, however, the proportion of homes with telephones is sufficiently large to obviate the problem. According to the U.S. Bureau of the Census (1979), about 97% of homes in the United States had at least one telephone, and that was back in the 1970s. At about the same time, Klecka and Tuchfarber (1978) used a telephone survey to replicate a survey done via face-to-face interviews and found no appreciable differences between the results of their survey and those of the original interviews. The bad reputation of telephone interviews is no longer justifiable.

The technique used to obtain respondents in Klecka and Tuchfarber's survey, and indeed in most telephone surveys, is known as random digit dialing. **Random digit dialing** is *a sampling procedure in which a valid telephone exchange is sampled from a region and the telephone number is completed with four randomly selected digits.* For national surveys, area codes are randomly selected; then valid exchanges within each area code are randomly selected, and then the final four digits are randomly selected from a random number table or generated by a computer program. Nonworking or invalid numbers (such as a business instead of a residence) are removed from the list of generated numbers as soon as their invalid status is determined.

Random digit dialing can be entirely computerized, and equipment that can both generate and dial the telephone number is available. Indeed, we all have received calls—usually attempts to sell us something—that even include a computer-generated message. Of course, researchers don't use a computer to generate the opening remarks in a survey, but computer dialing is easier on the fingers. One of the disadvantages to random digit dialing is that it is extremely difficult to obtain a specific sample, such as members of a particular economic, religious, or political group. The researcher may have to make many phone calls before he or she reaches enough of the right type of respondents. On the other hand, random digit dialing does overcome the problem of unlisted phone numbers.

Telephone interviews can overcome one of the major disadvantages of face-to-face interviews—generally low response rates. Steeh (1981), for example, observed a trend of declining response rates for face-to-face interviews. Since the 1950s, willingness to be interviewed in person has steadily decreased, making it more difficult to complete a sample. Hawkins (1977) studied face-to-face interview response rates in the Detroit area and noted a decline from an 85% response rate in the 1950s to a 70% response rate in the early 1970s. On the other hand, Dillman, Gallegos, and Frey (1976) obtained very good response rates for telephone interviews during the same time period.

Another major disadvantage of face-to-face interviews is their cost (Dillman, 1978, 2007). Nederhof (1981) noted that some face-to-face interviews can cost as much as $100 per respondent. Hawkins (1977) pointed out that interviews can require as many as 17 repeated attempts to locate and talk to a given respondent. Of course, using the telephone won't necessarily reduce the number of attempts to locate a respondent, but a phone call is certainly less expensive than a drive to the respondent's home.

There are other advantages to telephone interviews. Although not necessarily a major advantage, telephone interviewers do not have to concern themselves with their physical appearance. Also, calls made from a central office allow the interviewer to consult with a supervisor if a problem develops or a question arises that the interviewer cannot handle. An interviewer in the field must deal with such matters without supervision, which makes it more difficult to implement a consistent strategy for such occurrences.

Telephone interviews, however, are not a miracle cure for problems encountered with face-to-face interviews. Indeed, if the interview schedule is very long or complex, a face-to-face interview is more appropriate than a telephone interview. It is generally accepted that telephone interviews ought not to exceed 15 minutes, which is not much time to complete a lengthy instrument. Similarly, focused and nondirective interviews are more difficult over the phone.

Another disadvantage to telephone interviews is the relative ease with which the respondent can break off the interview (Institute for Social Research, 1976). It is considerably easier to refuse to begin or continue an interview when not facing the interviewer. Furthermore, the telephone interviewer must obtain all information through direct questions. One cannot unobtrusively measure such variables as race, age, or relative economic status over the telephone.

Mail Surveys

Distributing survey instruments through the mail to a predetermined sample is an example of a **self-administered survey**—*a survey in which respondents complete the instrument without intervention by the researcher*. Self-administered surveys provide greater privacy for the respondent, but they also increase the likelihood of misunderstood items or incomplete responses. There is no opportunity to follow up a seemingly inconsistent response, which makes instructions for a self-administered survey more important than those for an interview.

As a means by which to *reach* a specific sample, a mailed survey is the least expensive, least time-consuming, and most effective administration method; indeed, most survey research about which you read will have been done through the mail or direct administration. However, mailed surveys also rank lowest among administration methods with respect to response rates for reasons we'll discuss next.

Surveys administered through the mail lack one very important ingredient— an interviewer. No one is there to answer questions about the items or explain instructions. It's also a great deal easier to throw a survey in the trash than to say no to an interviewer. Essentially, the more distant—physically and psychologically—the maker of a request, the more likely it is that the request will be refused (Latané & Liu, 1996). A survey researcher at the other end of a mailed questionnaire is about as distant as one can be. For this reason, a variety of practices have been developed to increase response rates by making the instrument, which is not distant, as inviting as possible.

Dillman (1978, 2007) has provided the most comprehensive set of practices designed to increase response rates. Known collectively as the Total Design Method or the Tailored-Design Method (or TDM for those who like acronyms), these practices have been supported by empirical research (e.g., Nederhof, 1981). Some of the individual practices may seem to be mere gimmicks, but they do enhance response rates. Dillman views the survey research process as a **social exchange**—*an interpersonal relationship in which an individual's willingness to enter or remain in the relationship depends on expectations of rewards and costs* (Kelley & Thibault, 1978). From that viewpoint, a researcher must make completing and returning a questionnaire worthwhile for the prospective respondent. Dillman's TDM involves making the instrument well organized and easy to complete, and, through it, the researcher attempts to reward respondents by offering them copies of the research results.

A variety of other specific recommendations are incorporated into the TDM, and I suggest you read one of Dillman's books if you are interested. As a consumer of research, however, you are not likely to have an opportunity to conduct the kind of full-scale mailed questionnaire survey to which Dillman is referring. Nevertheless, the ideas and intentions underlying TDM can be incorporated into any survey research project. Essentially, getting a good response rate boils down to making respondents feel as though they are doing something worthwhile that also happens to be enjoyable and making sure respondents know that the researcher appreciates the effort they made. Good response rates, as you learned in Chapter 5, make it more likely that the sample represents the population of interest.

Comparisons Among Administration Methods

As mentioned earlier, each survey method has some advantages (+) and some disadvantages (0). Table 9.1 contains a summary of those discussed thus far. The comparisons are grouped into five areas: sampling, response rates, instrument construction, validity, and efficiency.

The ratings given to each method in each category are based on the assumption that the method is competently administered. A poorly done survey, regardless of which method is used, is not likely to provide any advantage at all, except, perhaps, as an example of what not to do next time.

Mixed-Method Surveys

After perusing Table 9.1, you should be able to conclude that there are only a few instances in which face-to-face, telephone, and mail surveys are equally effective for a given research purpose. Just because one method is better in one or another category, however, does not mean that researchers must necessarily accept shortcomings in their research projects. Mixing methods, normally not a good idea in research, can be extremely beneficial in survey research. One can, for example, call respondents who have returned a mailed instrument to obtain clarification on incomplete or seemingly inconsistent responses.

Certain circumstances may lead to mixing administration methods intentionally. If it were necessary, for example, to use a complex instrument that also dealt with sensitive topics, the researcher might adopt a proctored questionnaire approach. By allowing respondents to complete the questionnaire privately, the researcher would be in a better position to avoid bias due to self-presentation. By having a proctor available for questions, the researcher also avoids problems that might arise from the complex format. A ballot box or similar receptacle for completed questionnaires could be used to further assure respondents of anonymity.

When it is possible for respondents to assemble in one place or when captive audiences (such as students in a class or a regular meeting of a civic group) are available, group administration is more convenient than a mailed questionnaire. An advertisement placed in a local newspaper or announcements to appropriate groups could be used to attract respondents. However, such techniques involve **accidental sampling,** *selection based on availability or ease of inclusion,* which limits generalizability. An accidental sample of students in a large class, for example, is a fairly homogeneous sample, and it would be difficult to generalize results obtained from them to a group of, say, retirees. Furthermore, the possibility of volunteer bias is much greater with such an accidental sample.

The most important aspect of survey administration methods is to understand the research needs when deciding on the propriety of a method or a sample. If a project both requires a very high response rate, low costs, and some open-ended responses and contains some boring and sensitive items, then a

Table 9.1	Face-to-Face, Telephone, and Mail Surveys Compared		
Category	Face to Face	Phone	Mail
Availability of a complete sample			
Completely listed population	+	+	+
Incompletely listed population	+	0	0
Ability to select respondents	+	+	0
Ability to locate specific respondents	0	+	+
Response rates			
For heterogeneous sample	+	+	0
For homogeneous sample	+	+	+
Ability to avoid volunteer bias	+	0	−
Instrument construction			
Tolerance for length	+	0	0
Tolerance for complexity	+	−	0
Success with open-ended items	+	+	−
Success with screening items	+	+	0
Sequence control/contingency items	+	+	0
Success with tedious items	+	0	−
Avoidance of incomplete responses	+	0	−
Flexibility of format	+	0	−
Validity			
Avoidance of self-presentation	−	0	+
Avoidance of interviewer bias	−	0	+
Avoidance of interference from nonrespondents	0	+	0
Avoidance of misunderstood items	0	−	0

Category	Face to Face	Phone	Mail
Efficiency			
Small staff requirements	–	+	+
Implementation speed	–	+	–
Low cost per respondent	–	0	+
Low cost for geographical dispersion	–	0	+

combination of face-to-face and mail methods may be best. Boring or complex items could be administered in the face-to-face interview, and the interviewer could leave a printed questionnaire containing the sensitive items for the respondent to complete and return by mail. As with all research, a little creativity tempered with knowledge is very helpful in survey research. As a consumer, you should allow the researcher to employ creative means when evaluating the study. Don't assume that there is only one way to obtain a particular kind of response; evaluate research based on the stated purposes and, of course, based on your purposes with respect to reinterpreting the results.

DATA ANALYSES IN SURVEY RESEARCH

How a researcher analyzes data depends on the research hypotheses and the types of measurement scales used. There are three general types of analyses appropriate for survey data: description, association, and elaboration. Within each of these types, you may encounter either categorical or continuous data. We'll examine each type of analysis in this section, with sufficient detail for you to be able to determine whether or not a particular researcher analyzed data acceptably. If you are unfamiliar with these analyses, read Chapter 4, which provides considerably more detail about data analyses. Also, the various references cited along the way are excellent sources for expanding your statistical knowledge.

Description

The analyses best suited for descriptive purposes are generally referred to as summary or exploratory statistics. They include frequency displays and measures of central tendency and variability. Tukey (1977) and Hartwig and Dearing (1979) are two of the many excellent volumes that describe these analyses in more detail.

Nominal data yield categories rather than amounts, which is why they are also called categorical data. Gender, religious denomination, and voting preferences are some examples of nominal variables. Frequency distributions are a common way to describe such data. Frequency distributions may also be expressed as percentages, such as, "75% of the respondents were in favor of the Patriot Act." You may encounter reports of the modal response—the most frequently chosen response alternative—for variables with more than three categories.

If the researcher has obtained a representative sample, you may read inferences about the population from which the sample was selected in the form of inferential statistics appropriate for nominal data. The most common of these, chi-square, usually involves a goodness-of-fit test. A **goodness-of-fit test** is *a test in which data values obtained from one sample are compared to theoretical values to determine whether or not the two sets of values are equivalent*. The ultimate outcome of a goodness-of-fit test is a probability value—the probability that the obtained data fit the theoretical data. Chi-square tests are particularly common for survey data in which comparisons to earlier data are to be made or when comparisons between subsamples are necessary.

One example of a chi-square goodness-of-fit analysis is when television network anchors declare the winner of an election based on only 2% or 3% of the election returns. They are really saying that the obtained returns do not fit distributions of returns that would enable any of the other candidates to win the election. The actual returns are the survey data; the predicted distributions are the theoretical values to which the actual data are fit. The probability associated with the obtained data (the declared winner) fitting the theoretical values (one of the other candidates winning) is so low that the network is willing to claim that the obtained data could never fit the theoretical data in which one of the other candidates is a winner. Of course, they don't say all of that when they report the projected winner; they just say so-and-so is projected to be the winner on the basis of scientific polls (surveys).

Frequency distributions and goodness-of-fit analyses are sometimes used to describe continuous data, but they are not the most efficient way to report such data. Continuous data reflect amounts—more or less of whatever is being measured—such as temperature, annual income, and so forth. For such data, a stem-and-leaf display is more informative and efficient than a simple frequency distribution. If you are unfamiliar with stem-and-leaf displays, you may want to consult Chapter 4 or read Tukey's (1977) volume on exploratory analyses. It would be common to include a stem-and-leaf display in a report to be read by other researchers, but probably not in a report for the general public, because most of the public does not know how to read a stem-and-leaf display.

Researchers will most likely report the mean for each variable, as well as describe the variability by calculating the standard deviation or variance. The mean and standard deviation are usually the most efficient way to describe continuous data distributions.

For inferential purposes, the standard error of the mean can be used to determine the probability that a theoretical population mean falls within a range about the sample mean. If you are unfamiliar with the concept of the standard error of the mean, consult Chapter 4. The standard error provides an indication of what the population mean should be if the sample is a random sample from the population. When the sample mean is very different from the theoretical mean, the researcher may conclude that the data are not from the theoretical population. It is essentially the same concept as a goodness-of-fit test except that it is based on sample means instead of categorical distributions.

When the U.S. Bureau of the Census reports that the population is getting older, for example, it is really indicating that the mean age of the latest sample is considerably higher than the mean age of the previous sample; that is, the probability that the two sample means came from the same population is very low, and the Bureau is confident that the two means could not have come from the same population. A probability smaller than .05—less than a 5 in 100 chance—is usually low enough to make such a decision. When several groups are being compared, it is common to use an analysis of variance test, which is also based on the standard error of the mean.

Whatever statistics you encounter in a report of group differences, you must keep in mind that the researcher is trying to describe the fact that the groups are different. Unless the researcher has met the condition of random assignment and a manipulated variable, he or she should not do much more than speculate about why the differences are there. Speculation is, of course, permitted so long as the researcher clearly labels it as such.

Association

Surveys for which association (or correlation) analyses are commonly reported are those for which the hypotheses involve relationships between variables. One of the appropriate association analyses for categorical data is, again, a chi-square statistic. The procedure for association analyses, however, is a contingency analysis. **Contingency analyses** are *used to determine the probability that the results for one variable are related to the results for another* *variable*. Recall Hill, Rubin, and Peplau's (1976) survey of romantically involved couples in the Boston area. They performed contingency analyses to determine whether remaining a couple was related to living together. If the two variables were associated, the researchers expected a greater proportion of one kind of couple to have lived together than another kind of couple. They did not find evidence for that association; the proportion of intact couples who had lived together was not sufficiently different from the proportion of unsuccessful couples who had lived together.

Another way to word the above conclusion is to report that the probability that an intact couple had lived together was the same as the probability that an unsuccessful couple had lived together. Similarly, a researcher might report that breaking up was not related to cohabitation. All three statements are different ways to convey the same idea—that remaining a couple and living together were not associated in their sample.

The most common association statistic for continuous data is the correlation coefficient, also covered in Chapter 4. Hill et al. calculated a number of correlations from their data. They found, for example, that the correlation between the age of one member of a couple and the age of the other member was positive, $r = .19$, meaning that couples tended to be composed of individuals of about the same age.

Reading the results of correlational analyses is fairly straightforward—you will see the correlation coefficient and the probability associated with it, along with the degrees of freedom for the sample size. Going beyond the results, however, can be very tempting but should be avoided. If a researcher reports that parents' income and children's income are related, $r (98) = .50$, for example, you might be tempted to conclude that wealthy parents tend to give their children more money than do poor parents. Although such a conclusion makes sense, you cannot draw that conclusion from the results. Unless the researcher has somehow managed to assign parents randomly to different levels of wealth, the researcher has not met the necessary conditions to claim a causal relationship. You know that parental and child wealth are related, but the methodology is not adequate to allow you to know why they are related.

Elaboration

The difficulty of being able to draw conclusions about causal relationships from survey data is one of the reasons why Lazarsfeld and his colleagues at Columbia University developed the elaboration model for analyzing survey data (Merton & Lazarsfeld, 1950). **Elaboration** is *a process in which data analyses are used to explore and interpret relationships among variables*. The logic of elaboration enables one to dissect a relationship by examining how it changes when additional variables are included in the analysis. The original outline of the method makes interesting reading, but a later volume by Lazarsfeld, Pasanella, and Rosenberg (1972) is a better source from which to get information if you want more details.

The starting point in elaboration is an observed relationship between two variables. For illustration, let's assume a researcher has conducted a survey and found a relationship between parents' and children's wealth; at age 22, wealthy respondents are more likely to have wealthy parents. The researcher doesn't believe this relationship exists merely because parents are giving money to their children but would like to examine that and other hypotheses in order to more fully understand what's going on:

Why?

Parents' wealth → Children's wealth

Luckily, the researcher has some data with which to test some of the hypotheses suspected to explain the relationship:

Education?

Employment?

Direct support?

Parents' wealth → Children's wealth

Using the logic of elaboration, the researcher might first determine whether respondents with college degrees exhibit the same relationship between parental and respondent wealth as those who do not have college degrees. That is, could the relationship exist because wealthy parents can better afford to provide a college education for their children? If the relationship remains unchanged after separating the sample into those with and those without college degrees, then the researcher can rule out education as one of the explanatory variables. If the relationship is different for the two subsamples, then education becomes part of the underlying mechanism:

Parents' wealth → Education → Children's wealth

Essentially, elaboration enables one to control variables statistically that may contribute to (elaborate on) the basic relationship identified in the initial data analyses. Again, keep in mind that statistical control is not the same as actual control through manipulation. Just as matching is only a second-best alternative for random assignment, statistical control is only a second-best alternative for manipulating the independent variable in a true experiment.

Despite the remaining inability to draw fully supportable causal explanations from survey data, elaboration has a decided advantage over simply guessing about underlying mechanisms. The hypotheses that remain viable after elaboration are more likely to be supported by additional research; that is, the data already collected are consistent with the hypotheses, and it makes sense that additional data will likely be equally consistent.

When reading about elaboration (which may not be called elaboration in the article) or about any analysis dealing with association, you should avoid falling into the trap of *ex post facto* explanations. ***Ex post facto* explanations** are *untested causal statements applied to observed relationships*. (The phrase is Latin for "after the fact.") Suppose, for example, that a researcher determined through elaboration that parental wealth was related to respondent wealth more strongly for males than for females. If you proceeded to interpret this elaboration by concluding that males are more likely to inherent the family fortune, you would be guilty of an *ex post facto* explanation. The difference between genders is real, but the underlying mechanism, inheritance, is not something that has been tested with the data. An *ex post facto* explanation recently resulted in a "color expert" claiming that men who drove red cars had unfulfilled sexual desires. The "expert" had read somewhere that male owners of red cars were more likely to be single than married and jumped to this conclusion about sexual desires. Whether or not male owners of red cars are more likely to be single, the existence of that relationship provides no information at all about their sexual desires, fulfilled or otherwise.

Elaboration and *ex post facto* explanation are often mistaken for the same process, but there is one very important difference between them. Applying the logic of elaboration provides a test of the proposed hypotheses; *ex post facto* explanation is nothing more than speculation. Granted, the test of a proposed hypothesis through elaboration is not as rigorous a test as would be obtained through an experiment or quasi-experiment, but it is a test.

There exists a chi-square analysis known as hierarchical chi-square, which can be used for elaboration when variables are categorical. Haberman (1978, 1979) has written two very technical books that require considerable math background. Lindeman, Merenda, and Gold's (1980) chapter on contingency analyses is less mathematically oriented but still rather technical. I suggest you not consult these sources without at least one basic course in statistics, preferably two. As a consumer of research, however, you may only need to know that hierarchical chi-square analyses enable the researcher to employ elaboration in order to follow the researcher's presentation of results.

Elaboration can be accomplished using correlation coefficients for continuous data in much the way described in the example concerning parental and child wealth: Separate the samples and recalculate the coefficient. For continuous data, however, multiple regression analyses are more efficient and more statistically correct. **Multiple regression** is *a statistical technique for estimating simultaneous correlations among any number of predictor variables and a single, continuous response variable.* When multiple regression is used, the coefficients are called regression coefficients, and they can be interpreted in much the same way as correlation coefficients. Kerlinger (1979) has an excellent chapter on multiple regression, one that doesn't require an extensive math background to understand.

With elaboration analyses, a researcher may find that some of the variables to be included are categorical and some are continuous. With such mixed data, multiple regression is appropriate if the response variable is continuous. Such is the case with children's wealth in the previous example. If the response variable is categorical, such as religious denomination, then a technique called discriminant analysis is best. **Discriminant analysis** is *a statistical technique designed to estimate the relationship between any number of predictor variables and one or more categorical response variables.* The logic of discriminant analysis is the same as that for multiple regression, but considerably more complex calculations are necessary.

Discriminant analysis involves finding a set of predictor variables that can be used to categorize respondents into groups defined by the response variable. A series of repeated estimations, called iterations, is used to determine discriminant function weights (analogous to regression or correlation coefficients) for the predictor variables. The iterations continue until the computer program determines the best combination of predictors that, literally, predict responses on the categorical response variable. By comparing the computer-generated responses with the actual responses in a type of goodness-of-fit test, the relative effect of the predictor variables can be estimated. Kerlinger (1979) also includes a chapter on discriminant analysis, although you probably want to have more than just a basic course in statistics before tackling it. Multiple regression and discriminant analysis are especially complex statistical techniques. Although you should be aware of them, it is not necessary for you to understand them fully in order to make sense of results that are generated through these techniques. Figure 9.1 contains an overview of various analyses appropriate for different types of data, samples, and research purposes. The types of analyses that are used depend on the types of data collected and the purposes of the analyses. More information about all of these analyses can be found in Chapter 4.

Figure 9.1   A Summary of the Types of Data Analyses That Can Be Applied to Survey Data

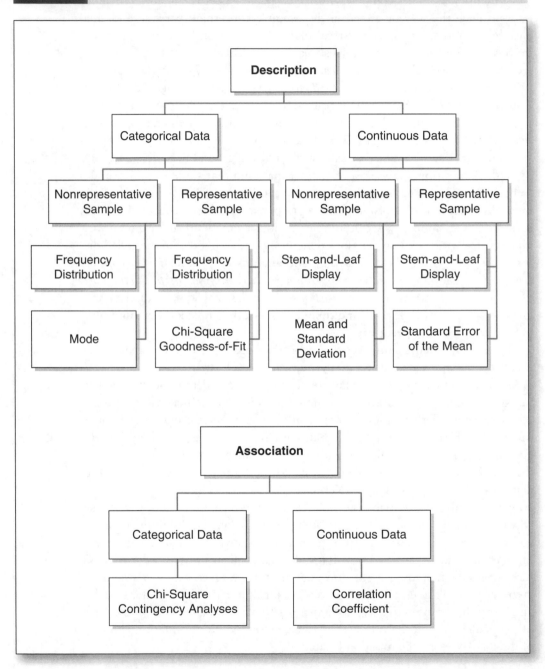

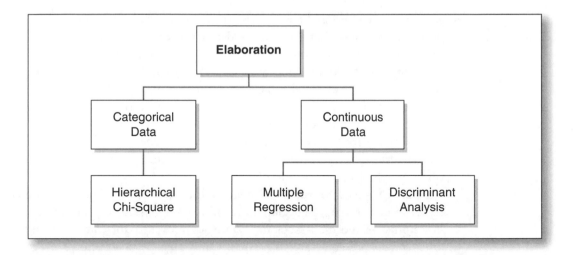

SUMMARY

- Survey research methods are used to obtain self-report information from research participants, mainly in order to accomplish descriptive or predictive goals. Although less efficient for such purposes, survey methods can be used for exploratory and action goals but rarely for explanation because it is usually too difficult to assign respondents randomly to different conditions produced by manipulating variables.

- The items contained in a survey instrument are used to measure facts, opinions, and behaviors. Facts are verifiable characteristics of respondents; opinions are preferences expressed by respondents; behaviors are reports of completed actions. Care must be taken to avoid response bias or incomplete responses to sensitive topics. Anonymity or confidentiality generally alleviates such bias.

- Instructions and formats should make it easy for respondents to complete the instrument. Pretesting should be used extensively to accomplish this goal.

- The face-to-face interview is the preferred method for administering relatively unstructured instruments, although it is also the most expensive method. Probes may be used more effectively with this than with any other method.

- Telephone interviews are less expensive than face-to-face interviews, but the acceptable length of a telephone interview is considerably shorter. The onetime problem of limited availability of samples because potential respondents lacked telephones is no longer relevant, but random digit dialing is necessary to reach respondents with unlisted numbers.

- Mail surveys can be used for relatively structured instruments, but care must be taken to ensure that the items and instructions can be understood by respondents. Mail surveys also produce lower response rates than interviews.
- The Total Design Method has been successfully used to increase response rates for mail surveys, and it has been demonstrated to be more successful than merely offering incentives. The Total Design Method involves a collection of procedures that make the instrument pleasant to complete as well as worth the respondent's investment of time and effort.
- As the need arises, various administration methods can be mixed to obtain the best combination of advantages.
- Data analyses used for surveys depend on the purpose of the research and the type of data collected. Summary statistics are most appropriate for descriptive purposes. Association statistics are used for data analyses when predictive goals are to be met. Care must be taken, however, to avoid unsupportable cause-effect conclusions from association analyses.
- Elaboration is a logical process for analyzing data that enables one to test tentative hypotheses about relationships among variables, but it is not as rigorous a form of causal analysis as a true experiment. *Ex post facto* explanations are untested assumptions about association data. Although similar to elaboration analyses in the final outcome, elaboration involves a statistical test of the hypothesis, whereas *ex post facto* explanations are nothing more than speculation.

EXERCISES

1. Find an article in which the authors report on survey research. For each variable, determine whether it can be considered fact, opinion, or behavior.

2. Using the same or a different article, determine whether or not the investigators pretested their survey instrument and identify the administration method employed.

3. Find an article in which the investigators employed a survey or interview for a descriptive purpose and explain to someone who did not read the article why the purpose is descriptive.

4. Find an article in which the investigators employed a survey or interview for some purpose other than description. Identify the researchers' purpose and explain to someone who has not read the article why you decided upon that purpose.

CHAPTER 10

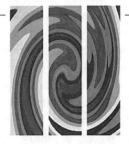

Field Research

Observation is a skill over and above passive reception of the raw data of sensory experience.

—Weimer (1979, p. 21)

Overview

In this chapter you will learn about methods that researchers use to conduct research on everyday events. You will learn about systematic observation—a method designed to examine behavior without actually being a part of it—and you will learn about participant observation, in which the researcher becomes a part of the event being observed. You will also learn about the advantages and disadvantages of intruding into the action being observed. As with other methods described in this text, you will learn about appropriate data analyses and conventions for reading reports about field research in order to enhance your ability to interpret field research reports.

INTRODUCTION

One of the continuing themes of this text is that every one of us conducts research every day but that scientific research is more objective and systematic than the informal research that merely satisfies our curiosity. In this chapter you will learn about research methods that are more similar to those of informal research than any other method. Just because field research methods are similar to informal practice does not mean that they are less scientific in any way. The principles and practices of field research provide one with the skills necessary to move beyond the notion of passive reception of everyday experience. However, don't let the label, field research, lead you to believe the methods described in this chapter can be used only outside the laboratory or to believe that research conducted outside the laboratory can be accomplished only through these methods. The label is an accident of tradition and not very descriptive. As a consumer of research, understanding the methodology underlying field research provides you with the means by which to apply field research, perhaps the most realistic of all research, to the policies and programs in which you are interested.

Field research is *the general label applied to a collection of research methods that includes direct observation of naturally occurring events*. The first characteristic of field research, direct observation, means that one examines the event as it happens, which sets it apart from the collection of retrospective data in survey research (Chapter 9). What is observed in field research, however, need not necessarily be live events; part of our discussion will include various techniques available to record events for later examination. Still, whether live or on tape, the emphasis is on observing events as they unfold.

The second characteristic of field research, naturally occurring events, involves a continuum of naturalness rather than a natural/artificial dichotomy. A **natural event** is *an event that is not created, sustained, or discontinued solely for research purposes* (Tunnell, 1977). The viewpoint used to assess naturalness is that of the research participant, which is why naturalness needs to be conceptualized as a continuum: The more the participant perceives the event to be part of the normal stream of experiences, the more natural the event is. The emphasis on natural events in field research is why field methods are sometimes called naturalistic methods.

Events may be artificially created by the researcher and still be perceived as natural by the participant. The research on helping behavior conducted by Piliavin, Rodin, and Piliavin (1969), discussed later in this chapter, is a good example of events that were artificially created for the purpose of conducting an experiment but were perceived as natural by the participants. Of course, events such as earthquakes or terrorist attacks are also considered natural, even though they may not qualify as part of the participant's normal stream of experience.

In Chapter 1 you learned that research methods may be used to address a variety of questions about our world, questions that were categorized in terms of exploration, description, prediction, explanation, and action. You also learned that certain research methods were more appropriate for some questions than for others. The naturalness of field research makes it difficult, but definitely not impossible, to assign participants randomly to different levels of an independent variable. Most explanatory questions, therefore, fall outside the purview of field research. For similar reasons, including the difficulty of extending hypotheses outside the preexisting situation, prediction is also somewhat inefficient when accomplished through field methods. Field research typically involves collecting data in order to form new hypotheses and is particularly suited to exploratory and descriptive goals (Butler, Rice, & Wagstaff, 1963).

As attempts to answer exploratory questions, field methods are very similar to the informal research of everyday living. More specifically, the method known as participant observation is ideally suited for the development of hypotheses about existing events. Participant observation generally involves studying events while simultaneously taking part in them, something we do as a part of life itself. On the other hand, the method known as systematic observation is more likely to lead to the discovery of new empirical relationships. Systematic observation involves studying events without participating in them, remaining all the while as unobtrusive as possible. We will more carefully and more comprehensively cover each of these methods later, but first let's address the general issues of validity and intrusion as they apply to field research.

VALIDITY OF FIELD RESEARCH

That field methods are most appropriate for exploratory and descriptive purposes does not necessarily mean that they cannot be used to address questions about relationships between variables. Rather, the limitation of field methods is that they cannot easily be used to test causal relationships—explanations—unless the field research is based on previous experimental research. Recall from Chapter 7 that testing causal relationships involves conducting an experiment, which involves manipulating the independent variable and randomly assigning participants to the different levels of the independent variable. Random assignment and manipulation are rather difficult in a natural setting, so explanations are rarely tested first through field research.

The way in which field research is typically used to test causal relationships involves taking an already experimentally tested phenomenon and applying it in a natural setting. Berkowitz and Donnerstein (1982), for example, have conducted numerous experiments through which they demonstrated that the presence of weapons (and other cues for violence) can cause people to become more aggressive. The causal relationship between the presence of violent cues and aggression, therefore, has been well established. Diener and Crandall (1979) used field research methods to evaluate the reverse of the causal relationship—the effects of removing cues for violence—in a natural setting in Jamaica. Anticrime legislation in that country included gun control regulations and banning gun-related segments from television shows and movies. Diener and Crandall measured the effects of this natural event and found rather dramatic decreases in crime rates, particularly for crimes involving firearms. The experimental research by Berkowitz and others tested the causal relationship, but the field research by Diener and Crandall described the impact that that relationship can have in everyday life. The field research wasn't the primary test of the causal relationship between weapons and aggression, but it was a demonstration of the impact of that causal relationship in more natural settings, in everyday life instead of the laboratory.

Internal Validity

Fassnacht (1982) noted that many people believe field research to be less valid than other methods, particularly experimental methods. If one defines internal validity solely in terms of testing causal relationships (see, e.g., Shadish, Cook, & Campbell, 2002), then this belief is somewhat correct. If, however, internal validity is defined as the extent to which research procedures enable one to draw reasonable conclusions, then field research, per se, is no more or less valid than any other method.

Diener and Crandall's (1979) research on the effects of gun control legislation in Jamaica is a valid test of what can happen when such laws are enacted. If they had gone so far as to conclude that censorship of gun segments on television is what *caused* the reduction in crime, however, then they would have gone beyond the limits of their research design and would have drawn an invalid conclusion. The experiments by Berkowitz and others make it reasonable to conclude that removing the cues for violence had something to do with the reduction in crime, but the Jamaican legislation involved more than removing cues for violence. As with any other research, conclusions drawn from field research methods should be limited to whatever effects actually were tested in the research.

External Validity

Internal validity is only part of the overall validity of a research project. We must also be concerned with **external validity**—*the extent to which the data may be generalized beyond the research project*. Field research generally suffers from a lack of external validity, mainly because either the setting studied is often unique or the common components of the setting cannot readily be demonstrated to be related to the results of the research. One could hardly claim, for example, that enacting the Jamaican legislation in another country would produce the same results. We do not know what aspects of Jamaican society may have contributed to the effectiveness of the legislation, aspects that may not exist in some other country. On the other hand, whenever a researcher is in a position to define the relevant aspects of the situation under investigation, field research probably has greater external validity than any other method because the naturalness of the situation more closely approximates everyday life.

INTRUSION IN FIELD RESEARCH

Earlier I described a natural event as one in which the researcher does not create, maintain, or restrict behavior for research purposes but also noted that naturalness must be determined from the viewpoint of the research participant. **Intrusion** is *anything that lessens the participants' perception of an event as natural* (Tunnell, 1977). Intrusion can involve any aspect of an event: the behavior that comprises the event, the setting in which it takes place, and the treatment of the participant by the researcher.

Intrusion Into Observations of Behaviors

Connecting participants to a polygraph machine and measuring their physiological reactions to a violent movie is behavioral intrusion, as is handing each participant a questionnaire in order to measure attitudes about violence. More natural ways to observe behaviors might involve unobtrusively watching physical reactions to a violent movie in a theater or eavesdropping on conversations about violence. Between the ends of the continuum is a host of moderately obtrusive ways to study behavior; the key element is the degree to which those engaging in the behavior are aware that they are being observed as part of a project.

Studying behavior naturally does not always exclude observation of artificially induced behavior. A study on helping behavior by Latané and Darley (1968) began with participants completing questionnaires in a waiting room, a procedure that is intrusive. Each participant was either alone in the room or with two others who were actually the experimenters' **confederates**—*people who appear to be research participants but are actually members of the research team.* After a while, white smoke began to pour through an air vent. At first, puffs of smoke escaped at somewhat irregular intervals. Eventually, enough smoke was discharged to fill the room. The behavior in which Latané and Darley were interested was whether or not participants would report the smoke to someone. Although certainly not an everyday event, to the extent that participants did not suspect that the smoke was part of the research procedure the behavior was natural (and the observation of it was unobtrusive). For those of you not familiar with this rather important experiment, participants who were alone were much more likely to report the smoke than were those who shared the room with two passive confederates.

Intrusiveness of Settings

The degree of intrusion into the setting is determined by the extent to which the event takes place in an environment the participant believes is a research setting. Laboratories, as in Latané and Darley's study, are clearly intrusive settings. Natural settings include those normally frequented for purposes other than participating in research. In a very different study, Piliavin, Rodin, and Piliavin (1969) used the Eighth Avenue subway in New York City as a natural setting in which to study helping behavior. A "victim" collapsed on the floor of the subway car, and observers were on hand to record the reactions of others in the car. By varying the apparent problem and race of the victim, Piliavin et al. were able to discover some rather clear differences in participants' behavior between their more natural setting and the more intrusive setting used by Latané and Darley. These differences led to considerable theoretical development as to why and under what circumstances people are willing to help others (Dane, 1988a). Note that both studies involved experimental research that took place in the field; naturalness and experimental design are not necessarily mutually exclusive.

Intrusiveness of Treatments

Intrusion with respect to treatment refers to the extent to which the event could have occurred without the researcher's presence or influence. In the Latané and Darley study, the treatment of the participants was intrusive; they would not have encountered the smoke if the researchers had not been manufacturing it. Indeed, a number of the participants later explained their failure to report the smoke by stating that they believed that the experimenter wanted them to experience a smoke-filled room. Piliavin et al.'s (1969) treatment was also intrusive, but not as much. That particular "victim" would not have collapsed without the influence of the researchers, but I know from experience that sooner or later in one or another subway car, there would have been a real victim. Diener and Crandall's treatment clearly qualifies as natural. Unless they have a great deal more power than most researchers, Diener and Crandall's absence would not have prevented the crime control legislation from being enacted by the Jamaican government.

The naturalness of the events being studied is a continuum, not a dichotomy. Participants' perceptions of naturalness can vary from one end of the continuum to the other. Also, the mixture of behavior, setting, and treatment makes some events more or less natural than others. Natural behaviors do not always occur in natural settings; they can arise from intrusive treatments or arise under unusual settings, and so forth. The key to determining the naturalness of an event is attempting to understand what is going on from the participant's point of view. With this in mind, let us move on to discuss specific field research methods.

SYSTEMATIC OBSERVATION IN FIELD RESEARCH

Unless you live in a sensory deprivation chamber, most of your waking hours are spent as an observer. You watch activity, listen to sounds, feel objects, taste flavors, and smell odors. Merely paying attention to sensory inputs, however, is not scientific—is not systematic—observation, although it does satisfy curiosity. **Systematic observation** is *a research method in which events are selected, recorded, coded into meaningful units, and interpreted by nonparticipants*. Because this is a rather long and involved definition, let's take it apart and deal separately with each component. Each component of the definition also is an opportunity to think critically about field research. Just because the research about which you are reading may seem like something that "everyone does" does not mean that the research results are not useful when you analyze a policy or program.

Selecting Events

When a researcher selects events, the researcher must first decide which events are of interest and then must decide how to sample the specific events to be observed. The first decision, of course, depends on the general kinds of behavior the researcher wishes to explore and the hypotheses to be examined. We don't have much in the way of critical commentary on these decisions, other than to decide whether or not the researcher's interests match our own interests. The second decision is dependent on the first, for the sampling procedures cannot be determined until the researcher decides which events to investigate. With respect to sampling, we have much to think about critically.

Deciding which events to observe is not as simple as you might think. One should not, for example, decide to go out and observe everything; that's not systematic. It is also not possible. If one concentrates on nothing in particular, that's pretty much what the researcher will observe—nothing. Weick (1968) has categorized events on the basis of behaviors in which field researchers are most interested: nonverbal, spatial, extralinguistic, and linguistic.

Nonverbal behaviors are body movements that convey information. They may include facial expressions, eye contact, hand movements, posture, and so on. Spatial behaviors involve maintaining or altering distances among people or between people and objects; again, such behaviors convey information or reactions to another's behavior. Extralinguistic behaviors include rate, tone, volume, and other similar characteristics of speech. Spoken in a normal tone and at even speed, for example, "Hey, Frank" means "Hello, Frank, how are you?" Spoken loudly with a pause between the two words, "Hey, Frank!" may mean anything from "wait for me" to "turn around and catch the softball about to hit you in the head." Finally, linguistic behaviors refer to the content of speech or written material. Which type of event is of interest to the researcher is a decision that must be made for each study; interest values of events vary as a function of hypotheses. If the hypothesis involves observing people from a distance in order to attain a high level of naturalness, for example, the researcher will be limited to nonverbal and spatial behaviors (unless the researcher uses a long-distance, directional microphone). The general principles of measurement (see Chapter 6) should be used to guide you in decisions about whether or not the researcher has chosen behaviors appropriate to the hypotheses stated in the introduction of the article. As critical consumers of research, we must understand the epistemic correlation between the variable measured and the concept represented by the variable. We must decide for ourselves whether that correlation applies to the issue, policy, or program we wish to clarify empirically.

Deciding how to select the actual events to be observed involves the general principles of sampling (see Chapter 5), but there are a few aspects specific to systematic observation. Generally, sampling events involves either time or event sampling. Time sampling, as the term implies, refers to selecting a specific interval of time during which observations will be made. It is used whenever duration of the event is of interest. If one wants to know how much time people spend lingering at the table after a restaurant meal, for example, then one needs to use time sampling.

In **continuous time sampling**, *the researcher observes every instance of the behavior for the entire duration of the event.* Continuous time sampling is usually limited to studies involving very short events or to studies in which measuring absolute duration is required. It is analogous to making a videotape of the entire event. Studies of the total time devoted to coffee breaks in an industrial setting, for example, may require continuous time sampling; the researcher needs to know exactly how much time people spend on their coffee breaks. More often than not, however, only relative measures of frequency or duration are required, such as whether people spend more time at the coffee machine than at their desks, and under such conditions one can use either time-point or time-interval sampling.

Time-point sampling involves *selecting only those behaviors that occur at the end of a specific time interval within the duration of the event.* Continuing with our coffee machine example, one could observe the coffee machine at the top of the hour and note which employees were present. Time-point sampling is analogous to photographing the participant and making observations from the photograph. Indeed, still photography is one of the ways in which permanent records of time-point-sampled events are created. With time-point sampling, one cannot measure every trip to the coffee machine or the total amount of time spent there, but one can determine whether one employee visited more often than another.

Time-interval sampling involves *observing whether a behavior occurs during a specified interval within the duration of the event.* One could, for example, observe the coffee machine for the last 10 minutes of each hour and record whether each employee was there at that time. Time-interval sampling is analogous to making a videotape of part of the entire event. The researcher gets more than just a snapshot of the event, but not the entire event. As with time-point sampling, only relative measures, and therefore relative conclusions, are possible with time-interval sampling.

Whether a researcher appropriately uses time-point or time-interval sampling depends on the duration of the event to be observed. If the behavior is very brief, time-interval sampling will probably be required, and longer intervals will be required for infrequent behaviors. If the behavior is long lasting, time-point sampling is more appropriate, particularly if the duration of the behavior is not relevant to the hypothesis.

Event sampling involves *observing one behavior contingent upon the presence of another behavior* and is usually used for hypotheses about relationships between two variables or when knowing the duration of the behavior is not necessary. A researcher may not, for example, be interested in how long people spend on their coffee breaks but may be interested in whether they take more coffee breaks when the boss is away from the office. Event sampling provides only relative information; only continuous time sampling will enable a researcher to make absolute measurements of the behavior. Regardless of the sampling procedure selected, the key is to sample systematically: every X minutes or every time behavior Y occurs. Researchers generally devise a sampling strategy and stick to it. As a consumer, you need to be able to understand the researcher's sampling process and decide whether or not it is appropriate to the questions the researcher wants to answer.

Recording Events

After a researcher has decided which, how often, and under what circumstances events are to be selected for observation, the next decision is how to record the observations. Although often done simultaneously, we will discuss recording and coding as separate processes. **Recording** refers to *the manner in which a permanent copy of the observation is made.* Taking photographs or video recordings, making notes, or making marks on a checklist or scale are all examples of recording observations. **Coding** involves *attaching some sort of meaning to the observation.* Deciding whether a baby's apparent smile means the baby is happy or has intestinal gas is part of the coding process. A researcher's decision about how to record observations depends on the research hypotheses and the resources available to the researcher. As consumers, we must decide whether or not the recording process is relevant to our interest in the research.

Recording, like any other measurement process, introduces some error. Even film or videotape involves error due to the camera angle, lighting, resolution, and other aspects of photography. If one cannot focus a camera on the behavior, one cannot record it. Therefore, recording is best accomplished with multiple observers so the researcher can estimate error through the amount of agreement between the observers (interobserver reliability). If six people make the same record of an observation, the record is more reliable than if only one person makes the record. There is, of course, no a priori reason to suspect recordings made by only one observer, but the number and type of observers should be part of your critical review process. Consider whether or not the researcher has convinced you that the recording was valid and reliable as you are reading the article.

Coding Events

As noted above, coding involves interpreting what has been recorded, and it is very often accomplished at the same time as recording. One may observe a baby's smile, interpret it as being happy and simply record that the baby was happy. Sometimes, coding is used to represent a behavior more efficiently—as a kind of shorthand system for recording observations. Leventhal and Sharp (1965), for example, developed an elaborate system of symbols used to record facial expressions. LaFrance (1979) used a similar system for arm positions in her study of the similarity of posture and its relation to attitude similarity. The symbols used are a shorthand for, or a representation of, the actual behavior, but they don't necessarily ascribe any meaning to the behavior.

More often than not, however, coding involves both recording and interpreting an observation. The most well known of such systems is the interaction process analysis (IPA) system developed by Bales (1950, 1970). IPA allows observers to record inferred meanings for linguistic, extralinguistic, and nonverbal behaviors among groups, using the categories listed in Table 10.1. As you can see from the table, IPA requires the coder/observer to decide not only whether the behavior has occurred but also to attach meaning to it. The IPA is one of many examples of **checklist coding schemes**—*coding systems for which the behaviors and their meanings are determined prior to making observations.*

An alternative to checklist systems is the unstructured or ethological system, also known as natural history. The **ethological system** involves *a detailed and comprehensive recording of behaviors with little or no inferred meaning.* When using an ethological system, a researcher might simply note that Ralph stuck out his tongue at Mary instead of checking the "seems unfriendly" category of the IPA. The emphasis is on making as few assumptions and interpretations as possible; hence its sometime name—natural history. McGrew (1972) used an ethological system to categorize 110 different behaviors of nursery school children's social interactions. Ethological systems, however, are not for the impatient. McGrew spent 15 hours coding each hour of videotape and another five hours coding each hour of audiotape. The advantage to an ethological system, however, is that the researcher has a permanent record that can be coded different

Table 10.1	Categories for Interaction Process Analysis (IPA)
Positive actions	1. seems friendly
	2. dramatizes
	3. agrees
Answers	4. gives suggestions
	5. gives opinion
	6. gives information
Questions	7. asks for information
	8. asks for opinion
	9. asks for suggestions
Negative actions	10. disagrees
	11. shows tension
	12. seems unfriendly

ways if later hypotheses require it. With a checklist system, all one has recorded are the codes themselves, not the behaviors that produced the codes.

Interpreting Events

Unless a researcher has invented infallible recording equipment and discovered an infallible operator, interpreting observations may begin before the behavior is recorded. **Interpretation** refers to *the process whereby recorded observations are used to describe events, generate hypotheses, or test hypotheses*. Any time one edits or otherwise imposes meaning on the event, one interprets the event. Recording involves interpretation, if for no other reason than one must decide what to record and what to leave out of the record.

Coding, too, involves some degree of interpretation, particularly when checklists are used for coding and recording. Refer again to Table 10.1 and notice that the IPA categories require considerable interpretation. In one context, sticking out one's tongue may seem unfriendly, but a different context may require that same behavior to be coded under "seems friendly" or "gives opinion." The observer/coder must first determine whether the action took place (recording interpretation) and then decide how to code it (coding interpretation).

When checklists or rating scales are used to record and code actions simultaneously, at least some interpretation occurs before any observations are made. Choosing the categories to be included on the checklist or choosing an existing checklist involves interpreting what will and will not be important before any observation occurs. When using the IPA, for example, a researcher is deciding that the 12 categories are relevant and that other actions or codes are not relevant. Using more than one checklist may help solve the problem but may also introduce problems of its own. Gellert (1955), among others, has noted that the number of different categories and the number of coding errors are directly related. Similarly, category abstractness and error are directly related: The more a coder/recorder must do in terms of interpretation, the more likely it is that he or she will make a mistake. As a consumer of research, part of your job is to determine whether or not the researcher chose a reasonable coding scheme and to assess, as best you can, the likelihood of coding errors in the chosen procedure.

Sources of Error

You may have realized that interpretation, whenever it occurs in the research, involves two concepts with which you are now rather familiar—reliability and validity. If observations are not measured reliably—measured consistently—then the researcher cannot describe the event or generate and test hypotheses about it. Similarly, if the observations are not valid—don't measure what they are supposed to measure—then only invalid or meaningless interpretations can be made. Dunnette (1966) described four sources of error that reduce reliability: inadequate sampling, chance response tendencies, changes in the participant, and changes in the situation.

The first of Dunnette's sources of error, **inadequate sampling,** *occurs when only a subset of events is recorded and the sampling process is not systematic.* When using IPA, for example, one must focus on linguistic, extralinguistic, and nonverbal behaviors. If one focuses on one type of behavior during part of the observation interval and focuses on a different behavior at another time, the observations are subject to inadequate sampling error. Comparing data obtained from the same observer at two different times will allow a researcher to assess the extent of this type of error, which may be corrected through additional training. As consumers, we must look for reports of assessments of the reliability and validity of the measurement system used.

Also correctable through additional training are **chance response tendencies**—*replacing formal category definitions with idiosyncratic definitions*. The most frequent source of chance response tendencies involves changing one's mind about what to observe after one has begun making observations. If one begins observing smiling, for example and then decides to include head nods in the same category, the researcher has introduced chance response tendencies. By including head nods, he or she has changed the measure from smiling to "friendly nonverbal behaviors." The observations made before the change are no longer valid, and the measure is therefore not reliable. Of course, you are not in a position to be able to detect such problems while reading a research article, but you should be reading carefully to determine the extent to which the researcher employed adequate observer training prior to collecting data.

Dunnette noted that chance response tendencies are more likely to occur when using abstract categories in a checklist system, although complex categories of any kind are generally sources of error. Essentially, the more confusing a coding or recording system is, the more likely the coder or recorder is to become confused when using it. When more than one participant is being observed, randomly splitting the sample into halves and comparing the two halves will enable the researcher to estimate the extent to which chance response tendencies are operating for a single observer. If one randomly splits the sample, the two halves should be more or less equal on all measures; if they are not equal, the researcher may have some reliability problems due to chance response tendencies. You may recognize this as a type of split-half reliability assessment. When reading about field research, look for efforts to assess reliability reported by the researcher.

Dunnette's other two sources of error refer to potential changes in the event being observed. Changes in the person being observed affect the consistency of observations, as would changes in the environment in which the observations are being made. If a researcher is observing smiling behavior and something happens to put the participant in an especially good or especially bad mood, the behavior is going to change. If the researcher is not aware of the event that caused the mood change, he or she cannot account for it when later interpreting the observations. You may recognize this as a history effect.

Correlating data from two independent observers provides a test of changes in the event. If something has changed, data from both observers should reflect the change. Of course, a high correlation between observers doesn't necessarily mean that no change has occurred, only that both observers have consistently detected the change. If changes in the event are not consistent with the research hypotheses, agreement between the raters will not correct such a failure to meet the conditions established for the research protocol.

Validity

You should be aware that reliability alone does not make good measurement. Categories for observation must be consistent, but they must also be valid; that is, they must measure the concept the researcher wants them to measure. The validity of observational measures becomes more difficult to establish as the observation categories become more abstract. It is easier to be sure that an observation fits the category "clapping hands" (McGrew, 1972) than that it fits the category "seems friendly" (Bales, 1970). Determining whether or not any particular measure is valid was covered in more detail in Chapter 6, and you should consult that chapter before attempting to read critically about any categorization system for observation.

PARTICIPANT OBSERVATION

Depending on the research hypotheses and the opportunities for observation, systematic observation may not be the most effective method for completing a research study. It is often impossible merely to sit back and watch events as they unfold. In such instances, participant observation is the method of choice. **Participant observation** is *an observational research method in which the researcher becomes part of the events being observed*. It differs from systematic observation not only in terms of the amount of researcher participation but also in terms of hypothesis formulation and data collection tactics.

Levels of Participation

Whenever one engages in field research, one must decide how much one will participate in the sequence of events. For systematic observation, participation is minimal and the researcher usually qualifies for Gold's (1969) label of **complete observer**—*one who observes an event without becoming part of it*. The participants may not be aware of the researcher at all. Depending on the level of intrusion, participants may not even be aware the researcher is conducting research. Gold has labeled three other points on the participation continuum: observer-as-participant, participant-as-observer, and complete participant.

According to Gold, the **observer-as-participant** is *known to the participants as a researcher but does not take an active part in the events*. In this capacity, the researcher's role is analogous to an announcer at a sporting event. Everyone knows the announcer is paying attention to the game, but the announcer is not one of the players. Because the observation is not entirely unobtrusive, some **reactivity effects**—*changes in the participants' behaviors because they know they are being watched*—may occur. In this role, however, reactivity can usually be avoided, and the researcher is more likely to be conducting systematic observation than participant observation.

Being a **participant-as-observer** involves *being known as a researcher but fully participating in the ongoing activities*. One classic example of this role is Liebow's (1967) study of low-income individuals in the ghetto area of the District of Columbia. Liebow was known to his participants as a researcher, but he also involved himself as much as an outsider could. He sat through and testified at legal hearings, visited employment agencies, and generally became a friend to a number of his participants.

Liebow did not, and probably could not, adopt the complete participant role in his research. A **complete participant** is *a researcher who fully participates in the events but is not known to the other participants as a researcher*. A complete observer is analogous to an undercover agent; no one knows his or her true identity as a researcher. Because Liebow was White, it would have been extremely difficult for him to have gone undercover in the predominantly Black D.C. ghetto. Whether pretending to participate or actively participating, the complete participant appears to be just another person in the sequence of events. One example of complete participation is Humphreys's (1975) study of homosexual activity in public restrooms. He served as a lookout while gathering data, and the participants were unaware of his status as a researcher.

Aside from reactivity, any level of participation has some effect on the events a researcher is observing. Whether such effects are intentional or not, you should be aware of them and their potential influence on the observations. Even remaining neutral during a group discussion or a focus group, for example, has some effect. The researcher may be creating the impression that not all participants in the decision process have a preference, which may make it more likely that other participants will alter their preferences. Making suggestions may also influence others, even if the researcher's suggestions are not adopted. Care must be taken to consider objectively the researcher's influence when interpreting any data collected through participant observation.

Selecting Settings

Whereas systematic observation involves selecting behaviors, participant observation is more likely to involve selecting a setting in which to observe the events of interest. Liebow's (1967) study of low-income individuals was set in the D.C. ghetto, for example, whereas Humphreys's (1975) research was set in public restrooms in St. Louis. The research in both cases was about people and their behaviors, but the selection of participants was based on the settings in which they behaved.

Given the emphasis on settings, sampling in participant observation is very different from sampling in systematic observation. Primarily, the researcher must first select the group of people to be observed and then attempt to locate settings in which those people can be found. Usually neither random selection nor random assignment is possible. Liebow, for example, could not randomly assign some participants to live in the ghetto and some to live in the suburbs. He could have obtained a list of all ghettos in the United States and randomly selected some of them to be observed, but that would have been incredibly inefficient for his research purpose.

More often than not, participant observers rely on informants for participant selection. An **informant** is *anyone who is knowledgeable about the participants to be observed.* Informants may or may not be coparticipants, and as you might expect, a researcher is rarely in a position to select informants randomly. After learning about the target group from an informant, including suggestions about the best settings in which to find a reasonable number of participants, the researcher may elect to use one of the three types of sampling suggested by McCall and Simmons (1969): quota, snowball, and deviant case.

Quota sampling—*selecting sampling elements on the basis of categories assumed to exist within the population*—involves purposefully searching out participants who fit the researcher's requirements. The researcher may want to include a certain number of men and women, young and old, Blacks and Whites, and so on. Once the researcher has enough of one type of participant, young men, for example, the researcher will avoid observing additional members of that subgroup. For each of the identified subgroups, the researcher may need to find different informants, who then lead him or her to other members of the subgroup and so on until the researcher has enough observations. Sometimes, the researcher may not become aware of the existence of a subgroup until after beginning the research, in which case the researcher may alter the sampling plan to include members of the newly discovered group.

More often than not, participant observers use a snowball sampling technique. **Snowball sampling** involves *obtaining suggestions for other participants from those the researcher has already observed*. Also called **key-informant sampling**, snowball sampling is analogous to a salesperson asking the most recent customer for names of prospective customers. If the research role is participant-as-observer, snowball sampling is fairly straightforward: All one has to do is ask the person one is interviewing for suggestions as to whom next to interview. As a complete participant, however, great care must be taken not to arouse suspicion while looking for key informants, particularly if some degree of secrecy surrounds membership in the group being studied. However, as a complete participant, one can more easily engage in passive sampling; one can allow the participants to make themselves known through the normal activity of the group.

McCall and Simmons's third sampling method, deviant case sampling, is not some weird sampling procedure. Rather, **deviant case sampling** involves *observing individuals who do not seem to fit some pattern exhibited by others who have been observed*. Insights into reasons for engaging in an activity can often be discovered from those who choose not to engage in the activity. In a study of religious cult membership, for example, a researcher might want to interview those who considered joining but did not or those who joined but later quit. Deviant case sampling depends on finding people who do not seem to fit a group pattern, which in turn depends on the researcher's ability to detect patterns. One can sometimes learn about patterns that enable one to identify deviant cases from participant observations conducted by others via perusal of existing research. Sometimes, the researcher must observe and detect patterns for him- or herself, which is what we turn to next.

Recording Observations

When using systematic observation methods, recording techniques such as checklists, video recorders, and other devices for creating permanent records are usually available. When conducting a participant observation study, the equipment will probably consist of little more than paper and pencil (and perhaps a computer). From time to time a researcher may need to rely on memory, but even the best memories are fallible.

The research tool of greatest importance in participant observation is the **field journal**—*a notebook into which the researcher enters all observations.* Entries in field journals fall into two categories—certain and uncertain—and it is essential that the researcher makes notes about which kind of entry is being made. For so-called certain entries a researcher might, for example, write, "Mary told Ralph to sit down and shut up." The researcher can be fairly certain about such an entry. The researcher might also note that Ralph appeared to take the comment as a joke, but Mary seemed to be fairly angry. These latter entries would be less certain; Ralph may have been trying to save face by treating it as a joke, or the researcher may not know Mary well enough to be able to tell whether she was angry or normally behaves that way. The intentions of others, as a general rule, are things about which we have little certainty. New information may lead one to believe that Mary was joking, and it would be easier to incorporate the note about her anger if the researcher had indicated that he or she was uncertain about the observation.

As easy as distinguishing between certain and uncertain events may seem to be, keep in mind that recording even seemingly straightforward events is often little more than logically filling in blanks in what we have observed. A number of researchers (see, for example, Forgas, 1982) have provided a very impressive amount of evidence about blank-filling-in recollection. If I tell you, for example, that I grabbed my motorcycle key and helmet and went for a ride, you would probably infer that I took that ride on my motorcycle. Of course, you have no direct information that I took the motorcycle, but it seems logical given the other information. At a later time, you could perhaps become certain that I had indeed taken the ride on the motorcycle. That's the way our memories work; assumptions we make today become the certain conclusions of tomorrow. In everyday life, assuming I used my motorcycle is probably of little consequence. After all, who cares what I drive? But in participant observation research, such assumptions can have disastrous effects. A researcher's field notes are his or her data, and the researcher does not want to make assumptions about them any more than one would want to assume a participant would have obtained a certain score on the dependent variable in experimental research. Collecting data involves measuring variables, not assuming values for them.

As with taking notes in the classroom, participant observers must decide how much detail to include in their field journals. Contrary to what your instructors may tell you about taking notes in the classroom, researchers should try to write down everything when conducting participant observation research. Because one may be formulating additional hypotheses after completing the observations, one cannot be sure what will and will not be important at the time one makes the observations. The rule for participant observation research is simple: If it happens, make a note of it.

Coding Observations

After a field researcher has a complete copy of the field journal, it is time to begin tearing it apart; that is, the researcher usually rearranges the entries in order to organize them into logical (rather than chronological) patterns. It is during this phase, coding the field journal entries, that the researcher may notice the development of conceptual patterns, the stuff of which hypotheses are made.

Researchers typically rework entries along whatever line of reasoning seems promising. They are likely to generate more than one working hypothesis during this process and may construct a different organizational pattern for each working hypothesis. Researchers often continue to generate additional hypotheses until the possibilities seem exhausted. Attempting to determine logically whether or not the data support any particular working hypothesis during the coding process makes generating additional working hypotheses more difficult. *Generating and revising working hypotheses* is known as **dynamic hypothesis formulation**. Essentially, it involves searching for patterns among the field notes.

Interpreting Observations

When a researcher has a collection of working hypotheses, he or she will test them. Testing hypotheses, particularly hypotheses involving some aspect of causality, requires differentiating between necessary and sufficient causes. A **necessary cause** is *something that must be present in order to produce the effect*. Carbon, hydrogen, oxygen, and nitrogen are all necessary causes for life as we know it; the absence of any one of these elements for an extended period of time precludes life. Certainly, other causes must also be present before someone or something is alive, but that does not diminish the extent to which these very simple elements are necessary causes for life. On the other hand, a **sufficient cause** is *something that will produce the effect*. The earth's atmosphere is a sufficient source of oxygen, but other sources serve equally well. The sometimes confusing aspect of causation is that necessary causes are not always sufficient; imagine trying to stay alive in a room full of carbon dust, water, and nitrogen gas. Similarly, sufficient causes are not always necessary: You can stay alive with scuba tanks; you don't need the earth's atmosphere.

When attempting to formulate causal hypotheses, the key is finding causes that can qualify as both necessary and sufficient. One method for doing this is **negative case analysis**—*searching for data that disconfirm a tentative hypothesis, revising the hypothesis to include the disconfirming data, searching for more data, and so on.* Whatever hypothesis survives this procedure is very likely to contain both necessary and sufficient causes. The researcher should not conclude that the remaining hypothesis is true or place as much faith in it as one could if one had tested it with experimental research. However, negative case analysis is about as close as one can come to providing empirical support for a hypothesis, short of experimental or quasi-experimental research.

NUMERICAL DATA ANALYSES

You may have gotten the impression that field research, whether systematic or participant observation, does not lend itself to numerical data analyses. If so, it is time to correct that impression. Natural observations are often analyzed qualitatively, but it is just as often the case that they can be subjected to quantitative analyses. Some researchers might consider the use of numerical analyses for ethnographic or participant observation research to be a sacrilege (Schwartz & Jacobs, 1979), but the key to proper analysis of any data is to consider numerical analyses as supplements to logic, not as replacements.

Description

As long as one observes more than one person or more than one behavior for a single person, regardless of the manner in which one collected the observations, one can always conduct descriptive analyses to summarize the sample. Such analyses may include mean or median ages; frequency histograms of racial, economic, educational, and ethnic backgrounds; or even a sociogram of relationships among participants. Which of these analyses, if any, a researcher will conduct and include in the research report depends on the number and characteristics of the people in the sample. If the researcher had only three participants, for example, it would be foolish to calculate a mean age. In general, if it takes less trouble or space to describe the participants in narrative form, most researchers will do so. Otherwise, summary statistics may save a considerable amount of time.

Frequency histograms may also be used to present summary information about the various types of activities observed. Again, researchers do not rely on numerical analyses to describe the activities, but do rely on them to summarize information about frequency of activity.

Correlation

Correlational analyses are always part of systematic observation research, if for no other reason than to assess interobserver reliability. (For more information on reliability analyses, consult Chapter 6.) It is also possible to use correlational analyses to assess reliability for participant observation research. Such analyses can provide useful information about the relative comprehensiveness of field journal notes.

It is nearly axiomatic that one gets better at participant observation the longer one does it, provided one is doing it correctly (Johnson, 1975). There are a number of different correlational analyses a researcher may use to gain insight into the progress of his or her note taking. One could, for example, simply correlate the day of the activity (1, 2, 3, and so on) with the length of the notes (number of lines per entry or some other measure). Although crude, the results would enable the researcher to determine whether he or she changed the thoroughness of note taking during the course of the study. Similarly, one could correlate the number of certain and uncertain entries, in which case each day's entry would provide a pair of data points. Or the researcher or another person could rate each day's notes on a subjective scale of detailedness and correlate one half of the notes with the other half. This analysis would provide information about consistency with respect to including detail in the notes.

The above analyses are only a few of the many possible correlational analyses a researcher could use to learn about the way in which he or she conducted the research. You are not likely to read about many of them in research articles, primarily because they are techniques used to assess training more than as techniques used to interpret data. However, if a researcher reports conducting such analyses, you can feel more confident that the researcher took his or her field research very seriously.

REPORT READING

Recording, coding, and interpreting observations do not define the limits of field research. The final phase of a field research project or any research project, for that matter, is reporting the results and conclusions. As with any other phase of research, the starting point for report writing is the literature review. As a consumer of research, you should pay attention to the researcher's descriptions of what others have done. Therein lies the opportunity to understand the reasons for conducting the research and the basis for your ability to decide whether or not the specific procedures are consistent with the intentions of the researcher.

It is not possible to tell someone what might or might not be in a field research article. By now you should be aware that Chapter 3 contains general guidelines for reading research reports. The remainder of this section includes aspects of reports that are specific to field research but are not necessarily specific to the research project about which you may be reading at any given point in time.

When more than one observer recorded or coded observations, the researcher should describe the procedures and results of any reliability analyses that were completed. Also, any training that was conducted should at least be mentioned if not fully described. The extent of the description depends on how unusual the procedures were. If, for example, a researcher used the IPA, you probably will read only a mention that the IPA was used and the observers were trained accordingly. If, on the other hand, the researcher developed his or her own checklist, then you should be able to read enough detail to understand the procedure.

You should also, of course, be able to learn how the researcher obtained the research participants, the sampling procedure. Important information includes how the researcher contacted informants, what his or her role as participant might have been, and so on. What the researcher told the participants about the study may have affected their behavior, and you should pay careful attention to such information as well.

Finally, evaluate critically the researcher's generalizations to make sure he or she did not go beyond or otherwise mistreat the data when drawing conclusions; that is, consider whether or not the researcher fell into one or another of the logical pitfalls surrounding data interpretation. Ask yourself whether the researcher is (1) using a narrow viewpoint when examining the data, (2) ignoring alternative conclusions that make equally good sense, (3) indeed measuring what he or she intended to measure, (4) ignoring data that should be included, and (5) setting up straw hypotheses in order to lead you (the reader) to unwarranted conclusions. (Straw hypotheses are hypotheses the researcher never intended to relate to the data but are included in order to make the researcher appear to be considering all points of view.)

Each time you read the equivalent of "it seems reasonable to conclude," consider the five points listed above. If you cannot rule out all five of these mistakes, you should probably not consider the conclusion to be reasonable. Of course, such difficulties may call into question the author's other conclusions, but you should not fall into this logical trap. That is, don't generalize from one faulty conclusion, presuming all conclusions to be faulty. Just because one conclusion may not be reasonable does not mean that all of the author's conclusions are unreasonable. Each conclusion should be evaluated on its own merits.

SUMMARY

- Field research includes any research applied to natural events—those not created, sustained, or discontinued solely for research purposes. How natural an event may be, however, must be determined from the viewpoint of the participant.
- Intrusion undermines naturalness and can affect the behavior of participants, the settings in which the behavior occurs, and treatments presented to participants. In general, anything perceived by participants as foreign to their normal experience may be intrusive.
- Field research methods are best applied to exploration, description, and action. They generally lack the external validity required for prediction and the internal validity required for explanation.
- Systematic observation involves observing activities without taking part in them. Events are selected on the basis of the types of behavior to be observed: nonverbal, spatial, extralinguistic, and linguistic. Selection usually involves choosing a sample of time periods during which the behavior occurs or choosing specific activities on the basis of some criterion related to the research hypothesis.
- Recording and coding events in systematic observation are often simultaneous processes. The former involves creating a permanent record of the activity, whereas the latter involves assigning to the activity meaning that is relevant to the research hypotheses. Regardless of the technique used for either process, recording and coding always involve some degree of measurement error.
- Participant observation involves making observations while taking part in the event sequence, sometimes while being recognized as a researcher and sometimes not.

- Sampling procedures in participant observation generally involve selecting a setting in which the activity occurs and then attempting to observe participants as a group or individually. If an activity of interest is not completed by all participants, deviant case sampling may be used to formulate hypotheses about participants' reasons for engaging in the activity.

- The primary research tool in participant observation is the field journal, a notebook into which all observations are entered. Good researchers keep the field journal as contemporary and accurate as possible because it contains the data that will be used to test research hypotheses.

- Coding and interpreting participant observations often involve rearranging chronological observations into patterns related to the research hypotheses, a process called dynamic hypothesis formulation. Necessary and sufficient causes should be differentiated when interpreting field journal entries.

- Negative case analysis involves attempting to find data that can be used to disconfirm a working hypothesis. When such data are found, the hypothesis is usually revised so as to include the disconfirming cases. Eventually, one or more hypotheses will be retained that can be used to account for all of the data.

- Although field research does not usually involve numerical analyses, they can be used to summarize information or to search for patterns related to research hypotheses.

- As with any research, field research should be critically scrutinized by consumers. The report should contain enough information about sampling, measurement, and interpretation procedures to enable you to understand and perhaps re-create the research.

EXERCISES

1. Find an article in which the authors report on field research and determine the levels of intrusion for the setting and treatment of the participants.

2. Using the same or a different article, determine the type of event selection used by the investigators.

3. Find an article in which the authors report on participation-observation research and determine the level of participation employed by the investigators.

CHAPTER 11

Archival Research

. . . but there is still no [person] who would not accept dog tracks in the mud against sworn testimony of a hundred eye-witnesses that no dog passed by.

—W. L. Prosser (1964, p. 216)

Overview

This chapter is about archival research—methods in which the sources of data are various types of documentation. You will learn about content analysis, a method for determining the meaning of recorded communication, as well as some special sampling problems relevant to content analysis. You will also be exposed to some of the techniques used to quantify information derived from content analysis. You will learn about the uses of existing data—measures that have been obtained by other researchers—as well as some ways in which such data may be used and analyzed. Finally, you will learn about research methods for investigating trends within a collection of related studies.

INTRODUCTION

The label *archival research* may suggest an image of an elderly scholar (with bad eyes, of course) bent over an ancient, dusty manuscript in the decrepit basement of a library. Indeed, many behavioral scientists have some disdain for archival research, the type of disdain reflected in the opening quote from Prosser (1964). One of the early reviewers of another text in which I described content analysis as a research technique (Dane, 1990), for example, commented, "I prefer to leave archival research to librarians and historians." Such images and comments notwithstanding, archival research has been firmly established as a research tradition in the behavioral and social sciences and, therefore, a type of research that you will encounter in your efforts to inform policies and programs empirically. One reason why archival research has gained acceptance may be that there are times when a researcher cannot find any "tracks in the mud" and must rely on the testimony of others. Such testimony may be found in dusty old manuscripts, but it is also found in newspapers, songs, novels, memoirs, movies, magazines, government reports, research reports, and a variety of other sources.

Archival research, like field research, is something every one of us does informally every day. We all read, watch, and listen. We may even be exposed to such statistical summaries as the gross national product, crime rates, or the batting averages of our favorite baseball players. Formal archival research, however, involves systematic examination of archives in order to formulate or test hypotheses and theories. For our purposes, then, **archival research** is *any research in which a public record is the unit of analysis.* What distinguishes archival research from other methods is that the researcher deals with information that was generated before the research began, and archival researchers deal with people's products rather than with the people themselves.

Archival research involves attempting to answer questions about people by investigating a portion of the seemingly infinite amount of recorded information they generate. Specific methods have been developed to allow researchers to find such records, obtain a sample of them, transform the collected information into usable data, analyze those data, and use the results to draw conclusions. Sometimes, research was not a consideration of those who originally compiled the information; in other instances the original information was gathered through the use of some research method. Literally any record of information is fair game for archival research.

Systematic archival methods can be separated into two types: content analysis and existing data analysis. Content analysis may involve interpreting any communication medium, whether written, pictorial, oral, or audiovisual. By studying such archives, researchers can test and formulate hypotheses about a variety of different behavioral phenomena, which in turn you can use to evaluate policies and programs. Existing data analysis generally involves using data for purposes other than those for which the data were gathered. Various archives, for example, may contain information about trends that could not have been detected when the data were first collected. Because the above descriptions are very general, more specific discussions follow.

CONTENT ANALYSIS

The amount of communication each of us experiences throughout a typical day is incredible. We converse with others; read what others have written; listen to live or taped conversations and songs; watch the actions of others on a television, movie, or computer screen; and pay attention to the various signs that surround us. All of this communication has some meaning for us, and content analysis is one research method that can be used to study that meaning.

The stuff of content analysis has been described very succinctly by Lasswell, Lerner, and Pool (1952) in the question, "Who says what, to whom, how, and with what effect?" (p. 12). Holsti (1968) adds "Why?" for the sake of completeness, although discovering why a particular message was sent is not always a part of content analysis. More formally, **content analysis** is *a research method used to make objective and systematic inferences about theoretically relevant messages*. Let's examine this formal definition in order to appreciate the potential power of content analysis as a research method.

As noted above, our world is full of messages—communication directed by someone to someone else for a specific purpose. These messages are the observations researchers investigate in content analysis. Messages contained in any medium can be analyzed, although the medium chosen for analysis depends on both theoretical and practical concerns. Content analysis is best used to test research hypotheses, and the content of archives thereby serve as operational definitions of theoretical concepts. Some media are easier to analyze than others, however, and practical concerns also become part of the planning process. Those practical concerns, then, have implications for our ability to use the research results for policy analysis.

Like all research, content analysis should be used to make inferences about events related to theory, policy, or program. In turn, a researcher's ability to make inferences depends on the sample studied. If one wants to investigate the violent content of television programs during the last 10 years, for example, it would be rather difficult to analyze all of the decade's programming. The messages one decides to sample systematically should represent the entire decade's programming, and one would need to be able to use a sampling procedure that ensures such representativeness (for more information about sampling, see Chapter 5).

In addition to being systematic, inferences must be objective; the inferences one makes about messages should be similar to the inferences someone else would make if he or she had access to the same information. Part of this objectivity is accomplished through careful construction of the operational definitions used in the research; another part of objectivity results from the consistency with which one uses the operational definitions one constructs, the reliability of measurement. Although reliability and validity are important in any research project, the ease with which communication can be misunderstood makes reliable measurement more difficult in content analysis.

The range of potential topics for content analysis is considerable but finite. Just because any question of the form "Who says what to whom, how, with what effect, and why?" can be answered through content analysis does not mean that content analysis is always the most appropriate method for such questions. Specifically, content analysis is best used as a comparative technique. It cannot, for example, be used to measure how conservative a particular newspaper's editorial policy is, but it can be used to determine whether one newspaper is more conservative than another.

Who—The Source of Messages

When the research question involves the "who" part of Lasswell et al.'s (1952) question, the researcher is concerned with describing the individual(s) who created the archives. The research hypothesis may concern disputed authorship or may involve making inferences about characteristics of the author(s). One example of disputed authorship was resolved by using content analysis of *The Federalist*, a series of 85 essays originally published under the *nom de plume* Publius. Alexander Hamilton, James Madison, and John Jay wrote the essays to persuade people to throw over the Articles of Confederation in favor of the Constitution. The authorship of 12 of the essays (Essays 49–58, 62, and 63) was uncertain; either Madison or Hamilton could have written them.

Mosteller and Wallace (1964) compared the relative frequency of certain common words—*and, in, the*, and *enough*—in essays known to have been written by the two authors with the same words in the disputed essays; their results were clearly consistent with the conclusion that Madison was the author. They demonstrated that even in the least convincing paper (No. 55), the odds were 80 to 1 in favor of Madison's authorship. Subsequently, Rokeach, Homant, and Penner (1970) compared values expressed in the papers—freedom, honor, equality, and comfort—and arrived at the same conclusion concerning authorship.

In both research projects, the researchers were able to address the question of authorship only because they had access to material known to have been written by Hamilton and Madison; without the undisputed essays, authorship could not have been settled. Using content analysis in the absence of comparative standards can cause a number of problems. Morton (1963), for example, used seven characteristics of an author's style to analyze the Epistles of St. Paul and concluded that there were at least six different authors for the Epistles. Responding to Morton's published challenge to others to repudiate his results, Ellison (1965) used the same procedure to demonstrate that Morton's own articles exhibited multiple authorship. Morton was repudiated, rather cleverly. Attempting to determine authorship in the absence of comparative standards usually leads to more ambiguity than clarity, and you should be wary of researchers who claim to have done so.

Rather than attempting to describe a single author's characteristics, Seider (1974) investigated ideologies and value systems of a group of authors—U.S. business executives. When Seider began his research, the predominant view was that most business executives shared a common ideology (Sutton, Harris, Kayson, & Tobin, 1956). Seider, however, hypothesized that different priorities among different industries would be mirrored in the language used by the executive officers.

By analyzing business speeches published in *Vital Speeches* from 1934 to 1970, Seider (1974) found support for his hypothesis. Three major ideologies were identified among the speeches: classical, social responsibility, and nationalistic. Classical ideology included such themes as free enterprise, profit, and self-regulation; social responsibility included solving social problems and improving conditions for employees and communities; and nationalism included themes protecting the United States and downgrading competing countries. The three ideologies appeared in 52%, 19%, and 31% of the speeches, respectively. Even though the classical ideology was prevalent, preferred ideologies did indeed differ across industries. Corporate officers in the aerospace industry, for example, emphasized nationalism more than they emphasized the other two ideologies.

Says What—The Content of Messages

Perhaps the most prevalent use of content analysis has been to investigate the content communicated in a message. Holsti (1968) separated this question into three distinct components: (1) changes in content over time, (2) the relationship between author characteristics and content, and (3) the extent to which content conforms to some external standard. Research by Zimbardo and Meadow (1974) provided a simultaneously encouraging and disconcerting example of the first of these components. The starting point for their research was the phenomenon known as **nonconscious ideology,** *a prejudice that has lost its label as prejudice and has become an implicit assumption that strongly affects the roles of certain members of a society* (Bem & Bem, 1970). For example, a man might consider the expectation that his male roommate would do all the cleaning to be unfair but would be perfectly willing to expect a female roommate to do the same. That there is apparently nothing wrong with expecting a female to do all the housework is a nonconscious ideology.

Zimbardo and Meadow (1974) reasoned that humor may be the most effective medium for preserving prejudicial attitudes and, therefore, changes in the content of humor should reflect the prevalence of a specific prejudice. They focused on stereotypes about women and analyzed the content of jokes taken from the "Cartoon Quips" and "Laughter, The Best Medicine" sections of *Reader's Digest* from 1947–48, 1957–58, and 1967–68. After identifying jokes with antiwomen bias, they discovered that the frequency of such jokes had declined over the 20-year period. Approximately 28% of the jokes were antiwomen in the 1940s, followed by 10% and 6% respectively, for the 1950s and 1960s. The total number of jokes in the sections increased over the years, but the proportion and absolute number of prejudicial jokes decreased. That's the encouraging aspect of Zimbardo and Meadow's (1974) research: general sexism declined over the years.

The disconcerting aspect of their research involves the analyses of specific stereotypes represented in the antiwomen jokes. Table 11.1 contains a list of the negative traits ascribed to women in the jokes and a representative quip for each trait. Zimbardo and Meadow's content analysis indicated that the amount of antiwomen sentiment decreased over the years, but the sentiments themselves remained relatively constant. The stereotypes remained current and understandable, even if they were becoming less popular among the editors of *Reader's Digest.*

Using content analysis to investigate what is said can involve any one of three components outlined by Holsti (1968). Zimbardo and Meadow's (1974) study

Table 11.1	A Partial List of Negative Traits Assigned to Women Based on Zimbardo and Meadows (1974)
Negative Trait	**Cartoon Setting and Quip**
Stupid, incompetent, foolish	(*"sweet young thing" to husband*) "Of course I know what's going on in this world! I just don't understand any of it, that's all."
Domineering, selfish	(*wife to husband picking out a three-piece suit*) "Well, go ahead and please yourself. After all, you're the one who will wear the suit." (*meek husband's reply*) "Well, dear, I figure I'll probably get to wear the coat and vest, anyway."
Exploiting men for their money	(*woman trying on a hat, to the salesperson*) "It's nice, but it's a little less than he can afford."
Jealous, catty	(*one woman to another*) "I've been wondering, my dear, why you weren't invited to the Asterbilts' last week?" (*other woman*) "Isn't that a coincidence? I was just wondering why you were."
Spendthrift, financially irresponsible	(*husband to guest*) "The decor is Helen's own blend of traditional, modern, and twenty-five hundred dollars."
Gossipy, nagging	(*one woman to another*) "I like her. She just gives you the straight gossip, without slanting or editorializing."
Man-hunting, overanxious to marry	(*young student explaining her choice of colleges*) "Well, I came here to get went with, but I ain't yet."

is just one example of temporal trends in content. Jacobs's (1967) content analysis of suicide notes (described in Chapter 1) is another example of archival research in which the content and author's characteristics were related. In the next section, the focus shifts from originators to receivers of messages.

To Whom—The Audience of Messages

It is no great revelation that people communicate different messages to different audiences. We all, for example, talk about different topics with fellow students than with nonstudents, and we talk about different topics with friends than with strangers. One purpose of content analysis is to determine the extent to which audience-specific messages really are different.

Berkman (1963), for example, analyzed the content of advertisements in *Life* and *Ebony* magazines and found that the major difference was the presumed economic status of prospective buyers. *Life* included a greater proportion of higher-priced products among its advertising. However, within any given price range for products, the only difference in the ads in the two magazines was the race of the models: Whites for *Life* and Blacks for *Ebony*. In all other respects the content of the advertisements was similar.

Differences among messages directed to different audiences can also be used to investigate theoretical issues. Levin and Spates (1970), for example, used content analysis to investigate Parson's (1951) propositions about the importance to subcultures of instrumental and expressive values. According to Levin and Spates, what had been labeled the "hippie" movement of the 1960s should be a prime example of an **expressive subculture**—one *characterized by an emphasis on feelings over accomplishment.*

They compared the content of various publications of the 1960s underground press to that of *Reader's Digest*, a much more traditional publication. They found that 46% of the content in underground publications included expressive themes, whereas only 10% of the content included instrumental themes. On the other hand, *Reader's Digest* included 23% expressive themes and 42% instrumental themes. Clearly, the communications directed toward hippies emphasized expressive themes, whereas the more traditional press emphasized instrumental themes. The communication of different messages to different audiences, although nothing new in and of itself, did provide supporting evidence for Parsons's (1951) theory.

How—Communication Techniques in Messages

Investigating the "how" of communication is a relatively rare application of content analysis, although the few investigations into this matter have been highly informative. Holsti's (1968) work, for example, provides an excellent starting point for research on propaganda, as does that of Crano and Brewer (1973). Another example is the work of McHugo, Lanzetta, Sullivan, Masters, and Englis (1985), which involved an analysis of Ronald Reagan's communication techniques.

McHugo et al. (1985) analyzed the content of a number of videotaped Reagan speeches, but they did not limit themselves to analyzing only the verbal content. Using a panel of judges, they separated videotapes into four groups based on Reagan's facial expressions: neutral, reassuring, threatening, and evasive. In order to examine the "how" of communication, McHugo et al. did something unusual for content analysis researchers: They brought the videotapes into a research laboratory and monitored viewers' reactions to the tapes.

Some people viewed the tapes intact (both picture and sound), whereas others watched only the video portion of the tapes. By comparing the two groups, McHugo et al. (1985) were able to demonstrate that Reagan's facial expressions were more influential than the verbal content of his speeches. The only exception to this general effect occurred among those whose attitudes were strongly anti-Reagan—these viewers were not affected by Reagan's reassuring facial expression, particularly when the content of the speech was not reassuring. This research illustrates the combination of content analysis and experimental methods, and it also demonstrates that content analysis of the "hows" of communication need not be limited to the manner in which people put words together.

With What Effect—The Effect of Messages

Assessing effects through content analysis can be approached in one of two ways. One way involves examining the effects of some phenomenon by analyzing the content of documents related to the phenomenon. A content analysis of interviews with first-grade children (Kounin & Gump, 1961), for example, provided evidence that the attitudes of children's teachers affected the children's perceptions of inappropriate behaviors. The other way to assess effects is to examine the effects produced by the content of the documents themselves. An example of this approach is Levin and Spates's (1970) analysis of the impact of the 1960s underground press on traditional publications.

Kounin and Gump (1961) studied the effects of teachers' styles through their pupils' beliefs about misbehavior. Using consensus among raters, they categorized teachers as either punitive or nonpunitive. The children were then asked to answer two questions: What's the worst thing a child can do at school? and Why is that so bad? The results clearly demonstrated that children who had punitive teachers were much more likely to consider fighting and other physical behaviors to be misconduct, whereas children with nonpunitive teachers were more likely to consider behaviors such as lying to be misconduct.

Of greater relevance to our educational system, children with punitive teachers were much less likely to consider poor academic performance to be misconduct. The authors concluded that a punitive teaching style is less likely than a nonpunitive style to produce high levels of academic performance. You may be thinking to yourself, "So what else is new?" but you should realize that the research was completed in 1961, when punitive teaching styles were considered the norm. This content analysis was influential in leading others to conduct research that has since made this conclusion old hat.

Why—The Reasons for Communications

Attempting to discover why various archives were created deals with one of the most difficult questions to answer using content analysis. Most research dealing with "why" has to do with biographical material and investigations of individuals' motivations for various actions. Using content analysis for such purposes has been variously labeled life history analysis, case study methodology, psychobiography, and psychohistory. Proponents of these different labels differ only a little in their specific methods and purposes but for the most part are highly similar (Runyan, 1982).

One use for investigating the "why" of archives is gaining an understanding of the social and political motives of biographers. Runyan (1982), for example, provided an insightful look at the motives of the Nixon administration through his analysis of two different archives concerning biographical material on Daniel Ellsberg. (Ellsberg leaked to the U.S. press the Pentagon Papers, classified documents that provided evidence of the deceitful and otherwise unethical activity of the Nixon administration during the Vietnam War.)

In summary, content analysis can be rather effectively used to answer a variety of questions. Understanding the variability of applications, however, is not the same thing as understanding the technique itself. For this reason, we turn next to procedural issues concerning content analysis.

METHODOLOGICAL ISSUES IN CONTENT ANALYSIS

The first step in any content analysis research is deciding what part of the "who says what to whom, how, with what effect, and why?" question is to be addressed. That decision, of course, depends on the researcher's interests, the theory with which he or she is working, and the research hypotheses developed from the theory. Making that decision, however, is only the beginning of content analysis. A researcher must also make a series of decisions concerning units of analysis, units of observation, sampling techniques, and coding before he or she can begin to collect data. Your understanding these decisions should provide considerable insight into how to interpret the results of content analysis.

Suppose, for example, that a researcher decides to investigate the degree of sexism displayed on television, as did Ellis (1988). The next decision would concern *the objects about which a researcher would like to answer a question*—the **units of analysis**. One could not, for example, analyze everything on television. Even if one chose to select a relatively small period of time—say, a day or two—one would still have a great deal of programming given the number of channels across the country (or the world, for that matter). One would have to choose a sample of programming that included network broadcasts, independent and cable channels, daytime programming, children's programs, news shows, commercials, and so forth to limit the research observations.

Deciding on units of analysis then enables one to choose the **units of observation**—*the specific material to be measured*. After deciding to use television commercials, for example, the researcher must refine the choice by deciding which of the myriad commercials will actually be examined for sexist content. Will the researcher deal only with a specific type of commercial, such as cleaning products? Or commercials presented at specific times of the day—say, during prime time? Or commercials aired during specific programs, such as during the news? The researcher must refine the choice until he or she has a concrete description of the archives to be examined.

Seider (1974), for example, decided to use speeches as units of observation in his study of corporate ideologies. He wanted to obtain a cross section of business leaders, and he decided that *Vital Speeches* sufficiently represented the range of material of interest to him. At the risk of second-guessing Seider, it may be that the annual reports of the various corporations would have served equally well as units of observation. Of course, it would have been more difficult to obtain copies of annual reports from the variety of businesses he wanted to include; copies of *Vital Speeches* were readily available in the library and were therefore more convenient. The point is not that there may have been better units of observation, just different units; of course, different units of observation can also lead to different results, so the issue is not moot. Once a researcher has selected the units of observation, the researcher must be aware that there are other units that also could have been observed. As the consumer of research, you also need to be aware of other units of observation, as well as understand the potential biases that might exist in the units selected by the researcher.

Deciding on the units of observation leads to a series of decisions about sampling, about how the researcher will select some representative group of the units. If, for example, a researcher decided to examine commercials presented during network news programs, he or she could probably look at every commercial during every newscast on every network for some specified period of time, but it would be unnecessary to do so. The researcher could instead, for example, plan a procedure that involved sequentially and randomly choosing a day of the week, a time period, a network, and a newscast to be observed for any given data collection session. With a programmable recorder, the researcher could record the newscasts he or she randomly selected and then view the commercials at a convenient time.

The reason for establishing a systematic sampling procedure is to avoid having to observe everything included in the units of observation. A systematic sampling procedure provides the researcher a representative sample from which he or she can generalize to the entire set of observational units. The researcher doesn't have to watch every television commercial to be able to draw conclusions about television commercials in general. Chapter 5 contains more detail about specific sampling procedures.

Having defined the sample, a researcher then must decide how to measure the variables contained in the research hypothesis. This, of course, involves determining the operational definitions the researcher will include in the research. One might, for example, simply decide to categorize commercials as either sexist or nonsexist, but even such a simple measure requires an operational definition. What makes a commercial sexist? Is there more than one way to define sexist? If there are different types of sexism, is the researcher going to consider all types or only some of them? How many examples of sexism must a commercial contain in order to categorize it as sexist? When dealing with content analysis, the researcher must decide between two different levels of content: manifest and latent.

Manifest content—*the physical or noninferential material that makes up an archive*—is usually coded in terms of words or letters in written material, words and pauses in audio material, concrete actions in visual material, and so forth. Kounin and Gump (1961), for example, used manifest content in their study of children's impressions of misconduct. Such words as "hitting," "pushing," and "kicking" were coded as assaultive behaviors; such phrases as "talking out of turn," "yelling at someone," or "lying to someone" were coded as nonassaultive. Manifest content is usually relatively easy to code reliably; few people would disagree about the presence or absence of a word or an action in an observation.

Latent content refers to *inferred, underlying, or hidden meaning in material that makes up an archive.* It may be coded in terms of words or actions, and it usually involves inferences from sentences, paragraphs, facial expressions, and tone of voice, as well as other indications of meaning. When someone says, "Nice try" during a softball game, for example, they may be complementing me on my effort, or they may be making a sarcastic appraisal of my relative incompetence. Cultural propriety, too, plays a role in coding latent content. When I moved to the South, for example, it took some time before I was comfortable with being greeted by the word "hey." In the North, saying "hey" is usually a warning or a threat, depending on the tone of voice. In the South, however, "hey" also merely means "hello."

Because coding latent content involves making inferences about the manifest content of an archive, latent content is generally less reliable than manifest content. On the other hand, latent content may be the only way to operationalize some concepts. Advertisers are not likely, for example, to come out and straightforwardly say, "Women are inferior decision makers" in their commercials. They may, however, show women deciding to buy a car because of its color and show men basing their decisions on gas mileage or investment value. Coding manifest content and coding latent content are not mutually exclusive practices. The same archive, *The Federalist*, was coded for manifest content by Mosteller and Wallace (1964) and for latent content by Rokeach et al. (1970); both research teams arrived at the same conclusions but used different coding practices in the process.

To summarize, a number of different, related decisions must be made in order to turn a research idea into a research hypothesis. One must decide what archives to analyze and which specific documents among those archives will actually be observed or measured. One must also decide how to obtain a representative sample of the archives and how operationally to define the variables included in the hypotheses. Having made all these decisions, the researcher is then in a position to begin to collect data—to measure the variables he or she has defined. As consumers of research, it's our job to consider each of those decisions critically to determine whether or not the decisions are consistent with the policy or issue we wish to inform empirically.

Quantification in Content Analysis

Virtually anything is quantifiable, provided the principles and procedures of measurement are followed correctly. Measurement in general is covered in

Chapter 6, but some measurement issues are specific to content analysis. It is these specific issues to which we turn our attention in this section. The type (or types) of quantification procedure selected for a content analysis project depends on the units of observation and the coding procedures the researcher has selected. One or more of the procedures outlined below will be appropriate for a content analysis study. As the procedures are discussed, we'll consider an example from my own research to illustrate the differences among the procedures.

The most common method of quantifying variables in content analysis involves measuring frequency—counting the number of times a given variable appears in the observational unit. In a study of simulated jury deliberations, for example, I counted the number of times jurors mentioned an item of evidence, a personal experience, the judge's instructions, and a few other variables in an effort to examine the relationship between the content of deliberations and the final verdict. By tallying the frequency with which each topic was discussed, I was able to determine that jurors made more remarks about evidence than about any other topic. I also discovered a relationship between the amount of evidence-related discussion and the verdict: More talk about evidence was associated with a greater likelihood of conviction.

One common difficulty associated with the frequency method of quantification, however, is deciding what to do with repetitions. One juror may say, "We have to remember that he had a knife," and another juror may echo that with, "Yeah, a knife." Do both statements count or only the first, or should there be a separate category for repetitions? If a researcher wants to measure the number of times a certain word occurs, as did Mosteller and Wallace (1964), then repetitions are no problem. But if a researcher wants to measure the number of times an idea is presented, repetition becomes a question that must be resolved. There is no single solution, for the decision depends on the hypotheses and other considerations. I decided not to count repetitions, partly because I was interested in counting how many times evidence was discussed, not simply how many times someone referred to any particular piece of evidence. As consumers, however, we need to pay attention to the decision made by the researcher and decide whether or not it is consistent with our purposes.

An alternative to frequency counts—one that also overcomes the potential problem of repetitions—involves measuring the amount of space (for written material) or time (for audio and visual material) appropriated to the variable. Using the same deliberations, I compared the amount of time jurors spent discussing evidence and other topics. With the temporal measure, however, I discovered that less time was devoted to discussion of the evidence, despite the fact that the frequency measure indicated that evidence statements were most frequent. That is, the jurors mentioned evidence more often than any other topic, but the amount of time spent discussing evidence was relatively brief. More to the point, using temporal coding resulted in no apparent relationship between discussion of evidence and verdict.

Different operational definitions of the variable produced different results, which is not unusual. One reason for the difference was that my unit of analysis was the sentence. There were more sentences about evidence than about any other topic, but the evidence-related sentences were also shorter than sentences about any other topic.

To avoid the problem introduced by differential sentence (or other unit) length, some researchers use a technique first developed by Osgood and his colleagues (Osgood, 1959; Osgood, Sporta, & Nunnally, 1956). The technique, called evaluative assertion analysis (EAA), involves breaking down statements into one of two structural forms: subject-connector-descriptor or subject-connector-object. Using EAA, the sentence "There are people who are unbalanced and pick up a knife" can be separated into two statements: Some people-are-unbalanced and unbalanced people-pick up-a knife. The first statement, according to my coding scheme, was categorized as general knowledge; the second was categorized as a remark about the defendant's character.

Of course, when one uses EAA, one cannot measure the amount of time devoted to a topic. When I used EAA on jury deliberations, I obtained essentially the same results as when I used simple frequency counts. Evidence was the most frequently discussed topic and was related to verdicts.

Perhaps the most difficult quantification method to use is the intensity method. Whenever the units of analysis might vary in intensity—some statements have more meaning or more relevance than others—it is often the case that simple frequency or space/time enumeration is insufficient. A number of different techniques can be used for intensity analysis, all of which involve using some sort of rating scale. For example, one of the coding categories I used in the content analysis of jury deliberations was verdict preference, an indication of the juror's intention to vote guilty, not guilty, or undecided. There are different ways, however, to indicate a preference. One juror might say, "I think he's guilty," whereas another might say, "He's definitely guilty." Clearly, these two jurors are expressing the same belief with different intensities.

Although there are a number of different ways to scale intensity (see, e.g., Chapter 6), I decided to ask several individuals to rate each statement on a scale from 1 to 10; the more intense the statement, the higher the rating. The first statement quoted above received an average rating of 5, and the second received an average rating of 8. I discovered that intensity ratings of statements about the incriminating nature of evidence—"No matter what his reasons, he still stabbed someone"—was the variable most strongly related to final verdicts, even more strongly related than were initial statements about verdict preferences.

Different quantification methods may lead to different results, although that does not mean that one method is necessarily better than another. In the above examples, the research question addressed by each method was slightly different. With frequency analysis, the analysis dealt with the relationship between frequency of occurrence and verdict; for the space/time analysis, the relationship examined was between verdicts and time spent discussing topics; the intensity method assessed the relationship between verdicts and strength of opinion. Once again, the questions asked have a great deal to do with the answers obtained. When reading research, you need to consider the decisions made by the researcher. Ask yourself whether or not the method enabled the researcher to answer the question(s) identified in the introduction and whether or not the method enables you to answer questions other than those addressed by the researcher.

EXISTING DATA ANALYSIS

Up to now our discussion has dealt with creating data from existing archives, typically archives not created for the purpose of research. In this section we consider research in which the data already exist. **Existing data** are *the archived results of research accomplished by someone else.* They are typically found in one of three formats: raw data, aggregate or summary data, and the results of completed data analyses (statistical results).

The raw data format generally contains measurements in the original units of observation. Thus, using existing raw data is analogous to hiring someone else to collect the researcher's data, except that the researcher doesn't have the latitude to determine which data are collected. The records stored by the registrar's office at your university, for example, contain raw data. The registrar collected the data and, if a researcher can obtain access to them, they may be analyzed however the researcher sees fit. Archived raw data are the most flexible of the forms of existing data.

Aggregate or summary data are not nearly as flexible as raw data. They typically are archived as one or more combinations of the original measures. For example, if the registrar would release only grade point averages, instead of grades for every course, those average or mean scores would be considered aggregate data. The original units of observation were the individual course grades, but they have been combined into a higher-order unit of analysis, the mean. Because the researcher doesn't have access to the original units of observation for aggregate data, his or her use of them is somewhat limited. The researcher could not, for example, use grade point average to investigate an individual's improvement during a given semester, although the researcher could use them to determine the extent to which the individual improved across semesters.

The third format for existing data, statistical results, is the format with which you are probably most familiar. The statistical results included in research reports are a form of existing data, although this format has the most restrictions. Consistent with the previous examples, the statistical result format would be analogous to the registrar releasing only correlations between semesters, not the GPA itself for each semester.

Applications of Existing Data Analysis

Regardless of their complexity or the format in which they are stored, all existing data have one thing in common: Someone else was responsible for their collection; all of the decisions about measurement have already been made by the time the researcher gets the data. If those decisions match the researcher's purposes, then he or she can use the data as they are. At other times, however, the researcher may need to build upon the decisions made by the original researcher. In this section, you will learn about how researchers accomplish such building by reading about examples of research completed with existing data.

In January 1973, the firm of Louis Harris and Associates conducted a survey of leisure activities and opinions in the United States. The raw data were archived at the Louis Harris Political Data Library of the Institute for Research in Social Science at the University of North Carolina. A number of years later, Marsden, Reed, Kennedy, and Stinson (1982) made use of those same data to investigate potential lifestyle differences between the northern and southern sections of the country. Their major intent was to determine the extent to which the considerable anecdotal and stereotypical information about North-South differences could be supported by empirical data.

The original survey data included responses on participation in 40 different leisure activities, far too many variables on which to measure North-South differences. To create a more manageable data set, Marsden et al. (1982) used **cluster analysis,** *a statistical technique that enables researchers to group variables* *according to the degree of similarity exhibited among the variables*. The mathematics of cluster analysis is well beyond the scope of this book, but the principle is simple. Categories of activities were formed on the basis of the extent to which people participated in the activities. For example, if many of the people who participated in spectator sports, such as watching car races, also participated in competitive sports, such as softball, then the two activities were grouped together in the same category. Table 11.2 contains a list of the various activities and the categories into which they were grouped.

Table 11.2	Examples of Activities Categorized by Marsden et al. (1982)
Category Label	Activities
Outdoor activities	Spectator sports, competitive sports, rock music
Social activities	Yoga, fashions, collecting things, nature studies, weekend trips
Cultural activities	Lectures, reading, museums, theater, concerts, dance recitals
Arts participation	Playing musical instrument, acting, performing for others, painting, dancing, singing
Music listening	Opera, classical, Broadway, jazz
Crafts	Sewing, gourmet cooking, gardening
Uncategorized	Country-western music, popular music, religious music

One way to interpret Table 11.2 is to consider the relative proximity of activities. For example, spectator sport participants are likely to participate in competitive sports but are not as likely to visit museums. On the other hand, those who collect things are equally likely to enjoy yoga and weekend trips. Category boundaries should be considered to represent "distance" as well. For example, those who play musical instruments are more likely to act than they are to attend dance recitals. The three activities at the bottom of the table—country-western, popular, and religious music—stood out as separate categories. People who listen to those three types of music are not any more or less likely to engage in any of the other activities.

Using the categories as dependent variables, Marsden et al. (1982) discovered that Northerners participated more than Southerners in every type of activity except two: Southerners were more likely to listen to country-western and religious music. Thus, even though the original data were not collected for such purposes, Marsden et al. were able to use them to demonstrate empirical support for anecdotal evidence about North-South differences—for the notion that Northerners are more active with respect to leisure activities.

Taking full advantage of the comprehensive nature of the original data set, Marsden et al. (1982) looked into some possible reasons for the North-South differences. The original survey included a great deal of demographic information, and Marsden et al. found that taking demographic variables into account reduced but did not eliminate the North-South differences. They concluded that "Southerners do less of almost everything—or at least almost everything it occurred to the [data collectors] to ask people about" (p. 1040).

The qualification in their conclusion points out one of the difficulties researchers have when analyzing existing data: Using existing data limits one to information that others consider important, not necessarily the same information the researcher may consider relevant to his or her purposes. Marsden et al. (1982) may have wanted to examine other types of leisure activities but were unable to do so because such activities were not included in the original survey. They were also required to use some rather sophisticated statistical analyses to adapt the original data to their purposes. Although the raw data format is the most flexible of the formats for existing data, existing data are rarely as flexible as those one collects for oneself—for one's own purposes and for testing one's own hypotheses. Thus, when consuming this type of archival research, we need to be a little more forgiving when researchers don't have certain types of data. By *forgiving* I mean that we don't necessarily fault the researchers for the limits of the data collection, as we would, say, if a researcher collecting his or her own data forgot to collect what obviously should have been an important variable. On the other hand, just because a researcher dealt with archival data does not excuse him or her for overgeneralizing from the data or from conducting inappropriate analyses.

The classic illustration of the use of aggregate data is Durkheim's (Durkheim, 1951/1897) research on environmental correlates of suicide. In an effort to address the question of why people take their own lives, Durkheim obtained and analyzed suicide rates and other demographic statistics from a number of different European countries. Although he identified a number of patterns in the suicide rates—including information that refuted the then-accepted explanation of uncomfortably hot weather—the most intriguing aspects of the data were the associations of suicide rates with both political activity and religious affiliations. Durkheim noted, for example, a dramatic increase in suicides during 1848, a particularly tumultuous year politically for many European countries. He also noted that countries with larger proportions of Catholic residents exhibited consistently lower suicide rates.

But Durkheim did not have access to information on the religious denominations of individuals who committed suicide. Instead, he investigated the religious connection by using the relative number of Catholics and Protestants within various countries. For example, predominantly Catholic Bavaria exhibited one-third fewer suicides than predominantly Protestant provinces. Generally, the greater the proportion of Catholics in a given region, the lower the suicide rate in that region.

Taken together, the associations of suicide rates with both religious affiliation and political turmoil led Durkheim (1951/1897) to conclude that **anomie**—*a general sense of instability or disintegration*—was an important contributory factor in suicide. Political changes led to instability in everyday life, which in turn produced anomie. Fewer suicides among Catholics may have been due to the fact that Catholicism in the 1800s was more structured and more authoritarian than were Protestant denominations, and the structure available to Catholics may have provided stability and prevented anomie.

Another example of the use of aggregate data is a study by Travis (1985), who used aggregate health statistics to demonstrate gender biases in elective surgery. Travis showed that hysterectomies were much more likely to be elective than other types of surgery, such as appendectomies (for men and women) or prostate removal (for men). More important, Travis was able to demonstrate that physicians were estimating risks and benefits in different ways for female and male patients.

In Chapter 3, you learned how to review existing literature, a process analogous to a qualitative content analysis. It is also possible to engage in a quantitative analysis of previous research using statistical results as data. When statistical results are the source of existing data, the research is called **meta-analysis,** *integrating research findings by statistically analyzing the results from individual studies* (Glass, McGraw, & Smith, 1981). Meta-analysis has become a means by which to determine how strong a particular empirical effect may be. (See Chapter 4 for more information on meta-analysis.)

For example, Wrightsman and I completed a qualitative review of research on the influence of defendant and victim characteristics on jury verdicts (Dane & Wrightsman, 1982). One of our conclusions was related to the finding that attractive defendants are generally treated more leniently than unattractive defendants. However, most of that research involved simulations of trials—legal and ethical restrictions on manipulating independent variables in actual trials made simulations necessary—and there has been considerable controversy about whether simulations can be generalized to actual trials (Bray & Kerr, 1982).

One of the major criticisms of the use of simulations is the limited amount of information presented to mock jurors. The amount of material ranges from half-page summaries to complete transcripts or videotapes of trials. Opponents of simulation claim that incomplete simulations overemphasize the influence of defendants' physical attractiveness and other independent variables. For example, viewing photographs of the defendant paired with a half-page summary of evidence might have a greater impact on jurors than seeing the defendant as one of many individuals in a videotape of a trial.

The controversy involved some very good arguments on both sides. But without a reasonable amount of empirical evidence, the debate could not advance beyond the equivalent of a shouting match. Rather than add more voices to either side, Linz, Slack, Kaiser, and Penrod (1981) used meta-analysis to provide the required empirical information. Their meta-analysis included 15 studies on the effects of defendants' physical attractiveness, and their results led them to estimate the odds that the effect was due to chance alone at less than one in a million. Of greater importance was the finding that the impact of manipulating physical attractiveness tended to increase with the amount of material included in simulations. Rather than being lost among the legitimate items of evidence presented in a full-scale simulation, physical attractiveness appears to have stronger effects. Thus, the controversy surrounding trial simulations was stilled, at least for physical attractiveness of defendants as the independent variable of interest.

METHODOLOGICAL ISSUES IN EXISTING DATA ANALYSIS

Just as with content analysis, researchers who use existing data require a specific purpose. Marsden et al. (1982) wanted to investigate stereotypes about leisure time, Durkheim's purpose was to consider environmental correlates of suicide, Travis (1985) wanted to examine gender bias in surgical procedures, and Linz et al. (1981) assessed the impact of defendants' physical attractiveness on verdicts. Each of these research projects included a specific hypothesis to be tested with existing data. Although a necessary first step, a specific hypothesis is not sufficient for analyzing existing data.

You may have noticed the rather wide range of units of analysis illustrated by these investigations. Marsden et al. (1982) analyzed individual responses to questionnaires, Durkheim (1951/1897) analyzed regional suicide rates, Travis (1985) analyzed rates of surgical procedures, and Linz et al. (1981) analyzed the results of statistical analysis. Great care must be taken to ensure that the units of analysis chosen are appropriate to the hypotheses tested and the conclusions drawn. Durkheim, for example, analyzed regional suicide rates but drew conclusions about individual suicide rates. *A mismatch between units of analysis and the research hypothesis* is known as an **ecological fallacy**. Durkheim's data dealt with groups, but his hypotheses were about individuals. Consider his conclusion regarding religious affiliation: Catholics committed fewer suicides because their religion reduced anomie. That hypothesis was tested by comparing the suicide rates in predominantly Catholic regions with the rates in predominantly Protestant regions. As Babbie (1983) has suggested, it may be that Catholics committed just as many suicides as Protestants but did so in predominantly Protestant areas. Certainly, Durkheim's explanation seems more plausible than the notion of Catholics (but not Protestants) traveling to faraway regions to commit suicide. On the other hand, proponents of either hypothesis cannot claim to have clear empirical support from Durkheim's data. Effects identified through research on aggregate data cannot be used to test hypotheses about the individual units that produced the aggregate.

Linz et al. (1981) did have a match between their hypotheses and their units of analysis; both dealt with research studies. However, someone might be tempted to conclude that Linz et al.'s findings also mean that attractive defendants may be treated more leniently in longer trials than in shorter trials. After all, the effect of attractiveness was stronger in the more complete (longer) simulations. This conclusion, however, would involve **reductionism**, *the logical fallacy of drawing conclusions about individuals' behaviors from units of analysis that do not deal with individuals.*

As noted earlier, one of the problems inherent in conducting research with existing data is that the hypotheses the researcher can test are limited to the data he or she can find. In addition to not being able to find relevant data, the researcher may also encounter a problem with the age of the data. Existing data, obviously, were collected in the past, and old data may not be appropriate to the researcher's hypotheses. The data used by Durkheim (1951/1897) are now almost 150 years old. Although ancient by research standards, they can still be used for valid tests of hypotheses, provided the hypotheses are about what happened 150 years ago. One could not, for example, use those data to predict next year's suicide rates in Europe.

Another threat to validity is the quality of the data. Consider Linz et al.'s (1981) meta-analysis. The essential aspect of meta-analysis involves comparing the size of effects across different studies. But the size of the effect in any given study depends on the quality of the study. If, for example, the studies that involved less complete simulations were also poorer in quality, the relationship identified by Linz et al. would be spurious. I should point out that such is not the case—the research included by Linz et al. was good research—but the potential effects of poor research procedures must be considered whenever one decides to use existing data.

Just as the researcher must rely on the original collectors of existing data for the data's validity, the researcher must also rely on them for the data's reliability. Again, consider Durkheim's (1951/1897) study. At the time the data were collected, suicide carried a much greater stigma for Catholics than for Protestants, and thus it is possible that some suicides in Catholic regions were mislabeled as accidental or due to some other cause. The suicide rates on which Durkheim depended for his research therefore may not have been reliable. Durkheim did not have direct experience with the data collection procedures, nor do most researchers who use existing data. Before drawing conclusions from research involving existing data, carefully examine the research procedures to ensure sufficient reliability and validity for your purposes.

SUMMARY

- Archival research includes any project in which existing documents or data are the units of observation. These may include novels, music, movies, and other reports, as well as raw, aggregate, or statistical data collected by others.
- Content analysis may be used to answer questions of the general form "Who says what to whom, how, with what effect, and why?" Although any communication medium can be content analyzed, it is more appropriate to compare two or more messages than to draw conclusions about a single message.
- Coding in content analysis can involve either manifest content or latent content. Coding manifest content—concrete denotations—usually results in more reliable data because the coding is more objective. Although sometimes less reliable, coding latent content may be the only way to operationalize complex theoretical concepts.
- Quantifying data in content analysis can involve recording either the frequency of variables or the amount of time or space devoted to a topic in the message; either may be used for manifest content or latent content. Evaluative assertion analysis can also be used for messages that contain complex statements.
- Archival research involving existing data relies on data collected in the past, usually by other researchers. Analyzing raw data is the most flexible

procedure, provided the operational definitions used to collect the data match those in the researcher's hypotheses. Aggregate data may be less flexible but may provide better operational definitions of complex concepts. Meta-analysis of statistical results limits the researcher to hypotheses about research studies but may be used to support conclusions drawn from qualitative literature reviews.

- The analysis of existing data includes the potential problems of ecological fallacy and reductionism. The former occurs when there is a mismatch between the units of analysis and the research hypotheses, and the latter occurs when conclusions about individuals are drawn from aggregate data.

- When reading about research involving data collected by others, it is sometimes more difficult to determine their reliability and validity. Because you lack direct experience with the data collection procedures, a careful reading of the original procedures is the only way to determine whether the data fit your purposes.

EXERCISES

1. Find an article in which the authors report on content analysis research. Determine how many answers to the "who says what to whom, how, with what effect, and why" questions were answered by the researchers.

2. Using the same or a different article, identify the unit(s) of observation employed in the research.

3. Find an article in which the researchers report on analyses of existing data. Identify the source of the data and what allowances the researchers had to make in order to use those data.

4. Find an article in which the researcher reports a meta-analysis. Identify the variables employed in the meta-analysis.

CHAPTER 12

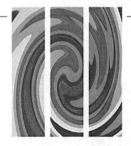

Evaluation Research

Modern nations should be ready for an experimental approach to social reforms.

—D. T. Campbell (1969, p. 409)

Overview

Although not truly a separate type of research method, program evaluation research involves sufficiently different issues to merit separate consideration. In this chapter you will learn about those issues, as well as some of the methods through which program effectiveness or planning can be evaluated. A review of operationalization will be presented, but the topics will be covered from the perspective of attempting to measure variables with minimum alteration of normal routines so that you have the information you need to evaluate program evaluation research. You will also learn about the political ramifications of evaluation research, which have obvious implications for the application of program evaluations to policies or programs. Finally, ethical issues will be reviewed with emphasis on the ways they apply to program evaluation research specifically.

INTRODUCTION

Let me begin this chapter by pointing out that evaluation research is not a method in the same way that experimental, quasi-experimental, and archival research are methods. Instead, in this context evaluation refers to the purpose for which research is completed, usually action, and it may involve any of the traditional research methods used for other purposes. It also involves assessing some aspect of a program designed to alter the world in which we live.

According to Rossi and Freeman (1982), "**evaluation research** is *the systematic application of . . . research procedures in assessing the conceptualization and design, implementation, and utility of social intervention programs*" (p. 20, emphasis added). This is a rather long, involved definition, and each of its parts deserves attention. The components illustrate the variety of questions that can be asked and answered through evaluation research.

Any attempt to alter the world may be considered a social intervention. When people attempt to change a particular situation, such as hunger, they implement a social intervention; that is, they do something to try to alter the conditions under which people live, presumably for the better. When such attempts involve a specific target group and are planned, social interventions become social programs. In this context, the school you are attending can be considered a social program.

From the perspective of social intervention, education is a planned attempt to alter the immediate experience of a specific target group: students. At a different level of analysis, education is also a program designed to increase the effectiveness of any number of unspecified programs; at least we are told in commencement speeches that educating people will improve the world in general. Other examples of social programs include Aid to Families with Dependent Children, community mental health centers, and (Product)Red (Buzztone, 2008), the program organized by Bono and Bobby Shriver to raise money for The Global Fund for treating HIV/AIDS in Sub-Saharan Africa.

Whenever a social intervention is evaluated, one very reasonable, simple, and appropriate question is asked: Does it work? The utility of a social program includes, in part, the effectiveness of the program—whether you are, for example, learning anything as a result of your education. To those paying for the program, another reasonable question centers on the cost of the program: Is it worth the money we are spending? Program utility, then, refers not only to the benefits received by its participants but also to the cost of the program relative to either its absence or an alternative program.

By definition, any social program includes a set of procedures for its administration—a plan for implementation. Evaluation research often involves examining implementations, sometimes in the planning stage and sometimes after they are underway. Indeed, evaluation of programs both as they are planned and as they are implemented is what Campbell (1969) was calling for in the opening quote for this chapter. To some extent, evaluating planning involves trying to predict the future, but that is pretty much what we do any time we generalize from existing research results. Evaluation research, then, generally involves the application of a variety of research methods to decide more effectively how to design and implement a social program and how to determine its effectiveness.

SUMMATIVE AND FORMATIVE EVALUATION

According to the above definition, evaluation research can be conducted at any phase of a program. The way in which evaluation research is practiced, however, actually falls into two major categories: summative and formative evaluations.

A **summative evaluation** is *an assessment of the outcome(s) of a program*. Also called outcome evaluation, summative research involves determining the goals that were actually reached by a completed program. For example, outcome evaluation may be used to determine the number of dollars delivered to The Global Fund directly from the Product(Red) campaign or the number of HIV/AIDS patients treated through those donations. The goals measured by a summative evaluation may or may not be those included in the original plan of the program, and the research is usually accomplished through archival, survey, experimental, or quasi-experimental methods. Because manipulations of independent variables are not always possible in evaluation research, quasi-experimental designs tend to be used more often than experimental designs.

A **formative evaluation** is *an assessment of the process(es) of a program*. Also called process evaluation, formative evaluation involves judging the means by which a program is operating. Questions about the effects of a program can be involved, but they are addressed with respect to how the effects are produced. Rather than using methods that measure differences among groups, formative evaluation researchers are more likely to concentrate on participant observation and other field research methods. Data tend to be qualitative but can be quantitative as well.

Summative and formative evaluations differ in terms of the questions asked about a program, what it has accomplished and how it is operating, respectively. Although there are methods that tend to be used more for one than the other purpose, any method that appropriately addresses the relevant question can be used for either type of evaluation research.

CONSUMERS OF EVALUATION RESEARCH

Perhaps one of the greatest differences between evaluation research and the other types of research discussed in this text concerns the consumers—the people who will use the results of the research. Thus far, most of our discussions have focused on other behavioral scientists as the major consumers of research results. Evaluation research, however, is action research conducted in order to produce a change in the way things are done, and its consumers include not only other scientists but also program administrators and recipients, policy makers, and anyone else with a vested interest in the program being evaluated, including you.

The fact that those with a vested interest in the program are also most likely to be the ones who commission or sponsor the evaluation research can produce some rather sticky ethical and practical problems for researchers. When someone's reputation or employment is on the line, the presumed objectivity with which the results may be considered tends to fade a bit. The experimenting society envisioned by Campbell (1969) and others does not yet exist. Primarily for this reason, the ways in which measures and procedures are determined for evaluation research may not be as straightforward as they may seem to be for other types of research. This, then, requires even more careful consideration of the research report as you attempt to apply the results of evaluation research to the particular policy or program of interest to you.

THE HARTFORD PROJECT:
AN EXAMPLE OF EVALUATION RESEARCH

Operationalization

Attempting to operationalize the concepts involved in any research project is no easy task. When the major reason for making the attempt is to evaluate a social program, the task can very quickly become extremely difficult. Program goals are often defined before anyone has contemplated doing research, and they are rarely as well defined as the theoretical concepts with which researchers work when conducting other types of research.

Throughout this section, we'll use a crime control intervention program designed to reduce burglaries and robberies in the Asylum Hill area of Hartford, CT (Fowler, 1981), as a continuing example. The program has been called both the Asylum Hill Project and the Hartford Project; we'll use the latter title, primarily because it is the better-known name. The project has become a classic in urban redesign as well as in community policing (Sherman, 1986).

Similarity to Basic Research

Like any research project, the Hartford Project was based on existing theory and research. For example, several researchers had pointed to the advantage of physical measures to control neighborhood crime. A high level of surveillance in a mixture of homes and businesses, together with a sense of cohesion or belongingness, was theorized to reduce or retard criminal activity. The Hartford Project was the first in a series of studies designed to examine these theoretical issues in an actual neighborhood setting.

Also like any other research project, evaluation research includes a great deal of decision making and planning before any data are collected. The variety of questions that can be asked about a program is as great as the variety of questions that can be asked about a theory; it is limitless. Whether there are questions about theory or about programs, a single study cannot address all questions. Indeed, one of the reasons we will study the Hartford Project as an exemplary piece of evaluation research is the combination of its similarity to the general research process and its inclusion of a wide range of evaluation-specific issues. The Hartford Project, for example, included both formative and summative purposes, but we're getting ahead of ourselves.

The Problem

In any evaluation research project, defining the problem is the first step. "What is the present situation?" and "What about it should be the target of the evaluation?" are the main questions involved in defining the research problem. If the program is ongoing, these questions can be addressed through archival research or interviews with key program personnel. In the Hartford Project, they were addressed through formative evaluations.

According to Fowler (1981) "from the outset, [the project] was intended to be an integrated, multifaceted program which included physical design, police, and citizen components working in concert to reduce criminal opportunities" (p. 167). Not only was the Hartford Project the first of its kind; it was also an effort to tackle a social problem—crime—that seems to invite more problems than solutions. Some form of preliminary assessment was necessary before the operationalization of the project could be finalized.

It was necessary to obtain descriptive data about the physical design of the neighborhood, and so a team of design experts studied Asylum Hill. For example, some of the conditions that required change included a great deal of traffic on residential streets, a high number of pedestrians who did not reside in the neighborhood, a public park that seemed overrun by drunks and teenagers, and the frequent use of private and semiprivate areas, such as backyards and parking lots, as alternatives to sidewalks.

Other preliminary information was obtained by surveying residents, particularly about their fear of crime and experience with victimization. Police records were examined to obtain baseline data about the frequency and patterns of criminal activity. The police officers working in the neighborhood were also surveyed, and observational research provided information about the activities of residential organizations.

The Program

As a result of the information collected during the planning stage of the program, a number of changes in the Asylum Hill neighborhood were suggested. These eventually became incorporated into a planned innovation, a social program for reducing crime. According to Fowler (1981), the program included three components:

1. A police team was to be permanently assigned to the area in order to increase police familiarity with the local crime problem and with criminals and to strengthen ties between police and citizens.

2. The vehicular traffic through the neighborhood was to be restructured by the use of street closings and the introduction of one-way streets. Through these changes and the introduction of visual neighborhood boundaries, it was hoped that the residential nature of the area would be emphasized and that residents would be more able and willing to exert control over the activities in their neighborhood, thereby making operation of outside offenders more difficult.

3. Resident organizations were to be developed and encouraged to provide a mechanism for residents to work with police, to participate in the planning of the details for the physical design changes and, perhaps, to involve residents directly in efforts to strengthen the neighborhood and reduce crime. (p. 169)

Just as a single research project can rarely test an entire theory, a single innovation can rarely affect the full range of difficulties included in a social problem or even the full range of measures in a single program. Those designing the project realized that a program may be designed to reduce all crime, but implementing and evaluating such a program would be impossible. Too many crimes are extremely difficult to detect, such as spouse and child abuse, and other crimes may be too infrequent, such as murder. Instead, the program was to focus on two crimes only: burglary and robbery. These two crimes were chosen because they were somewhat common in the area and were typically committed by perpetrators unknown to the victims and because the program designers believed they produced fear.

In the Hartford Project, the ability to measure processes and outcomes was considered in the planning of the program. This is one advantage inherent in deciding to evaluate a program before it is fully designed and implemented. Not all programs, however, are implemented with evaluation in mind; many researchers find themselves having to deal with program goals that cannot be measured.

The Questions

The most obvious question to be addressed was simply whether the project reduced crime. As a program designed specifically for that purpose, perhaps it is the only question of merit. The Hartford Project, however, was not designed only to reduce crime. Again, because the project was planned with evaluation in mind, there were actually four questions:

1. In what ways was the program as implemented similar to or different from the one that was planned?

2. Did the rates of burglary and robbery and the residents' concerns about those crimes decrease as a result of the program?

3. If so, what features of the program produced those results? If not, for what reason did this program fail to produce those results?

4. What, if anything, does this experience teach us about how to affect crime and fear in other neighborhoods? (Fowler, 1981, p. 170)

As pointed out earlier, the Hartford Project included both formative and summative evaluations. Formative evaluation was used in the design of the program. The first question restates the general purpose of formative evaluation but does so from a summative perspective: Did we do what we planned to do? The second question is most clearly an outcome issue, a summative evaluation question: Did the program accomplish what it was designed to accomplish? The third question involves causal analysis, an attempt to determine the cause(s) of whatever effects were produced by the program. The fourth question is a crossover question; from the viewpoint of the Hartford Project it is summative, but from the viewpoint of a continuing series of crime control projects it is formative. How these questions were answered or not answered through the data collected is the issue to which we next turn.

The Measures

Fowler (1981) pointed out several difficulties encountered in attempting to obtain reliable and valid measures for the project. These difficulties, or at least some of them, are likely to be encountered by most evaluation researchers (see, for example, Reicken & Boruch, 1974).

The first of these difficulties stemmed from what Fowler (1981) described as "vague, meaningless, or extremely complex" (p. 172) concepts. One of those concepts is fear of crime, for which reliable and valid measures were required at the outset of the project in order to obtain baseline information. Because previous research (as of 1973) was of little help in operationalizing fear of crime, the researchers relied on theory (see, for example, Parsons, 1951) to derive their measures. Eventually, fear of crime was operationalized as a combination of the likelihood of personal victimization and a subjective assessment of the general severity of victimization for a particular crime. That is, an individual's level of fear was related both to the perceived chances of becoming a victim and a belief about how dangerous and uncomfortable being a victim might be.

Another problem inherent in attempting to operationalize various concepts surfaced because the evaluation team was composed of researchers from different disciplines. No small amount of effort was devoted to becoming familiar with one another's specialized jargon and measurement processes. The social psychologists, sociologists, criminologists, and urban designers all were required to translate terms and concepts—the meanings of which they took for granted—for the benefit of the others. Such communication difficulties are more common than you might think because those conducting evaluation research are typically outsiders with respect to the program. Evaluation researchers must communicate with practitioners, administrators, clients, and others who may be unfamiliar with the jargon of research and may have their own brand of jargon (Dane, 2008). Just think back, for example, about how much jargon you have picked up reading this textbook. Did you know, for example, what *quasi-experimental*, *sampling distribution*, or *regression artifact* meant? How many of your friends who haven't taken this course would understand these terms? The glossary is full of jargon, and you're just beginning to deal with research.

The second problem encountered in the project was attempting to measure systematically processes that were not systematic. Describing or measuring changes in everyday human behavior is often problematic in summative evaluation research but is equally as often necessary in formative evaluations. One of the processes to be evaluated in the Hartford Project was the use of space by those residing in and outside of the neighborhood. To measure vehicular traffic, for example, mechanical counters were deployed day and night to monitor traffic at strategic locations in the neighborhood. To measure pedestrian traffic, observers counted pedestrians at certain times of the day. The observers also coded the direction of movement and estimated age, ethnic status, and other demographic characteristics. The combination of research strategies for the purpose of measurement was necessary to measure all of the components of the project.

The third problem centered on attempting to measure the impact of the program. In basic research, replications or random assignment aid in causal analysis, the logical process of attributing an effect to the treatment of participants. In evaluation research, however, replications are extremely rare. Funds were not available in the Hartford Project, for example, to redesign several neighborhoods, nor could the researchers randomly assign people to live in different neighborhoods or randomly assign some outsiders to visit or stay out of the neighborhood.

More often than not, the impact of a new program is assessed by comparing the preexisting conditions with conditions after the program. Without random assignment, however, this before-after design is highly susceptible to a variety of alternative explanations. When the research environment is a city neighborhood, history and mortality effects are of particular concern. Another approach, more often used with existing programs, is to identify a similar unit of analysis—a neighborhood, individuals, and so on—not involved in the program and use it for comparison. For the Hartford Project, the difficulty of finding another neighborhood similar to Asylum Hill precluded that approach.

A combination of approaches was used instead. Baseline data were collected in the Asylum Hill neighborhood, and the outcome measures were compared to those data. Also, two neighborhoods adjacent to Asylum Hill were selected as control neighborhoods. The adjacent areas were chosen, in part, because one possible outcome of the physical redesign was displacement, movement of criminal activities out of Asylum Hill and into some other neighborhood. Although displacement solves the problem of crime in one location, it does not produce any net reduction in crime.

Ecosystem Measures

Measuring victimization rates and fear of crime were attempts to measure the impact of the program from the perspective of the recipients or clients. The Hartford Project researchers had an advantage over other evaluation researchers because they had a pretty good idea of the clients' desired level of service: The residents of Asylum Hill presumably desired zero victimization and zero fear of crime. A zero-level outcome, however, cannot always be assumed to be the desired level.

Developed from the concept of stakeholder evaluations (Bryk, 1983; N. Gold, 1981), **ecosystem measurement** involves *the simultaneous measurement of level of service received and level of service desired by clients*. In an educational program, for example, students may be asked to describe both the depth of coverage provided for a particular topic and the depth of coverage they desired for the topic. Ecosystem measures and stakeholder evaluation in general are based on the assumption that those who have a stake in the program are valuable resources for determining the desired level of service.

Ecosystem measures enable one to determine whether the perceived level of service was less than, equal to, or greater than the desired level of service. Regardless of the extent to which such information is to be used to determine the level of service that should be provided, ecosystem measures provide information beyond a simple satisfactory/unsatisfactory measure of the program. The more that clients can be assumed to be competent judges of the desired level of service, the more informative and valuable ecosystem measures become.

The Results

In case you are wondering about the outcome of the Hartford Project, the program did both lower crime rates and reduce residents' fears about crime. The complete results are too lengthy to outline in this chapter, but you can read about them in Fowler's (1981) report. It is an interesting report, and it is fascinating if you are interested in program evaluation or criminal justice issues. Now, however, we must turn to the relative advantages and disadvantages of the use of experimental designs for evaluation.

THE CONTROVERSY OVER THE USE OF EXPERIMENTS IN EVALUATION RESEARCH

Boruch (1975) provided what is perhaps the best elucidation of the controversy over the use of experiments in evaluation research. The controversy involves four major issues: difficulty, qualitative information, innovation, and ethics. Almost 40 years later, no straightforward solutions appear to be forthcoming, although there are guidelines that are beneficial to both beginning and experienced scientists. As well, understanding these difficulties might eliminate some frustration as you search unsuccessfully for experimental research relevant to a particular program or policy.

Difficulties With Experiments in Evaluation Research

The *possibility* of using experimental designs in evaluation research is not part of the controversy; it is possible (and has been for some time) to manipulate variables and randomly assign participants to different conditions within almost any program that can be evaluated. Boruch (1975) provided over 200 examples of experimentally evaluated programs, including programs in job training, criminal justice, social welfare, and many other fields. It is not, however, always *easy* to use experimental designs in evaluation research.

The difficulties inherent in the use of experimental designs are not difficulties with the designs per se. After all, random assignment is not a difficult procedure, nor is manipulating a variety of different variables likely to be included in program evaluation. Instead, the difficulties appear to revolve around the willingness of program administrators to allow the use of experimental designs, as well as the ability of other research procedures to measure up to experiments.

The key factor appears to be the type of program being evaluated. Boruch points out that the difficulty is directly related to the extent to which the effects being evaluated are dependent on program staff and personal skills. Social service programs, for example, involve greater difficulty than do programs involving technological innovations. Administrators of social service programs often resist the use of experiments for evaluation simply because an experiment is too often perceived to be a perfect test of a program. The argument is not with the use of experimental designs but with the perceived inability of scientists to measure the effects of social service programs. A potentially good idea for social service may be deemed a bad idea not because it is ineffective but because a supposedly perfect experiment did not include an accurate measure of the benefits of the program. That is, the problem is not with determining the cause but with measuring the effect.

Similarly, Boruch (1975) points out that critics of experiments consider them to be too narrow in scope (to test only a few variables) or too brief in duration (only one measurement of the dependent variable[s] instead of multiple measurements over a period of time). Again, however, these criticisms are not related to design considerations but rather to the financial and political considerations that are a part of all evaluation research. Interviews, for example, are more expensive than questionnaires, which in turn are more expensive than archival measures. It is often the case that waiting a number of years in order to monitor longitudinally the progress of a program is not politically feasible. Research takes time, and both proponents and opponents of social programs are usually anxious to learn of a program's effectiveness as quickly as possible.

The above viewpoint from the administrators' perspective is clearly based on a lack of familiarity with experimental designs and research in general. There is, of course, no perfect experiment, nor should anyone ever consider the results of a single experiment to be the final word on any issue. What is required to overcome this problem, in addition to better measures of outcome variables, is education about the value of experimental research as well as its limitations.

Qualitative Information in Evaluation Research

The second issue in the controversy also appears to revolve around misperceptions of experimental research. Specifically, experimental research is perceived to preclude the collection of qualitative data. Clearly, researchers who use experimental designs tend to favor quantitative measures, but that preference has little to do with experimental design itself. Instead, it would seem to be more reasonable to conclude that those who prefer quantitative data also prefer experimental designs. Neither randomly assigning participants to conditions nor manipulating independent variables necessarily requires the use of quantitative dependent variables. Although design and measurement are related, the relationship between them is simply not that strong.

Innovation in Evaluation Research

The third issue connected with using experimental designs for evaluation research is that such designs, when used to test the outcome of a program, cannot provide information about what other new programs might work. An experimental test of a traffic safety program, for example, might answer whether the program produces a lower accident rate; but if the answer is no, it doesn't lower the accident rate, then the experiment does not provide information about the potential effectiveness of alternative programs.

Although this is a valid criticism, it is not new. Indeed, this same criticism can be directed at all research in which theories are tested. If only one theory is tested in a research project, the researcher is limited to information about that theory. The theory is either supported or not; a program either works or it doesn't. Regardless of the research design, one obtains information only about what is tested.

Campbell (1971) has offered one solution to the innovation problem, a solution based on what has been done in theory testing research to overcome the same problem. The solution is, very simply, to use experimental designs to test the relative effectiveness of two or more programs, just as many experiments test the relative effectiveness of competing theories. The question then becomes whether one program is better than the other. If more than one alternative exists for a social service program or any other program, for that matter, but enough money is available to fund only one of them, Campbell suggests implementing a simultaneous test of alternatives rather than what is typically done now, a sequential test of first one program, then the other.

Also within the context of innovation, Boruch (1975) pointed out that many opponents of experiments in evaluation claim that rigorous—that is, experimental—tests of programs will limit creativity for developing new programs. Essentially, the argument is that incentives to be creative will be reduced if those responsible for development fear that their creations will be shot down by an evaluator armed with an experiment. This issue is similar to one addressed earlier, that of the unwillingness of administrators to accept the results of experiments because they perceive them to be final. Drawing an analogy between theory testing and evaluation research, however, destroys the logic of this criticism. Certainly, creativity in terms of theory development has not suffered from the use of experimental designs, and there is no reason to assume that creativity with respect to program development will also suffer.

What may be affected, however, are the careers of those who propose innovative programs. If the effectiveness of a proposed program is used to determine whether or not a program administrator or developer will be retained, for example, then not too many administrators or developers are going to be open to rigorous evaluation. Again, Campbell (1969) suggested adopting an experimentation approach to program development to solve this problem. If evaluation of administrative and development performance is based on a track record of success, as opposed to the success of a single program, then individuals may be more willing to try something new.

Ethics in Evaluation Research

Perhaps the greatest controversy over the use of experimental designs for evaluation revolves around the ethical issues of random assignment. Opponents of experiments have likened random assignment to denying treatment randomly to those who would otherwise receive a program's services. However, failing to test a program adequately before implementing also constitutes a potential breach of ethics (Dane, 2007a).

Most program evaluations involve a test of whether the program is beneficial or ineffective. More often than not, limitations on the number of participants in most programs are based on financial rather than methodological considerations. That is, with or without random assignment, monetary constraints limit the number of participants who could potentially benefit from the services being evaluated. In such cases, holding lotteries to select and assign participants may be the fairest means by which to implement an experiment (Reicken & Boruch, 1974). When the individuals involved have equivalent needs, lotteries are perceived as fair, and the procedures for a lottery are not much different from those normally involved in random assignment.

Although ethical questions rarely have easy answers, the general balancing act concerns whether random assignment places a greater burden on participants than does a nonexperimental design. If the answer is yes, then a quasi-experimental design should be used to complete the evaluation. Withholding benefits to potential program clients through random assignment is not the only ethical issue involved in evaluation research, and so we turn now to some other ethical considerations.

ETHICAL CONSIDERATIONS IN EVALUATION RESEARCH

Like all research, evaluation research does not occur in an ethical vacuum. Indeed, because evaluation research is often contracted for or paid for by those running the program being evaluated, evaluation research poses some ethical issues not normally considered in other types of research. Evaluation research involves trying to serve four masters: the researcher, the program clients, the program staff, and the program administrator(s). In the ideal world of Campbell's (1971) experimenting society, these four masters share the common goal of obtaining sufficient information to decide the best way to implement a program to solve a social problem.

In the not-so-ideal world of practicing evaluation research, the four groups may have very different and sometimes competing interests. The researcher wants to complete a high-quality research project, the clients want their problem solved, the staff members want to be able to function effectively and efficiently, and the administrators want a low-cost, favorable evaluation of the program. The American Evaluation Association (2004) has published a set of principles to aid evaluation researchers in their attempts to promote the ideal while working in the not-so-ideal. If you peruse that document, you'll find that the principles are much the same as ethical principles for all researchers whose research includes human participants (e.g., National Commission for the Protection of Human Subjects of Biomedical and Behavioral Research, 1979). The discussion below is based on an earlier set of standards (Evaluation Research Society Standards Committee, 1982) that were more broadly based on the issues of interest to all stakeholders. Understanding the ethical issues involved in evaluation research will not only better enable you to apply evaluation research to your interests but, as one involved in the policies and programs, will also enable you to avoid pitfalls should you have occasion to commission evaluation research.

Formulation and Negotiation

Before beginning an evaluation project, all parties involved should reach a mutual understanding of the task, the methods, the rationale, and the shortcomings of the project. The rights of all individuals involved in the project should be of major importance, and no stakeholder should attempt a project that is beyond his or her expertise and resources. Any agreements reached during the negotiation and formulation stages should be specified in writing, for the documents may clarify subsequent misunderstandings.

The agreement should contain a clear statement of the purpose and description of the program to be evaluated, including identification of the expectations and needs of clients, decision makers, and other potential users of the results. The objectives of the evaluation should be clearly specified, as should any reasonable estimate of the cost of the evaluation. Within the context of outlining any possible conflicts of interests, the feasibility of the evaluation and any restrictions on dissemination of the results should also be specified.

Structure and Design

In addition to methodological interests, the design of an evaluation project is influenced by "logistical, ethical, political and fiscal concerns" (Evaluation Research Society Standards Committee, 1982, p. 13). Such influences are not, however, sufficient reason for failing to provide the best possible design, regardless of the type of evaluation chosen during the negotiation phase. The design should be clearly specified and should be appropriate for the purposes of the evaluation. For outcome studies, for example, the design should be adequate for identifying the relative differences between treatment and control groups. Sampling methods should be specified and justified in terms of the purposes of the evaluation.

Any measures involved in the project should be clearly described, including their levels of established reliability and validity. Finally, the cooperation of any individuals involved in implementing the actual data collection procedures should be obtained. If you plan to involve staff members in data collection, for example, the best possible design will be worthless if the staff cannot collect the data.

Data Collection and Preparation

Like any good research project, the procedures and means for data collection should be planned in advance and should include some way to determine whether the plan is being followed. Training and supervising may be required to ensure that those collecting the data are following the proper procedures. To whatever extent possible, the plan for data collection should include an effort to assess the reliability and validity of the data as they are collected. That a pre-existing measure has exhibited reliability and validity in previous studies is not an absolute guarantee that the same will hold true for the way in which it is used in a different context. As you critically read about evaluation research, check to make sure the researchers assessed reliability and validity.

The actual data collection procedures should involve a minimum amount of disruption to the routine of the program. Staff members usually have enough to do without being asked to take on the extra burden of collecting data. Informed consent should be monitored, particularly if those who are clients or data collectors are to be exposed to any risks. Depending on the sensitivity of the data, safeguards should be established to protect confidentiality or anonymity. Also, safeguards must be developed to ensure against loss of the data, including documentation of the sources, collection procedures, and preparation of the data.

Data Analysis and Interpretation

The data analyses should be chosen to match the purpose and design of the project and the data collected. Rather than simply relying on what others have done or what is convenient, the chosen analyses should be clearly justified in light of the underlying assumptions and limitations inherent in them. Care must be taken to match analyses with the type of data collected. Sufficient documentation should be maintained so that others may replicate the analyses, including procedures used to clean or transform variables.

When interpreting data, care must be taken to avoid drawing conclusions beyond the limitations of the data and their analyses. If the decision makers are not well versed in the use of statistics, the difference between statistical significance and practical significance should be clearly explained. Cause-effect conclusions should be drawn only when appropriate with clear reference to any remaining alternative explanations. The report should clearly distinguish among empirical results, opinions, judgments, and speculations.

Communication and Disclosure

In addition to care concerning the differences among results, opinions, judgments, and speculations, the final report should clearly convey the research findings. Any assumptions made during the project should be explicitly included, particularly those assumptions relevant to the final recommendations or conclusions. Any limitations of the research, within or without the researcher's control, should also be specified and related to the final recommendations.

Dissemination of the final or any preliminary reports should be completed within the guidelines specified in the initial agreement. Only those authorized to publicize the results should do so. Those who have contributed to the project should be acknowledged and should receive whatever feedback is appropriate. Finally, preparation of a database and its documentation should be completed as outlined in the initial agreement.

Use of Results

Because evaluation research is invariably conducted to provide information to those who must make decisions about the program, it is essential that the results be made available in sufficient time to allow them to be used. And although one cannot be responsible for others' misinterpretations of results, there is an ethical requirement to attempt to prevent misinterpretations, as well as to attempt to correct them when they become known.

Because the researcher is probably the most fully informed about the results, the researcher may be called upon to make policy recommendations. Personal interests may lead a researcher to adopt an advocate role. Although policy recommendations and advocacy are not unethical themselves, care must be taken to separate them from the results. Understanding research results does not necessarily make one an expert on policies and implications. As with any research, departures from reasonable conclusions drawn from the data must be labeled as such.

SUMMARY

- Evaluation involves the use of behavioral research methods to assess the conceptualization, design, implementation, and utility of intervention programs. In order to be effectively evaluated, a program should have specific procedures and goals, although formative evaluation can be used to develop them. Summative evaluations deal with program outcomes.
- For evaluation research, administrators, clients, staff, and others with a vested interest must be included with behavioral scientists in the research audience. Operationalizing concepts in evaluation research involves translating goals and procedures into reliable and valid variables. The expanded audience for evaluation research poses an additional burden with respect to ensuring that consumers understand the variables involved in the research.

- When the desired level of some dependent variable is something other than zero, ecosystem measures can be used to compare desired outcomes to obtained outcomes. Using ecosystem measures, however, requires an assumption that those being measured are in a position to know what levels of service they desire.

- Although experimental designs provide the best way to test cause-effect relationships, some controversy exists about their use for evaluation. With the exception of the ethics of random assignment, however, most of the controversial issues result from misunderstandings about the use and utility of experimental designs. When more potential clients exist than can be served by a program, a lottery may be the solution to problems concerning random assignment and decisions about who will or will not receive services.

- There are a number of other ethical issues of significance to evaluation research. The Evaluation Research Society has published standards for ethical conduct that should be used as guidelines by those who conduct evaluation research.

EXERCISES

1. Find an article in which the authors report on an evaluation research project. Determine whether the evaluation was summative or formative (or both).

2. Using the same or a different article, identify the type of research method and, if appropriate, the type of design used in the research.

3. Find an article in which the researchers used ecosystem measures and identify what concept they were trying to measure in the research.

Epilogue

We have come to the end of our exploration of evaluating research. At this point, you should have a solid understanding of a general framework for evaluating just about any research project you may encounter, and I hope you have a better appreciation for the utility of research, including its limitations. Along the way, you learned that the phrase *research proves* is meaningless, at least when taken literally. Researchers can demonstrate phenomena, can predict outcomes, and can test explanations to determine which is more probable, but they cannot prove that a particular explanation is true or prove that a particular phenomenon will happen in the future. You are able to distinguish among a priori logic, appeals to authority, tradition, and science, and you know the differences among the purposes of research—description, prediction, exploration, explanation, and action. You also know to ask, and answer, the important questions about research—who, what, where, when, how, and why. In short, you have a way "to counteract and eliminate as much intellectual error as possible" (Bartley, 1962, p. 140).

You have learned about sampling and how the sampling process affects the conclusions you may draw from the research, and you have learned about research design. Indeed, you probably learned more about research design than you thought you ever wanted to know, but now you can identify the flaws in most any research project. More importantly, you know that there always are flaws, that more research is always needed, but that need does not prevent you from forming tentative conclusions about a phenomenon, an explanation, or the implementation of a policy.

So, now what? Well, the short answer is, "Use it!" If you are in a position to evaluate public policy, use what you know about evaluating research to identify and promote reliable and valid research in furtherance of the policy. Make sure those who need to know about the research actually know about it. Help them to understand how the results can be applied to improve the policy, its implementation, and reactions to the policy. As well, make sure that you know about unreliable and invalid research and can correct the errors of those who are using less-than-worthy research to inform their opinions about public policy. Help those who know less than you about evaluating research to distinguish between good research and not-so-good research and between relevant and irrelevant research. In short, do what you can to bring about Donald Campbell's (1969) experimenting society.

Admittedly, the task may seem daunting at first, in part because it is much easier to rely on authority or tradition and move on to implementation. In the middle of another long meeting, when someone says, "So-and-so did a study, so we know this will work," it can be difficult to ask "who, what, where, when, how, and why"; everyone just wants to make a decision and get on with the real work of implementing the policy and helping people. You know now that the real work might never get done if the policy makes little empirical sense, if there is no evidence that the program can produce the intended effects. Indeed, without critical evaluation of research applied to a policy, the resulting programs might have unintended effects and make real work even more difficult or do real damage.

Even though the task is somewhat daunting, you are well prepared to help bring about an empirical approach to policy analysis. You know a great deal about research design and methodology and know how to apply that knowledge. You also have many resources, in the form of the references for this book, to consult when you need additional information. You may not have a great deal of confidence, but you are a knowledgeable person. Go, use that knowledge; make the world a better place.

Glossary

accidental sample or sampling: selection based on availability or ease of inclusion.

action research: refers to research conducted to solve a social problem.

activity: extent to which the concept is associated with action or motion in a semantic differential scale.

alternate-forms reliability: consistency estimated by comparing two different but equivalent versions of the same measure.

analysis of variance: also known as ANOVA.

anomie: a feeling that stems from a lack of integration into a social network; general sense of instability or disintegration.

anonymity: exists when no one, including the researcher, can relate an individual's identity to any information pertaining to the project; when no one knows the identity of the person who provides the information.

ANOVA: analysis of variance. The principle underlying *t* tests, ANOVA is the assumption that both (or all) groups, whatever they may be, represent samples from the same population. Men and women, for example, represent two different samples from the same population (humans).

a priori method (of knowing): in epistemology, this method defines knowledge as anything that appears to make sense, to be reasonable.

archival research: any research in which a public record is the unit of analysis.

attrition: *see* **mortality effects.**

authoritarianism: personality trait characterized by submission to authority figures, ethnocentrism, and preoccupation with strength or power.

authority: in epistemology, believing something because the source of the knowledge is accepted as inherently truthful.

autonomy: the ability to direct oneself, particularly through the exercise of independent processing of information.

baseline design: preindependent variable measures are compared with postindependent measures for a single participant.

behavior: an action or actions completed by a respondent.

beneficent subject effect: occurs when participants are aware of the research hypothesis and attempt to respond so as to support it.

between-subjects design: a research design, usually factorial, in which each participant experiences one and only one manipulation of each independent variable. In factorial design, each participant experiences only one cell of the design.

blind rater: someone who is unaware of either the research hypothesis or the experimental group from which the responses came.

case study: intensive study of a single participant over an extended period of time.

categorical measure(ment): *see* **nominal measurement.**

causal analysis: the logical process through which we attempt to explain why an event occurs.

chance response tendencies: replacing formal category definitions with idiosyncratic definitions in a coding scheme.

checklist coding schemes: coding systems for which the behaviors and their meanings are determined prior to making observations.

chi-square analyses: statistical techniques used to determine whether the frequencies of scores in the categories defined by the variable match the frequencies one would expect on the basis of chance or on the basis of predictions from a theory.

cluster analysis: a statistical technique that enables researchers to group variables according to the degree of similarity exhibited among the variables.

cluster sampling: randomly selecting hierarchical groups from a sampling frame.

coding: attaching some sort of meaning to the observation.

coefficient of reproducibility (CR): proportion of fit between a perfect Guttman scale and one's data.

comparative format: a response format in which direct comparisons among various positions are provided to respondents.

compensatory education: raising the educational level of individuals whose education has been disadvantaged.

complete observer: one who observes an event without becoming part of it.

complete participant: a researcher who fully participates in the event but is not known to the other participants as a researcher.

concept: abstract word that is used to represent concrete phenomena.

concurrent validity: comparing a new measure to an existing, valid measure.

confederate: someone who is seemingly a research participant but is actually a member of the research team.

confidence interval: the inclusive, probabilistic range of values around any calculated statistic.

confidence level: probability associated with the accuracy of an inferential statistic.

confidentiality: exists when only the researchers are aware of the participants' identities and have promised not to reveal those identities to others.

construct validity: extent to which a measure represents concepts it should represent and does not represent concepts it should not represent.

content analysis: research method used to make objective and systematic inferences about theoretically relevant messages.

content validity: *see* **face validity**.

contingency analyses: statistical procedures used to determine the probability that the results for one variable are related to the results for another variable.

contingency item: an item on a survey that is relevant only if a certain response was provided for a previous item.

continuous time sampling: observing every instance of the behavior for the entire duration of the event.

control condition: the level of an independent variable that represents the absence of manipulation; *see also* **control group**.

control group: the group in a study composed of individuals who received the "old" treatment or no treatment at all; the group to which the treatment group is compared.

convergent validity: extent to which a measure correlates with existing measures of the same concept.

correlation: a statistical procedure used to estimate the extent to which changes in one variable are associated with changes in another.

criteria for growth: standards that can be used to decide one explanation or theory is better than another.

crossbreak analysis: also known as chi-square.

cross-sectional design: one measurement of different groups that represents different time periods.

cumulative scale: *see* **Guttman scale**.

deception: providing false information about the research project.

definitional operationism: failure to recognize the difference between a theoretical concept and its operational definition.

definitive study: a research project that completely answers a question; such a study does not exist.

dependent variable: the effect under investigation in an experiment.

descriptive research: a research goal that involves examining a phenomenon to characterize it more fully or to differentiate it from other phenomena.

design: the number and arrangement of independent variable levels in a research project.

determinism: the philosophical assumption that every event has at least one discoverable cause.

deviant case sampling: observing individuals who do not seem to fit a pattern exhibited by other individuals who have been observed.

dimensionality: the number of different qualities inherent in a theoretical concept.

discriminant analysis: statistical technique designed to estimate the relationship between any number of predictor variables and one or more categorical response variables.

divergent validity: extent to which a measure does not correlate with measures of a different concept.

double-barreled item: a single item that contains two or more questions or statements.

double-blind procedure: the raters (or investigators) and participants are unaware of the research hypothesis or of group memberships related to that hypothesis.

dynamic hypothesis formulation: the process of generating and revising working hypotheses in field research.

ecological fallacy: mismatch between units of analysis and the research hypothesis.

ecosystem measurement: the simultaneous measurement of level of service received and level of service desired by clients.

effect size: a statistical term for the estimate of the magnitude of the difference between groups or the relationship between variables.

elaboration: process in which data analyses are used to explore and interpret relationships among variables.

element: a single thing selected for inclusion in a research project; *see* **sampling element.**

epistemic correlation: theoretical relationship between the true component of a measure and the concept it represents.

epistemology: the study of the nature of knowledge, of how we know what we know.

equal-appearing interval technique: a scaling technique that produces a series of items, each of which represents a particular point value on the continuum being measured; also known as a Thurstone scale.

ethological system: detailed and comprehensive recording of behaviors with little or no inferred meaning.

evaluation: overall positive or negative meaning attached to the concept in a semantic differential scale.

evaluation apprehension: concern about being observed.

evaluation research: the systematic application of research procedures in assessing the conceptualization and design, implementation, and utility of social intervention programs.

event sampling: observing one behavior contingent upon the presence of another behavior.

existing data: the archived results of research accomplished by someone else.

experimental research: general label applied to methods developed for the specific purpose of testing causal relationships.

experimenter bias: researcher's differential treatment of experimental groups.

expert validity: *see* **face validity.**

explanatory research: a research goal that involves testing a cause-effect relationship between two or more phenomena.

exploratory research: a research goal that involves an attempt to determine whether or not a phenomenon exists.

ex post facto explanations: untested causal statements applied to observed relationships.

expressive subculture: one characterized by an emphasis on feelings over accomplishment.

external validity: the relationship between the research experience and every day experience; the similarity between the physical and social aspects of the research environment and the target environment; the extent to which the data may be generalized beyond the research project.

face validity: consensus that a measure represents a particular concept, sometimes called *expert validity.*

fact: an objectively verifiable phenomenon or characteristic available to anyone who knows how to observe it.

factor analysis: statistical technique used to separate continuous variables into groups of variables that can be interpreted as single dimensions of a multidimensional concept.

factorial design: a research design that includes more than one independent variable.

field journal: notebook into which a researcher enters all observations.

field research: general label applied to a collection of research methods that includes direct observation of naturally occurring events.

focused interview: technique in which an interviewer poses a few predetermined questions but has considerable flexibility concerning follow-up questions.

forced-choice format: item response format in which the respondents must choose between discrete and mutually exclusive options.

formative evaluation: an assessment of the process(es) of a program.

generalize: to relate the findings gathered from the research situation to other situations.

goodness-of-fit test: one in which data values obtained from one sample are compared to theoretical values to determine whether the two sets of values are equivalent.

graphic format: an item on which responses are presented along a graded continuum and the respondent chooses one of the options.

Guttman scale: scale on which it is possible to order both the items and the respondents on a single, identifiable continuum of measurement.

heuristic value: the quality associated with stimulating a great deal of additional research activity.

history effect: a potential alternative explanation to the results of an experiment, produced whenever some uncontrolled event alters participants' responses.

hypothesis: a statement that describes a relationship between variables (plural is *hypotheses*).

inadequate sampling: occurs when only a subset of events is recorded and the sampling process is not systematic.

independent variable: the suspected cause under consideration in a research project.

inductive reasoning: generalization; applying specific information to a general situation or future events.

inferential statistics: values calculated from a sample and used to estimate the same value for a population.

informant: usually in field research, anyone who is knowledgeable about the participants to be observed.

informed consent: the process by which potential research participants are provided with all of the information necessary to allow them to make a reasonable decision concerning their participation.

instrumentation effects: changes in the manner in which the dependent variable is measured.

intellectual honesty: individual scientist's ability to justify the use of science itself.

interaction: a result that occurs when the effect of one variable depends upon which level of another variable is present.

internal validity: the extent to which the independent variable is the only systematic difference among experimental groups.

interpretation: process whereby recorded observations are used to describe events, generate hypotheses, or test hypotheses.

interrater reliability: the consistency with which raters or observers make judgments.

interrupted time-series design: a design in which the implementation of the independent variable is experienced as a change in the normal stream of events in participants' lives.

interval measurement: a level of measurement that involves a continuum divided into equally spaced or equally valued parts.

interview: a structured conversation used to complete a survey.

intrusion: anything that lessens the participants' perception of an event as natural (usually of greatest concern in field research).

item bias: extent to which the wording or placement of an item (question, rating, etc.) affects someone's response to the item.

itemized format: any response format that involves presenting a continuum of statements representing various choice options.

item-total reliability: an estimate of the consistency of one item with respect to other items on a measure.

key-informant sampling: *see* **snowball sampling.**

latent content: inferred, underlying, or hidden meaning in material that makes up an archive.

Likert scale: a unidimensional measure containing items reflecting extreme positions on a continuum, items with which people are likely either to agree or to disagree.

literature: generic term used to refer the collection of articles, chapters, and books that contain research results relevant to a particular topic.

longitudinal designs: any design in which the same participants are repeatedly measured over time.

main effect: an effect produced by a single independent variable.

maleficent subject effect: occurs when participants are aware of the research hypothesis and attempt to respond in a way that will undermine it.

manifest content: the physical or noninferential material that makes up an archive.

MANOVA: multivariate analysis of variance; one of the more complicated forms of ANOVA; employed whenever two or more dependent variables are analyzed simultaneously, usually because there is reason to believe that the multiple dependent variables are related in some way.

matching: assigning participants to groups in order to equalize scores across groups on any relevant variable.

maturation: any process that involves systematic change over time, regardless of specific events.

mean: arithmetical average of a set of scores.

measurement: process through which the kind or intensity of something is determined.

median: the 50th percentile score; it separates the lower and upper halves of a distribution of scores.

meta-analysis: collective name for the various quantitative techniques used to combine the results of empirical studies; integrating research findings by statistically analyzing the results from individual studies.

mode: most frequent score in a set of scores.

mortality effects: caused by the loss of participants during the project.

multiple regression: statistical technique for estimating simultaneous correlations among any number of predictor variables and a single, continuous response variable.

multivariate analysis: *see* MANOVA.

mundane realism: the extent to which the experience of the participants in a study is similar to the experiences of everyday life.

natural event: an event that is not created, sustained, or discontinued solely for research purposes.

necessary cause: something that must be present in order to produce the effect.

negative case analysis: searching for data that disconfirm a tentative hypothesis, revising the hypothesis to include the disconfirming data, searching for more data, and so on.

nominal measurement: determining the presence or absence of a characteristic; naming a quality.

nonconscious ideology: a prejudice that has lost its label as prejudice and has become an implicit assumption that strongly affects the roles of certain members of a society.

nondirective interview: technique in which the interviewer encourages the respondent to discuss a topic but provides little or no guidance and very few direct questions.

nonjustificationism: a philosophy of science in which the major premise is that we cannot logically prove that the way we go about doing research is correct in any absolute sense.

nonprobability sampling: any procedure in which elements have unequal chances for being included in the sample.

objective: adjective applied to a process, observation, or anything else that can be replicated (observed by more than one person under a variety of different conditions).

objectivity: an observation that can be replicated (observed by more than one person under a variety of different conditions).

observer-as-participant: one who is known to the participants as a researcher but does not take an active part in the events.

operational definitions: concrete representations of abstract theoretical concepts.

opinion: an expression of a respondent's preference, feeling, or behavioral intention.

order effects: changes in participant responses resulting from the sequence in which they experience multiple levels of an independent variable.

ordinal measurement: a level of measurement in which scores are ranked or otherwise placed in order with respect to the intensity for a quality.

overgeneralization: drawing conclusions too far beyond the scope of immediate observation.

paradigm: logical system that encompasses theories, concepts, models, procedures, and techniques.

parameter: a value associated with a population.

participant-as-observer: one who is known as a researcher but fully participates in the ongoing activities.

participant bias: any intentional effort on the part of participants to alter responses for the purpose of self-presentation.

participant characteristics: variables that differentiate participants but cannot be manipulated and are not subject to random assignment; sometimes called *subject variables.*

participant observation: observational research method in which the researcher becomes part of the events being observed.

periodic trends: cyclic changes that repeat throughout a sampling frame.

philosophy of science: any set of rules that defines what is acceptable, empirical knowledge.

pilot study: small-scale version of a research project in which the researcher practices or tests the procedures to be used in the full-scale project.

population: all possible units or elements that could be included in research.

potency: overall strength or importance of the concept in a semantic differential scale.

pragmatic action: the process chosen to answer the question of how we should go about putting a scientific approach into practice.

predestination: philosophical assumption that events are unalterable and that, once initiated, events cannot be changed.

prediction: a research goal that involves identifying relationships that enable us to speculate about one thing by knowing about some other thing.

predictive research: involves any study in which the purpose is to determine whether a relationship between variables exists such that one can use one of the variables in place of another.

predictive validity: comparing a measure with the future occurrence of another, highly valid measure.

predictor variable: the measure one hopes will predict the response or outcome variable in predictive research.

pretesting: administering research measures or procedures under special conditions in order to evaluate the validity or reliability of the measures or procedures.

probability sampling: any technique that ensures a random sample.

probe: a phrase or question used by the interviewer to prompt the respondent to elaborate on a particular response.

purposive sampling: procedures directed toward obtaining a certain type of element.

Q-sort: a scaling technique used to measure an individual's relative positioning or ranking of a variety of different concepts.

qualitative analyses: nonnumerical data analyses concerning quality rather than quantity.

quasi-experimental designs: research designs that approximate experimental designs but do not include random assignment to conditions.

quota sampling: selecting sampling elements on the basis of categories assumed to exist within the population.

random assignment: any procedure that provides all participants with an equal opportunity to experience any given level of the independent variable.

random digit dialing: sampling procedure in which a valid telephone exchange is sampled from a region and the telephone number is completed with four randomly selected numbers.

random sampling: any technique that provides each population element an equal probability of being included in the sample; also known as *random selection*.

random selection: any technique that provides each population element an equal probability of being included in the sample; also known as *random sampling*.

ratio measurement: a level of measurement that involves a continuum that includes an absolute zero, a value of zero that represents the complete absence of a quality.

rational inference: a philosophical problem concerning the difficulty inherent in supporting any claim about the existence of a universal truth.

reactance: the proposition that whenever someone's perceived freedom is threatened, the person is motivated to reassert the freedom.

reactivity effects: changes in the participants' behaviors because they know they are being watched.

recording: the manner in which a permanent copy of the observation is made, usually in field research but relevant to all research.

reductionism: the logical fallacy of drawing conclusions about individuals' behaviors from units of analysis that do not deal with individuals.

regression equation: formula for predicting a score on the response variable from the score on the predictor variable.

repeated measures design: a specific factorial design in which the same participants are exposed to more than one level of an independent variable.

representative sample: a sample that resembles the population within an acceptable margin of error.

research: a critical process for asking and attempting to answer questions about the world.

response variable: the measure one would like to predict in predictive research, the outcome variable.

sample: a portion of the elements in a population.

sampling: the process by which participants are selected for a research project.

sampling distribution: a collection (or distribution) of statistics created by repeatedly selecting random samples from a population.

sampling element: the single thing selected for inclusion in a research project; *see also* **sampling unit.**

sampling error: the extent to which a sample statistic incorrectly estimates a population parameter.

sampling frame: concrete listing of the elements in a population.

sampling unit: the single thing selected for inclusion in a research project; *see* **sampling element**.

scale: measurement instrument that contains a number of slightly different operational definitions of the same concept.

scalogram analysis: determination of the extent to which the pattern of actual responses fits the ideal pattern of a Guttman scale.

scalogram scale: *see* **Guttman scale**.

scatterplot: graph in which corresponding codes from two variables are displayed on two axes.

schedules: survey instruments that are essentially orally administered questionnaires.

science: the process of using systematic, empirical observation to improve theories about phenomena based on a set of rules that defines what is acceptable knowledge.

selection effect: produced by the manner in which the participants were recruited or recruited themselves.

self-administered survey: an instrument the respondent completes without intervention by the researcher.

self-presentation: concern for the impression one makes upon others.

self-selection: any circumstances in which the participants are already at different levels of an independent variable.

semantic differential scale: designed to measure the psychological meaning of concepts along three different dimensions: evaluation, potency, and activity.

semi-interquartile range: a measure of variability or degree of dispersion calculated by halving the difference between the values representing the 75th and 25th percentiles in a distribution of scores.

simple random sampling: any technique that involves an unsystematic random selection process.

simple trends: systematic and consistent changes in some quality inherent in sampling frame elements.

single-participant designs: designs specifically tailored to include only one participant in the study; also known as *single subject designs*.

snowball sampling: obtaining suggestions for other participants from those one has already observed.

social exchange: interpersonal relationship in which an individual's willingness to enter or remain in the relationship depends on expectations of rewards and costs.

sociometric scale: measurement instrument designed specifically for measuring relationships among individuals within a group.

split-half reliability: consistency measured by creating two scores for each participant by dividing the measure into equivalent halves and correlating the halves.

SQ3R: survey, query, read, recite, and review; a technique designed to enhance understanding while reading.

standard error: the standard deviation of the sampling distribution of a statistic.

statistic: any numerical value calculated from a sample (as opposed to a parameter, which is a value estimated for the population).

statistical regression effect: artifact of measurement that occurs when extreme scores are obtained. The more extreme a score the first time a measurement is taken, the more likely that the second measure will produce a more average score.

stem-and-leaf display: allows view of entire data set as a distribution of scores, without having to lose information about what the specific scores are; also enables informal examination of differences among groups.

stratified random sampling: employing random selection separately for each subgroup in a sampling frame.

subject variables: *see* **participant characteristics.**

sufficient cause: something that will produce the effect.

summative evaluation: an assessment of the outcome(s) of a program.

summative scale: any measurement scale for which scores are calculated by summing responses to individual items.

survey research: directly obtaining retrospective information from a group of individuals.

systematic observation: field research method in which events are selected, recorded, coded into meaningful units, and interpreted by nonparticipants.

systematic random sampling: choosing elements from a randomly arranged sampling frame according to ordered criteria.

temporal priority: the requirement that causes precede their effects.

testing effects: changes in responses caused by measuring the dependent variable.

testing-treatment interaction: participants experiencing one level of the independent variable may be more sensitive to testing effects than participants experiencing a different level of the independent variable.

test-retest reliability: measurement consistency estimated by comparing two or more repeated administrations of the same measurement.

Thurstone scale: *see* **equal-appearing interval technique.**

time-interval sampling: observing whether a behavior occurs during a specified interval within the event duration.

time-point sampling: selecting only behavior that occurs at the end of a specific time interval within the event duration.

time-series design: a type of extended repeated measures design in which the dependent variable is measured several times before and after the introduction of the independent variable.

tradition: in epistemology, believing something because of historical precedent, because it has always been believed.

_t_ test: a parametric statistical analysis used to determine the probability that two group means are different.

units of analysis: objects about which a researcher would like to answer a research question.

units of observation: the specific material, objects, or people to be measured in a research project.

validation by consensus: _see_ **face validity.**

validity: in general, the extent to which a claim or conclusion can be defended on the basis of logic; in measurement, the extent to which a variable measures the theoretical concept it is supposed to measure.

variable: a measurable entity that exhibits more than one level or value and serves as an operational definition of a theoretical concept.

withdrawal design: independent variable (treatment) is presented and removed several times for a single participant.

worldview: basic set of untestable assumptions underlying all theory and research.

References

Adams, G. R. (1977). Physical attractiveness research: Toward a developmental social psychology of beauty. *Human Development, 20*(4), 217–239.

Adams, G. S. (1964). *Measurement and evaluation in education, psychology, and guidance.* New York: Holt, Rinehart & Winston.

Adams, P. J. (2007). Assessing whether to receive funding support from tobacco, alcohol, gambling and other dangerous consumption industries. *Addiction, 102*(7), 1027–1033.

Adorno, T. W., Frenkel-Brunswick, E., Levinson, O. J., & Sanford, R. N. (1950). *The authoritarian personality.* New York: Harper.

Allen, M. J., & Yen, W. M. (1979). *Introduction to measurement theory.* Belmont, CA: Wadsworth.

American Evaluation Association. (2004). *American Evaluation Association guiding principles for evaluators.* Fairhaven, MA: Author.

American Psychological Association. (2010). *Publication manual of the American Psychological Association* (6th ed.). Washington, DC: Author.

Anastasi, A. (1982). *Psychological testing.* New York: Macmillan.

Aronson, E. (1980). Persuasion via self-justification: Large commitments for small rewards. In L. Festinger (Ed.), *Retrospections on social psychology.* (pp. 3–21). New York: Oxford University Press.

Babbie, E. R. (1983). *The practice of social research.* Belmont, CA: Wadsworth.

Bachrach, A. J. (1981). *Psychological research: An introduction.* New York: Random House.

Back, K. W. (1980). The role of social psychology in population control. In L. Festinger (Ed.), *Retrospections on social psychology* (pp. 22–45). New York: Oxford University Press.

Balay, R. (Ed.). (1996). *Guide to reference books* (11th ed.). Chicago: American Library Association.

Bales, R. F. (1950). A set of categories for the analysis of small group interaction. *American Sociological Review, 15,* 257–263.

Bales, R. F. (1970). *Personality and interpersonal behavior.* New York: Holt, Rinehart & Winston.

Baron, R. A. (1980). A note on rude awakenings: Some effects of being fleeced. *SASP Newsletter, 6*(6), 1.

Bartley, W. W., III. (1962). *The retreat to commitment*. New York: Knopf.

Becker, L. J., & Seligman, C. (1978). Reducing air conditioning waste by signaling it is cool outside. *Personality & Social Psychology Bulletin, 4*(3), 412–415.

Bem, S. L., & Bem, D. J. (1970). Case study of a nonconscious ideology: Training the woman to know her place. In D. J. Bem (Ed.), *Beliefs, attitudes, and human affairs* (pp. 89–99). Belmont, CA: Brooks/Cole.

Berkman, D. (1963). Advertising in *Ebony* and *Life*: Negro aspirations vs. reality. *Journalism Quarterly, 40*, 53–64.

Berkowitz, L., & Donnerstein, E. (1982). External validity is more than skin deep: Some answers to criticisms of laboratory experiments. *American Psychologist, 37*, 245–257.

Bingham, W. V. D., & Moore, B. V. (1924). *How to interview*. New York: Harper & Row.

Bland, J. M., & Altman, D. G. (1986). Statistical methods for assessing agreement between two methods of clinical measurement. *The Lancet, 29*, 307–309.

Bobkowski, C. J. (2007). A proposed model for defining common ground between science and religion [Electronic Version]. *Forum on Public Policy Online, 2007*. Retrieved January 1, 2008, from http://www.forumonpublicpolicy.com/archivespring07/bobkowski.pdf

Boruch, R. F. (1975). On common contentions about randomized field experiments. In R. F. Boruch & H. W. Reicken (Eds.), *Experimental tests of public policy* (pp. 107–142). Boulder, CO: Westview Press.

Bowen, D. J., Bradford, J. B., Powers, D., McMorrow, P., Linde, R., Murphy, B. C., et al. (2004). Comparing women of differing sexual orientations using population-based sampling. *Women & Health, 40*(3), 19–34.

Bray, R. M., & Kerr, N. L. (1982). Methodological considerations in the study of the psychology of the courtroom. In N. L. Kerr & R. M. Bray (Eds.), *The psychology of the courtroom* (pp. 287–323). New York: Academic Press.

Brazzill, W. (1969). A letter from the south. *Harvard Educational Review, 39*, 348–356.

Brehm, J. W. (1966). *A theory of psychological reactance*. New York: Academic Press.

Bryk, A. S. (Ed.). (1983). *Stakeholder-based evaluation*. San Francisco: Jossey-Bass.

Butler, J. M., Rice, L. N., & Wagstaff, A. K. (1963). *Quantitative naturalistic research*. Englewood Cliffs, NJ: Prentice Hall.

Buzztone. (2008). Product(Red). Retrieved July 7, 2008, from http://www.joinred.com/red/Learn.aspx

Cain, D. M., Loewenstein, G., & Moore, D. A. (2005). Coming clean but playing dirtier: The shortcomings of disclosure as a solution to conflicts of interest. In D. A. Moore, D. M. Cain, G. Loewenstein, & M. H. Bazerman (Eds.), *Conflicts of interest: Challenges and solutions in business, law, medicine, and public policy* (pp. 104–125). New York: Cambridge University Press.

Camara, W. J., & Kimmel, E. W. (Eds.). (2005). *Choosing students: Higher education admissions tools for the 21st century*. Mahwah, NJ: Lawrence Erlbaum.

Campbell, D. T. (1969). Reforms as experiments. *American Psychologist, 24*, 409–429.

Campbell, D. T. (1971, September). *Methods for the experimenting society*. Paper presented at the American Psychological Association, Washington, DC.

Campbell, D. T., & Fiske, D. W. (1959). Convergent and divergent validation by the multitrait-multimethod matrix. *Psychological Bulletin, 56*, 81–105.

Campbell, D. T., & Stanley, J. C. (1963). *Experimental and quasi-experimental designs for research*. Chicago: Rand McNally.

Carroll, R. T. (2005). Alien abduction. In *The skeptics dictionary*. Retrieved December 2005 from http://www.skepdic.com/aliens.html

Chaplin, W. F., Phillips, J. B., Brown, J. D., Cianton, N. R., & Stein, J. L. (2000). Handshaking, gender, personality, and first impressions. *Journal of Personality and Social Psychology, 79*(1), 110–117.

Committee on Assessing Integrity in Research Environments. (2002). *Integrity in scientific research: Creating an environment that promotes responsible conduct*. Washington, DC: National Academies Press.

Conover, W. J. (1998). *Practical nonparametric statistics* (3rd ed.). New York: Wiley.

Cook, S. (1981). Ethical implications. In L. H. Kidder (Ed.), Selltiz, Wrightsman and Cook's *research methods in social relations*. New York: Holt, Rinehart & Winston.

Cook, T. D., & Campbell, D. T. (1979). *Quasi-experimentation: Design & analysis for field settings*. Chicago: Rand McNally.

Cooper, T. L. (1998). *The responsible administrator: An approach to ethics for the administrative role* (4th ed.). San Francisco: Jossey-Bass.

Copenhaver, M. M., & Dane, F. C. (1987, March). *Effects of quantified instructions for reasonable doubt: Upper limits and reactance*. Paper presented at the Southeastern Psychological Association, Atlanta, GA.

Crano, W. D., & Brewer, M. B. (1973). *Principles of research in social psychology*. New York: McGraw-Hill.

Crawford, J., & Crawford, T. E. (1978). Development and construct validation of a measure of attitudes toward public exposure to sexual stimuli. *Journal of Personality Measurement, 42,* 392–400.

Dane, F. C. (1985). In search of reasonable doubt: A systematic examination of selected quantification approaches. *Law and Human Behavior, 9,* 141–158.

Dane, F. C. (1988a). *The common and uncommon sense of social behavior*. Pacific Grove, CA: Brooks/Cole.

Dane, F. C. (1988b). *Community reactions to field testing genetically altered organisms*. Unpublished manuscript, Clemson, SC.

Dane, F.C. (1990). *Research methods*. Pacific Grove, CA: Brooks/Cole.

Dane, F. C. (2006). Ethical issues in statistical analyses: An argument for collective moral responsibility. *C-Stat News, 2*(3), 1, 3, 4.

Dane, F. C. (2007a). Ethics of stem-cell research: A framework for ethical dialogue regarding sources of conflict [Electronic Version]. *Forum on Public Policy Online, Spring 2007,* from http://www.forumonpublicpolicy.com/archivespring07/dane.pdf

Dane, F. C. (2007b, March). *Ethics of stem cell research: Sources of conflict*. Paper presented at the Oxford Roundtable Conference—Science and Religion: Is There Common Ground? Oxford, England.

Dane, F. C. (2008). Evaluation and restorative justice. In C. K. Dorne (Ed.), *Introduction to restorative justice in the United States* (pp. 367–371). Upper Saddle River, NJ: Pearson/Prentice Hall.

Dane, F. C., & McPartland, F. (1983). *Attitudes toward public displays of intimacy: An exploratory study*. Unpublished manuscript, Oswego, NY.

Dane, F. C., & Parish, D. C. (2006). Ethical issues in registry research: In-hospital resuscitation as a case study. *Journal of Empirical Research on Human Research Ethics, 1*(4), 69–75.

Dane, F. C., Russell-Lindgren, K. S., Parish, D. C., Durham, M. D., & Brown, T. D., Jr. (2000). In-hospital resuscitation: Association between ACLS training and survival to discharge. *Resuscitation, 47,* 83–87.

Dane, F. C., & Thompson, J. K. (1985). Asymmetrical facial expressions: A different interpretation. *Cortex, 21,* 301–303.

Dane, F. C., & Wrightsman, L. S. (1982). Effects of defendants' and victims' characteristics upon verdicts. In N. L. Kerr & R. M. Bray (Eds.), *Psychology in the courtroom* (pp. 83–115). New York: Academic Press.

Deaux, K., & Major, B. (1987). Putting gender into context: An interactive model of gender-related behavior. *Psychological Review, 94,* 369–389.

Dermer, M. L., & Hoch, T. A. (1999). Improving descriptions of single-subject experiments in research texts written for undergraduates. *Psychological Record, 49,* 49–66.

Descartes, R. (1637/1993). *Discourse on the method of rightly conducting the reason in the search for truth in the sciences.* Salt Lake City, UT: Project Gutenberg.

Deutsch, M. (1980). Fifty years of conflict. In L. Festinger (Ed.), *Retrospections on social psychology* (pp. 46–77). New York: Oxford University Press.

Devine, D. J., Clayton, L. D., Dunford, B. B., Seying, R., & Pryce, J. (2001). Jury decision making: 45 years of empirical research on deliberating groups. *Psychology, Public Policy, and Law, 7*(3), 622–727.

Diener, E., & Crandall, R. (1979). An evaluation of the Jamaican anticrime program. *Journal of Applied Social Psychology, 9,* 135–146.

Dillman, D. A. (1978). *Mail and telephone surveys: The total design method.* New York: Wiley.

Dillman, D. A. (2007). *Mail and Internet surveys: The tailored design method* (2nd ed.). New York: Wiley.

Dillman, D. A., Gallegos, J. G., & Frey, J. H. (1976). Reducing refusal rates for telephone surveys. *Public Opinion Quarterly, 40,* 360–369.

Dillon, M. (2006). D.A.R.E. effectiveness reports. Retrieved January 8, 2008, from http://www.sayno.com/effectiv.html

Doniger, A. S., Riley, J. S., Utter, C. A., & Adams, E. (2001). Impact evaluation of the "Not Me, Not Now" abstinence-oriented, adolescent pregnancy prevention communications program, Monroe County, NY. *Journal of Health Communication, 6*(1), 45–60.

Dunnette, M. D. (1966). *Personnel selection and placement.* Belmont, CA: Wadsworth.

Durant, J. (Ed.). (1985). *Darwinism and divinity: Essays on evolution and religious beliefs.* New York: Blackwell.

Durkheim, E. (1951/1897). *Suicide.* Glencoe, IL: Free Press.

Educational Testing Service. (1981). *Guide to the use of the Graduate Record Examination.* Princeton, NJ: Educational Testing Service.

Edwards, A. (1957). *Techniques of attitude scale construction.* Englewood Cliffs, NJ: Prentice Hall.

Ellis, L. (1988, April). *The influence of feminist values on television viewing habits.* Paper presented at the Southeastern Psychological Association, New Orleans, LA.

Ellison, J. W. (1965). Computers and testaments. In J. W. Ellison (Ed.), *Computers for the humanities* (pp. 72–74). New Haven, CT: Yale University Press.

Ellison, K. W., & Buckhout, R. (1981). *Psychology and criminal justice.* New York: Harper & Row.

Evaluation Research Society Standards Committee. (1982). Evaluation Research Society standards for program evaluation. *New Directions for Program Evaluation, 15,* 7–19.

Fassnacht, G. (1982). *Theory and practice for observing behaviour* (C. Bryant, Trans.). London: Academic Press.

Flanagan, T. J., & McLeod, M. (Eds.). (1983). *Sourcebook of criminal justice statistics—1982.* Washington, DC: Government Printing Office.

Fleck, L. (1979). *Genesis and development of a scientific fact* (F. Bradley & T. J. Trenn, Trans.). Chicago: University of Chicago Press.

Fogerty, J. C. (1970). Who'll stop the rain? On *Cosmo's Factory.* San Francisco: Fantasy Records.

Forgas, J. P. (1982). Episode recognition: Internal representation of interaction routines. In L. Berkowitz (Ed.), *Advances in experimental social psychology* (pp. 59–101). New York: Academic Press.

Fowler, F. J., Jr. (1981). Evaluating a complex crime control experiment. In L. Bickman (Ed.), *Applied social psychology annual* (Vol. 2, pp. 165–187). Beverly Hills, CA: Sage.

Frank, J. (1981). Social psychology and the prevention of nuclear war: What is our responsibility? *SASP Newsletter,* 7(2), 8.

Gejman, P. V., & Weilbaecher, A. (2002). History of the eugenic movement. *Israel Journal of Psychiatry and Related Sciences, 39*(4), 217–232.

Gellert, E. (1955). Systematic observation: A method in child study. *Harvard Educational Review, 25,* 179–195.

Gilligan, P., Bhatarcharjee, C., Knight, G., Smith, M., Hegarty, D., Shenton, A., et al. (2005). To lead or not to lead? Prospective controlled study of emergency nurses' provision of advanced life support team leadership. *Emergency Medicine Journal, 22*(9), 628–632.

Glass, G. V. (1976). Primary, secondary, and meta-analysis of research. *Educational Researcher, 5,* 3–8.

Glass, G. V., McGraw, B., & Smith, M. L. (1981). *Meta-analysis in social research.* Beverly Hills, CA: Sage.

Gold, N. (1981). *The stakeholder process in educational program evaluation.* Washington, DC: National Institute of Education.

Gold, R. L. (1969). Roles in sociological field observation. In G. J. McCall & J. L. Simmons (Eds.), *Issues in participant observation* (pp. 30–39). Reading, MA: Addison-Wesley.

Gorden, R. L. (1969). *Interviewing: Strategy, techniques, and tactics.* Homewood, IL: Dorsey.

Gorman, H. M., & Dane, F. C. (1994). Balancing methodological rigour and ethical treatment: The necessity of voluntary, informed consent. In P. P. DeDeyn (Ed.), *Animal and human experimentation* (pp. 35–41). London: John Libbey.

Greenberg, M. S., & Ruback, R. B. (1982). *Social psychology of the criminal justice system.* Monterey, CA: Brooks/Cole.

Gross, A. E., Green, S. K., Storck, J. T., & Vanyur, J. M. (1980). Disclosure of sexual orientation and impressions of male and female homosexuals. *Personality and Social Psychology Bulletin, 6,* 307–314.

Guttman, L. L. (1944). A basis for scaling qualitative data. *American Sociological Review, 9,* 139–150.

Haberman, S. J. (1978). *Analysis of qualitative data: Vo. 1. Introductory topics.* New York: Academic Press.

Haberman, S. J. (1979). *Analysis of qualitative data: Vol. 2. New developments.* New York: Academic Press.

Hall, E. T. (1959). *The silent language.* New York: Doubleday.

Hartwig, F., & Dearing, B. E. (1979). *Exploratory data analyses.* Beverly Hills, CA: Sage.

Hawkins, D. F. (1977). *Nonresponse in Detroit area study surveys: A ten-year analysis.* Chapel Hill, NC: Institute for Research in Social Sciences.

Hearnshaw, C. S. (1979). *Cyril Burt: Psychologist.* Ithaca, NY: Cornell University Press.

Hill, C. T., Rubin, A., & Peplau, L. A. (1976). Breakups before marriage: The end of 103 affairs. *Journal of Social Issues, 32* (1), 147–168.

Hilton, T. F. (1981). The moral majority and social psychology: An issue for the profession. *SASP Newsletter, 7*(2), 5.

Holsti, O. R. (1968). Content analysis. In G. Lindzey & E. Aronson (Eds.), *The handbook of social psychology* (pp. 596–692). Menlo Park, CA: Addison-Wesley.

Human Genome Project. (2007, July 24). *What are genetically modified (GM) foods?* Retrieved March 6, 2008, from http://www.ornl.gov/sci/techresources/Human_Genome/elsi/gmfood.shtml

Humphreys, L. (1975). *Tearoom trade: Impersonal sex in public places.* Chicago: Aldine.

Hunt, M. (1974). *Sexual behavior in the 1970s.* Chicago: Playboy.

Institute for Social Research. (1976). *Newsletter, 4,* 4.

Jacobs, J. (1967). A phenomenological study of suicide notes. *Social Problems, 15,* 60–72.

Jenkins, J., & Russell, W. (1958). An atlas of semantic profiles for 360 words. *American Journal of Psychology, 71,* 688–699.

Jenkins, K. E. (2003). Intimate diversity: The presentation of multiculturalism and multiracialism in a high-boundary religious movement. *Journal for the Scientific Study of Religion, 42*(3), 393–409.

Jensen, A. (1969a). How much can we boost IQ and scholastic achievement? *Harvard Educational Review, 39,* 1–123.

Jensen, A. (1969b). Reducing the heredity-environment uncertainty: A reply. *Harvard Educational Review, 39,* 449–483.

Johnson, J. M. (1975). *Doing field research.* New York: Free Press.

Jones, J. H. (1993). *Bad blood: The Tuskegee syphilis experiment.* New York: Free Press.

Judd, C. M., & Park, B. (1993). Definition and assessment of accuracy in social stereotypes. *Psychological Review, 100*(1), 109–128.

Kamin, L. J. (1974). *The science and politics of IQ.* Potomac, MD: Erlbaum.

Kant, I. (1788/1997). *Critique of practical reason* (M. Gregor, Trans.). Cambridge, UK: Cambridge University Press.

Kelley, H. H., & Thibault, J. W. (1978). *Interpersonal relations: A theory of interdependence.* New York: Wiley-Interscience.

Kerlinger, F. N. (1972). The structure and content of social attitude referents: A preliminary study. *Educational and Psychological Measurement, 32,* 613–630.

Kerlinger, F. N. (1973). *Foundations of behavioral science research.* New York: Holt, Rinehart & Winston.

Kerlinger, F. N. (1979). *Behavioral research: A conceptual approach.* New York: Holt, Rinehart & Winston.

Kerr, N. L. (1998). HARKing: Hypothesizing after the results are known. *Personality and Social Psychology Review, 2*(3), 196–217.

Kerr, N. L., & Bray, R. M. (Eds.). (1982). *The psychology of the courtroom.* New York: Academic Press.

Kimmelman, J. (2007). Inventors as investigators: The ethics of patents in clinical trials. *Academic Medicine, 82*(1), 24–31.

Kinsey, A., Pomeroy, W. B., & Martin, C. E. (1948). *Sexual behavior in the human male.* Philadelphia: W. B. Saunders.

Kinsey, A., Pomeroy, W. B., Martin, C. E., & Gebhard, P. H. (1953). *Sexual behavior in the human female.* Philadelphia: W. B. Saunders.

Klecka, W. R., & Tuchfarber, A. J. (1978). Random digit dialing: A comparison to personal survey. *Public Opinion Quarterly, 42,* 105–114.

Kleinke, C. K. (1975). *First impressions.* Englewood Cliffs, NJ: Prentice Hall.

Kounin, J., & Gump, P. (1961). The comparative influence of punitive and nonpunitive teachers upon children's concepts of school misconduct. *Journal of Educational Psychology, 52,* 44–49.

Kuder, G. F., & Richardson, M. W. (1937). The theory of estimation of test reliability. *Psychometrica, 2,* 151–160.

Kuhn, T. (1962). *The structure of scientific revolution.* Chicago: University of Chicago Press.

Kulik, J. A., Kulik, C.-L. C., & Bangert, R. L. (1984). Effects of practice on aptitude and achievement test scores. *American Educational Research Journal, 21*(2), 435–447.

Kuncel, N. R., Hezlett, S. A., & Ones, D. S. (2001). A comprehensive meta-analysis of the predictive validity of the graduate record examinations: Implications for graduate student selection and performance. *Psychological Bulletin, 127*(1), 162–181.

LaFrance, M. (1979). Nonverbal synchrony and rapport: Analysis by the cross-lagged panel technique. *Social Psychology Quarterly, 42,* 66–70.

Landon, 1,293,669: Roosevelt, 972,897. (1936). *The Literary Digest,* pp. 5–6.

Lasswell, H. D., Lerner, D., & Pool, I. d. S. (1952). *The comparative study of symbols.* Stanford, CA: Stanford University Press.

Latané, B., & Liu, J. H. (1996). The intersubjective geometry of social space. *Journal of Communication, 46*(4), 26–34.

Latané, B., & Darley, J. M. (1968). Group inhibition of bystander intervention in emergencies. *Journal of Personality and Social Psychology, 10,* 215–221.

Laurent, J., Swerdlik, M., & Ryburn, M. (1992). Review of validity research on the Stanford-Binet Intelligence Scale. *Psychological Assessment, 4*(1), 102–112.

Lazarsfeld, P. F., Pasanella, A., & Rosenberg, M. (Eds.). (1972). *Continuities in social research.* New York: Free Press.

Lea, S. E. G., & Webley, P. (2006). Money: Motivation, metaphors, and mores. *Behavioral and Brain Sciences, 29*(2), 196–204.

Leahey, T. H. (1980). The myth of operationism. *Journal of Mind and Behavior, 1*(2), 126–143.

Lennon, R. T. (1982). Testing and the law. *Florida Journal of Educational Research, 24,* 39–50.

Leventhal, H., & Sharp, E. (1965). Facial expressions as indicators of distress. In S. Thompkins & C. Izard (Eds.), *Affect, cognition, and personality* (pp. 296–318). New York: Springer.

Levin, J., & Spates, J. (1970). Hippie values: An analysis of the underground press. *Youth & Society, 2,* 59–72.

Levine, J. M., & Russo, E. M. (1987). Majority and minority influence. In C. Hendrick (Ed.), *Review of personality and social psychology* (Vol. 8, pp. 13–54). Beverly Hills, CA: Sage.

Lewin, K. (1946). Action research and minority problems. *Journal of Social Issues, 2,* 34–46.

Liebow, E. (1967). *Tally's corner.* Boston: Little, Brown.

Likert, R. (1932). A technique for the measurement of attitudes. *Archives of Psychology* (140).

Lindeman, R. H., Merenda, P. F., & Gold, R. (1980). *Introduction to bivariate and multivariate analysis.* New York: Scott, Foresman, & Co.

Linz, D., Slack, A., Kaiser, K., & Penrod, S. (1981, October). *Meta-analysis of defendant characteristic studies.* Paper presented at the Bicennial Convention of the American Psychology-Law Society, Cambridge, MA.

Lynam, D. R., Milich, R., Zimmerman, R., Novak, S. P., Logan, T. K., Martin, C., et al. (1999). Project DARE: No effects at 10-year follow-up. *Journal of Consulting and Clinical Psychology, 67*(4), 590–593.

Malandro, L. A., & Barker, L. (1983). *Nonverbal communication.* Reading, MA: Addison-Wesley.

Marsden, P. V., Reed, J. S., Kennedy, M. D., & Stinson, K. M. (1982). American regional cultures and differences in leisure time activities. *Social Forces, 60,* 1023–1049.

Mastroianni, A. C., Faden, R., & Federman, D. (Eds.). (1999). *Women and health research: Ethical and legal issues of including women in clinical studies: Vol. 2. Workshop and commissioned papers.* Washington, DC: National Academy Press.

Mazis, M. B. (1975). Antipollution measures and psychological reactance theory: A field experiment. *Journal of Personality and Social Psychology, 31,* 654–660.

McCall, G. C., & Simmons, J. L. (Eds.). (1969). *Issues in participant observation.* Reading, MA: Addison-Wesley.

McDougall, W. (1908). *Introduction to social psychology.* London: Methuen.

McDowall, D., McCleary, R., Meidinger, E. E., & Hay, R. A., Jr. (1980). *Interrupted time series analysis.* Beverly Hills, CA: Sage.

McGrew, W. C. (1972). *An ethological study of children's behavior.* New York: Academic Press.

McHugo, G. J., Lanzetta, J. T., Sullivan, D. G., Masters, R. D., & Englis, B. G. (1985). Emotional reactivity to a political leader's expressive displays. *Journal of Personality and Social Psychology, 49,* 1513–1529.

Mead, M. (1969). Research with human beings: A model derived from anthropological field practice. *Daedalus,* 361–386.

Merton, R. K., Fiske, M., & Kendall, P. L. (1956). *The focused interview.* Glencoe, IL: Free Press.

Merton, R. K., & Lazarsfeld, P. F. (Eds.). (1950). *Continuities in social research: Studies in the scope and method of "The American soldier."* New York: Free Press.

Milgram, S. (1963). Behavioral study of obedience. *Journal of Abnormal and Social Psychology, 67*(4), 371–378.

Miliotis, M., & Watkins, W. (2005). Quantitative risk assessment on the public health impact of pathogenic Vibrio parahaemolyticus in raw oysters (Executive Summary). Washington, DC: Food and Drug Administration. Retrieved from http://www.fda.gov/Food/ScienceResearch/ResearchAreas/RiskAssessmentSafetyAssessment/ucm050421.htm

Mindick, B. (1982). When we practice to deceive: The ethics of metascientific inquiry. *The Brain and Behavioral Sciences, 5*(2), 226–227.

Moore, D. A., & Loewenstein, G. (2004). Self-interest, automaticity, and the psychology of conflict of interest. *Social Justice Research, 17*(2), 189–202.

Morris, D. (1971). *Intimate behaviour.* London: Jonathan Cape.

Morton, A. Q. (1963, November 3). A computer challenges the church. *The Observer,* p. 21.

Mosteller, F., & Wallace, D. L. (1964). *Inference and disputed authorship: The Federalist.* Reading, MA: Addison-Wesley.

Munsterberg, H. (1913). *On the witness stand.* New York: Doubleday.

Nachmias, D., & Nachmias, C. (1981). *Research methods in the social sciences.* New York: St. Martin's Press.

National Commission for the Protection of Human Subjects of Biomedical and Behavioral Research. (1979). *The Belmont report: Ethical principles and guidelines for the protection of human subjects of research.* Washington, DC: Author.

Nederhof, A. J. (1981). *Some sources of artifact in social science research: Nonresponse, volunteering and research experience of subjects.* Unpublished doctoral dissertation, Rijksuniversiteit te Leiden, Netherlands.

Nowaczyk, R. H. (1988). *Introductory statistics for behavioral research.* New York: Holt, Rinehart & Winston.

Nuremberg Military Tribunal. (1949). *Trials of war criminals before the Nuremberg military tribunals under Control Council Law No. 10* (Vol. 2). Washington, DC: Government Printing Office.

O'Donnell, L., Wilson-Simmons, R., Dash, K., Jeanbaptiste, V., Myint-U, A., Moss, J., et al. (2007). Saving sex for later: Developing a parent-child communication intervention to delay sexual initiation among young adolescents. *Sex Education, 7*(2), 107–125.

Office for Human Research Protections. (2007). *International compilation of human subject research protections.* Retrieved from http://www.hhs.gov/ohrp/international/HSPCompilation.pdf

Okpala, C. O. (1996). Gender-related differences in classroom interaction. *Journal of Instructional Psychology, 23*(4), 275–285.

Osgood, C. E. (1959). The representational model and relevant research methods. In I. d. S. Pool (Ed.), *Trends in content analysis* (pp. 33–88). Urbana: University of Illinois Press.

Osgood, C. E., Sporta, S., & Nunnally, J. C. (1956). Evaluative assertion analysis. *Litera, 3,* 47–52.

Osgood, C. E., Suci, G., & Tannenbaum, P. (1957). *The measurement of meaning.* Urbana, IL: University of Illinois Press.

Ostrom, C. W., Jr. (1978). *Time series analysis: Regression techniques.* Beverly Hills, CA: Sage.

Pachter, W. S., Fox, R. E., Zimbardo, P., & Antonuccio, D. O. (2007). Corporate funding and conflicts of interest: A primer for psychologists. *American Psychologist, 62*(9), 1005–1015.

Parish, D. C., Dane, F. C., Montgomery, M., Wynn, L. J., Durham, M. D., & Brown, T. D. (2000). Resuscitation in the hospital: Relationship of year and rhythm to outcome. *Resuscitation, 47*(3), 219–229.

Parker, L. C., Jr. (1980). *Legal psychology.* Springfield, IL: Charles C Thomas.

Parsons, T. (1951). *The social system*. New York: Macmillan.

Patterson, M. L. (1976). An arousal model of interpersonal intimacy. *Psychological Review, 83,* 235–245.

Patterson, M. L. (1982). A sequential functioning model of nonverbal exchange. *Psychological Review, 89,* 231–249.

Paul, W., Weinrich, J. D., Gonsoriek, J. C., & Hotvedt, M. E. (1982). *Homosexuality: Social, psychological, and biological issues.* Beverly Hills, CA: Sage.

Peele, S., & DeGrandpre, R. J. (1998). Cocaine and the concept of addiction: Environmental factors in drug compulsions. *Addiction Research, 6,* 235–263.

Peirce, C. S. (1877). The fixation of belief. *Popular Science Monthly, 12*(November), 1–15.

Peter, L. J. (1980). *Peter's quotations: Ideas for our time.* New York: Bantam.

Phillips, D. (1971). *Knowledge from what? Theories and methods in social research.* Chicago: Rand McNally.

Piaget, J. (1984). Piaget's theory. In P. Mussen (Ed.), *Handbook of child psychology* (4th ed., Vol. 1). New York: Wiley.

Piliavin, I. M., Rodin, J., & Piliavin, J. A. (1969). Good samaritanism: An underground phenomenon? *Journal of Personality and Social Psychology, 13,* 289–299.

Plato. (2005). *Early Socratic dialogues* (T. J. Saunders, Trans.). New York: Penguin Classic.

Poling, D. A., & Evans, E. M. (2004). Religious belief, scientific expertise, and folk ecology. *Journal of Cognition and Culture, 4*(3–4), 485–524.

Posavac, E. J. (1994). Misusing program evaluation by asking the wrong question. *New Directions for Program Evaluation, 1994*(64), 69–78.

Proctor, C., & Loomis, C. (1951). Analysis of sociometric data. In M. Jahoda, M. Deutsch & S. Cook (Eds.), *Research methods in social relations.* New York: Holt, Rinehart & Winston.

Prosser, W. L. (1964). *Handbook of the law of torts.* St. Paul, MN: West.

Protection of Human Subjects, 45 CFR 46 (2001).

Rector, R. (2002). The effectiveness of abstinence education programs in reducing sexual activity among youth [Electronic Version]. *The Heritage Foundation Backgrounder.* Retrieved January 2, 2008, from http://www.heritage.org/Research/Abstinence/BG1533.cfm

Reicken, H. W., & Boruch, R. F. (Eds.). (1974). *Social experimentation: A method for planning and evaluating social intervention.* New York: Academic Press.

Revkin, A.C. (2005, June 8). Bush aide softened greenhouse gas links to global warming. *The New York Times.* Retrieved January 1, 2007, from http://www.nytimes.com/2005/06/08/politics/08climate.html?pagewanted=1#

Rhodes, G., Halberstadt, J., Jeffery, L., & Palermo, R. (2005). The attractiveness of average faces is not a generalized mere exposure effect. *Social Cognition, 23*(3), 205–217.

Robinson, F. P. (1970). *Effective study* (4th ed.). New York: Harper & Row.

Roche, W. P., III, Scheetz, A. P., Dane, F. C., Parish, D. C., & O'Shea, J. T. (2003). Medical students' attitudes in a PBL curriculum: Trust, altruism, and cynicism. *Academic Medicine, 78*(4), 398–402.

Rokeach, M., Homant, R., & Penner, L. (1970). A value analysis of the disputed Federalist papers. *Journal of Personality and Social Psychology, 16,* 245–250.

Rooney, A. (1982). *And more by Andy Rooney.* New York: Athenium.

Rooney, A. (2003). *Years of minutes.* New York: Public Affairs.

Rosenthal, R., & Fode, K. L. (1963). The effect of experimenter bias on the performance of the albino rat. *Behavioral Science, 8*(3), 183–189.

Rosenthal, R., & Jacobson, L. (1966). Teachers' expectancies: Determinants of pupils' IQ gains. *Psychological Reports, 19,* 115–118.

Rossi, P. H., & Freeman, H. E. (1982). *Evaluation: A systematic approach.* Beverly Hills, CA: Sage.

Rulon, P. J. (1932). A simplified procedure for determining the reliability of a test by split-halves. *Harvard Educational Review, 9,* 99–103.

Runyan, W. M. (1982). *Life histories and psychobiography: Explorations in theory and method.* New York: Oxford University Press.

Russell, J. B. (1991). *Inventing the flat Earth.* Westport, CT: Praeger.

Ryan, J. J., & Ward, L. C. (1999). Validity, reliability, and standard errors of measurement for two seven-subtest short forms of the Wechsler Adult Intelligence Scale—III. *Psychological Assessment, 11*(2), 207–211.

Sagan, C. (1980). *Cosmos.* New York: Random House.

Sales, S. M. (1972). Economic threat as a determinant of conversion rates in authoritarian and nonauthoritarian churches. *Journal of Personality and Social Psychology, 23,* 420–428.

Schwartz, H., & Jacobs, J. (1979). *Qualitative sociology: A method to the madness.* New York: Free Press.

Seider, M. S. (1974). American big business ideology: A content analysis of executive speeches. *American Sociological Review, 39,* 802–815.

Seiler, L. H., & Murtha, J. M. (1981). Victory at HHS: Final regulations for the protection of human subjects of research provide a balanced compromise. *SASP Newsletter, 7*(2), 6–7.

Shadish, W. R., Cook, T. D., & Campbell, D. T. (2002). *Experimental and quasi-experimental designs for generalized causal inference.* Boston, MA: Houghton Mifflin.

Shaver, K. G. (1981). Federal funding for social psychology: The end of an era? *SASP Newsletter, 7*(2), 1, 3–4.

Shaver, K. G. (1982). NSF and social psychology: Past trends and future prospects. *SASP Newsletter, 8*(2), 1, 3–5.

Shepperd, J. (1997, November). *Maladaptive self-presentation.* Paper presented at the 20th Annual Meeting of the Society of Southeastern Social Psychologists, Research Triangle Park, NC.

Sherman, L. W. (1986). Policing communities: What works? *Crime and Justice, 8,* 343–386.

Simon, R. J. (Ed.). (1975). *The jury system in America: A critical overview.* Beverly Hills, CA: Sage.

Snider, J., & Osgood, C. (Eds.). (1969). *Semantic differential technique: A sourcebook.* Chicago: Aldine.

Snyder, M. (1987). *Public appearances and private realities.* New York: W. H. Freeman.

Solomon, R. L. (1949). An extension of control group design. *Psychological Bulletin, 46,* 137–150.

Steeh, C. G. (1981). Trends in nonresponse rates, 1952–1979. *Public Opinion Quarterly, 45,* 40–57.

Stephenson, W. (1953). *The study of behavior*. Chicago: University of Chicago Press.

Stone, G. R. (2002). Discussion: Above the law: Research methods, ethics, and the law of privilege. *Sociological Methodology, 32,* 19–27.

Sutton, F. X., Harris, S. E., Kayson, C., & Tobin, J. (1956). *The American business creed*. New York: Schocken.

Svara, J. (2007). *The ethics primer for public administrators in government and non-profit organizations*. Sudbury, MA: Jones and Bartlett.

Thurstone, L. L. (1929). Theory of attitude measurement. *Psychological Bulletin, 36,* 222–241.

Thurstone, L. L. (1931). The measurement of social attitudes. *Journal of Abnormal and Social Psychology, 26,* 249–269.

Thurstone, L. L., & Chave, E. J. (1929). *The measurement of attitudes*. Chicago: University of Chicago Press.

Toglia, M. P., Read, J. D., Ross, D. F., & Lindsay, R. C. L. (Eds.). (2007). *The handbook of eyewitness psychology, Vol. I: Memory for events*. Mahwah, NJ: Lawrence Erlbaum.

Travis, C. B. (1985). Medical decision making and elective surgery: The case of hysterectomy. *Risk Analysis, 5,* 241–251.

Tukey, J. W. (1977). *Exploratory data analyses*. Reading, MA: Addison-Wesley.

Tunnell, G. B. (1977). Three dimensions of naturalness: An expanded definition of field research. *Psychological Bulletin, 84,* 426–437.

Union Carbide Company. (2007). *Bhopal Information Center*. Retrieved March 6, 2008, from http://www.bhopal.com/

Union of Concerned Scientists. (2006). *Scientific knowledge on abstinence-only education distorted* [Electronic Version]. Retrieved January 2, 2008, from http://www.ucsusa.org/scientific_integrity/interference/abstinenceonly-education.html?print=t

U.S. Bureau of the Census. (1979). *Statistical abstracts of the United States*. Washington, DC: Government Printing Office.

U.S. Bureau of the Census. (2008). *U.S. Census Bureau*. Retrieved from http://www.census.gov/

U.S. Department of Health and Human Services. (1981). Final regulations amending basic HHS policy for the protection of human research subjects, 46 Fed. Reg., 8366–8391 (45 C.F.R. pt. 46).

Vacca, R. T., & Vacca, J. A. L. (1999). *Content area reading: Literacy and learning across the curriculum*. New York: Longman.

Wachter, K. W., & Straf, M. L. (Eds.). (1990). *The future of meta-analysis*. New York: Russell Sage Foundation.

Wartofsky, M. W. (1968). *Conceptual foundations of scientific thought*. New York: Macmillan.

Watson, R. I. (1967). Psychology: A prescriptive science. *American Psychologist, 22,* 435–443.

Weick, K. E. (1968). Systematic observational methods. In G. Lindzey & E. Aronson (Eds.), *The handbook of social psychology* (Vol. 2, pp. 357–451). Reading, MA: Addison-Wesley.

Weimer, W. B. (1979). *Notes on the methodology of scientific research*. Hillsdale, NJ: Erlbaum.

Whitman, D., & Dane, F. C. (1980). The use of psychology in jury selection. *American Business Law Association Regional Proceedings*, 78–90.

Wike, E. L. (1985). *Numbers: A primer of data analysis*. Columbus, OH: Charles E. Merrill.

Willey, S. (2002). The book of Jerry Falwell: Fundamentalist language and politics. *Journal of Media & Religion, 1*(4), 253–255

Winer, B. J. (1971). *Statistical principles in experimental design*. New York: McGraw-Hill.

Witte, R. S., & Witte, J. S. (2006). *Statistics* (8th ed.). New York: Wiley.

World Medical Association. (1964). Declaration of Helsinki. *British Medical Journal 313*(7070), 1448–1449.

Wrightsman, L. S. (1987). *Psychology of the legal system*. Monterey, CA: Brooks/Cole.

Zimbardo, P. G., & Meadow, W. (1974, April). *Sexism springs eternal in the* Reader's Digest. Paper presented at the Western Psychological Association, San Francisco, CA.

Author Index

Subject Index

Pages with a t or an f indicate table or figure, respectively.

About the Author

Frank Dane received a B.S. in psychology from the University of Wisconsin–Milwaukee and a Ph.D. in social psychology from the University of Kansas. His advisor was Larry Wrightsman, and he has certainly followed in Dr. Wrightsman's footsteps in terms of staying active in publishing and doing research. He was Associate Professor of Psychology at Clemson University from 1983 to 1988 and then moved to Mercer University in Georgia, where he was Associate Professor and Department Chair of Psychology. He stayed at Mercer as the William Heard Kilpatrick Professor of Psychology in the College of Liberal Arts and as Professor of Internal Medicine at Mercer University School of Medicine until 2002 and then moved to his current position as James V. Finkbeiner Endowed Chair of Ethics and Public Policy in the College of Arts and Behavioral Sciences at Saginaw Valley State University in University Center, Michigan.